Admission to the United Nations

Legal Aspects of International Organization

Volume 50

Admission to the United Nations

Charter Article 4 and the Rise of
Universal Organization

By

Thomas D. Grant

MARTINUS
NIJHOFF
PUBLISHERS

LEIDEN • BOSTON
2009

This book is printed on acid-free paper.

Library of Congress Cataloging-in-Publication Data

Grant, Thomas D., 1969–
    Admission to the United Nations Charter : Article 4 and the rise of universal organization /
by Thomas D. Grant.
        p. cm. — (Legal aspects of international organization ; v. 50)
    Includes bibliographical references and index.
    ISBN 978-90-04-17363-7 (hardback : alk. paper) 1. United Nations. Charter—Membership.
2. United Nations—Membership. 3. International organization. I. Title.
    KZ4997.G73 2009
    341.23'3—dc22

                                                                                    2008055206

ISSN   0924-4883
ISBN   978 90 04 17363 7

Copyright 2009 by Koninklijke Brill NV, Leiden, The Netherlands.
Koninklijke Brill NV incorporates the imprints Brill, Hotei Publishing,
IDC Publishers, Martinus Nijhoff Publishers and VSP.

PRINTED IN THE NETHERLANDS

Contents

Preface and Acknowledgments

In March 2006, I gave a lecture at Washington University School of Law in St. Louis, Missouri, USA, entitled 'Legitimacy, Efficacy, and Universality in International Organization: What the First Fifty Years of the United Nations Tells Us About the Future.' This was by invitation of the Whitney R. Harris Institute for Global Legal Studies which had asked for a lecture on a topic of current interest respecting international organization. Work at the time on a number of longer-term projects had led me to consider the significance of the admission provisions of the United Nations Charter and their counterparts in the constitutive instruments of other international organizations. The impact within the Organization alone is certainly enough to merit examination: the efficacy of the UN, as of any international organization, will be determined, in part, by the States admitted to its membership. However, the implementation of UN Charter Article 4 in practice has had effects ranging well beyond the organs of the United Nations. In light of the on-going process of UN reform, the internal consequences of universal membership make the topic noteworthy. In light of the ever-present need in international society for ordering mechanisms to co-ordinate inter-State action, the external consequences do as well.

Though UN admission has been addressed before, work to date has been largely piecemeal. There is the Repertory of the United Nations, now complete through the 1990s, which contains surveys of Article 4, but these offer only a sketch of the field and little by way of synthesis or historical and legal analysis. Amerasinghe, Bühler, Rosenne, Schermers, and Zacklin have produced studies of international organization practice, and these touch on admission, but as one part of a larger whole and without a full presentation of the relevant practice or an assessment of its impact.[1] Crawford's *The Creation of States in International*

[1] Amerasinghe *Principles of the Institutional Law of International Organizations* 2nd rev edn (2005); Bühler *State Succession and Membership in International Organizations. Legal Theories versus Political Pragmatism* (2001); Rosenne *Developments in the Law of Treaties 1945–1986* (1989)) esp. 181–258, 353–447; Schermers *International Institutional Law* 2nd edn (1980); and Schermers & Blokker *International Institutional Law: Unity within Diversity* 4th rev edn (2003); Zacklin *The Amendment of the Constitutive Instruments of the United Nations and Specialized Agencies* (1968, reissued with forward by Schermers, 2005).

Law and Dugard's *Recognition and the United Nations* consider, *inter alia*, the relation between admission and general issues of statehood.[2] These are more detailed expositions of a theme taken up earlier by Rosalyn Higgins.[3]

The present work aims to fill the ellipsis. The evolution of Charter Article 4 which led to the eventual displacement of substantive criteria for admission in favour of universal membership of States is the story of how the United Nations assumed its now-familiar shape. This is a story of transformation. A wartime alliance including only States actively committed to a particular goal turned into a universal organization admitting any State regardless of political programme, internal government, or strategic priority. The transformation was momentous. How the Charter accommodated it is a little-considered question and one on which the present work seeks to shed light. In so doing, the practice of the UN on admission of States from 1945 to the present is set out in detail, ending with the march to universality and questions of participation in recent disputed cases.

Words of thanks are due John O. Haley, Wiley B. Rutledge Professor of Law, and F. Scott Kieff, Professor of Law, both of the Washington University School of Law. Professors Haley and Kieff kindly arranged the invitation for me to lecture at the Harris Institute in 2006. Dr. Tom D'Andrea, of Wolfson College, University of Cambridge, organized the College Research Colloquium at which a preliminary version of the lecture was presented. Parts of earlier drafts were presented at the University of Swansea, Wales, in a round table organized by Professor Volker Roeben in March 2008; and at a conference organized by Chen Yi-Yeh at the Taiwan Think Tank in Taipei in April 2008. Input from participants in all of these places helped refine the work.

Damon Wischik, University College, London, assisted with the graph of UN membership. A more extensive treatment of data concerning participation in the specialized UN organs is anticipated in a co-authored article with Dr Wischik (in progress at time of press). Alison Quentin-Baxter, in correspondence to which I was more a spectator than active participant, noted a point in New Zealand legislation that would seem to confirm the 1949 Geneva Conventions as history's first genuinely universal treaty (even as there arguably is yet to be a universal organization in the same, complete sense). Iruthisham Adam of the UN Permanent Mission of the Republic of the Maldives in New York furnished useful references to certain recent UN documents. Kate Parlett helped with the occasional intervention on human rights law. Russ Burns, Chris Holbrook, Stephanie Ierino, and Federica Paddeu assisted with copyediting.

---

[2] Crawford *The Creation of States in International Law* 2nd edn (2006) 174–95; Dugard *Recognition and the United Nations* (1987) 41–170.

[3] Cohen 'The Concept of Statehood in United Nations Practice' (1961) 109 *U Pa LR* 1127.

I completed much of the drafting and research for this work as a visiting fellow of the Max Planck Institute for International Law in Heidelberg, Germany during spring of 2007. Professor Rüdiger Wolfrum kindly arranged three months of research support at the Institute, including access to its library. During the final drafting work, the John Wolff International and Comparative Law Library of the Georgetown Law Center kindly extended access to its collection, and David Wills and his staff at the Squire Law Library, Cambridge were helpful throughout. Final drafting was done in the first part of a ten-month sabbatical as a Jennings Randolph Senior Fellow of the U.S. Institute of Peace in Washington, DC.

Finally, I must thank James Crawford, my work for whom over the past five years was the germ of many of the ideas (though none of the errors or debatable assertions) contained in the chapters which follow. Opinions expressed in the present work are those of the author and not necessarily those of any of the institutions with which he is or has been affiliated.

The work is current so far as possible as at 14 October 2008.

December 2008
Washington, DC

Table of Cases

Table of Treaties and Other Instruments

Table and Figures

List of Abbreviations

ARSIWA	Articles on Responsibility of States for Internationally Wrongful Acts (2001)
AdV	Archiv des Völkerrechts
RIAA	Reports of International Arbitral Awards
New York Rev Books	New York Review of Books
AFDI	Annuaire français de droit international
AJ	American Journal of International Law
AJ Supp	Supplement to the American Journal of International Law
Am J Comp L	American Journal of Comparative Law
Am U ILR	American University International Law Review
Am U JIL & Pol'y	American University Journal of International Law and Policy
Ann Surv Int'l & Comp L	Annual Survey of International and Comparative Law
ASIL Proc	Proceedings of the American Society of International Law
Austral YBIL	Australian Yearbook of International Law
Baltic YBIL	Baltic Yearbook of International Law
Berkeley JIL	Berkeley Journal of International Law
BverGE	Reports of the Bundesverfassungsgericht
BY	British Yearbook of International Law
Ca L Rev	California Law Review
Can Ybk	Canadian Yearbook of International Law
Chicago JIL	Chicago Journal of International Law
Colum J Trans'l L	Columbia Journal of Transnational Law
Cornell ILJ	Cornell International Law Journal
Duke LJ	Duke Law Journal
ECR	Reports of the European Court of Justice
EJIL	European Journal of International Law
Florida J Int'l L	Florida Journal of International Law
Ford ILJ	Fordham International Law Journal
GAOR	General Assembly Official Records

Georgetown JIL	Georgetown Journal of International Law
Georgia J Int'l & Comp L	Georgia Journal of International & Comparative Law
Harv ILJ	Harvard International Law Journal
Harv JL & Pub Pol	Harvard Journal of Law and Public Policy
Harv LR	Harvard Law Review
HC Debs	House of Commons (UK) Debates
HL Debs	House of Lords (UK) Debates
Hum Rts LR	Human Rights Law Review
Hum Rts Q	Human Rights Quarterly
ICJ Pldgs	Pleadings in the International Court of Justice
ICJ Rep	Reports of the International Court of Justice
ICLQ	International and Comparative Law Quarterly
ICSID Rep	Reports of decisions under the International Center for the Settlement of Investment Disputes
ILC	International Law Commission
ILC Ybk	Yearbook of the International Law Commission
ILM	International Legal Materials
ILR	International Law Reports
Ind Int'l & Comp LR	Indiana International and Comparative Law Review
Int'l Org	International Organization
J Trans L & Pol'y	Journal of Transnational Law and Policy
Keesing's	Keesing's Record of World Events
LNTS	League of Nations Treaty Series
LONSOJ	Official Journal of the League of Nations
Max Planck Ybk UN Law	Max Planck Yearbook of United Nations Law
N Car LR	North Carolina Law Review
NYU J Int'l L & Pol	New York University Journal of International Law and Politics
Pace YBIL	Pace Yearbook of International Law
Rep SC	Repertoire of the Practice of the Security Council
Rep UN	Repertory of Practice of United Nations Organs
RGDIP	Revue Générale de Droit International Public
SCOR	Security Council Official Records
Stan JIL	Stanford Journal of International Law
Tex ILJ	Texas International Law Journal
U Miami Int'l & Comp LR	University of Miami International and Comparative Law Review
U Pa LR	University of Pennsylvania Law Review
UCLA J Env L & Pol'y	University of California at Los Angeles Journal of Environmental Law and Policy

UN Jurid Ybk	United Nations Juridical Yearbook
UN Ybk	Yearbook of the United Nations
UNTS	United Nations Treaty Series
Virg JIL	Virginia Journal of International Law
Wash Q'ly	Washington Quarterly
Wash U J Law & Pol'y	Washington University Journal of Law and Policy
William & Mary LR	William and Mary Law Review
Yale LJ	Yale Law Journal
ZaöRV	Zeitschrift für ausländisches öffentliches Recht und Völkerrecht

Introduction

What are the considerations that the United Nations takes into account, when deciding whether to elect to membership a candidate seeking admission? The question may sound faintly anachronistic, for, it might be asked, have not all States now been admitted to membership, and, even if not, is it not inevitable that any State seeking admission will be granted admission? An initial response is that the number of States in the world at a given time perhaps looks like a fixed quantity, but to examine the composition of international society over a period of years is to disclose longer or shorter periods of stability punctuated by major episodes of change. A welter of principalities underwent rapid consolidation during the Napoleonic occupation of Germany; the remaining thirty-odd States two generations later submerged within a new central European State. The break-up of Romanov, Ottoman, and Habsburg States constituted the next major episode of change – this one, in and after 1918, rather than reducing, added to the ranks of States. Decolonization after the Second World War brought about an even more striking increase in the number of States. Scarcely anybody thought the socialist States would give way to nearly two dozen new States in the 1990s. And latent possibilities remain.

The number of States has fluctuated, and greatly, over time, and the present international order, even as international law favours the preservation of existing relations, by no means forecloses the creation – and extinction – of States. As for a presumption that any State seeking to be admitted to the United Nations will be admitted, such a presumption well may now prevail, but to posit its prevalence does not tell us where it came from. The United Nations started as a wartime alliance; it became the universal organization of States. The present work describes how that happened.

This entails a close look at practice within the UN by which universal membership was attained. The UN did not start as a universal organization. Moreover, the Charter did not explicitly require that it become one. Far from requiring universality, the Charter contains substantive criteria for admission; and it sets out a basic constitutional mechanism by which to apply the criteria. It was a momentous change for the Organization to become universal. The question therefore is of inherent interest, how universal admission of States came to be entrenched in the UN.

The present work addresses admission of States to the United Nations, by surveying the development of UN admission practice since 1945, including the two advisory opinions of the International Court in which admission was the main concern.* The result eventually reached was that the UN is open to all States, so that it came to be the world's first international organization that might properly be called universal. Of main relevance here, then, is the meaning of UN Charter Article 4, under which admission to the UN is to be open to 'all other peace-loving states which accept the obligations contained in the... Charter and, in the judgment of the Organization, are able and willing to carry out these obligations.' The language very well could invite a vetting process, a filtration of compliant from non-compliant States. That the Charter excluded 'enemy States,' and that the San Francisco Conference on International Organization did not include various States that had remained ostensibly neutral during the war, also supports a restrictive interpretation. Yet restrictions on membership did not prevail. By the mid-1950s, famously, they disappeared almost entirely.

This is a story of policy judgments, especially the judgment that to achieve and keep international peace and stability requires an organization of universal membership. The evolution of an organization governed by law, including the law of its constitutive instrument, however, cannot be referred entirely to policy. The decision to develop the UN into an all-inclusive organization well may have sprung from considerations of policy, but to implement the decision entailed working within the terms of the Charter. How the terms of the Charter came to accommodate universality requires a legal explanation as well.

At the same time as legal interpretations concerning admission open the doors to all States, universality has been maintained by legal interpretations concerning suspension and expulsion. States which are members must remain members, if an organization which is universal is to remain universal. Expressed in the negative, for an organization to be universal, it cannot expel a State. The story of universality, then, also includes how the UN, in practice, has retired from operation those terms of the Charter which provided for suspension of membership or expulsion of a State.

The work proceeds in seven chapters. The first chapter considers the formal provisions of the Charter concerning admission of States as new members. These include provisions respecting admission mechanisms (i.e., procedural modalities for admission), and provisions respecting admission criteria (i.e., legal standards or rules governing eligibility for admission). The present position in respect of admission of States as new members is not self-evident in the text of the Charter.

---

* *Conditions of Admission of a State for Membership in the United Nations* Advisory Opinion ICJ Rep 1948 p. 57; *Competence of the General Assembly for Admission of a State to the United Nations* Advisory Opinion ICJ Rep 1950 p. 4.

Admission developed through practice. One thus must consider the practice, if one is to understand how the United Nations has become what it is today.

It is necessary in particular to consider the shift from more rigorous application of the criteria for admission to an approach that largely, or wholly, accepts a presumption that an applicant State is admissible as a member State. The practice would be of little interest, if universal admission were inscribed on the face of the Charter; or, even if not required by the Charter, if universal admission had been the prevailing position from the start. There were indications early in the Charter era however that admission was to entail rigorous assessment of every candidate. Chapter 2 considers instances in which the substantive criteria for admission were accorded due juridical weight and indeed implemented in practice. The procedural mechanisms adopted to this end, now largely forgotten, suggest the outline of what would have been a very different international organization.

By the early 1950s, a large number of States seeking admission had not been granted admission. Some applications met delay at the hands of Permanent Members casting Security Council vetoes. The so-called logjam of the first Charter decade owed to Superpower deadlock, but it led the protagonists to adopt legal arguments which are among the fullest articulations of Charter law on admission. Chapter 3 considers the period when admission became a contested issue on the UN agenda, and it recalls the positions set out by opponents of the admission of various new applicant States. Yet this was also the period when arguments in support of universality took shape. So the vestiges of a restrictive rule, which had the consequence for some States of a decade-long delay in admission, existed side by side the groundwork of a presumption of universality.

The attempt to put the substantive criteria of Charter Article 4 into practice turned out to be only a tentative experiment in admission policy; and the political deadlock over new applicants did not last indefinitely. Though the early practice might have foretold a future in which the UN rigorously vetted applicants for admission, the UN did not develop in that direction. The shift after the mid-1950s to a permissive admission practice, by which the substantive criteria largely were set aside, has given the United Nations its present-day shape. The 'package deal' of 1955–6 by which a large number of applicants were admitted in a single General Assembly session marked the start in earnest of the march to universal membership. The substantive admission criteria of Article 4 fell into eclipse.

This is the momentous development in the history of the UN. Its grounding in considerations of policy becomes evident, on study of the deliberations of member States during the controversy over admission in the late 1940s and early 1950s. Member States, as participants in a constitutional system, also sought a legal basis for the shift to universality. It was said that universality was inherent in the Charter, that sovereign equality impelled the Organization to accept all States, and that the principles and purposes of the UN also militated in favour of widest possible membership. Such positions, however, do not address the salient feature of the Charter already noted: the Charter requires that applicants satisfy certain, even if basic, criteria before the principal organs recommend and vote to admit them as members. Chapter 4 below considers the fate of Charter Article 4, with a view in particular to the processes of amendment or interpretation that seem to have cemented universality as a presumption in Charter law.

Chapter 5 continues the narrative of UN practice from the point at which the presumption had firmly entrenched itself that the Organization would deny no State admission. One criterion of admission contained in Charter Article 4 remained – to be admitted, the applicant has to be a State. The focal point of most (but not quite all) controversies over admission of new members, after 1955–6, thus would be the identity of the applicant as a State. Insofar as admission practice bore relevance to general international law, it did so from then on in connection with questions of statehood, rather than in connection with any putative rules governing the conduct of States in fields like human rights or democracy. This whittling down of the relevance of admission as a legal measure of the applicant was not complete, as will be seen from the real controversies that arose over statehood during certain applications, but the controversies after the mid-1950s were few and their resolution in most (but not quite all) instances rapid. The few long-lasting controversies over admission arose, with one or two exceptions, in connection with the divided States. Special considerations of international peace and security were presented in most of the divided States cases; Kosovo and Taiwan, the remaining special cases, have given rise to their own particular problems.

Chapter 6 brings the narrative up to the present day. Universality, though entrenched as a presumption by the second Charter decade, has taken considerably longer to become an achieved fact. New States emerging out of the disappearance of the socialist bloc indeed gained admission rapidly, thus confirming the universalist presumption. Other States, however, existed as States for some time before becoming member States. A number of small island developing States – residue of the European colonial empires – and Switzerland – a special case in light of its ancient neutrality – were the remaining non-members in the 1990s and early 2000s. The decisions eventually reached by each of these States to seek admission complete the tale of universality.

As admission to the UN for some time has been a presumption seemingly attaching as an incident to statehood, it may be asked what if any particular consequences arise from admission to the UN, and – to put a related question – how, if at all, can the consequences of admission be disentangled from the general concept of the State in international law. These are matters which Chapter 7 addresses.

Chapter 1

Admission under the UN Charter

1.1   *The Constitutive Function of Admission*

An international organization is an entity comprised, in the main, of States.[1] Those creating a new international organization do so by adopting an international instrument that expresses their intention to do so and prescribes the form and function of the intended new entity.[2] An international organization has the purpose of coordinating the action of its constituents in a particular field or

---

[1] Existing international organizations also may constitute a new international organization: see Art. 5, Vienna Convention on the Law of Treaties between States and International Organizations or between International Organizations, adopted 21 Mar 1986 (not yet entered into force). The overwhelming majority of international organization constituents, however, are States.

[2] As acknowledged in the definition of 'international organization' proposed by Fitzmaurice and accepted by El-Erian in his First Report as 'gather[ing] all the essential elements':

> The term "international organization" means a collectivity of States established by treaty, with a constitution and common organs, having a personality distinct from that of its member States, and being a subject of international law with treaty-making capacity.

Fitzmaurice at A/CN.4/100, art. 3, quoted by El-Erian in First Report ¶ 59, *ILC Ybk* 1963 Vol. 2 p. 167. The constitutive function of the treaty also is acknowledged in draft article 2 adopted by the drafting committee on the topic of Responsibility of International Organizations. Treaty-making capacity is not included in the definition there: 'The term "international organization" refers to an organization established by a treaty or other instrument governed by international law and possessing its own legal personality.' The matter of finding a definition universally acceptable however has not entirely been resolved. It arose again, for example, in connection with the ILC's work leading to the 1986 Vienna Convention on the Law of Treaties between States and International Organizations or between International Organizations: see ILC 34th sess 1750th mtg, 21 July 1982, *ILC Ybk* 1982 Vol. II Pt Two pp. 20–1, Comments (22) and (23); in connection with the topic of Relations between States and international organizations: see ILC 41st sess 2133rd mtg 7 July 1989 ¶¶ 9–11, *ILC Ybk* 1989 Vol. I pp. 282–3; ILC 55th sess 4 June 2003: A/CN.4/L.632. El-Erian said that one of the earliest attempts to define the term was Anzilotti's:

fields over which their individual competence would not be effective or over which joint action promises some other advantage.

The States existing in the early twenty-first century display a remarkable heterogeneity in terms of their political and social configurations. As a legal formation, however, the modern State has conformed more and more to a uniform template.[3] International organizations, by contrast, are both juridically and functionally heterogeneous.[4] Each organization has its own constitutive instrument. Whether it is called a charter, a treaty, or by some other name, the constitutive instrument of an organization may set out, *inter alia*, the purposes and principles of the organization, its procedures, dispute settlement provisions, and, as in the case of the conventions establishing the various river commissions, even substantive rules governing multinational use of a resource.[5]

> Sont organs collectives ceux qui sont institués par plusieurs Etats ensemble et dont la déclaration de volonté est rapporté par le droit international à une collectivité de sujets et, comme telle, rendue la présupposition de conséquences juridiquement déterminées.

Anzilotti *Cours de Droit International* 3rd edn, trans to French from Italian by Gidel (1929) 283 quoted in El-Erian First Report ¶ 40, *ILC Ybk* 1963 Vol. 2 p. 165. One of the most recent is that in art. 2 of the draft articles on responsibility of international organizations, defining 'international organization' as 'an organization established by treaty or other instrument governed by international law and possessing its own international legal personality': ILC 55th sess: A/CN.4/L.632, 4 June 2003 p. 1. The matter of definition was discussed in Giorgio Gaja (Spec Rapp) First Report on responsibility of international organizations: ILC 55th sess A/CN.4/532, 26 March 2003 pp. 7–9, 12–18 ¶¶ 12–15, 22–34. See also Alvarez *International Organizations as Law-makers* (2005) 4–17; Rosenne *Developments in the Law of Treaties 1945–1986* (1989) 199, observing hesitation to settle on a definition of 'international organization.'

[3] Crawford *Creation* 2nd edn 254. Cf. Petra Minnerop 'The Classification of States and the Creation of Status within the International Community' (2003) 7 *Max Planck Ybk UN Law* 79.

[4] This point was acknowledged in the commentary to article 3 of the draft articles on the representation of States in their relations with international organizations: *ILC Ybk* 1971 Vol. II Pt One p. 287 (commentary ¶ 2: '…given the diversity of international organizations and their heterogeneous character…'). A typology had been proposed as part of the historical background notes in El-Erian's First Report as Special Rapporteur for Relations between States and Inter-Governmental Organizations: *ILC Ybk* 1963 Vol. 2 pp. 167–9 ¶¶ 64–81. The European Commission, in comments and observations on the draft articles on responsibility of international organizations, 'recall[ed] the diversity of the structures, forms and functions of international organizations…': A/CN.4/582, 1 May 2007 p. 14. See also the taxonomic section in Schermers *International Institutional Law* (1980) §§ 29–39 pp. 21–6.

[5] This was one purpose of the treaty often identified as having constituted the first international organization in the modern sense, the European Commission of the Danube: General Treaty of Peace between Austria, France, Great Britain, Prussia, Russia, Sardinia, and the Ottoman Porte, Paris, 30 Mar 1856, Arts 16–7, 114 CTS 410, 415–6, about which see *Jurisdiction of the European Commission of the Danube between Galatz and Braila (France, Great Britain and Italy v Roumania)* Advisory Opinion of 8 Dec 1927, 1927 PCIJ Ser B No 14 pp. 5, 11.

There exists considerable interest in the role of the UN Charter and of general international law as sources of a global 'constitution,'[6] and a contrast is sometimes drawn between conceptions of international law as a system of essentially contractual undertakings and as a constitutional system for the provision of public order.[7] Judge De Visscher said that 'in the interpretation of a great international constitutional instrument, like the United Nations Charter, the individualistic concepts which are generally adequate in the interpretation of ordinary treaties, do not suffice.'[8] Writers earlier referred to a distinction between law-making and contractual treaties.[9] The interest here is on specific provisions of the UN Charter (which have been adopted by all member States and thus can be addressed at least partly by ordinary methods of treaty interpretation) and on certain more general constitutive effects that those provisions may have on the UN, and, through the UN, on the world of States in which the Organization exists.

---

[6] See e.g. Breau 'The constitutionalisation of the international legal order' (2008) 21 *Leiden JIL* 545 and works cited ibid. 545 n. 1, 546, esp. Tomuschat & Thouvenin eds *The Fundamental Rules of the International Legal Order: Jus Cogens and Obligations Erga Omnes* (2006); Slaughter *A New World Order* (2004); Noortmann *Enforcing International Law: From Self-help to Self-contained Regimes* (2005). See also Fischer-Lescano 'Die Emergenz der Globalverfassung' (2003) 63 *ZaöVR* 715; Dupuy 'The Constitutional Dimension of the Charter of the United Nations Revisited' (1997) 1 *Max Planck Ybk UN Law* 1.

[7] See essays in St John MacDonald & Johnston eds *Towards World Constitutionalism, Issues in the Legal Ordering of the World Community* (2005); Warbrick & Tierney eds *Towards an International Legal Community? The Sovereignty of States and the Sovereignty of International Law* (2006). Sir Humphrey Waldock forty years before already had posited that the UN Charter is a constitution as well as a treaty: Waldock (1962) 106(II) *Hag Rec* 20. The history of the idea of an international constitutional law is reviewed by Orrego Vicuña *International dispute settlement in an evolving global society: constitutionalization, accessibility, privatization* (2004) 10–13. For an interesting, if somewhat vague, statement of the distinction between the UN Charter as treaty and UN Charter as constitution, see Statement of Greece in the *Admission* case: ICJ Pldgs 1948 p. 21. cf. overview of the distinction between *traité-loi* and *traité-contrat*: Rosenne *Treaties* 182–90; and acknowledgment of a constitutional and a contract theory of the UN Charter: Soder *Die Vereinten Nationen und die Nichtmitglieder. Zum Problem der Weltstaatenorganisation* (1956) 22–3. Alvarez rejects analogies to national constitutions but notes that the treaty-making power which the UN Charter and other constitutive instruments confer on international organizations is not found in ordinary contractual treaties: op. cit. 65–74, 273–9.

This long-running debate is distinct from a somewhat more modern one concerning the relation between the internal law of international organizations (e.g., the administrative law of the UN) and international law. For the position that internal law is not part of international law see works cited ILC Commentary to draft article 8 on international responsibility of international organizations, Comment (5) n 103: ILC Rpt on the work of its 57th sess 2 May to 3 June and 11 July to 5 Aug 2005 GAOR 60th sess Supp No 10: A/60/10 ¶ 206 p. 88.

[8] *International Status of South-West Africa* Advisory Opinion of 11 July 1950, Dis Op Judge De Visscher ICJ Rep 1950 pp. 128, 189.

[9] Zacklin 8–9; and cf. Rosenne *Treaties* 181–258 for examination of the legal character of constitutive instruments.

The provisions of the constitutive instrument of an international organization, as suggested in passing immediately above, may address diverse matters. Some provisions may state the matters that the organization has been established to regulate. This is the 'scope of their activities' to which UN Charter Article 96(2) refers. Provisions defining the 'scope of their activities' may be highly significant. For example, they may determine questions of jurisdiction when a non-principal organ or specialized agency has made a request for an advisory opinion to the International Court of Justice under Article 96(2). Presented such a request, the Court must ask whether the request relates to a question arising within the scope of the activities of the organ or agency making the request. Thus the Court has considered the scope of activities of UNESCO,[10] IMCO,[11] and the WHO.[12]

Other provisions may contain the design of the internal structures and specify the composition that the States creating the organization wish it to possess. In somewhat formal terms, then, it may be said that the constitutive instrument has

---

[10] *Judgments of the Administrative Tribunal of the International Labour Organisation upon Complaints Made Against the United Nations Educational, Scientific and Cultural Organization* Order, ICJ Rep 1955 p. 127; Advisory Opinion, ICJ Rep 1956 pp. 77, 83–4. cf. Sep Op Klaestad ibid. 112–13.

[11] *Constitution of the Maritime Safety Committee of the Inter-Governmental Maritime Consultative Organization* Order, ICJ Rep 1959 pp. 267, 267–68; Advisory Opinion, ICJ Rep 1960 pp. 150, 153.

[12] *Interpretation of the Agreement of 25 March 1951 between the WHO and Egypt* Order, ICJ Rep 1980 pp. 67, 67–8 ¶ 2; Advisory Opinion, ICJ Rep 1980 pp. 73, 76–7 ¶¶ 11–12. To the request in 1993 by the World Health Organization (ICJ Rep 1993 p. 467), the Court determined however that it could not exercise advisory jurisdiction. The Court said as follows:

> Interpreted in accordance with their ordinary meaning, in their context and in the light of the object and purpose of the WHO Constitution, as well as of the practice followed by the Organization, the provisions of its Article 2 may be read as authorizing the Organization to deal with the effects on health of the use of nuclear weapons, or of any other hazardous activity, and to take preventive measures aimed at protecting the health of populations in the event of such weapons being used or such activities engaged in.
>
> The question put to the Court in the present case relates, however, *not to the effects* of the use of nuclear weapons on health, but to the *legality* of the use of such weapons *in view of their health and environmental effects*. Whatever those effects might be, the competence of the WHO to deal with them is not dependent on the legality of the acts that caused them. Accordingly, it does not seem to the Court that the provisions of Article 2 of the WHO Constitution...can be understood as conferring upon the Organization a competence to address the legality of the use of nuclear weapons, and thus in turn a competence to ask the Court about that.

Legality of the Use by a State of Nuclear Weapons in Armed Conflict Advisory Opinion, ICJ Rep 1996 pp. 66, 76 ¶ 21. See also ibid., pp. 72–3, 74–81 ¶¶ 13, 18–26. The Court's analysis here, it is respectfully submitted, was too formal; and it was arguably unnecessary, in view of the separation of powers problem which itself deprived the WHO of authority to ask for an Advisory Opinion on a matter belonging to the Security Council or General Assembly.

both provisions with an external orientation – i.e., provisions dealing expressly with problems in the world at large in response to which the organization was established – and provisions with an internal orientation – provisions dealing expressly with how the organization is built. The ILC had something like this distinction in mind when dealing with the law concerning treaties to which international organizations are parties – and added a cautionary note that the 'internal law' of the organization cannot in all respects be separated from its 'international aspect.'[13]

Thus, as José Alvarez has put it, on considering an international organization one may observe ' "external" ripples of [its] "internal" law.'[14] Something like the converse also holds: if the organization is to fulfil the purposes its constituents wish it to fulfil, then those purposes will guide how they design the organization. The external casts a reflection on the internal. A formal division between external function and internal structure, on examination, then, may be less operative in practice, even as each part of the constitutive text of the organization retains independent significance in particular circumstances – such as in requests for advisory opinions. The matter which interests us here is that of admission criteria as specified in the UN Charter and as interpreted since 1945.

If there were no differences among States, it would be difficult to see how criteria could be adopted to control which States are eligible for admission to an international organization. A legal system that posits – and to a large extent has realized – the principle of sovereign equality of States is a system in which States are legal equals. So in an important respect, all States are the same under the international legal system. Significant heterogeneity obtains, however, in other respects.

States may be said to be heterogeneous in two main respects. First, any given State holds specific legal rights and obligations, and no two States, in practice,

---

[13] Treaties concluded between States and international organizations or between two or more international organizations, draft articles, ILC 34th sess 1750th mtg 21 July 1982, *ILC Ybk* 1982 Vol. II Pt Two p. 21 Comment (25):

> [A] question which occupied the Commission for some considerable time was that of the terms referring to the organization's own law, or that body of law which is known as "the internal law" of a State and which the Commission has called "the rules" of an international organization. The Commission has, finally, left its definition unchanged. There would have been problems in referring to the "internal law" of an organization, for while it has an internal aspect, this law also has in other respects an international aspect...

cf. remark of El-Erian, Spec Rapp for Relations between States and inter-governmental organizations, ILC 20th sess 948th mtg 6 June 1968 ¶ 66, *ILC Ybk* 1968 Vol. I p. 34. Whether that 'internal law' is governed by general international law or is solely a matter of the law of the constitutive instrument has occasioned debate: Gaja Third Report A/CN.4/553, 13 May 2005 pp. 7–9 ¶¶ 18–23.

[14] Op. cit. 122.

hold identical legal rights and obligations. Colin Warbrick even wonders, in view of the wide variation in treaty rights from State to State, 'in what sense... [it is] possible to refer usefully and accurately to the equality of states.'[15] That is to say, a given State through its voluntary transactions with other States and with international organizations has acquired a unique set of rights and obligations, and this has led to diversity among States.[16] Second, a given State has a unique portfolio of non-legal attributes. This includes incidents of geography, natural resources, human resources, physical infrastructure, military capability, etc. It

---

[15] Warbrick 'The principle of sovereign equality' in Lowe & Warbrick eds *The United Nations and the Principles of International Law: Essays in memory of Michael Akehurst* (1994) 204, 207.

[16] Consider the diverse rights and obligations under bilateral investment treaties (BITs). An example was brought to light by international tribunals considering, separately, two of Switzerland's BITs – one with Pakistan, one with the Philippines. In *SGS Société Générale de Surveillance SA v Republic of the Philippines*, ICSID Case No ARB/02/6, Decision on Objections to Jurisdiction, 29 Jan 2004 (El-Kosheri, President; Crawford & Crivellaro, members), 8 ICSID Rep 515, the Tribunal considered the effect of an 'umbrella clause,' providing that '[e]ach Contracting Party shall observe any obligation it has assumed with regard to specific investments in its territory by investors of the other Contracting Party' (art. X(2) of Agreement on the Promotion and Protection of Investments (Swiss Confederation and Republic of the Philippines), signed 31 Mar 1997, entered into force 23 Apr 1999, RO 2001 438). A slightly earlier case had involved Switzerland's BIT with Pakistan (and the same Swiss investor), and the Tribunal there had had to apply a similar, but not identical, umbrella clause. The Tribunal in *SGS Société Générale de Surveillance SA v Islamic Republic of Pakistan*, ICSID Case No ARB/01/13, Decision on Objections to Jurisdiction, 6 Aug 2003 (Feliciano, President; Faurès & Thomas, members), 8 ICSID Rep 383, determined that the umbrella clause in the Swiss-Pakistani BIT (Agreement on the Promotion and Reciprocal Protection of Investments (Swiss Confederation and Islamic Republic of Pakistan), signed 11 July 1995, entered into force 6 May 1996, RO 1998 2601) had the effect of placing under the law of the BIT certain disputes arising out of contracts between Swiss investors and Pakistan and making the disputes subject to arbitral jurisdiction.

The tribunal in the later case determined that the umbrella clause in the Swiss-Philippine BIT had a different effect. According to the tribunal, under the Swiss-Philippine BIT, Philippine courts retain jurisdiction over disputes arising out of State contracts: the BIT umbrella clause may make the Philippines responsible at international level if its courts fail to afford the foreign investor fair process, but it does not 'internationalize' contracts between Swiss investors and the Philippine State, where national law is the designated law of the contract: 8 ICSID Rep at 552 ¶ 125. The Swiss-Pakistani BIT, by contrast, apparently can take jurisdiction away from Pakistani courts, for, at least under 'exceptional circumstances' (8 ICSID Rep at 445–6 ¶ 172), whatever those may be, disputes arising under State contracts are subject to the law of the BIT, including the arbitral jurisdiction it establishes. Thus, in their international treaty relations with a particular third State, Pakistan and the Philippines are not homogeneous States, and the difference, as it controls the way proceedings in international investment disputes are instituted and resolved, is consequential.

The relevant BITs are available through the investment instruments facility at http://www .unctadxi.org/templates/DocSearch____779.aspx.

is in the sense of the unique legal relations and power resources of every State
that States may be said to be heterogeneous.

A constitutive instrument may take one or more of several approaches to
indicating which among this community of States, diverse in the senses just
described, may be admitted as members. The instrument may incorporate a closed
list of specific, existing States; the constitutive instruments of various fisheries
organizations are examples.[17] It may invite States from a particular region to
apply for admission – for example, as in the European treaties[18] and the Charter
of the OAS.[19] Special constitutional criteria might define the membership; the
Commonwealth requires its member States to have had a constitutional link
to the United Kingdom (or to another Commonwealth member).[20] Religious
qualifications may control membership, as under Article VIII of the Charter of
the Islamic Conference.[21] The provisions governing admission to an organization
are central to the constitution of the organization in the following respect: those
provisions provide the terms for deciding which States become constituents of
the organization.

The United Nations has been shaped fundamentally by the admission provisions of the Charter and, moreover, the manner in which those provisions have
been implemented in practice since 1945. Because the United Nations occupies
an influential position among States, implementation of the admission provisions
also has significance beyond the contours of the UN itself. As will be discussed in
the final Chapter, below, admission to membership in the United Nations, as it

---

[17] E.g. the Interim Convention on Conservation of North Pacific Fur Seals, signed 9 Feb 1957,
entered into force 14 Oct 1957, 314 UNTS 106, 109–10, by Art. V of which was established
the North Pacific Fur Seal Commission (USA-Canada-Japan-USSR); the International Convention for the High Seas Fisheries of the North Pacific Ocean, signed 9 May 1952, entered into
force 12 June 1953, 205 UNTS 80, 82–4, by Art. II of which was established the International
North Pacific Fisheries Commission (USA-Canada-Japan); the Convention for the Protection,
Preservation and Extension of the Sockeye Salmon Fisheries of the Fraser River System, signed
26 May 1930, entered into force 28 July 1937, 184 LNTS 306, 308–10, by Art. II of which
was established the International Pacific Salmon Fisheries Commission (USA-Canada).

[18] See esp. Title VII, Art. O (Final Provisions) of the Treaty on European Union, signed 7 Feb
1992, entered into force 1 Nov 1993: 1757 UNTS 4, 156.

[19] Chap III, Arts 4–8. The OAS Charter in original form was published at 119 UNTS 3,
adopted 30 Apr 1948, entered into force 13 Dec 1951. The membership provisions resulted
from subsequent amendments, starting with those adopted at Buenos Aires, 27 Feb 1967 and
entered into force 27 Feb 1970: 721 UNTS 326–8, about which see Bühler *State Succession
and Membership in International Organizations* (2001) 23 n. 95.

[20] Commonwealth Heads of Government Meeting, Edinburgh, 24–27 Oct 1997: *The Edinburgh
Communique* ¶ 20.

[21] Adopted 4 Mar 1972, entered into force 28 Feb 1973: 914 UNTS 110, 115. On the admission provisions, see Moinuddin *The Charter of the Islamic Conference and Legal Framework of
Economic Co-operation among its Member States* (1987) 100–4.

has developed under the Charter in practice, entails various consequences, political and legal, for the admitted State. It also affects global public order generally, even, perhaps, exerting an influence on the creation of States. As States remain the chief building blocks of global public order, this would number among the most consequential effects of admission.

The admission provisions of the Charter are significant in another sense: they are unlikely to change, which is to say the words of Article 4 have been the same since 1945, and amendment is unlikely. The political hurdles to amendment are considerable, so the UN Charter has only rarely been revised by way of the formal mechanisms of amendment.[22] The provisions of the Charter governing admission of States to the Organization have never been formally amended, and so the relevant language has been a fixed quantity. Any changes in UN practice with respect to admission of States since 1945 have taken place within the parameters of Article 4.

The framers of the Charter could have drafted it in 1945 to leave no choice as to the development of admission practice thereafter. An admission provision designed to include every State and giving no legal basis for excluding a State would scarcely have been susceptible to a restrictive interpretation. No State could have been kept out, if the text had called for all to be let in. If the plain language of the Charter in truth were deterministic as to admission practice, then there would be no call for considering how the Charter came to create a universal organization.

The first step, then, in understanding how the UN has evolved to be a universal organization of States is to consider the plain text of the Charter relative to admission. Admission of States to membership in the UN is dealt with chiefly in Article 4 of the Charter, though, as will be seen below, other aspects of the constitution of the Organization and, moreover, the practical implementation of admission, have had significant effect on the composition of the UN. Admission involves two distinct matters: the procedural mechanisms by which an application for admission is considered; and the legal conditions or criteria to be applied

---

[22] Luck 'Prospects for Reform: Principal Organs' in Weiss & Daws eds *Oxford Handbook* 653, 654–5. See also Lupu 'Rules, Gaps and Power: Assessing Reform of the U.N. Charter' (2006) 24 *Berkeley JIL* 881. The difficulty of achieving the agreement necessary to effect change under Chapter XVIII has been demonstrated, for example, on the matter of increasing Security Council membership (from 11 to 15), one of the few major changes to the 1945 text and achieved only after some struggle; the others were to increase ECOSOC membership from 18 to 27, and then to 54: Wilson 'Changing the Charter: The United Nations Prepares for the Twenty-first Century' (1996) 90 *AJ* 115, 117. See also de Marco & Bartolo *A Second Generation United Nations for Peace and Freedom in the 21st Century* new edn (2002) 23–35. Amerasinghe lists the instances in which the Charter and the constitutions of the specialized agencies have been amended: *Principles of the institutional law of international organizations* 2nd edn (2005) 447.

when evaluating applications for admission under the designated mechanisms. This is a recognized division, Scelle for example having distinguished admission from admissibility – the former concerning the constitutional and procedural modalities for determining whether to admit a State; the latter concerning the criteria that a candidate must meet if it is to be eligible to be considered for admission.[23] The former matter – the modalities – can be dealt with in brief. Then we will turn to the question of criteria for admission.

1.2 Admission Mechanisms: Article 4(2)

The decision whether to admit an applicant State to membership in the United Nations is a competence shared by the Security Council and General Assembly. This is a constitutional allocation of competence, Article 4, paragraph 2 of the Charter providing as follows:

> The admission of any such state to membership in the United Nations will be effected by a decision of the General Assembly upon the recommendation of the Security Council.

This is to say that two steps must be taken, in order for an applicant State to be admitted: (i) admission must be recommended by the Security Council; and (ii) admission must be decided by the General Assembly. Some States took this to present ambiguities. Two putative ambiguities were instanced.

First, Article 4(2) does not say which voting rule applies to reaching a recommendation in the Council – the ordinary Security Council voting rule, under which nine members must affirm including the five permanent members (Article 27(3)); or the voting rule for procedural matters, under which permanent members have no veto (Article 27(2)).

Second, some States said, paragraph 2 does not specify what effect the recommendation has on General Assembly discretion. This, they said, gives rise to a question: does the Assembly have to follow the recommendation? The answer the States raising this question sought was that the Assembly can approve admission, as against a negative recommendation. At least one writer, well after the matter would appear to have been settled in the UN, said, as a general matter of international institutional law, that '[r]ecommendations addressed to other organs have no binding effect.'[24] The meaning of the word 'recommendation' in Article 4(2) thus, perhaps, required clarification. Some States at least maintained that it did. The legal effect of a recommendation within the Organization was a matter

---

[23] ICJ Pldgs 1950 p. 159.
[24] Schermers § 1099 p. 609.

of disagreement early in the Charter era and, as will be seen shortly, occasioned one of a pair of advisory opinions concerning Article 4 of the Charter.

The first question instanced above (voting procedure) ultimately was dealt with without resort to the Court. As a matter of interpretation, the matter is probably settled by cross-reference to Article 18(2), by which decisions of the General Assembly 'on important questions' shall be made by a two-thirds majority – and included in the category 'important questions' is 'the admission of new Members to the United Nations.' It is true that the General Assembly and Security Council have different functions in the Charter scheme and, thus, it is not impossible that how a particular matter is to be characterized for one of the principal organs differs from how it is to be characterized for another. At a minimum, however, one would presume that the two organs treat a given matter under the same voting rule; differences would require a showing of some good reason. With respect to admission, whatever reason one might adduce for different treatment as between Security Council and General Assembly would be more than counterbalanced by the constitutive consideration: the decision to admit a State as a new member affects not just one but all Charter organs. Admission thus would be strange to characterize as a procedural matter subject to separate treatment. The logic of the Charter is clear enough that the Security Council votes on recommendations for admission under Article 27(3) – that is to say, the permanent members have the authority to veto a proposed recommendation of admission.[25]

The apparent clarity of the UN Charter on the voting procedure point notwithstanding, both supposed ambiguities in Article 4(2) gave rise to dispute

---

[25] The position that the veto of the permanent five member States should not apply in Security Council decisions on admission had no chance of securing the support of the permanent five member States: see, e.g., Sir Pierson Dixon (United Kingdom) SCOR 10th Year 701st mtg 10 Dec 1955 ¶ 46. The position nevertheless was voiced on a number of occasions, including when the chance for testing it in the International Court practically had passed. The Chairman of the Delegation of India, for example, said in 1955 that the Security Council veto of the admission of Japan and Mongolia was contrary to the 'doctrine of universality': Mr Menon (India) GAOR 10th sess 556th mtg 15 Dec 1955 ¶133. The United States – though apparently as a decision of policy, not a requirement of Charter law – said it would 'avoid thwarting the will of a qualified majority by use...of the veto': Mr Lodge (USA) SCOR 10th yr 701st mtg 10 Dec 1955 ¶ 85. The U.S. Senate in paragraph 1 of the Vandenberg Resolution (S. Res. 239, 80th Cong., 2d sess., 11 June 1948) had stated as a goal of U.S. foreign policy '[v]oluntary agreement to remove the veto from all questions involving pacific settlements of international disputes and situations, and from the admission of new members.' cf. GA res 267 (III) ('The problem of voting in the Security Council') 14 Apr 1949, esp. annex. The Soviet Union made clear from the start that the expression 'procedural matters' was to be narrowly construed: Fuller 'Soviet Policy in the United Nations' (1949) 263 *Annals of the Am Acad of Pol & Soc'l Science* 141, 144–5.

in the early years. It might have seemed uncontroversial, too, to say that, for the General Assembly to vote on an application, the 'recommendation' of the Security Council has to be an *affirmative* recommendation. Otherwise, the Security Council – chief executive mechanism of the organized international community – would be relegated to a passive role when membership applications are received. Alternative interpretations nevertheless were put forward. It was said that the provision in Article 4(2) that the General Assembly consider a State for admission 'on the recommendation of' the Security Council does not require that the Security Council make an affirmative recommendation.[26] Questions of admission, in this view, belonged to the General Assembly's 'paramount right of decision under Article 4.'[27] The position also was taken, in the alternative, that the voting procedure in the Security Council on whether to recommend admission was not subject to the veto power of the permanent five member States.[28] Its adherents referred this position to a number of arguments. It was said that the principle of universality superseded the veto; that the veto could not extend to matters that were not exclusively within the competence of the Security Council;[29] that the veto is inadmissible, if it is exercised against admission of an applicant State satisfying the criteria of Article 4; and that the General Assembly has the power to take action where a veto has resulted in deadlock in the Council.[30]

Neither the voting procedure position nor the 'recommendation' position attracted much support,[31] and States forcefully rejected both.[32] The latter position – that an affirmative Security Council recommendation is not necessary for the General Assembly to vote on admission – was tested by the International

---

[26] See the Argentine exposition on this point: Report of the Special Committee on Admission of New Members, 25 June 1953, A/2400, GAOR 8th sess, annexes, agenda item 22 ¶ 20.

[27] Ibid. ¶ 38.

[28] See the El Salvadoran interpretation: ibid. ¶ 16. See also the comments of Cuba: ibid. ¶¶ 30–1.

[29] Ibid. ¶ 15.

[30] The arguments are summarized in the above-cited Report, ¶ 8. The Special Committee which produced the report had been established under GA res 620A (VII), 21 Dec 1952.

[31] Argentina espoused the alternative theories, which, apparently, were chiefly the personal project of its UN representative. A group of other Latin American States, in particular Cuba, El Salvador, and Peru, sometimes espoused the theories as well. The proposals that the Organization interpret Article 4(2) in this way are covered in detail in Pomerance 'Seeking Judicial Legitimation in the Cold War: U.S. Foreign Policy and the World Court, 1948–1962' (1995) 5 *Ind Int'l & Comp LR* 303. On the (successful) efforts of the United States to keep the veto question from the International Court, see, ibid. at 309–12.

[32] E.g., Belgium, the United Kingdom, Greece, France, Canada, the Philippines, China, Norway, the Netherlands, and New Zealand: Report of the Special Committee on Admission of New Members, 25 June 1953, A/2400, GAOR 8th sess, annexes, agenda item 22 ¶¶ 51–75.

Court of Justice at the Assembly's request.[33] A request for an Advisory Opinion
was made, on the following question:

> Can the admission of a State to membership in the United Nations, pursuant to
> Article 4, paragraph 2, of the Charter, be effected by a decision of the General
> Assembly when the Security Council has made no recommendation for admission
> by reason of the candidate failing to obtain the requisite majority or of the negative
> vote of a permanent Member upon a resolution so to recommend?[34]

The Court, in a notably brief Advisory Opinion,[35] said that a recommendation is necessary – and explicitly rejected the theory that 'recommendation'
in Article 4 could be taken to include a negative recommendation. First, the
Court said that the scheme of institutional powers established by the Charter
must be respected:

> To hold that the General Assembly has power to admit a State to membership
> in the absence of a recommendation of the Security Council would be to deprive
> the Security Council of an important power which has been entrusted to it by the

---

[33] *Competence of the General Assembly for Admission of a State to the United Nations* Advisory Opinion, ICJ Rep 1950 pp. 4, 9, about which see Hudson 'The Twenty-Ninth Year of the World
Court' (1951) 45 *AJ* 1, 2; Honig 'The International Court of Justice 1947–1950' (1951/52)
14 *ZaöRV* 497, 523–4.

[34] GA res 296J (IV), 22 Nov 1949.

[35] Rosenne says that the question 'from the legal point of view was not of sufficient gravity or
difficulty to warrant the request for the advisory opinion': *Treaties* 229. The Court has referred
to the *Competence* Advisory Opinion most frequently to support the proposition that, when the
'clarity of…provisions, viewed in their context, admits of no doubt,' the Court must apply the
provisions 'as they stand': *LaGrand Case (Germany v United States of America)* ICJ Rep 2001 pp.
466, 494 ¶ 77. See also *Case Concerning the Arbitral Award of 31 July 1989 (Guinea-Bissau v
Senegal)* ICJ Rep 1991 pp. 53, 69 ¶ 48; *Fisheries Jurisdiction (UK v Iceland)* ICJ Rep 1973 pp.
3, 9–10 ¶ 17; *Fisheries Jurisdiction (Federal Republic of Germany v Iceland)* ICJ Rep 1973 pp. 49,
56 ¶ 18; *IMCO* Advisory Opinion of 8 June 1960, ICJ Rep 1960 pp. 150, 159–60. Yet clarity
may be in the eye of the beholder. See *Case Concerning the Aerial Incident of 10 August 1999
(Pakistan v India)* (Jurisdiction) Dis Op Judge *ad hoc* Pirzada ICJ Rep 2000 pp. 12, 96–7 ¶ 76;
*Case Concerning Application of the Convention on the Prevention and Punishment of the Crime of
Genocide (Bosnia and Herzegovina v Yugoslavia (Serbia and Montenegro))* (Further Requests for
the Indication of Provisional Measures) Order of 13 Sept 1993, Dis Op Judge *ad hoc* Kreča ICJ
Rep 1993 pp. 325, 458–9; *North Sea Continental Shelf (Federal Republic of Germany/Denmark;
Federal Republic of Germany/Netherlands)* Sep Op Judge Fouad Ammoun ICJ Rep 1969 pp.
3, 102 ¶ 2; *South West Africa (Ethiopia v South Africa; Liberia v South Africa)* (Second Phase)
Judgement of 18 July 1966, Dis Op Judge *ad hoc* Sir Louis Mbanefo ICJ Rep 1966 pp. 6, 501;
Case Concerning the Aerial Incident of July 27th, 1955 (Israel v Bulgaria) Judgement of 26 May
1959 (Preliminary Objections) Sep Op Judge Armand-Ugon ICJ rep 1959 pp. 127, 152 ¶ 2;
Effects of Awards of Compensation Made by the United Nations Administrative Tribunal Advisory
Opinion of 13 July 1954, Dis Op Judge Levi Carneiro ICJ Rep 1954 pp. 47, 92; *Ambatielos
Case (Greece v UK)* Dis Op Sir Arnold McNair, President, Judges Basdevant, Klaestad, and
Read ICJ Rep 1953 pp. 10, 30.

Charter. It would almost nullify the role of the Security Council in the exercise of one of the essential functions of the Organization.[36]

Operating here is the principle that all the words of the constitutive text are to be given meaning. An interpretation that took the Security Council out of the picture on admission would deprive of meaning the final clause of Article 4(2) ('upon the recommendation of the Security Council'), thus 'depriving' the Security Council of an assigned (or 'entrusted') power. To avoid such a result, Article 4(2) had to be interpreted so as to require the Security Council to exercise the function concerned, and as one prior to the corresponding function of the General Assembly. The Court went so far as to call this 'one of the essential functions' in the scheme of the Organization as a whole.

The Court then made clear that Article 4(2) means that the Security Council must give a favourable recommendation if the predicate for General Assembly action is to have been established:

> In the opinion of the Court, Article 4, paragraph 2, envisages a favourable recommendation of the Security Council and that only. An unfavourable recommendation would not correspond to the provisions of Article 4, paragraph 2.[37]

This finding may be referred to the same general principle of construction as above: 'recommendation' has little, if any, meaning if it is interpreted to include any recommendation at all regardless of content. The Court in the 1950 Advisory Opinion thus affirmed admission to be a task of the Security Council and the General Assembly as set out in Article 4(2).[38] In connection with the ILC's work on the responsibility of international organizations, the International Monetary Fund in 2007 would make the observation, applicable to the advisory request in 1950, that '[w]hatever politics may be involved in reaching particular decisions, compliance with the decision-making process is not a political choice.'[39]

---

[36] *Competence of the General Assembly for Admission of a State to the United Nations* Advisory Opinion, ICJ Rep 1950 p. 4.

[37] ICJ Rep 1950 at 9.

[38] As was to be expected, the Security Council itself did not contest the Advisory Opinion, though it did throw a sharp elbow at the Court as if to reserve the matter of reviewability of Security Council actions. See statement of the President of the Security Council, SCOR 10th yr 701st mtg 10 Dec 1955 ¶ 3: 'The Security Council is a principal organ of the United Nations, and it is an autonomous organ. In reaching decisions on matters within its competence, it is not subject to direction from the Assembly *or any other body*' [emphasis supplied].

[39] Responsibility of international organizations, Comments and observations received from international organizations: ILC 59th sess, A/CN.4/581, 1 May 2007 pp. 6–7.

A number of States made submissions in connection with the advisory proceedings on *Competence of the General Assembly*.[40] The East Bloc States objected to jurisdiction,[41] the Soviet Union going so far as to question whether the Court could ever have jurisdiction to interpret 'a quite peculiar document as the Charter.'[42] Egypt took the position which the Court would say was right – i.e., that an affirmative recommendation by the Security Council is necessary.[43] Venezuela, breaking from other Latin American States, agreed that concurrence of the Security Council and General Assembly is needed to effectuate admission. Venezuela also noted that Articles 10 and 12 as well place limitations on the powers of the General Assembly and that admission is not the only Charter function requiring concurrence of Assembly and Council.[44] The United States expressed the view that the question presented in the request 'does not involve serious difficulty,'[45] a view shared by France, which said that the text of the Charter was clear.[46] The Court itself, as might be inferred from the brevity of its opinion, concurred.

Argentina, main protagonist during discussions in the Assembly, in the advisory proceedings set out the most developed argument against the prevailing view. The General Assembly had not adopted Argentina's proposals which would have included in the question addressed to the Court the matter of Security Council voting procedure; Argentina nevertheless made submissions on that matter. The veto, Argentina said, when applied to applications for admission, was 'illegal.'[47] Addressing more closely the question as actually presented, Argentina posited that a 'recommendation' is not the same thing as a 'decision.' Though Argentina identified support for this in evidence of general usage,[48] the need for an *affirmative* recommendation by the Security Council was too clear for the Court to accept a contrary position. A rather persistent attempt to remove the Security Council from the admission equation failed as a legal strategy. It however reflected an emerging politics of the General Assembly, in which member States

---

[40] Among them USSR, Ukraine, Belorussia, Egypt, Czechoslovakia, USA, Argentina, Venezuela, and France.

[41] E.g., Ukraine ICJ Pldgs 1950 pp. 102–3; Belorussia ibid. 104–5; Czechoslovakia ibid. 108–9.

[42] ICJ Pldgs 1950 p. 100.

[43] ICJ Pldgs 1950 pp. 106–7.

[44] Others mentioned were expulsion (Charter Art. 6), election of the Secretary-General (Charter Art. 97) and election of judges to the International Court of Justice (Statute of the Court Art. 4): ICJ Pldgs 1950 pp. 149–51.

[45] ICJ Pldgs 1950 p. 111.

[46] ICJ Pldgs 1950 p. 163.

[47] ICJ Pldgs 1950 p. 145. See also ibid., pp. 123–4.

[48] ICJ Pldgs 1950 pp. 124, 132.

assert rights as against the permanent members of the Security Council. The transformation of the General Assembly through the admission of scores of new States in the decades following the *Competence* Advisory Opinion would make this the prevailing politics of the Assembly. The attempt to re-work Article 4(2), its weakness as legal argument notwithstanding, was a premonition of changes soon to occur in the constituency of the UN.

A short point may be made, in light of later practice, about the degree of specificity required when the Security Council recommends a State for admission. The Security Council by resolution 139 of 28 June 1960 recommended to the General Assembly that the Federation of Mali be admitted to membership.[49] The Federation of Mali, as a whole, had applied for admission on 23 June 1960.[50] The Federation, after the Security Council recommendation and before General Assembly action, however broke into two separate States, Senegal and Mali. According to one writer, the single recommendation, contained in resolution 139, referring as it did to the Federation which had contained them, sufficed for both States. The General Assembly proceeded to admit Senegal and Mali. It was said admission was 'without any further recommendation from the Security Council.'[51] This is not correct. The General Assembly, by resolution 1490 (XV) of 28 September 1960 admitted Senegal; and by resolution 1491 (XV) of the same date admitted Mali. In fact, the two States had submitted separate applications for membership – Senegal on 20 September 1960 (or late in August)[52] and Mali on 22 September 1960;[53] and the Security Council adopted two separate

---

[49]   SC res 139, 28 June 1960.

[50]   S/4347, Cable dated 23 June 1960 from the President of the Federal Government of Mali addressed to the Secretary-General. Note the contemporaneous cable from the Permanent Representative of France affirming the independence of the Federation of Mali and its possession of 'all the qualifications for United Nations membership': S/4348.

[51]   Young 'The State of Syria: New or Old?' (1962) 56 *AJ* 484, 485–6 n. 11.

[52]   Letter dated 20 Sept 1960 from the Minister of Foreign Affairs of the Republic of Senegal addressed to the Secretary-General. The letter confirmed cables dated 20 and 24 August 1960 from the Government of Senegal requesting admission. The 20 September letter notes that Senegal adopted a new constitution on 25 August 1960 and, thereby, had 'acceded to full and complete independence.' The letter also contained Senegal's formal acceptance of Charter obligations. It was distributed under the title 'Application of the Republic of Senegal for Admission to Membership in the United Nations': A/4511 dated 27 Sept 1960.

[53]   Cable dated 22 September 1960 from the President of the Government of the Republic of Mali addressed to the Secretary-General, saying '[B]y Act No. 60–35/AL/Rs of 22 September 1960 the Republic of Mali has been proclaimed an independent and sovereign State. The Republic of Mali requests admission to the United Nations': A/4512.

recommendations, one for Senegal[54] and one for Mali,[55] that is to say, after (and superseding) the earlier recommendation to admit the now-defunct Federation. Article 4(2) does not say the form the Security Council recommendation is to take; the recommendation apparently may be contained in a resolution or other decision. But the recommendation, as the *Competence* Advisory Opinion would suggest, must be affirmative *as to the State seeking admission.* It would appear from practice that a recommendation does not apply to an applicant's successor. As will be seen in connection with treatment of the former Yugoslavia (Chapter 6), this is consistent with the relation between State succession and UN membership generally.

The constitutional apparatus of Article 4(2) has been further specified in UN procedure. The Provisional Rules of Procedure of the Security Council and the Rules of Procedure of the General Assembly set out the procedural steps which a State seeking admission must follow.[56] A State submits an application for membership to the Security Council, and this must contain a formal declaration that the State is willing to accept the obligations of the Charter.[57] The Security Council considers whether the State satisfies the criteria for admission set out in Article 4(1).[58] The General Assembly does the same, relative to those applications which the Council has recommended.[59] An application for admission, '[u]nless the Security Council decides otherwise,' is to be referred for further examination

---

[54] SC res 158, 28 Sept 1960. In a letter dated 28 September 1960 addressed to the Secretary-General, the President of the Security Council said that resolution 158 'supersedes the recommendation made by the Council at its 869th meeting on 28 June 1960 regarding the application which had been made by the Federation of Mali.' The letter and resolution 158 were distributed under the title 'Application of the Republic of Senegal for Membership in the United Nations': A/4513. The General Assembly, in its resolution admitting Senegal to membership, refers to the 'Security Council recommendation of 28 September 1960': GA res 1490 (XV), 28 Sept 1960.

[55] SC res 159, 28 Sept 1960. This was sent to the Secretary-General with a letter taking the same form as the letter accompanying the Senegal recommendation: A/4514. GA res 1491 (XV), 28 Sept 1960 refers to 'the recommendation of the Security Council of 28 September 1960.'

[56] The procedures are summarized by Ginther 'Article 4' in Simma ed p. 184 ¶ 32. The content of the paragraph above derives from Ginther. The Provisional Rules of Procedure of the Security Council were adopted by the Security Council at its 1st meeting and amended at its 31st, 41st, 42nd, 44th and 48th meetings, on 9 Apr, 16 and 17 May, 6 and 24 June 1946; 138th and 222nd meetings, on 4 June and 9 Dec 1947; 468th meeting, on 28 Feb 1950; 1463rd meeting, on 24 Jan 1969; 1761st meeting, on 17 Jan 1974; and 2410th meeting, on 21 Dec 1982: S/96/Rev.7. For the Rules of Procedure of the General Assembly, as amended, see A/520/Rev.15, 31 Dec 1984.

[57] Provisional Rules of Procedure of the Security Council, Rule 58; Rules of Procedure of the General Assembly, Rule 135.

[58] Provisional Rules of Procedure of the Security Council, Rule 60.

[59] Rules of Procedure of the General Assembly, Rule 137.

to a committee on admission of new members.[60] The referral procedure has not been consistently used.[61] More will be said in the next Chapter, about the relation of the procedural rules and the substantive criteria for admission.

On the basis of the *Competence* Advisory Opinion, the constitutional allocation of authority over admission as between the Security Council and General Assembly was to remain as envisaged under the Charter; no serious interpretative question has since been raised as to how the authority is to be shared. By contrast, in the five years after the 1950 Advisory Opinion, how to apply the substantive criteria for admission – that is to say, how to apply Article 4, paragraph 1 – would occupy the member States at length.

1.3   *Admission Criteria: Article 4(1)*

Article 4, paragraph 1 of the UN Charter is the main location of the criteria for admission of States to the Organization.

A core group of fifty-one States, most of which were adherents to the anti-Axis alliance of World War II, comprise the 'original members' of the United Nations. Other States, to seek admission, do so under Article 4, paragraph 1:

> Membership in the United Nations is open to all other peace-loving states which accept the obligations contained in the present Charter and, in the judgment of the Organization, are able and willing to carry out these obligations.

The expression 'judgment of the Organization' is to be read in connection with paragraph 2 of Article 4, providing that the UN may admit a State as member, upon the recommendation of the Security Council and affirmative vote of the General Assembly (see preceding section). Thus, States are not born members of the United Nations; they are admitted under decisions taken by existing members. There was for a time the suggestion that the substantive criteria of Article 4(1) would be applied restrictively when the UN considered non-member States for admission. This can be traced to the Conference on International Organization in 1945; followed through the ICJ Advisory Opinion of 1948 on *Conditions of Admission*, and then to the debates of the early and mid-1950s occasioned by the so-called 'logjam,' after which a permissive interpretation of Article 4(1) prevailed and the journey began to universal membership in the Organization. It is to this train of developments of admission criteria in practice that we now will turn.

---

[60] Provisional Rules of Procedure of the Security Council, Rule 59.
[61] *UN Ybk* 1972 p. 215.

Chapter 2

The Early Years: Implementing Article 4?

2.1 *Introductory*

Article 4, paragraph 2 of the Charter sets out an admission procedure. Article 4, paragraph 1 sets out criteria for admission. Both the procedure and the criteria are set out only in general terms. Further detail was required, if admission was to be implemented as a rigorous process. The present Chapter examines steps taken early in the UN era to develop Article 4 into a workable system of institutional mechanisms and legal rules to control admission of States to the Organization. The fate of early efforts to establish and implement Article 4, especially the criteria contained in paragraph 1, we will see would prove a significant influence on the future shape of the United Nations.

Like other parts of the UN Charter, the provisions on admission were described broadly, so it remained for the member States and the Organization to develop their specific meaning through practice. It is a basic and accepted proposition that the practice of States and of international organizations is the material element in the formation of customary international law rules,[1] and, so, too that practice can be the basis of interpretations of rules adopted initially in a treaty.[2] As will be seen in Chapter 4 below, beyond that basic position, the effect of practice may be considerably murkier – e.g., as respects amendment of treaties and the constitutional evolution of an international organization.

---

[1] *North Sea Continental Shelf (Federal Republic of Germany/Denmark; Federal Republic of Germany/Netherlands)* ICJ Rep 1969 pp. 3, 37–46 ¶¶ 60–82; *Judgments of the Administrative Tribunal of the International Labour Organisation upon Complaints made against the United Nations Educational, Scientific and Cultural Organization* Advisory Opinion ICJ Rep 1956 pp. 77, 91.

[2] See *Air Transport Services Case*, Decision of 22 Dec 1963 (Ago, President; Reuter and De Vries, Members): 3 ILM 668, 713 (1963); *Temple of Preah Vihear (Cambodia v Thailand)*, ICJ Rep 1962 pp. 6, 33. For writers, see Murphy 'Assessing the Legality of Invading Iraq' (2004) 92 *Georgetown LJ* 173, 203 n. 127; Sloane 'The United Nations as a Constitution' (1989) 1 *Pace YBIL* 61, 103–21.

It is not however to be doubted that practice is relevant when considering Charter Article 4. As the United States submitted in the *Competence* advisory proceedings, '[T]he Court will wish to give great weight to the construction which has in practice been placed on Article 4, paragraph 2, by the organs of the United Nations which have the responsibility for giving effect to this provision.'[3] Though the allocation of competence between the Security Council and General Assembly was not a difficult problem for the Court, the further development of admission rules and procedures was not a simple technical matter, nor was it resolved by a plain reading of the Charter text. The constitutional law of the Charter concerning substantive criteria for admission, as will be seen in the present Chapter, was a matter of disagreement among the member States in the first decade of the Organization. Charter law would involve the politics of Cold War rivalry, the interests of voting blocs in the General Assembly, and separation of powers among the principal organs of the Organization. The practice that resulted from these competing influences has been instrumental in determining how the UN has implemented Article 4.

Even before the formal adoption of the Charter in 1945 at San Francisco, dispute arose as to which States should be participants. The Argentine controversy, which concerned seating the delegation of Argentina in the Conference on International Organization, may be seen as the first test of admission criteria under the UN system. In itself, this was a short-lived dispute. It was enmeshed however in a nascent rivalry between the United States and the USSR and foretold impending difficulties. It also foretold future lines of development under Article 4. The Argentine controversy encapsulated competing legal positions which would form poles in the coming decade of disputed applications for admission.

The 1946 session of the UN witnessed adoption of rules of procedure, and under these rules the Committee on Admission of New Members showed some initial energy in the discharge of its assigned function. This was the function of fact-finding and evaluation with respect to applications for admission. Inquiries into the fitness of applicants under the substantive criteria of Article 4(1) were carried out in several instances. As controversy began to brew over new applicants however, the mechanism tentatively employed in 1946 by the Committee fell into disuse.

Controversy over admission would intensify thereafter. The General Assembly, seeking to resolve the matter, would request and obtain an Advisory Opinion on admission in 1948, but judicial guidance did not settle outstanding differences over how to manage pending applications. The World War II neutrals and various States allied with one or the other rival Cold War bloc were delayed admission,

---

[3] ICJ Pldgs 1950 p. 112.

producing the so-called logjam. Far from admission being further proceduralized and the substantive criteria consolidated, the period from the late 1940s through the mid-1950s brought a breakdown of the admission process. States seeking admission accumulated, until the delay surrounding their candidatures came to be seen as a crisis in urgent need of solution. The breakdown of admission processes in the late 1940s and early 1950s was in time addressed, but the way it was addressed did not build upon the initial practice. The solution to the logjam will be considered in Chapter 3 below.

The early practice is nevertheless instructive, for it shows how substantive criteria for admission might have been implemented – and it also shows how the UN and its member States failed to establish the basis which otherwise might have supported rigorous application of Article 4. These developments must be understood, if the present constitution of the Organization is to be understood and, so, starting with the Argentine Controversy of June 1945, each now will be addressed in turn.

2.2 *The Argentine Controversy*

At the Conference on International Organization in San Francisco, a question arose as to the identity of the Original Members. The wartime allies convened the Conference, and their goal was to proceed from the Dumbarton Oaks drafts and adopt a final instrument so as to constitute the United Nations as a permanent body. Argentina sent a delegation. The Latin American States favoured including them in the Conference. They also favoured including Argentina as an Original Member State of the United Nations. The Soviet Union protested. Argentina, it was noted, had declared war against Germany on 27 March 1945. This was scarcely six weeks before final victory in Europe. Up to that point, Argentina had been closer to the Axis than to the Allies. The Soviet Union argued that Argentina had been in effect part of the Axis camp, and too late in its conversion – a conversion, it was plain for all to see, prompted by the Allies' progress on their own road to Berlin. In the Soviet view, Argentina simply did not classify as a 'peace-loving State.'

The problem occasioned heated pronouncements at the Conference on International Organization. The Soviets contrasted Argentina with Poland, which had fought the Nazis from literally the first shot of the war to the end. Soviet Foreign Minister Molotov made the following statement at the Conference:

> Imagine what would happen if we acted rashly and invite Argentina to this Conference, although in the present war she has been assisting the Fascists who are our enemies, and failed to invite Poland which is an Ally. Poland is known to hold in this war an honourable place among Allied nations which have devoted all their

efforts to the struggle against our common foe. The heroic Polish people have been fighting in our ranks and making innumerable sacrifices. We cannot afford to forget about all this. To invite Argentina, which has been helping our common enemy throughout this war, and not to invite the Provisional Polish Government, which is now functioning in liberated Poland and enjoys enormous prestige among the Polish people, would be taking a course that might affect adversely the prestige of this Conference.[4]

As would be the case in future East-West disagreements in the UN framework (there was as yet no United Nations Organization as such – only the Conference for its establishment), more than one consideration determined the positions staked out. The western Allies were struggling against Soviet insistence that the Soviet-sponsored Polish government be the only public body recognized as having authority in Poland. It was far from clear that the pro-Soviet government 'enjoy[ed] enormous prestige,' and Molotov's attack on Argentine participation was notably expressed as a comparison to put pressure on the Allies to accept the Polish delegation. (The London-based exile government in the event was pushed aside in favour of its Soviet-sponsored competitor.) Also considered were western relations with Latin America. The United States in particular aimed to foster good relations with other States in the western hemisphere where the question of Argentine participation in the Conference had excited public sentiment.

Amid the tumult of negotiations at the conference, Argentina at length was admitted and included as an Original Member. Various compromises were involved, in particular respecting the two Soviet republics, Belorussia and Ukraine.[5] The Soviet objections to Argentina are nonetheless instructive. They

---

[4] 5th Plen Sess 30 Apr 1945, Verbatim Minutes, Doc 42/ P/10 *UN Conference on International Organization: Documents* vol. I p. 346.

[5] On the membership question at the Conference on International Organization, see Russell *A History of the United Nations Charter: The Role of the United States 1940–1945* (1958) 433–9, 551–72, 631–9. The question of admission of Argentina specifically is addressed, with extensive reference to the diplomatic record, by Woods 'Conflict or Community? The United States and Argentina's Admission to the United Nations' (1977) 46(3) *Pacific Historical Review* 363. Bailey mentions the question only in passing: *Diplomatic History of the American People* 10th edn (1980) 769. See also Trask 'Spruille Braden versus George Messersmith: World War II, The Cold War, and Argentine Policy, 1945–1947' (1984) 26(1) *Journal of Interamerican Studies & World Affairs* 69, 73, 88. The admission of Ukraine and Belorussia, both non-State entities at the time, generally has been recognized as anomalous: Dugard *Recognition and the United Nations* (1987) 54–5. As Union Republics of the USSR, these had very limited international relations outside the UN: Dolan 'The Member-Republics of the USSR as Subjects of the Law of Nations' (1955) 4 *ICLQ* 629, 631, which is not to say that some federal units do not exercise even fairly extensive international competences: see Audeoud 'Les Collectivités Intra-Étatiques dans la Vie Internationale' in Société française pour le droit international *Colloque de Nancy: L'Etat souverain à l'aube du XXIᵉ siècle* (1994) 139–69; David 'La Responsabilité des États Fédéraux dans les Relations Internationales' in Institut de sociologie *Les États fédéraux dans les relations internationales:*

illustrate how a State could argue on principles concerning the fitness of another State to participate in the UN. The Soviet Union argued that the Conference should have excluded Argentina on grounds that that State had acted contrary to the objects and purposes of the (then-nascent) Organization. Also foretelling future developments, the Argentine dispute led to an essentially political compromise – admission of candidates championed by the opposing power. As of 1945 however there still was ample scope for developing the Charter admission criteria as part of a legal system.

Not long after the Charter was adopted, application of the Article 4(1) criteria was subject to a request by the General Assembly for an opinion under the advisory jurisdiction of the International Court of Justice.[6] This would invite the most thorough statements to date from States on the matter of substantive criteria for admission and the particular meaning to be ascribed the multiple elements of Article 4(1).

2.3   *Advisory Opinion on* Conditions of Admission *(1948)*

The International Court of Justice in *Conditions of Admission of a State for Membership in the United Nations* (1948)[7] was asked by the General Assembly, *inter alia*, whether a State member of the UN, voting on an application for admission under Article 4, is legally entitled to condition its vote on criteria not expressly set out in paragraph 1 of Article 4. The question as put to the Court was as follows:

> Is a Member of the United Nations which is called upon, in virtue of Article 4 of the Charter, to pronounce itself by its vote, either in the Security Council or in the General Assembly, on the admission of a State to membership in the United Nations, juridically entitled to make its consent to the admission dependent on conditions not expressly provided by paragraph 1 of the said Article? In particular, can such a Member, while it recognizes the conditions set forth in that provision to be fulfilled by the State concerned, subject its affirmative vote to the additional

---

actes du colloque de Bruxelles (1984) 483; and documents collected by Lejeune 'Les Competences des Communautés et des Regions Belges en Matière Internationale' ibid. 511.

[6] UN Charter Art 96; ICJ Statute Arts 36(1), 65.

[7] ICJ Rep 1948 p. 57, about which see Honig 'The International Court of Justice 1947–1950' (1951/52) 14 *ZaöRV* 497, 519–23; Liang 'Conditions of Admission of a State to Membership in the United Nations' (1949) 43 *AJ* 288; 'Advisory Opinion of the International Court of Justice Concerning Conditions of Admission of a State to Membership in the United Nations, May 28, 1948' (1948) 2 *Int'l Org* 568. See also Koskenniemi *From Apology to Utopia. The Structure of International Legal Argument* (2005) 371–9.

condition that other States be admitted to membership in the United Nations together with that State?[8]

This occasioned the first advisory opinion of the International Court of Justice.[9] In the advisory opinion, the Court had the chance to clarify the substance of the criteria for admission of States to the United Nations, an urgent matter at the time, for the backlog in applications to membership by then was rising to the level of a political crisis. The advisory proceedings also gave States the chance, in oral and written submissions, to set out their views, significant in their own right as indicators of State legal opinion, as to the meaning of Article 4(1).

The Court answered the General Assembly's question in four parts, and the substance of its answer was as follows: (i) The question of membership is a legal question. (ii) The criteria listed in Article 4(1) are the sole criteria on which membership applications are to be considered. (iii) The autonomy of member States to come to a decision as to how to cast their votes is not to be infringed, it being for each member State according to its own internal processes to determine whether the Article 4(1) criteria are met. (iv) The factual and other circumstances which the member States properly may consider when reaching the determination whether an applicant has met the Article 4(1) criteria are wide in scope. The Court's analysis of the main points merits consideration.

2.3.1   *The Court's Analysis*

The advisory request on *Conditions of Admission* led the Court to give its most significant analysis of the legal requirements for admission. Of concern to the Court throughout was the balance between the discretion of a State as a fact-finder and its obligations under Charter Article 4(1). The Court set down an interpretation of the Charter tempering the bolder assertions of State discretion posited by certain member States.

---

[8] GA res 113B(II), 17 Nov 1947; ICJ Rep 1948 pp. 57, 58.

[9] Rosenne *The law and practice of the International Court, 1920–2005* 4th ed (2006) vol. II p. 1019. As an advisory opinion at the beginning of the ICJ era, the *Conditions* Advisory Opinion has been significant for its guidance on a number of points in addition to the substantive ones, e.g., justiciability of legal questions having political aspects: *Legal Consequences of the Construction of a Wall in the Occupied Palestinian Territory* Advisory Opinion of 9 July 2004 ICJ Rep 2004 pp. 136, 155 ¶ 41. Judge Oda identified the opinion as the first in a series of seven advisory opinions early in the Charter era developing the constitutional law of the Organization: *Legality of the Threat or Use of Nuclear Weapons* Advisory Opinion of 8 July 1996, Dis Op Judge Oda, ICJ Rep 1996 pp. 226, 370 ¶ 49.

With respect to the autonomy of States in their internal deliberations as to how to vote, the Court said the following:

> Although the Members are bound to conform to the requirements of Article 4 in giving their votes, the General Assembly can hardly be supposed to have intended to ask the Court's opinion as to the reasons which, in the mind of a Member, may prompt its vote. Such reasons, which enter into a mental process, are obviously subject to no control. Nor does the request concern a Member's freedom of expressing its opinion. Since it concerns a condition or conditions on which a Member 'makes its consent dependent,' the question can only relate to the statements made by a Member concerning the vote it proposes to give.
>
> It is clear from the General Assembly's Resolution of November 17th, 1947 [setting out the questions for which answers were requested of the Court], that the Court is not called upon either to define the meaning and scope of the conditions on which admission is made dependent, or to specify the elements which may serve in a concrete case to verify the existence of the requisite conditions.[10]

According to the Court in this passage, a member State when it considers the question of admission of an applicant State possesses a certain discretion and is also subject to a certain control. On the one hand, 'Members are bound to conform to the requirements of Article 4.' The substantive criteria of Article 4, the Court thus made clear, are 'requirements' – not merely a list furnished by way of example or standards for guidance. This is the aspect of control which the Court identified. On the other hand, the Court acknowledged that States, in evaluating an application for admission, have internal mechanisms for doing so. This is the purport of the language concerning 'reasons...in the mind of a Member [which] may prompt its vote' and 'enter[ing] into a mental process.' The language refers to the internal processes of decision of each member State, and it is those processes that are 'subject to no control.' By 'no control' is meant no control exogenous to the State. No other State or States subject the member State to control in the process of decision, nor does the UN itself. The decision in question is how to cast the State's vote in the Council or Assembly with respect to an application for admission to membership. This is the discretionary aspect.

Taken on its own, the passage would raise the question whether anything is left of legal criteria for admission. The words 'obviously subject to no control' appear categorical. The discretionary aspect in this light might seem to consume the rest. On examination, however, it is clear that the Court was referring to a particular part of the decision-making operation, not to the whole. In particular, the Court was referring to the fact-finding process in which each member State engages when considering how to cast its vote on an application. The

---

[10] ICJ Rep 1948 pp. 57, 60.

subordinate clause in the second question of the General Assembly's request postulated a situation in which a member State 'recognizes the conditions set forth in [Article 4(1)] to be fulfilled by the State concerned.' It was not for the Court to say what factual circumstances might properly lead a member State to 'recognize [that] the conditions' obtain in a given case; this was not the direction of the General Assembly's query, thus it was not the direction of the Court's response. The Court was clear that the advisory opinion was not the place for it to specify 'elements which may serve in a concrete case to verify the existence of the requisite conditions.'

Even if the General Assembly had asked the Court to give examples of such elements 'verify[ing] the existence of the requisite conditions' (i.e., verifying that the applicant State satisfied the Article 4(1) criteria), according to the Court no agency other than the member State's chosen internal process has authority to say whether the elements obtain in a given case. This holding is consequential with respect to the UN's efforts to proceduralize Article 4. More will be said below in this Chapter about the inquiries carried out in the Committee on Admission of New Members as to the fitness of applicants under Article 4(1). The inquiries, in the form of questionnaires directed to applicants, were an exercise of fact-finding by the Committee. Here it may be observed that the Court's statement in the 1948 Advisory Opinion casts doubt on whether such inquiries were constitutional under the Charter, for they would appear to have had the effect of relieving the member States of fact-finding authority in respect of applications for admission. If a UN committee were to make the determination whether an applicant satisfied the criteria for admission (and assuming that such a determination were to have binding effect), then it could not be said that the member States are 'subject to no control.'

The discretion to which the Court referred with the phrase 'subject to no control' is discretion with respect to the fact-finding required when a State is asked to vote. Such discretion is significant. It is a far cry, however, from discretion to add to (or to ignore) the substantive criteria for admission as provided in the Charter. The Court here, at least in theory, placed a limit on the discretion of each State. A State had a margin of appreciation in reaching a judgment as to whether the facts of an application satisfied the five criteria of paragraph 1 and the margin was wide – 'subject to no control.' The limit lay in the Court's judgment that no member State could lawfully add new criteria to those provided.

In saying this, the Court was establishing a position in distinct contrast to that submitted by certain States in connection with the advisory proceedings. According to Czechoslovakia,

> [L]e texte du paragraphe 1 de l'article 4 n'exclut nullement que les Membres des Nations Unies peuvent considérer l'admission de Membres nouveaux, en exerçant leur pouvoir discrétionnaire, non seulement par rapport à certaines conditions qui sont expressément énumérées... mais encore sous l'angle d'autres conditions

dictées par leur jugement politique et qui ne sont pas indiquées expressément dans l'article.[11]

Poland said, 'This set of conditions does not create a right to be admitted to the United Nations,'[12] from which it might be inferred that the member State has the right to impose further conditions on its affirmative vote. The Court however rejected the proposition that the Charter allows a member State to add further conditions. So, while the Court may appear to have left a great deal of discretion in the hands of the member States, this was restricted to the field of fact finding. The Court drew a line, as against the view that the criteria of Article 4(1) were a mere starting point rather than the exhaustive list of conditions of admission. This met resistance from states (e.g., Czechoslovakia and Poland). As will be seen shortly, the Court's conclusion was doubted by several members of the bench as well.

The Court also spoke of the legal character of admission. The Court emphasized that fact-finding in connection with an application for admission, though it well may have a political and discretionary aspect, is subject to legal regulation:

> Understood in this light, the question, in its two parts, is and can only be a purely legal one. To determine the meaning of a treaty provision – to determine, as in this case, the character (exhaustive or otherwise) of the conditions for admission stated therein – is a problem of interpretation and consequently a legal question.
>
> The requisite conditions are five in number: to be admitted to membership in the United Nations, an applicant must (1) be a State; (2) be peace-loving; (3) accept the obligations of the Charter; (4) be able to carry out these obligations; and (5) be willing to do so.
>
> All these conditions are subject to the judgment of the Organization. The judgment of the Organization means the judgment of the two organs mentioned in paragraph 2 of Article 4, and, in the last analysis, that of its Members. The question put is concerned with the individual attitude of each Member called upon to pronounce itself on the question of admission.

The Court characterized the decision as one resting ultimately with each member State – subject to 'the individual attitude of each.' Nevertheless, the criteria on which an applicant is to be evaluated are prescribed by the Charter; they are legal criteria; and the Court took notice of them. The five criteria are set out in the Charter – not formulated by the member States, even as the member States hold the discretion to evaluate factual circumstances with a view to deciding whether, in the circumstances, the criteria have been met. The message most often drawn from the Advisory Opinion has been that no new criteria may be added to those in Article 4(1). In placing so much emphasis on the five criteria

---

[11] ICJ Pldgs 1948 p. 117.
[12] Ibid., p. 100.

comprising Article 4(1), however, the Court equally might be taken as having admonished States not to elide them.

In the Advisory Opinion as received, the main point indeed was generally taken to be the exhaustiveness of Article 4(1). A number of States had supported this point in the proceedings. According to Honduras, 'admission...cannot be based on conditions other than those clearly and precisely set out in paragraph 1 of Article 4 of the Charter.'[13] India said States were 'wrong to import extraneous considerations into this matter.'[14] Canada noted that other conditions had been proposed at the Conference on International Organization but that these had been rejected, a drafting history supporting the position that the criteria in Article 4 are the only ones properly considered.[15]

The Court came to the same judgment. The criteria in Article 4(1) are exhaustive:

> The terms 'Membership in the United Nations is open to all other peace-loving States which....' ...indicate that States which fulfil the conditions stated have the qualifications requisite for admission. The natural meaning of the words used leads to the conclusion that these conditions constitute an exhaustive enumeration and are not merely stated by way of guidance or example. The provision would lose its significance and weight, if other conditions, unconnected with those laid down, could be demanded. The conditions stated in paragraph 1 of Article 4 must therefore be regarded not merely as the necessary conditions, but also as the conditions which suffice.
>
> Nor can it be argued that the conditions enumerated represent only an indispensable minimum, in the sense that political considerations could be superimposed upon them, and prevent the admission of an applicant which fulfils them. Such an interpretation would be inconsistent with the terms of paragraph 2 of Article 4, which provide for the admission of...'any such State [fulfilling these conditions].' It would lead to conferring upon Members an indefinite and practically unlimited power of discretion in the imposition of new conditions. Such a power would be inconsistent with the very character of paragraph 1 of Article 4 which, by reason of the close connexion which it establishes between membership and the observance of the principles and obligations of the Charter, clearly constitutes a legal regulation of the question of the admission of new States. To warrant an interpretation other than that which ensues from the natural meaning of the words, a decisive reason would be required which has not been established.[16]

If, as suggested in our discussion above, one effect of the Court's advisory opinion was to emphasize the legal significance of the five criteria set out in Article 4(1), then it was equally the purpose of the Court to foreclose the imposition

---

[13] Ibid., p. 17.
[14] Ibid., p. 18.
[15] Ibid., p. 19. See also statement of Iraq ibid. 27; and written observations of Belgium ibid. 24. The drafting history is considered further in Chapter 4, pp. 128–30 below.
[16] ICJ Rep 1948 pp. 57, 62–3.

of any further conditions on States seeking admission. The criteria set out in Article 4(1) are exhaustive, and no others may be 'superimposed upon them.' To interpret the criteria set out therein as mere examples would give member States an 'indefinite and practically unlimited power of discretion' – a power inconsistent with the character of Article 4(1) as a 'legal regulation of the question of the admission of new States.' This legal regulation consists of the 'close connexion…between membership and the observance of the principles and obligations of the Charter': Article 4 governs admission to membership, and admission to membership is to be granted only those applicants which observe the principles and obligations of the Charter. The criteria in Article 4(1) must be applied when considering an application for admission; applying the criteria is not elective, for they are indeed 'the *necessary* conditions.' So too are the criteria complete. The main concern in the Advisory Opinion was to establish the completeness of the criteria enumerated in Article 4(1), for certain member States at the time were inclined to condition their votes on factors not belonging to the five enumerated criteria, factors 'unconnected with those laid down.' If member States were to do so, then, according to the Court, Article 4(1) would 'lose its significance and weight.' It was the preservation of the constitutional significance of Article 4(1) that chiefly concerned the Court in the *Admission* Advisory Opinion. To the General Assembly's question whether, in general terms, 'conditions not expressly provided' could be added by member States when considering applications for admission, the Court, then, was clear.

The General Assembly also asked a further, specific question. In addition to the general question whether States are permitted to consider conditions not contained in Article 4(1), the General Assembly asked whether it would be proper for a member State to condition its vote on admission of one State on admission of another State. This was a lesser included case of the situation addressed in the first question: if, as a general matter, no conditions not expressly provided could be added, then no particular condition not expressly provided could be either. The Court's answer in the Advisory Opinion therefore also was negative:

> The second part of the question concerns a demand on the part of a Member making its consent to the admission of an applicant dependent on the admission of other applicants.
>
> Judged on the basis of the rule which the Court adopts in its interpretation of Article 4, such a demand clearly constitutes a new condition, since it is entirely unconnected with those prescribed in Article 4. It is also in an entirely different category from those conditions, since it makes admission dependent, not on the conditions required of applicants, qualifications which are supposed to be fulfilled, but on an extraneous consideration concerning States other than the applicant State.
>
> The provisions of Article 4 necessarily imply that every application for admission should be examined and voted on separately and on its own merits; otherwise it would be impossible to determine whether a particular applicant fulfils the necessary conditions. To subject an affirmative vote for the admission of an applicant

State to the condition that other States be admitted with that State would prevent Members from exercising their judgment in each case with complete liberty, within the scope of the prescribed conditions. Such a demand is incompatible with the letter and spirit of Article 4 of the Charter.[17]

This is clear enough as far as it goes. It follows logically from the general restriction against additive conditions. It also further specifies that restriction by instructing member States that linkage of one applicant to another constitutes an additive, and thus prohibited, condition. What the Court did not do however is furnish a general rule of interpretation to tell whether any given factual or legal consideration constitutes an additive condition. A question of appreciation well may arise when examining a member State's conduct for consistency with the Advisory Opinion: no additional criteria may be added, but what exactly constitutes an additional criterion? Australia, in its submission in the advisory proceedings, said that the position taken by the Soviet Union is incorrect that the absence of diplomatic relations is ground for a negative vote. It also was no ground to cast a negative vote, according to Australia, that the applicant had been neutral during World War II.[18] Both Australia and Siam (Thailand) expressly rejected linking admission of one applicant to admission of another,[19] a position they shared with France which, however, as will be seen, otherwise held distinct views as to the scope of the discretion possessed by a member State.[20] Such considerations, then, in those States' views, were tantamount to criteria extraneous to Article 4(1) and thus *contra legem*.

There is an intrinsic difficulty in distinguishing extrinsic criteria from facts going to the existence of the criteria provided. This is not to say that clear cases do not exist. The Court believed that the General Assembly's second question presented a clear case. According to the Court, linking admission of one State to admission of another 'clearly constitutes a new condition.' The situations in which it is not so clear that a proposed consideration is 'an extraneous consideration' however are easy to hypothesize. What if the absence of diplomatic relations was one fact among others indicative of hostile intention inconsistent with the requirement that the applicant be 'peace-loving'? Or what if it cast doubt on the ability of an applicant to fulfil other Charter obligations? A State might suspend diplomatic relations with another because, for example, it wishes to express its displeasure at sanctions instituted for the purpose of compelling it to cease gross violations of its citizens' human rights. The question would have to be decided where it arose whether a given consideration really is extraneous – or, instead,

---

[17] ICJ Rep 1948 pp. 57, 64–5.
[18] ICJ Pldgs 1948 pp. 30–1.
[19] Ibid., pp. 32, 33.
[20] Ibid., p. 79.

simply one of the five enumerated criteria, perhaps in occluded form. Judge Azevedo attached an individual opinion, which we will consider below, in which he suggested that just such a consideration as absence of diplomatic relations well may enter into a State's decision – and nevertheless remain within bounds of Article 4(1). Again, in the example given in the General Assembly's request – conditioning admission of one State upon admission of another – the position seemed clear enough. As far as the Court was concerned, if criteria extraneous to Article 4(1) are to be excluded, then a member State cannot be permitted to link admission of one applicant to admission of another. The Court did not think that this point required much analysis for purposes of the advisory opinion.

The Court nevertheless saw the question of linked admissions as inviting a further observation. The problem with linked admissions is that such a practice would make it 'impossible to determine whether a particular applicant fulfils the necessary conditions.' The determination for one applicant would be intertwined with that for another, and, thus, in effect, the applicant would be denied its own day in the UN admission process. The Court was shifting its emphasis here from substance – what considerations may go to determining whether the Article 4(1) criteria are fulfilled? – to process – how is the relevant determination to be reached? One may conclude from the Court's observations that determining whether the 'necessary conditions' are fulfilled is a significant process under the Charter. The process is not to be encumbered by 'extraneous' considerations or 'a new condition...entirely unconnected with those prescribed in Article 4.' The necessary conditions must be determined to be met, before a given applicant is admitted to membership, and the Court believed it necessary to describe this for what it was – a rule guaranteeing separate process for each applicant: '[E]very application for admission should be examined and voted on separately and on its own merits.' As considered later in this Chapter, procedures indeed were established through which the merits of 'every application' might be examined, and, in some early cases, the procedures were utilized as intended. This matter of process would have implications for the overall structure of the international organization.

The Court also was concerned with process as carried out by each member State. According to the Court, determining whether the necessary conditions are met is a fact-finding process that each State not only is entitled but also is obliged to undertake. The Court determined the breadth of the facts that a member State may consider, when forming its decision as to how to vote on an application. The facts which a member State may consider are not to be narrowly circumscribed:

> It does not...follow from the exhaustive character of paragraph 1 of Article 4 that an appreciation is precluded of such circumstances of fact as would enable the existence of the requisite conditions to be verified.

> Article 4 does not forbid the taking into account of any factor which it is pos-
> sible reasonably and in good faith to connect with the conditions laid down in that
> Article. The taking into account of such factors is implied in the very wide and
> very elastic nature of the prescribed conditions; no relevant political factor – that
> is to say, none connected with the conditions of admission – is excluded.[21]

Member States are to consider 'such circumstances of fact' as are relevant to
determining an applicant's suitability for admission. And those circumstances
include 'any factor which it is possible reasonably and in good faith to connect'
to the Article 4 criteria. These are extremely open terms. The Court made clear
in the Advisory Opinion that Article 4(1) sets limits to the considerations permissible in evaluating an application for admission, but that the considerations are
'very wide and very elastic [in] nature.' The admission criteria are legal criteria
and thus constrained by the terms of the Charter; but States have an active role
in determining their fulfilment in each application for admission. No particular
factual circumstances in a given application are excluded from a member State's
analysis, when the member State is forming an internal judgment whether an
applicant has met the Article 4(1) criteria. This was a position wide enough that
it is to be wondered whether a State, in spite of the Court's interpretation, might
add an 'extraneous consideration' by folding it into the internal processes of fact-
finding which the Court essentially declared immune from judicial examination.
The possibility was highlighted in the individual opinions.

Judge Azevedo, for example, did not view additional political considerations
as necessarily problematic. He did apparently think it likely in some cases that
States would introduce such considerations:

> It would be difficult to say that any one of the required conditions has a purely
> objective character, and that it could be appraised algebraically; and despite the place
> allotted to the word "judgment," it is precisely in the matter of the peace-loving
> nature of a State that a wide scope has been given to the political views of those
> who are called upon to pronounce themselves...In short, all political considerations
> may intervene in determining the judgment of the organs of the United Nations
> regarding the qualifications laid down in Article 4 of the Charter. Hence, objections
> that have been raised regarding the protection of the rights of man, the attitude
> of countries during the last war, the extent of diplomatic relations, etc., may, in
> principle, justify the rejection of an application.[22]

'Political considerations,' in Judge Azevedo's judgment, well may 'intervene' in
the process by which member States decide whether an applicant satisfies the
criteria of Article 4(1). As Judge Azevedo signed his opinion as an individual
opinion and not a dissent, he is to be taken as having accepted the result reached
by the Court. This means that the intervening 'political considerations,' in Judge

---

[21] ICJ Rep 1948 pp. 57, 63.
[22] Judge Azevedo, Individual Opinion, ICJ Rep 1948 pp. 57, 77–8.

Azevedo's view, were readily assimilated into one or more of the criteria of Article 4(1). This was to distinguish between referring to relevant and lawful factual considerations (including political considerations) and adding new conditions of admission.

Judge Alvarez, also by way of an individual opinion, even rejected the position that no State's admission could be linked to another's. States emerging from the disappearance of a colony or predecessor State, for example, 'should be considered simultaneously.'[23] These he considered to be exceptional situations, but, in his view, they nevertheless required that one qualify the Court's more categorical view. Judge Alvarez's position would be vindicated to some extent by the dual admissions of East and West Germany and North and South Korea, though these were not exactly the situation the judge identified as inviting an exceptional resort to linkage. Judge Alvarez also said that rejecting an application might be justified on non-Article 4(1) grounds where 'admission is liable to disturb the international situation.'[24] This seems to have been the rationale behind the two cases of dual admission, about which more will be said in Chapter 5 below. Longer-term considerations concerning 'the international situation' also may be relevant, a matter also to be addressed below.

Judges Basdevant, Winiarski, Sir Arnold McNair, and Read took a different approach. In contrast to Judges Azevedo and Alvarez, they could not agree with the Court that the criteria under Article 4(1) are exhaustive. According to their joint dissenting opinion,

> [W]hile the Charter makes the qualifications specified in paragraph 1 of Article 4 essential, it does not make them sufficient. If it had regarded them as sufficient, it would not have failed to say so. The point was one of too great importance to be left in obscurity. It is easy to understand why the authors of the Charter, after having rejected the principle of universality, should deem it undesirable to exclude the consideration of the very diverse political factors which the question of admission can in certain cases involve. When one considers the variety in the political conditions of the States which were not original Members of the United Nations – some ex-enemy, some ex-neutral, one permanently neutral by treaty, some with empires and some without, some unitary and some consisting of federal or other unions of States – and when one considers the political repercussions attending the union of existing States, or the emergence of new States and their entry into the United Nations – perhaps, the framers of the Charter, after having decided in this connexion to entrust a special mission to the Security Council, were wise in their generation in taking the view (as we submit they did) that it was impossible to do more than to prescribe certain preliminary and essential qualifications for membership and to leave the question of admission to the good faith and the good sense of the Security Council and the General Assembly, and particularly the former by

---

[23] Judge Alvarez, Individual Opinion, ICJ Rep 1948 pp. 57, 72.
[24] Ibid. 71.

reason of the special responsibilities laid upon it. For the authors of the Charter had to look beyond the year 1945 and endeavour to provide for events which the future had in store. A little reflection upon the changes in the map of the world during the short period which has elapsed since June 1945 suggests to us that they were prescient and prudent in the plan which they adopted.[25]

The prohibition that the Court set out against additive political considerations, in the dissenting view, was not part of the Charter. Instead, according to the dissenting judges, the Charter merely set a minimum standard. The question this opens is what further conditions might be imposed. The dissentients could not have meant that the standard for admission is limitlessly flexible. Enrique Armand-Ugon, as judge *ad hoc* in the 1964 *Barcelona Traction* judgment, said that the UN could not impose on Spain 'as a supplementary condition for Membership of the United Nations, the acceptance of a specific jurisdiction of the International Court.'[26] If this is correct, then one limit, at least, would be that admission to the UN cannot be with special conditions formulated with respect to one State.[27] The dissenting opinion in 1948 was not concerned with additive criteria that were so narrow and case-specific. The main consideration evident in the dissenting opinion was that criteria not expressly provided in

---

[25] Judges Basdevant, Winiarski, Sir Arnold McNair, and Read, Dissenting Opinion, ICJ Rep 1948 pp. 57, 90–1 ¶ 18. cf. Judge Krylov, Dissenting Opinion, ICJ Rep 1948 pp. 57, 110 § II ¶ 3.

[26] *Case Concerning the Barcelona Traction, Light and Power Company Ltd (New Application: 1962) (Belgium v Spain)* Dis Op Judge *Ad Hoc* Armand-Ugon, ICJ Rep 1964 pp. 6, 150.

[27] Under the general law concerning international organizations, insofar as it reaches the matter of admission of States to membership, there is no restriction preventing an organization from adding special criteria to a particular State applicant. The EU's admission provisions, for example, subject each candidate State's accession to a separate agreement. The central provision for accession is contained in Title VII, Art O (Final Provisions) of the Treaty on European Union, signed 7 Feb 1992, entered into force 1 Nov 1993: 1757 UNTS 4, 156:

> Any European State may apply to become a Member of the Union. It shall address its application to the Council, which shall act unanimously after consulting the Commission and after receiving the assent of the European Parliament, which shall act by an absolute majority of its component members.
>
> The conditions of admission and the adjustments to the Treaties on which the Union is founded which such admission entails shall be the subject of an agreement between the Member States and the applicant State. This agreement shall be submitted for ratification by all the Contracting States in accordance with their respective constitutional requirements.

Apart, then, from the condition, generally applicable, that the applicant be a 'European State,' conditions of admission are set out in the agreement with the applicant. As to the practice of the EU relative to accession, see Hoffmeister 'Changing requirements for membership' in Ott & Inglis eds *Handbook on European Enlargement: A Commentary on the Enlargement Process* (2002) 90–102. Each constitutive instrument governs the matter; the UN Charter establishes one set of criteria, and, on the plain terms of Article 4 at least, these apply in all instances without modification.

Article 4(1) might be required by the role of the UN as guarantor of international peace. Given the instability of geopolitics, States were free, perhaps even required, to apply political considerations to their judgment whether to vote to admit an applicant to membership. The underlying rationale to the dissentients' position, it is submitted, concerned the obligations of the UN and its member States within a system of public order. The dissenting view did not prevail in 1948, as against the apparent urgency of the Court to enjoin any addition to the Charter criteria for admission.

It must be said that there was a fineness to the reasoning in the various opinions in the *Admission* case. What was the difference between a 'political consideration' – which Judge Azevedo thought was permissible and consistent with the majority opinion – and the 'very diverse political factors' which the dissenting judges said were also permissible but which they felt had to be staked out in a dissent? It is submitted that there was a shared consideration in the several opinions, namely that it would be very difficult to say with any certainty what precisely influences a State in reaching its decision under Article 4(1) – and, conversely, that it would be very easy for a State to act according to a criterion not enumerated in Article 4(1) but to characterize its vote with reference to one of the express criteria. 'Reasonableness' and 'good faith' were, perhaps, the true counterpoise against the 'very wide and very elastic nature of the prescribed conditions.' Whatever the considerations leading to the Advisory Opinion as adopted, applying additional criteria, as we will see below, would not, in practice, be the problem.

Certain other objections were raised to the *Admission* Advisory Opinion by writers and by dissenting judges. For example, DW Grieg said that the General Assembly had put to the Court a political question which was outside the Court's competence to answer.[28] This was the position Judge Zoričić and Judge Krylov adopted in their Dissenting Opinions.[29] It was also the position submitted by several States.[30] The admission problem already however had proved a difficult thicket from which to extricate the Security Council, the struggle over the problem by 1947 having illustrated the depth of paralysis it was capable of causing.[31] Moreover, whatever political considerations might motivate a decision respecting an application for admission, the Charter had been crafted to address

---

[28] Grieg 'The Advisory Jurisdiction of the International Court and the Settlement of Disputes between States' (1966) 15 *ICLQ* 325, 340–45.

[29] ICJ Rep 1948 pp. 57, 94–106; ibid. 107–9.

[30] Yugoslavia ICJ Pldgs 1948 pp. 22–3, Ukraine ibid. 29, USSR ibid. 29, Poland ibid. 105–12, Czechoslovakia ibid. 113–7. Yugoslavia also made a separation of powers argument against jurisdiction: ibid. 84–90.

[31] On the transactions leading to requests for Advisory Opinions relative to Article 4 see Michla Pomerance 'Seeking Judicial Legitimation in the Cold War: U.S. Foreign Policy and the World Court, 1948–1962' (1995) 5 *Ind Int'l & Comp LR* 303, 306–7.

admission under legal provisions. Politics between UN member States necessi-
tated an authoritative interpretation of Article 4(1), but it is hard to see how a
contest over the meaning of a Charter provision is not a question containing a
significant legal aspect such that it is a proper question for an Advisory Opinion
of the Court.[32] There will be political motivations behind all, or very nearly all,
requests for Advisory Opinions; to require that they be absent from requests
would virtually have put an end to the advisory jurisdiction of the Court.[33]

2.3.2   *Negative Votes and Non-application of the Substantive Criteria*

The Court in the *Admission* case was involved mainly with the problem that States
might add criteria not enumerated in Article 4(1). Contemporary interpretation
by the General Assembly reflected this.[34] At the same time, in its clarity as to
the completeness of Article 4(1), the Court drew attention to the significance of
the criteria set out therein and to the fact-finding function to be performed by
each member State when determining how to vote on a question of admission.
The Article 4(1) criteria, the Court said, 'clearly constitute a legal regulation
of the question of the admission of new States.' Though States were limited to
the criteria enumerated in Article 4(1), they were intended to apply those cri-

---

[32] The *Conditions of Admission* Advisory Opinion later would be cited to the effect that the Court
may interpret the Charter (or other treaty) in response to an advisory request: e.g. *Difference
Relating to Immunity from Legal Process of a Special Rapporteur of the Commission on Human
Rights* Advisory Opinion of 29 Apr 1999, ICJ Rep 1999 pp. 62, 77 ¶ 26. Cf. *Legality of the
Threat or Use of Nuclear Weapons* Advisory Opinion of 8 July 1996, ICJ Rep 1996 pp. 226, 234
¶ 13; *Certain Expenses of the United Nations (Article 17, Paragraph 2, of the Charter)* Advisory
Opinion of 20 July 1962, ICJ Rep 1962 pp. 151, 156.

[33] And the Court has avoided this result, repeatedly reaching determinations which establish the
'effectiveness' of its advisory jurisdiction: Hersch Lauterpacht *The Development of International
Law by the International Court* (1958) 248–50, noting in particular *Reservations to the Convention
on the Prevention and Punishment of the Crime of Genocide* Advisory Opinion of 28 May 1951,
ICJ Rep 1951 p. 19; *Interpretation of Peace Treaties with Bulgaria, Hungary and Romania (First
Phase)* Advisory Opinion of 30 March 1950, ICJ Rep 1950 p. 65. See also *Interpretation of the
Agreement of 25 March 1951 between the WHO and Egypt* Advisory Opinion of 20 Dec 1980,
ICJ Rep 1980 pp. 73, 87 ¶ 33; *Western Sahara* Advisory Opinion of 16 Oct 1975, ICJ Rep
1975 pp. 12, 19 ¶ 18. This does not deny that there are political considerations which may cast
serious doubt on the jurisdiction of the Court. The International Court determined that the
General Assembly's advisory request in GA res ES-10/14, 8 Dec 2003 (10th Emergency Spec
Sess) presented no such considerations, and so an opinion could be given: *Legal Consequences of
the Construction of a Wall in the Occupied Palestinian Territory* Advisory Opinion of 9 July 2004,
ICJ Rep 2004 pp. 136, 155 ¶ 41. Writers asked, with reason, whether the Court in so doing
interfered in a complicated multilateral peace process: see esp Wedgwood 'The ICJ Advisory
Opinion on the Israeli Security Fence and the Limits of Self-Defense' (2005) 99 *AJ* 52.

[34] The Advisory Opinion was noted and recommended to the member States in GA res 197A(III),
8 Dec 1948. cf. GA res 306 (VI), 1 Feb 1952.

teria – and to apply them in every instance of an application for admission to membership. As to the extent of State discretion in applying the criteria – this being in large part a fact-finding operation – the Court also was clear: member States are within their rights to take into account a very wide category of facts – so long as they still apply the criteria set out in Article 4(1) by way of legal regulation of admission.

Two matters are raised by the *Admission* Advisory Opinion which the Court did not have occasion to address.

First, the Court did not address whether a problem of Charter law arises, where a member State conditions a *negative* vote, cast to block admission of an applicant State, on extraneous criteria – for example, on the non-admission of another State. The Advisory Opinion was clear that a member State is not permitted under the Charter to condition an affirmative vote to admit an applicant State on extraneous criteria, and this logically entails the same position with respect to a negative vote. The negative vote was not the matter put to the Court by the General Assembly, and so the Court did not explicitly address it. The two positions are so closely linked as perhaps not to require an explicit statement of their connection: a rule forbidding linkage of admissions has the corollary that non-admission of a State is not to be linked to non-admission of another. However self-evident it may be, such reflexivity does not appear to have been established in practice. The United States Permanent Representative was clear that the American veto of application for admission of the two Viet Nams, for example, was linked to rejection earlier the same month of the application of the Republic of Korea (South Korea):

> What in the end changed our mind was the decisions of the Security Council taken on 6 August...It became absolutely clear on that occasion that the Council, far from being prepared to support the principle of universal membership, was denying to one applicant even the right to have its case considered.[35]

The United States veto of the Viet Nam applications was criticized with reference to the advisory opinion in the *Admission* case.[36] The veto, of course, stood, and protest was relatively restrained.

A second unaddressed question was what to do, if, instead of applying additional criteria when voting on admission, a member State declined to apply one or more of the criteria provided. The main concern in the *Admission* Advisory Opinion was that States might apply additional criteria. The Court was clear that the Charter forbids this. The main substantive objection of the dissenting judges was that the Charter might be interpreted to allow additional criteria.

---

[35] Mr Moynihan (USA) SCOR 30th yr 1836th mtg 11 Aug 1975 p. 13 ¶ 112.

[36] Mr Salim (Tanzania) ibid. pp. 15–16 ¶ 132; Mr García Robles (Mexico) SCOR 30th yr 1846th mtg 30 Sept 1975 p. 5 ¶ 39.

The focus on possible additions to Article 4(1) was logical enough in view of the context. The advisory request was spurred by a situation in which States in the Security Council had been refusing to recommend certain applicant States for admission and were referring this explicitly to additional criteria – chiefly to the refusal of other member States to support admission of their own preferred candidates.

The other problem – possible failure to apply the criteria which everyone agreed were at least a minimum requirement – to be sure was not altogether ignored. Greece, in its submissions in the proceedings, raised the question of the affirmative vote cast without regard to one or more Article 4(1) criteria. Greece's view was that such a vote is not permissible:

> [A]ucun Membre des Nations Unies, en votant, soit dans l'Assemblée générale, soit dans le Conseil de Sécurité, sur une demande d'admission d'un État non membre de l'organisation n'a le droit de donner un vote affirmatif tant qu'il ne s'est pas persuadé que l'État demandant l'admission ait rempli *toutes les conditions* d'admission prévues par l'article 4, alinéa 1, de la Charte.[37]

If a State 'does not have the right to give an affirmative vote' unless it is persuaded that the applicant 'has fulfilled *all the conditions*' of Article 4(1), then it follows that it is the State's obligation, in casting an affirmative vote, to verify that all the conditions are fulfilled.

France expressed a similar view in even more definite terms. According to France, if a member of the Security Council or General Assembly comes to the

> *bona fide*...conviction...que les conditions ne sont pas remplies, il est obligatoirement tenu d'émettre un vote négatif. C'est une obligation juridique pour les membres des deux organes de se refuser à admettre l'admissibilité, si toutes les conditions posées à l'article 4, paragraphe 1, ne sont pas intégralement remplies...En conclusion, ni le Conseil de Sécurité ni l'Assemblée ne peuvent légalement admettre un candidat ne remplissant pas les conditions d'admissibilité posées à l'article 4, paragraphe 1.[38]

Both the statements of Greece and France had gone somewhat beyond the advisory request, for the request had not concerned challenges to affirmative votes where the problem was non-application of admission criteria.[39] The Court, appropriately, did not address the situation in which a State affirming admission has failed to apply the enumerated criteria. That situation, however, is logically just as much a problem, if the Court's position is correct that the five criteria of Article 4(1) are necessary as well as sufficient. As will be seen in the Chap-

---

[37] Emphasis added. ICJ Pldgs 1948 p. 21.
[38] ICJ Pldgs 1948 p. 69.
[39] A point made by Belgium: ICJ Pldgs 1948 p. 24.

ters below, non-application of the criteria turned out to be the situation more frequently arising in practice.

2.3.3   *Elaborating the Criteria for Admission*

The Court itself declined to say more about the five criteria of Article 4(1), the General Assembly having 'not called upon [it] to define... or to specify the elements' of the criteria. A number of States in their written or oral submissions did attempt to define or specify Article 4(1).[40] From the State submissions, a sketch is available of opinion respecting possible definitions of the criteria for admission.

The most extensive statement on the five criteria of Article 4(1) was that of France. Represented by Georges Scelle, the French Republic set out a number of observations, including a scheme of at least partial elaboration of the five specified admission criteria. Scelle began by noting that the Charter gives no definition of 'State.' The omission has proved problematic in a number of respects, including with respect to the admission provisions of Article 4. To be admitted, the applicant must be a State, but those evaluating the application do not have the benefit of an authoritative definition of this threshold criterion. Scelle suggested that the first criterion is satisfied where the entity seeking admission displays self-government and is free to take its own decisions, especially with respect to its international transactions.[41]

The requirement that the applicant declare its acceptance of the principles of the Charter Scelle saw as 'purely formal,' its juridical importance being that the declaration must be made in conformity with national constitutional requirements (presumably the requirements applicable to the ratification of international agreements).[42] The third criterion treated in the French submission, capability of fulfilling the obligations of the Charter, Scelle characterized as a component of statehood and described it as a criterion of 'effectiveness of government.'[43] If effectiveness of government indeed were applied as a requirement for admission, and applied rigorously, it is possible that a number of applicants since 1945 would have been delayed in their admission as member States. Scelle's formulation of the criterion of capability therefore is noteworthy.

The requirement that a State be peace-loving Scelle said is 'a condition that implicates diverse elements of appreciation.' Scelle referred to the opinion of

---

[40] States submitting written statements were China, El Salvador, Guatemala, Honduras, USA, Greece, Yugoslavia, Belgium, Canada, India, Iraq, Ukraine, USSR, Australia, and Siam (Thailand); oral presentations were made by France, Yugoslavia, Belgium, Poland, and Czechoslovakia.
[41] ICJ Pldgs 1948 p. 66.
[42] Ibid., p. 67.
[43] Ibid.

governments – and even the sentiment of 'the populations of interested States.'[44] This would suggest that recent victims of armed aggression (e.g., the French) had a legal interest under the Charter in the substantive evaluation of certain States' applications for admission. Though somewhat less committal, Yugoslavia, in its own submission merely noted that the Charter contains no definition of 'peace-loving.'[45] This is consistent with France's observation that 'diverse elements' properly may be considered in determining whether an applicant meets the criterion. As for the condition that the applicant have the intention to fulfil the obligations of the Charter, Scelle referred to this as 'singularly close to a discretionary competence.' A wide range of considerations would seem to fall under the intention criterion, and, said Scelle, it therefore would be difficult to scrutinize a member State's voting behaviour with respect to the criterion.[46] The wide berth that the Court in the Advisory Opinion gave States carrying out fact-finding under Article 4 tends to affirm Scelle's position on the point.

According to Poland, for which Manfred Lachs acted as representative, the criterion of capability can be measured by reference to indicia of actual independence. The application of Austria, on this view, was inadmissible at the time, because the Allied control machinery continued to act in effect as the government of Austria; thus, it was said, preventing that State from carrying out its obligations.[47] Lachs did not consider the continuity of the Austrian State relevant. The important consideration, in his view, was instead the as yet provisional character of Austria's government arrangements. Insofar as this was an objection that Austria at the time was not in truth an independent State, it may be submitted that Lachs's objection would have been better referred to the criterion of statehood.

2.4   *Substantive Criteria and the Procedures for Admission*

The submissions by States noted above are far from complete, if what is sought is to fill out the substance of the five criteria of Article 4(1). Some hints were offered as to what certain criteria might mean in practical terms, but no State fully defined all five elements that the Charter requires be present for an applicant to be admissible, and nor did the Court.[48] It is a noteworthy ellipsis in

---

[44] Ibid., p. 68.
[45] Ibid., p. 81.
[46] Ibid., p. 68.
[47] Ibid., pp. 103–5.
[48] ICJ Rep 1948 pp. 57, 60.

United Nations practice that no authoritative statement has been adopted on the matter.[49]

Even if a full and generally applicable statement existed as to what precisely the five criteria mean, it would remain for the UN to adhere to a procedure for their implementation. As will be seen, admission procedure in time was treated in most cases as an essentially *pro forma* exercise, institutional mechanisms left unused under which more rigorous implementation of the Article 4(1) criteria may have been possible. This outcome was not inevitable from the start. As the Court noted in 1948, linking the admission of a State to that of another presents a procedural problem as well as a substantive one; and the Court required that every applicant be given a sort of Charter due process. It is not the case that all opportunities to substantively evaluate applications were let pass. In the remainder of this Chapter, the earlier practice of implementing the substantive criteria under UN admission procedures will be considered.

2.4.1   *Rules of Procedure*

The procedural rules of the Security Council and General Assembly contain chapters addressing admission of new members. These were adverted to in Chapter 1 above. Now we will consider them in detail.

The Provisional Rules of Procedure of the Security Council were originally adopted at the first meeting of the Council. The Rules were subsequently amended six times, most recently in 1982.[50] The rules concerning admission, which together comprise Chapter X of the Security Council Provisional Rules, provide as follows:

Rule 58

Any State which desires to become a Member of the United Nations shall submit an application to the Secretary-General. This application shall contain a declaration made in a formal instrument that it accepts the obligations contained in the Charter.

Rule 59

The Secretary-General shall immediately place the application for membership before the representatives on the Security Council. Unless the Security Council decides otherwise, the application shall be referred by the President to a committee of the Security Council upon which each member of the Security Council shall be represented. The committee shall examine any application referred to it and report its conclusions thereon to the Council not less than thirty-five days in advance of

---

[49] Successive volumes of the *UN Repertory* observe that no attempt has been made 'to define their meaning in any general sense': *Rep UN* (1945–54) p. 19 ¶ 45; ibid. (1954–5) p. 83 ¶ 22; ibid. (1955–9) p. 190 ¶ 19; ibid. (1959–66) p. 185 ¶ 19; ibid. (1979–84) p. 124 ¶ 14.

[50] SCOR 37th yr 2410th mtg 21 Dec 1982.

a regular session of the General Assembly or, if a special session of the General Assembly is called, not less than fourteen days in advance of such session.

Rule 60

The Security Council shall decide whether in its judgement the applicant is a peace-loving State and is able and willing to carry out the obligations contained in the Charter and, accordingly, whether to recommend the applicant State for membership.

If the Security Council recommends the applicant State for membership, it shall forward to the General Assembly the recommendation with a complete record of the discussion.

If the Security Council does not recommend the applicant State for membership or postpones the consideration of the application, it shall submit a special report to the General Assembly with a complete record of the discussion.

In order to ensure the consideration of its recommendation at the next session of the General Assembly following the receipt of the application, the Security Council shall make its recommendation not less than twenty-five days in advance of a regular session of the General Assembly, nor less than four days in advance of a special session.

In special circumstances, the Security Council may decide to make a recommendation to the General Assembly concerning an application for membership subsequent to the expiration of the time limits set forth in the preceding paragraph.[51]

Articles 59 and 60 merit a brief word.

The terms of Article 59 appear to comprehend an examination procedure. In mandatory language ('the application shall be referred by the President'), Rule 59 calls for reference of applications for admission to a 'committee of the Security Council.' The Committee, which is to be comprised of representatives of all Security Council members, 'shall examine any application referred to it and report its conclusions thereon to the Council.' Again, the language is mandatory, and the steps prescribed are proceduralized to a degree: the Committee shall reach 'conclusions' and 'report' these conclusions – language suggesting that the Committee is to produce a formal result – and time limits are specified, the Committee being required to report to the Council by a date not less than thirty-five days in advance of a regular session of the General Assembly; or, in the event of a special General Assembly session being called, not less than 14 days in advance of the special session. The steps to be taken are not entirely free-form. However, the rule contains an escape clause: '[u]nless the Security Council decides otherwise.' That is to say, an application 'shall be referred by the

---

[51] S/96/Rev.7: as adopted by the Security Council, 1st yr 1st mtg 17 Jan 1946 and as amended, 1st yr 31st, 41st, 42nd, 44th and 48th meetings, 9 Apr, 16 and 17 May, 6 and 24 June 1946; 2nd yr 138th and 222nd mtgs, 4 June and 9 Dec 1947; 5th yr 468th mtg 28 Feb 1950; 24th yr 1463rd mtg 24 Jan 1969; 29th yr 1761st mtg 17 Jan 1974; and 37th yr 2410th mtg 21 Dec 1982.

President' to the Committee for examination, so long as the Security Council does not decide to follow an alternative procedure. No alternative procedure is specified. The rule simply says that the procedure it specifies may be by-passed. The alternative procedure in practice most often followed has been to send the application directly to a vote of the Council. The procedural mechanism for implementing the substantive criteria for admission in this way readily could be (and has been) taken out of the picture.

Even if the Security Council does not 'decide otherwise,' and the application goes to the Committee, the Rules of Procedure say little as to what the Committee is to do with the application. It is to 'examine' the application. It is to 'report' on its examination, back to the Council. This does not specify a formal procedure. It instead merely hints at the outline of one. The provisions of Rule 59 are incomplete as a guide for implementing the substantive criteria for admission.

Whether or not resort is made to the Committee, Rule 60 says that the Security Council itself 'shall decide whether in its judgement the applicant is a peace-loving State and is able and willing to carry out the obligations contained in the Charter.' The words 'decide' and 'judgement' suggest that the process is not fully discretionary, requiring as they do in their ordinary sense that reasons be given for results reached. A transmittal requirement is contained in Rule 60: the Security Council, if recommending admission, is to 'forward to the General Assembly the recommendation with a complete record of the discussion.' If deciding not to recommend admission, the Council is also obliged to transmit a 'complete record of the discussion.' While this says nothing as to the procedures for carrying out that discussion, some guidance is furnished as to the substantive matters that are to be discussed. The first paragraph of Rule 60 says that the Council 'shall decide whether in its judgement the applicant is a peace-loving State and is able and willing to carry out the obligations contained in the Charter.' This follows Article 4(1) of the Charter nearly verbatim. The choice of words suggests that the Security Council is to examine the substantive criteria for admission when reaching a decision. However, the rule adds no further substance to the criteria which, as noted above, are under-specified. It sets down no clear mechanism for the Security Council to follow in discussions concerning admission. Nor does it say the degree of particularity with which the Council must report its findings.

The General Assembly adopted Provisional Rules of Procedure at its first regular session.[52] The Rules subsequently were amended a number of times.[53]

---

[52] A/71/Rev.1; A/520/Rev.15, 15 Dec 1946.

[53] *Inter alia*, by GA resns 173 (II), 21 Nov 1947; 262 (III), 11 Dec 1948; 362 (IV), 22 Oct 1949; 377A (V), 3 Nov 1950; 689B (VII), 21 Dec 1952; 791 (VIII), 23 Oct 1953; 1104

The rules concerning admission, which together comprise Chapter XIV of the General Assembly Rules, provide as follows:

Applications
Rule 134
Any State which desires to become a Member of the United Nations shall submit an application to the Secretary-General. Such application shall contain a declaration, made in a formal instrument, that the State in question accepts the obligations contained in the Charter.

Notification of applications
Rule 135
The Secretary-General shall, for information, send a copy of the application to the General Assembly, or to the Members of the United Nations if the Assembly is not in session.

Consideration of applications and decision thereon
Rule 136
If the Security Council recommends the applicant State for membership, the General Assembly shall consider whether the applicant is a peace-loving State and is able and willing to carry out the obligations contained in the Charter and shall decide, by a two-thirds majority of the members present and voting, upon its application for membership.

Rule 137
If the Security Council does not recommend the applicant State for membership or postpones the consideration of the application, the General Assembly may, after full consideration of the special report of the Security Council, send the application back to the Council, together with a full record of the discussion in the Assembly, for further consideration and recommendation or report.

Notification of decision and effective date of membership
Rule 138
The Secretary-General shall inform the applicant State of the decision of the General Assembly. If the application is approved, membership shall become effective on the date on which the General Assembly takes its decision on the application.[54]

Rule 136, it will be noted, calls on the General Assembly to carry out its own evaluation of the substantive criteria for admission. This is additive to the first paragraph of Rule 60 of the Security Council rules. As such, there are at least two stages at which substantive examination of the applicant may be carried

---

(XI), 18 Dec 1956; 1192 (XII), 12 Dec 1957; 1659 (XVI), 28 Nov 1961; 1990 (XVIII), 17 Dec 1963; 2046 (XX), 8 Dec 1965; 2323 (XXII), 16 Dec 1967; 2390 (XXIII), 25 Nov 1968; 2553 (XXIV), 12 Dec 1969; 2837 (XXVI), 17 Dec 1971; 2913 (XXVII), 9 Nov 1972; 3191 (XXVIII), 18 Dec 1973; 31/95, 14 Dec 1976; 32/103, 14 Dec 1977; 33/138, 19 Dec 1978; 35/219A&B, 17 Dec 1980.

[54] A/520/Rev.15: as adopted by the General Assembly, 1st sess 15 Dec 1946.

out: first, on presentation of the application to the Security Council, then on reference to the General Assembly following Security Council recommendation. Assuming no Security Council decision to by-pass the Committee on Admission, these two stages are preceded by the Committee's examination. Two or even three opportunities thus are presented to consider an application under the criteria of Article 4(1).

A few further observations may be made with respect to the General Assembly Rules of Procedure.

Membership becomes effective immediately upon the decision of the General Assembly to admit the applicant as a member State. Rule 138 of the General Assembly rules says that 'membership shall become effective on the date' of the General Assembly's (affirmative) decision; effectiveness in practice is immediate, the delegation of the applicant typically being seated directly after the affirmative two-thirds majority vote of the General Assembly members present and voting (Rule 136). This is slightly different timing from that set out in the original rules. Under the Provisional Rules of Procedure as originally adopted,[55] membership did not become effective immediately upon the decision of the General Assembly to admit. Instead, an applicant had been required, *after* the General Assembly voted to admit it as a member State, to 'present[ ] to the Secretary-General an instrument of adherence.'[56] It was upon presentation of the instrument of adherence that membership became effective. The rules as amended now require a 'declaration made in a formal instrument' (Rule 58 (Security Council rules), Rule 134 (General Assembly rules)), and this is to be contained in the application for membership. No further formal assurance is required to effectuate membership. It has been suggested that requiring the instrument of acceptance (or 'declaration') be deposited before the General Assembly votes on admission is in stricter conformity with Article 4 than requiring it afterward, for Article 4(2) identifies only decisions of the Security Council and General Assembly as determining admission – not subsequent action by the applicant.[57] The change to immediate effectiveness well may have streamlined proceedings under municipal law as well. The earlier procedure under some national constitutions would have required two operations by the applicant – one to reach the decision to make application; and a second to adopt the formal instrument following affirmative vote by the General Assembly. Under the procedure now in effect, an applicant State becomes a member without further municipal law steps. This too perhaps makes admission procedure more consistent with the Charter, which contains

---

[55] Which remained in effect until 21 Nov 1947 (General Assembly rules) and 9 Dec 1947 (Security Council rules).

[56] Provisional Rules of the General Assembly, Rule 116: A/71/Rev.1.

[57] See *Rep UN* (1945–54) pp. 176–7 § 38.

no express requirement that applicants ratify their acceptance of Charter obligations under the normal treaty ratification provisions of municipal law. Original
members had had to ratify the Charter, so the absence of a ratification requirement for 'other States' seems deliberate.[58]

It may be asked, as a matter of international law, what, if any, significance
is to be attributed to the 'declaration made in a formal instrument.' It is clear
enough that this procedural element corresponds to the clause of Article 4(1)
restricting admission to applicants 'which accept the obligations contained in
the present Charter.' The requirement that Charter obligations be accepted may
be seen as the most objective of the five elements of Article 4(1), in that there
is little or no margin of appreciation to the matter of whether an applicant has
made a formal statement that it accepts the obligations. Scelle, as noted above,
thought that this requirement was purely formal. The Rules of Procedure are not
inconsistent with Scelle's view: where the Rules set out the substantive criteria
for admission which the two principal organs assigned the competence to decide
admission applications are to consider, they do not mention the requirement that
the applicant 'accept' the obligations of the Charter.[59] Nevertheless, it should
not be rejected out of hand that the declaration performs something in addition
to its admittedly formal function. The declaration, after all, establishes in clear
terms as part of the conventional practice of the applicant State that that State
will abide by Charter law.[60] The registration in the UN Treaty Series of formal
instruments adopted pursuant to Rule 58 (SC)/Rule 134(GA), besides furnishing a convenient reference, further suggests the conventional character of the
instruments.[61] As '[d]eclarations publicly made and manifesting the will to be
bound' they well may 'have the effect of creating legal obligations.'[62]

---

[58] Rosenne *Treaties* 214 n. 35.

[59] Security Council Rules of Procedure, Rule 60, first paragraph; General Assembly Rules of
Procedure, Rule 136.

[60] Consider *Case Concerning Military and Paramilitary Activities in and Against Nicaragua (Nicaragua v United States of America)* Merits, ICJ Rep 1986 pp. 14, 106 ¶ 202, relative to 'statements whereby States avow their recognition of the principles of international law set forth
in the United Nations Charter.' cf. ICJ Pldgs 1950 p. 126 (Argentina): '[T]he Organization
does not select States in order to suggest their admission; States desiring it voluntarily apply
for admission.' Rosenne sees the principle *ex consensus advenit vinculum* at work in applications
by States to the UN: *Treaties* 215.

[61] See e.g. the instrument of acceptance of Burma, by which that applicant 'accept[ed] without
any reservation the obligations of the Charter of the United Nations and promise[d] to keep
them inviolably from the day when it becomes a Member of the United Nations': 15 UNTS
4, 17 Mar 1948.

[62] Guiding Principle 1, Guiding Principles applicable to unilateral declarations of States, ILC 58th
sess, A/61/10, *ILC Ybk* 2006 Vol. II Pt 2 p. 370. Guiding Principle 1 further states, 'When the
conditions for this are met, the binding character of such declarations is based on good faith;

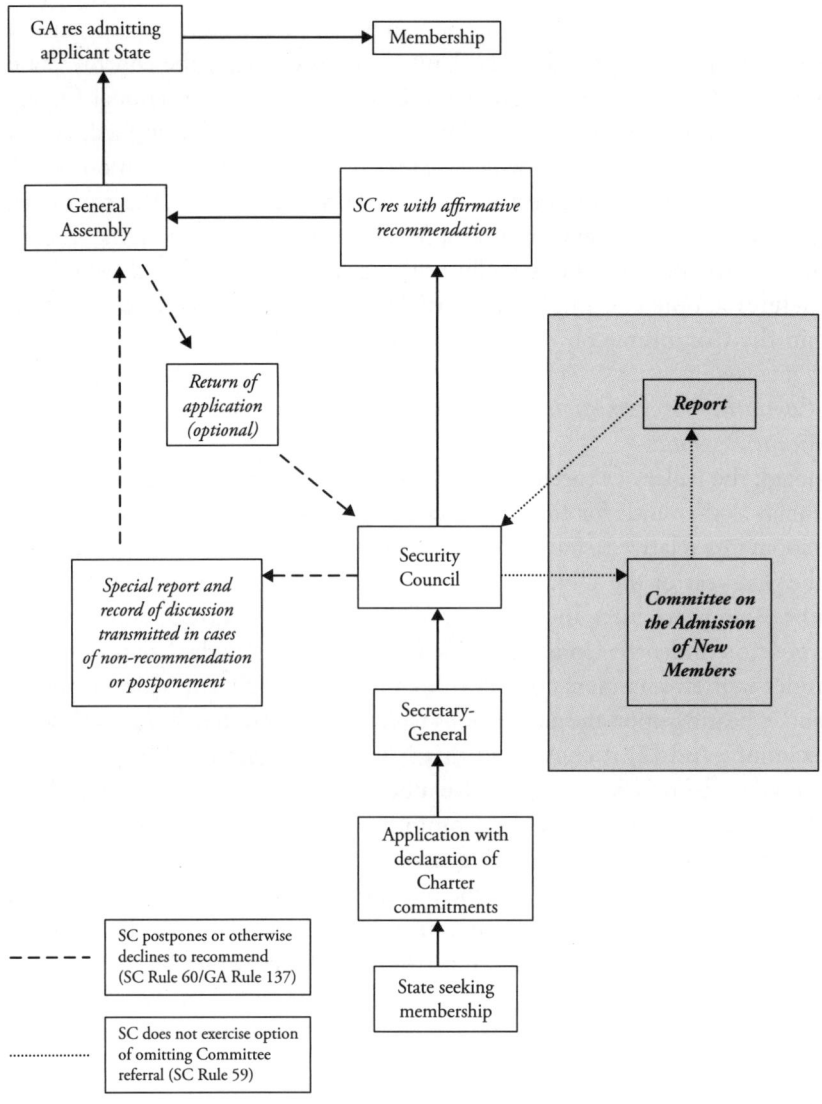

Figure 1: Procedure for Admission to the United Nations

2.4.2   *Implementation*

A certain apparatus thus was adopted under the Rules of Procedure for the purpose of handling applications for admission of States as new UN members. The apparatus eventually fell into disuse; and, in time, the substantive criteria for admission came scarcely to be implemented at all. Nevertheless, particular episodes in the early period of the United Nations – e.g., the controversy over seating the Argentine delegation at the Conference on International Organization – suggest how criteria might have been more rigorously applied. As noted already, controversies arose in which States expressed differing positions as to the substantive meaning and effect of the criteria for admission. The controversies suggest an early movement toward more fully elaborating the criteria. There also were tentative steps toward actually utilizing, and even further developing, the procedures adopted to implement Article 4(1). These took place in particular within the Committee on Admission of New Members.

(i) *Committee on Admission of New Members: Questionnaires and Applicant Responses*

As noted, the Rules of Procedure identified the Committee on Admission of New Members as the venue for consideration of applications; so it is not surprising that developments relative to admission procedure took place within the Committee. In the first year of the UN, the Committee adopted two resolutions pertaining to admission procedure. These were confirmed by the Security Council as valid.[63] The position under the Committee resolutions was that (1) the Committee 'would consider written statements of fact from any of the applicant States or from any Member, bearing upon the applications which the Committee had been instructed to examine'; and (2) it considered that it was the Committee's right 'to ask for information from Governments of Member States or applicants having a bearing upon the applications before the Committee.'[64] The phrasing used – 'from any of *the* applicant States' and 'bearing upon *the* applications before the Committee' – raises the question whether the position adopted was intended to relate to all applications, pending and future, or only to those of which the Committee was seized at the time. The latter, more limited, effect would be consistent with the phrasing. It also would be consistent with the rather evanescent character of early UN procedural statements: amendments to the Rules in the early years

---

States concerned may then take them into consideration and rely on them; such States are entitled to require that such obligations be respected': ibid. Any legal obligations so created could be as between the applicant State and the UN, the applicant State and other States, or the applicant State and 'the international community as a whole': see Guiding Principle 6, ibid. 376.

[63] *Rep UN* (1945–54) p. 183 ¶ 53 7 Aug 1946.

[64] Ibid.

were many. A statement of procedure intended to have effect with respect to future applications, however, cannot be ruled out on the basis of the text and the circumstances of its adoption. New applications were increasing in number already, so it would have been short-sighted to say the least, if the Committee had assumed that the UN was not to receive further applications.

The Committee sent questionnaires to certain applicants. The questionnaire sent to Transjordan (Jordan) read as follows:

> The Committee on the Admission of New Members would be appreciative if you would be kind enough to supply additional information on the following points to assist the Committee in preparing its report.
> 1. The means of maintaining the territorial integrity and political independence of the Hashemite Kingdom of Transjordan.
> 2. The budget of the Hashemite Kingdom of Transjordan with as much detail as possible concerning sources of revenue and headings of expenditure.
> 3. The effect of the application of the annex of the Treaty of Alliance between the United Kingdom and the Hashemite Kingdom of Transjordan of 22 March 1946 on the maintenance of Transjordan's territorial integrity and political independence.
> The asking of these questions is not in any way an expression of opinion by the Committee on the Hashemite Kingdom of Transjordan's application.[65]

The points on which the Committee elicited information related chiefly to the question of the independence of the applicant. The questionnaire reflected concern as to both the actual and legal dimensions of independence. The first two points in the questionnaire went to the capability of the applicant, focusing as they did on 'means of maintaining' and 'sources of revenue.' The third point, though also directed toward the effectiveness of Transjordan as a State, was concerned particularly with formal indicia of independence, in particular with the effect of Transjordan's treaty relations.[66]

Transjordan responded to the questionnaire point for point. According to the response, Transjordan's

> [m]eans of maintaining... territorial integrity and political independence... are threefold. First, the Charter of the United Nations Organization; secondly, the Arab Legion military units which consist of 6,000 highly trained and equipped personnel; thirdly, the defensive alliance with Great Britain.[67]

---

[65] Contained in Letter from the Chairman of the Committee on Admission of New Members to the Representative of the Hashemite Kingdom of Transjorden in New York: SCOR 1st yr 2nd ser p. 143 supp no 4 annex 7 appendix 18, 15 Aug 1946.

[66] The first point, too – 'means of maintaining... territorial integrity and political independence' – contained a relation to independence as well as to capability.

[67] Contained in Letter from Djamil Tutanji Pasha, Representative of the Hashemite Kingdom of Jordan in New York addressed to the Chairman, Committee on the Admission of New Members, SCOR 1st yr 2nd ser p. 144 supp no 4 annex 7 appendix 18, undated.

The letter went on to disclose, in tabular form, the Kingdom's public revenue, set out by source, and a schedule of expenditures.[68] With respect to the third point in the Committee questionnaire, Transjordan said as follows:

> The maintenance of the territorial integrity and political independence of Trans-
> jordan has not been affected by the application of the military annex which has
> amounted in effect to nothing more than closer co-operation between the two allied
> forces. It is to be noted that since the conclusion of the Treaty, Great Britain has
> not increased its forces in Transjordan or asked that this should be done.[69]

The Committee on Admission of New Members thus exercised its mandate to require an applicant State to adduce specific considerations supporting its candidacy. Questions of independence, capacity, and treaty relations were the chief concern with respect to Transjordan. The applicant co-operated with the Committee, thus suggesting the viability of a nascent admission procedure.

This was not isolated practice, though the form that Committee scrutiny took varied among the States which it put to the test. The substantive matters which the Committee examined also differed depending on the situation of the particular applicant. Siam (Thailand) communicated its desire to be admitted to the UN in 1946.[70] Two members of the Security Council, in the Committee on Admission, expressed concern about the fitness of Siam for admission. France said that Siam had seized territory from Cambodia and Laos (under cover of Japanese forces during the war); and that France 'would continue to consider herself in an actual state of war with Siam' until Siam acceded to a mechanism for pacific resolution of the territorial dispute.[71] The Soviet Union said that it did not maintain diplomatic relations with Siam. France and the Soviet Union said that Siam could not be admitted to the United Nations.

Siam responded to the objections to its candidacy. It said that Siam and France had never been in a formal state of war with one another. It said that the Siamese resistance organization which had fought Japan during World War II now governed Siam. It mentioned a *compromis* of August 1946 by which Siam had accepted a French proposal to refer the territorial dispute to the International Court of Justice.[72] As for recent armed incidents on the Siam-Indo-China border, which France said had resulted from attacks by Siamese forces, Siam acknowledged that these had occurred, but the real cause, according to

---

[68] Ibid., pp. 144–5.

[69] Ibid., p. 145.

[70] Letter dated 20 May 1946: SCOR 1st yr 2nd ser p. 68 supp no. 4 annex 6(3).

[71] SCOR 1st yr 2nd ser supp no. 4 p. 76 (summary of discussion in Committee on Admission).

[72] This, incidentally, did not lead to a definitive settlement of all frontier differences, though the two States did refer certain outstanding questions to a Franco-Siamese Conciliation Commission in 1947, noted in *Case Concerning the Temple of Preah Vihear (Cambodia-Thailand)* ICJ Rep 1962 pp. 6, 28–9.

the Siam government, was instability in French Indo-China, a matter outside Siam's responsibility: 'His Majesty's Government sincerely realizes the difficulties the French authorities are confronting, but [could] in no way accept any responsibility for what happens in Indo-China.'[73] Siam responded to the Soviet objection by stating that it was the intention of Siam to establish diplomatic relations with the USSR 'as soon as possible.'[74] It might have been said, but was not, that maintenance of diplomatic relations was not in itself clearly a criterion for admission. In light of the objection having been that of a Permanent Member of the Security Council, it is understandable that Siam chose instead to respond on the terms of the Soviet objection.

Certain concerns arose as well in connection with the application for admission of Mongolia. As with Transjordan, the concerns were set out in the form of a questionnaire. The Committee on Admission of New Members asked the following:

1. What is the present extent of Mongolia's foreign relations including political, economic, social and cultural?
2. What is the attitude of the Mongolian Government regarding the development of her foreign relations and in particular the exchange of diplomatic or consular representatives?
3. What countries other than the Soviet Union and China have hitherto proposed to enter into diplomatic or consular exchanges with the Mongolian Peoples' Republic, and what replies have been given?
4. It would also assist the Committee if it could be given more detailed information regarding:
   (a) The Constitution of the Mongolian People's Republic and other pertinent facts relating to its system of government and the conduct of its foreign relations.
   (b) The budget, particularly the appropriation in respect to international affairs.[75]

Mongolia replied in considerable detail. It included a review of the history of Mongolia's international status; its cooperation with the USSR against the Axis during World War II; and the commencement of international relations by the People's Republic, including, Mongolia said, with China in 1946. (A protocol for establishing diplomatic relations apparently had been signed but not implemented). As for the extent of diplomatic relations (Question 2), Mongolia replied that it had maintained diplomatic relations with Russia since 1921, but did not indicate any other States with which it maintained diplomatic relations. Under

---

[73] Letter from the Siamese Representative to the Secretary-General, 24 Aug 1946: SCOR 1st yr 2nd ser supp no. 4 pp. 146–7.

[74] Ibid., p. 147.

[75] SCOR 1st yr 2nd ser supp no. 4 appendix 12 pp. 123–4.

the constitutional points, Mongolia replied in considerable detail, expounding its constitutional history, government institutions, electoral law, women's rights and other human rights, and social welfare provisions. On the budgetary point, Mongolia described the (relatively recent) creation of national financial and monetary institutions, and affirmed that a 'small part of the budget' is for the maintenance of the foreign ministry, trade ministry, and Mongolia's one overseas diplomatic mission.[76]

The application of Albania presented particular difficulties and occasioned a correspondingly detailed inquiry from the Committee on Admission. The Committee asked seven questions. This was perhaps the most extensive use of the Committee's competence to inquire into the fitness of an applicant for admission. The questions were as follows:

1. Does Albania consider itself in a state of war with Greece?
2. If so, how, in the view of Albania, is this state of war to be ended?
3. Is the Albanian Government prepared to accept the peaceful means of settlement provided by the Charter in connection with territorial claims or other disputes with another State?
4. Has the Albanian Government terminated the treaties existing between Albania and other States prior to 7 April 1939?
5. What is the attitude of Albania towards the continued validity of treaties and agreements in effect on that date between Albania and other States now Members of the United Nations?
6. Can the Albanian Government give information on the following matters which have been brought to the attention of the Committee?
   (a) the report of twenty-one incidents on the Greek-Albanian frontier since early 1946...
   (b) the report that on 15 May 1946 two British warships were fired on by batteries on the Albanian coast;
   (c) the report of the seizing of Greek citizens and their detention in Albanian concentration camps, denial of access to these camps of representatives of the International Red Cross and alleged ill-treatment of the inmates...
   What representations have been made by other Governments in respect of the above-mentioned matters and what action has the Albanian Government taken in regard to these representations?
7. In addition, it would assist the Committee in making its report to the Security Council if it could be supplied with official information regarding the results of the general election of 2 December 1945, including the total number of electors enrolled; the number of electors who cast votes; the distribution of votes.[77]

---

[76] SCOR 1st yr 2nd ser supp no. 4 appendix 12 Addendum pp. 124–30.

[77] Letter from the Chairman of the Committee on Admission of New Members to Colonel Tuk Jakova, Minister of State of the Albanian People's Republic dated 9 August 1946 and the Reply Dated 14 August 1946: SCOR 1st yr 2nd ser supp no. 4 Appendix 7 pp. 91–2.

As with other questionnaires it issued, the Committee stated that the questions did not 'in any way' express an opinion on the application in question. However, the substance of the questionnaire implied definite concerns. In particular, it is clear from the questions posed to Albania that member States – including Greece and the United Kingdom – had doubts as to the character of Albania as a 'peace-loving State.' The persistence of border incidents and, generally, unfriendly relations between Albania and Greece posed a possible obstacle to admission. The inquiry as to treaty obligations (Question 5) might have been to establish a clear position with respect to succession and thus to avoid confusion and conflicting claims as to the application of particular instruments. However, one may detect a systemic concern there as well: an applicant ready to disregard treaty obligations was, arguably, not ready to accept the principles and purposes of the Charter, one of which certainly is the maintenance of rule of law as reflected in fulfilment by all States of such obligations. The last question went to the popular basis of the Albanian government and its commitment to democracy.

Albania responded to the Committee's questions in considerable detail. According to Albania, no state of war existed with Greece, and aggression carried out against Greece during World War II from Albanian territory was the responsibility of Italy, which had annexed Albania by force in 1939. Albania had resisted Italy during the war and did not collaborate, much less provide army units in support of Italy's Balkan adventures. Albania was 'ready to assume all the obligations deriving from the Charter of the United Nations.' Albania abrogated all treaties entered into under pressure by Italy and which 'impaired the independence and sovereignty' of Albania – but Albania affirmed that it would respect 'all treaties *in effect prior to 1939, which do not impair the independence and sovereignty of Albania.*'[78] This was, perhaps, a concession, as against the policy of other socialist States to treat treaty law as a 'clean slate' after revolution.[79]

Albania said that the reports of border incidents set out by Greece were 'fanciful inventions and fabrications' and claimed, instead, that Greece had instigated incidents against Albania. The firing by Albanian batteries on British naval vessels, Albania said, was an 'unwished-for incident.' Albania suggested that its gunners actually thought their targets were Greeks. Albania denied that it maintained concentration camps, and indicated that it had received no protests in connection with detainees from any foreign Government. The Albanian response also included a tally of the results of the recent elections (the government party

---

[78] Emphasis original: ibid., p. 95.

[79] The USSR, though in practice moderating its position after the initial post-revolutionary period, did not abandon it completely: see observation of USSR on Categories of Succession of States: Sir Francis Vallat, Spec Rapp, First Report on Succession of States in respect of treaties, 19 & 22 Apr, 24 & 31 May, 10 & 21 June 1974 ¶ 50 *ILC Ybk* 1974 Vol. 2 Pt One p. 14.

received 93.16 per cent of the vote). Extensive supporting documents were attached to the response, concerning, *inter alia,* relations between Albania and Italy during the period of annexation.[80]

A certain correspondence can be seen between the substance of an applicant's response and the success of its application. Mongolia's reply well may have given rise to doubt at the time as to the independence of that State *vis* the USSR and as to its ability to carry out Charter obligations with limited resources. The newness of its main institutions, too, perhaps raised doubt as to the permanence of Mongolia as a State.[81] Albania's reply tended to show that significant differences continued to exist between Albania and Greece and that no immediate prospect of pacific resolution was in sight. For both Mongolia and Albania, admission would be considerably delayed. By contrast, Transjordan and Siam, arguably, gave satisfactory replies. In Siam's case, the main point adduced in its reply was that it had agreed to submit its dispute with France to pacific means of settlement. Transjordan gave the requested details of its treaty relations and fiscal situation. Siam was admitted in 1946. Transjordan, however, would have to wait until 1955, showing that the correspondence between the Committee's procedure and outcome in the Security Council was not complete. Nevertheless, the specificity of the Committee questionnaires and the responsiveness of applicants to them suggest how the criteria of Article 4(1) well could have been developed and implemented in practice. The procedural means existed. It was up to the member States whether to use them.

(ii) *Disuse of the Committee on Admission*
The deadlock over admission in the late 1940s and 1950s led the General Assembly to call on the Security Council to expedite its consideration of applications. In so doing, the Assembly also further developed the Article 4(1) criteria by way of listing specific factors that might bear on evaluating an application. A resolution of 1952 is of particular interest. Peru had proposed a draft by which, *inter alia,* applicants would be invited to submit documents as proof of their qualifications. The provision to invite submission of documents was opposed by a number of States, which noted that the Charter contains no provision for such measures. They were clearly right that the Charter contains no such provision, but this in itself hardly means that it would be outside the authority of the Council or Assembly to invite submission of documents. The functions and powers of the

---

[80] Ibid. 97 ff.

[81] Permanence probably has little bearing on statehood in cases where statehood is clearly established. It may bear more in a close case, especially where one of the core criteria is in doubt: see Crawford *Creation* 2nd edn 90–1 esp the comparison there between the Second (1965) and Third (1987) *Restatements of Foreign Relations Law of the United States,* § 100 and § 202 respectively.

General Assembly as set down in Chapter IV are not inelastic;[82] and Article 4(1) calls on the UN to reach a 'judgment.' The better view would be that reaching a judgment for purposes of Article 4(1) requires at least a degree of development at forensic level; calling on applicants to submit evidence of their qualifications would seem a modest step in that direction.

By the resolution as adopted, the General Assembly, *inter alia*

> *Consider[ed]* that the judgment of the Organization that they are willing and able to carry out these obligations and are otherwise qualified for membership ought to be based on facts such as: the maintenance of friendly relations with other States, the fulfilment of international obligations and the record of a State's willingness and present disposition to submit international claims or controversies to pacific means of settlement established by international law...
>
> *Recommend[ed]* that the Security Council reconsider all pending applications for the admission of new Members; that in this reconsideration, as well as in the consideration of all future applications, the members of the Council take into account such facts and evidence as States applicants for membership may present.[83]

The General Assembly resolution, like the earlier questionnaires of the Committee on Admission, developed the substance of the criteria of Article 4(1). The evaluation of each applicant 'ought to be based on facts' and should 'take into account...facts and evidence' – an important, if basic, assertion. Whether the applicant kept 'friendly relations with other States' was a question that might lead to concrete information about the applicant's conduct. Whether the applicant 'submit[s] international claims or controversies to pacific means of settlement' even more so was susceptible to objective evaluation: appearance in international proceedings and adherence to the judgments and orders of international

---

[82] 'Under international law, the Organization must be deemed to have those powers which, though not expressly provided in the Charter, are conferred upon it by necessary implication as being essential to the performance of its duties': *Reparation for Injuries Suffered in the Service of the United Nations* Advisory Opinion of 11 Apr 1949, ICJ Rep 1949 pp. 174, 182. It has been said that in some situations 'those powers' include *compétence-de-compétence*: see Argentine submission, *Competence of the General Assembly* Advisory Proceedings, ICJ Pldgs 1950 p. 146. As would be expected, the extent of the elasticity of implied powers has been contentious and its full definition is to be referred to specific disputes: see, e.g., *Case Concerning the Land, Island and Maritime Frontier Dispute (El Salvador/Honduras)* Application for Permission to Intervene, Order of 28 Feb 1990, Dis Op Shahabuddeen, ICJ Rep 1990 pp. 3, 41–2:
> However elastic may be the test to be applied in determining the existence and extent of implied powers – and undue rigidity is surely to be avoided – it seems in any event clear that a constituent instrument cannot be read as implying the existence of powers which contradict the essential nature of the organization which it creates to exercise them.
Establishing fuller mechanisms for the evaluation of applications for admission hardly would seem to 'contradict' the UN's 'essential nature,' for the UN is an organization of States, admission to which is controlled by its member States.

[83] GA res 506A (VI) pream ¶ 2, operative ¶ 2, 1 Feb 1952 (43–8:7).

tribunals were (relatively) measurable indicia, even as in individual cases parties might dispute the extent of their obligations.[84] The specification by the General Assembly of such elements may be seen as a step toward fuller implementation of the Article 4(1) criteria.

As will be seen in Chapters 4, 5 and 6 below, however, this was not the beginning of a sustained development in UN procedure. What suggestions were made after the early 1950s more fully to implement the criteria of Article 4(1) were incidental to other issues and failed to take root as a means for rigorous control over admission.

The increase in number of very small States seeking admission was the main development leading the UN, briefly, again to consider possible means for implementing the substantive criteria. Admission of the Maldive Islands as a member State in 1965[85] in particular seems to have been the incident which occasioned renewed concern over very small States. A large number of such States then were acceding to independence, and their admission was said to put strains on the politics and bureaucracy of the UN. The United States and France raised a point whether extremely small States would be 'able' in the sense of Article 4(1) to carry out Charter obligations. 'Today,' it was said, 'many of the small emerging entities, however willing, probably do not have the human or economic resources at this stage to meet this secondary criterion.'[86] France referred to Rule 59 of the Security Council Provisional Rules of Procedure, which, according to France, 'lays down an examination procedure offering further opportunities for reflection and judgement, which, it would seem, must be put to good use henceforth if we do not wish to risk seeing the effectiveness of the Organization diminished in the future.'[87] The examination procedure to which France referred is that envisaged by the provision in Rule 59 for 'a committee of the Security Council upon which each member of the Security Council shall be represented' and which 'shall examine any application referred to it and report its conclusions thereon to the Council.' The limits of this mandatory language are noted above; the Security Council has authority to decline to refer an application to the Committee. When exercised, this authority removes substantive examination from the agenda. France seems to have recognized the limits, having not stated

---

[84] The General Assembly's inclusion of the 'international claims and controversies' point is perhaps to be counted among the after-effects of the *Corfu Channel* case: *The Corfu Channel Case (United Kingdom v Albania)* Compensation, ICJ Rep 1949 pp. 244, 247–8. On non-appearance generally, see Thirlway *Non-Appearance before the International Court of Justice* (1985).

[85] Application by letter dated 26 Aug 1965 from the Prime Minister of the Government of Maldive Islands to the Secretary-General, S/6645; recommendation by SC res 212, 20 Sept 1965; admission by GA res 2009 (XX), 21 Sept 1965.

[86] SCOR 20th yr 1243rd mtg 20 Sept 1965 ¶ 89.

[87] Ibid. ¶ 76.

that the rule *requires* an examination procedure but, rather, merely 'lays down' a procedure. France based its call for resort to the examination procedure on a consideration of policy ('if we do not wish to risk seeing the effectiveness of the Organization diminished in the future'), not on an application of procedural requirements. The weakness of Rule 59 is suggested by these transactions: the mechanism for substantive evaluation set out in the rule is subject to a policy decision and, thus, by no means is its operation assured. This amounts to a procedural gap, by way of which implementation of the substantive criteria for admission has readily been set aside.

The United States supported France's call for examination under Rule 59 at the time.[88] Two sessions later, the United States proposed re-activating the Security Council Committee on Admission of New Members, 'with a view to providing the members and the Security Council with appropriate information and advice.'[89] The Committee had functioned between 1946 and 1949, but applications until 1971 were addressed directly by the Security Council.[90] Thereafter, the Committee on Admission indeed was put back into use. However, the gap in the Rules of Procedure, noted above, was such that the mere formal reference of applications to the Committee by no means guaranteed that the Committee would serve as an effective mechanism for implementing the substantive criteria for admission. Applications henceforward would go to the Secretary-General (as provided in Rule 58); then to the Security Council; then to the Committee on Admission; then back to the Council; and then, if recommended, to the General Assembly, but this procedure produced no indication that the Security Council or the Committee on the Admission of New Members evaluated applications on their substance.

The Security Council, in rare instances, when recommending an applicant for admission to the General Assembly departed (slightly) from a standard formulation. For example, the Council stated a special political rationale for admitting the two Koreas:

> The aspirations of the peoples and Governments of the Democratic People's Republic of Korea and the Republic of Korea have harmoniously coincided. That is why the Council decided to consider and take a simultaneous decision on the admission of both parts of the Korean Peninsula.[91]

---

[88] Ibid. ¶ 90.

[89] Letter dated 13 December 1967 from the USA to the President of the Security Council, SCOR 22nd yr Supp Oct–Dec pp. 321–2, S/8296.

[90] The vicissitudes are described in Sydney Bailey & Sam Daws *The Procedure of the UN Security Council* 2nd edn (1998) 339–44.

[91] Security Council Presidential Statement, S/22911, 8 Aug 1991.

It must be submitted, however, that harmonious coincidence does not bear clear relation to any particular criterion under Article 4(1); and there certainly was reason to explain the Council's recommendation in greater detail, if not for its substance, then at least for its form, for it was unusual to admit two States by way of a single resolution.[92] The statement in connection with the Korean case in any event was the exception. More typical is the following Security Council Presidential Statement, issued in connection with the recommendation to admit East Timor:

> The Security Council has decided to recommend to the General Assembly that the Democratic Republic of East Timor be admitted as a Member of the United Nations. On behalf of the members of the Security Council, I wish to extend my congratulations to the Democratic Republic of East Timor on this historic occasion.
>
> The Council notes with great satisfaction the solemn commitment of the Democratic Republic of East Timor to uphold the purposes and principles of the Charter of the United Nations and to fulfil all the obligations contained therein.
>
> We look forward to the day in the near future when the Democratic Republic of East Timor will join us as a Member of the United Nations and to working closely with its representatives.[93]

The language adopted in connection with other Security Council recommendations on admission has been very similar.[94]

The re-activation of the Committee on Admission of New Members proved to be an addition of procedure with no addition of substance. The *pro forma* treatment of applications for admission was by then firmly installed in UN practice.[95]

---

[92] This is not to say that good ground was lacking for dual admission. See Chapter 5, pp. 155–6, 158–60, 161, below on the systemic considerations of international security relevant to the dual admissions of the Germanies and Koreas and, perhaps, to admission more generally.

[93] S/PRST/2002/15, 23 May 2002. For the recommendation itself, see S/2002/566, SC res 1414, 23 May 2002.

[94] E.g., that for Switzerland: S/PRST/2002/23, 24 July 2002.

[95] The *pro forma* character of admission practice has drawn general comment from writers: e.g. O'Keefe 'The Admission to the United Nations of the Ex-Soviet and Ex-Yugoslav States' (2001) 1 *Baltic Yearbook of International Law* 167, 170–1; Ginther 'Article 4' in Simma ed *Commentary* 2nd edn p. 185 ¶ 34; Bailey & Daws *The Procedure of the United Nations Security Council* 3rd edn 339–44.

Chapter 3

The Road to Universality: the Admissions of 1955–6

> The universal character of an organization receives its practical application in its attitude as regards admission of new members.[1]

Architects designing the physical premises to be built on the banks of the East River reportedly asked Oscar Schachter, then one of the senior legal counsellors at headquarters, how many seats the UN General Assembly meeting hall should include. Schachter told the architects to include seats for an additional twenty member States.[2] From that early vantage, such an allowance seemed enough. The possibility existed early in the UN era to apply criteria for admission with a rigour likely to bring due scrutiny upon all applicants. Nobody thought that the fifty-one seats for Original Members would suffice for long, but a stampede for admission seemed unlikely. The possibility for controlling admission had been illustrated even before the Charter was adopted: the principle that States should be rigorously vetted was the basis of objection to Argentina participating in the Conference on International Organization. Shortly after, the Committee on Admission of New Members, in issuing admission questionnaires, demonstrated a willingness to subject applicants to factual and legal inquiry as to their Article 4(1) fitness. Article 4 itself was expounded by the International Court in the *Admission* and *Competence* Advisory Opinions. The General Assembly in 1952 proposed further specifications of the criteria for admission.

These and related steps, which the preceding Chapter described, were however sporadic and insufficiently connected to develop into a coherent substantive position or procedural apparatus. After that, for a short time – chiefly in the tenth and eleventh sessions (1955 and 1956) – States debated the admission of

---

[1] El-Erian, Special Rapporteur, First Report on Relations between States and Inter-Governmental Organizations: 11 June 1963 ¶ 70, *ILC Ybk* 1963 Vol. 2 p. 168.

[2] Personal anecdote related by Robert John Araujo 'Objective Meaning of Constituent Instruments and Responsibility of International Organizations' in Ragazzi ed *International Responsibility Today. Essays in Memory of Oscar Schachter* (2005) 343, 344.

new members with reference to the legal criteria under Article 4. Recalling the Argentine controversy, the debate during this time again suggested the possibility of applying the admission criteria restrictively – but the failure in the first decade to establish a process that might actually delay or prevent admission of an applicant meant that little by way of consistent practice now existed for the member States to build upon.

3.1   *The 'Logjam'*[3]

After the fifty-one Original Members adopted the Charter, a group of States remained outside the ranks of the Organization. For a number of these, no particular hurdle stood in the way of admission. Three States which had been neutrals during World War II were admitted in 1946.[4] Pakistan, recently independent, and Yemen were admitted in 1947.[5] One newly independent State was admitted in each General Assembly session from 1948 to 1950 – Burma, Israel, and Indonesia.[6] It was clear by 1950, however, that a remaining group of States

---

[3] Writers summarizing the struggle over admission between 1945 and 1955 include Louis Sohn *Cases and Materials on United Nations Law* (1956) 1–8; Grieg 'The Advisory Jurisdiction of the International Court and the Settlement of Disputes between States' (1966) 15 *ICLQ* 325, 350. See also *Rep SC* (1946–51) pp. 248–56; and the chart recording Security Council votes (including vetoes) in the sessions from 1952–55 in *Rep SC* (1952–5) pp. 87–90.

[4] Afghanistan, Iceland, and Sweden: SC res 8 (1946), 29 Aug 1946, GA res 34 (I), 9 Nov 1946; and Thailand (Siam): SC res 13 (1946), 12 Dec 1946, GA res 101 (I), 15 Dec 1946. See Humber 'Admission to the United Nations' (1947) 24 *BY* 96, 96–7. In later years the Security Council would address almost all applications in separate resolutions or decisions. SC res 8, in addition to recommending three States simultaneously for admission, noted consideration by the Committee on Admission of applications of Albania, Mongolia, Jordan, Portugal, Ireland, and Siam – but did not recommend those applicants for admission at the time.

[5] On the recommendation of the Security Council in SC res 29 (1947), 12 Aug 1947 and by vote of the General Assembly in GA res 108 (II), 30 Sept 1947. On the admission of Pakistan and Yemen, see 24 *BY* at 90, 98. SC res 29 noted consideration by the Committee on Admission of applications of Albania, Mongolia, Jordan, Ireland, Portugal, Hungary, Romania, Austria, and Bulgaria. These were not recommended for admission at the time.

[6] In the 1948 session (3rd session), the General Assembly admitted Burma (currently titled 'Myanmar'): SC res 45 (1948), 10 Apr 1948, GA res 188 (II), 19 Apr 1948. See Liang 'Admission of Indian States to the United Nations' (1949) 43 *AJ* 144.

In 1949, Israel was admitted: SC res 69 (1949), 4 Mar 1949, GA res 273 (III), 11 May 1949, about which see Dugard *Recognition and the United Nations* 60–63; Liang 'Conditions of Admission' (1949) 43 *AJ* 299. After an initial postponement of the matter of Israel's application, it was proposed to request an advisory opinion on the matter, but agreement was not reached to make the request before Israel was in fact admitted. For references to committee discussions on this, see Rosenne vol. I p. 300 n. 66. As GA res 273 (III) refers to prior General Assembly practice, including observations about refugee status, certain writers and States have asked

would be problematic. Some, such as Hungary and Mongolia, were favoured by the Soviet Union. These were Soviet allies – perhaps more accurately described, as some States did describe them, as Soviet 'satellites.'[7] Others, like Japan and Spain, were favoured by the United States and the other western Allies. From the opposite Cold War side, they, too, met objection. The first decade of the United Nations, even as an appreciable number of States actively sought admission, thus saw few admissions. The period between 1950 and 1955 saw no admissions at all. Indeed, so far from breaking the deadlock were the member States at the time, that in the 1953–4 session the Security Council did not discuss the question of admission.[8]

Yet the existing non-member States were not content to be excluded, and, with the independence of former colonial territories, the number of States seeking admission grew. The words 'logjam' and 'deadlock' were used by State representatives in the UN at the time.[9] Writers picked the words up, so they became part of the vocabulary of the history of the UN.[10]

The logjam was a result of Cold War politics: neither side in the international contest wished the other to gain the advantage that the admission of friendly States to the United Nations was thought to entail.[11] The balance of votes in

---

whether admission of Israel was 'conditional': see Lewis Saideman 'Do Palestinian Refugees Have a Right of Return to Israel?' (2004) 44 *Virg JIL* 829, 836–41. The better view, in light of the completeness of the Art. 4 criteria for admission, is that no special obligation is entailed in GA res 273 (III). Leo Gross took this position: (1983) 77 *AJ* 569, 581 n. 51.

Indonesia was admitted in 1950: SC res 86 (1950), 26 Sept 1950, GA res 491 (V), 28 Sept 1950.

[7] E.g., Mr Tsiang (China) SCOR 10th yr 703rd mtg 13 Dec 1955 ¶¶ 51–2; Mr Lodge (USA) SCOR 10th yr 704th mtg. 13 Dec 1955 ¶ 99.

[8] *Rep SC* (1952–5) p. 88 n. b.

[9] For example, on adoption of GA res 918(X), 8 Dec 1955, José Maza of Chile, in the capacity of President of the General Assembly said,

> The Assembly has just, by a majority eloquent in itself, approved a resolution which, for the first time in ten years, offers us some possibility of extricating the United Nations from the *dead-lock* which has prevented any progress over the admission of new Members.

[emphasis added] GAOR 10th sess 553rd mtg 8 Dec 1955 ¶ 158. Sir Percy Spender (Australia) GAOR 10th sess 555th mtg 4 Dec 1955 ¶ 55, called it a 'log jam.' See also Mr Katz-Suchy (Poland) GAOR 12th sess 552nd mtg 8 Dec 1957 ¶¶ 110–11; Sir Leslie Munro (New Zealand) GAOR 10th sess 555th mtg 14 Dec 1955 ¶ 46; Sir Pierson Dixon (United Kingdom) GAOR 10th sess 555th mtg 14 Dec 1955 ¶ 70; Mr Sobolev (USSR) GAOR 12th sess 663rd mtg 28 Feb 1957 ¶ 4.

[10] E.g., Finkelstein 'International Cooperation in a Changing World: A Challenge to United States Foreign Policy' (1969) 23(3) *Int'l Org* 559, 568; Feinberg 'L'admission de nouveaux membres à l'Organisation des Nations Unies' (1952) LXXX *Hag Rec* 299.

[11] It is generally accepted that this was the relevant political background: see, e.g., the passing references by Scharf 'Musical Chairs: The Dissolution of States and Membership in the United Nations' (1995) 28 *Cornell ILJ* 29, 40; Lloyd 'Succession, Secession, and State Membership in

the General Assembly in particular was perceived as a matter of some political significance by the major powers, for it was there that the in-built protection of the veto was lacking. Questions of prestige also may have been in play, a successful blockade of the other side's candidates for admission perhaps enhancing the political standing of a power, acceptance of new members from the opposing block having the opposite effect.[12] Whatever the political background, protagonists in the resultant debate in the United Nations frequently expressed themselves in terms of the criteria of Article 4(1). It was in fact the logjam that triggered the request for an Advisory Opinion on conditions of admission of States to membership in the United Nations.[13]

In the end, all States constituting the 'logjam' would be admitted, and it was during the discussions concerning their admission, particularly in the 1955 and 1956 sessions, that the view decisively took hold that the interests of the Organization and its members would be served by universal admission, rather than by an exacting application of the substantive criteria of Article 4(1). Yet the position was far from clear to all member States that a legal basis existed for universal admission, or, as a corollary, that the Charter permitted the effective suppression of substantive criteria for admission. In the General Assembly meeting of 14 December 1955, at which a then-record number of States – sixteen – were admitted to membership and the door thus opened to universal membership, the Permanent Representative of El Salvador said, '[N]or is universality prescribed in the Charter. The Charter in fact does not... lay down the principle of universality, but the General Assembly has been able to lay it down to a certain extent.'[14] This would determine the future face of the United Nations. The constitutional development that led the General Assembly to 'lay down the

---

the United Nations' (1994) 26 *NYU JIL & Pol* 761, 768–9. For a fuller account, see Roberts & Kingsbury 'Introduction: The UN's Roles in International Society since 1945' in Roberts & Kingsbury eds *United Nations, Divided World: The UN's Roles in International Relations* 2nd edn (1993) 1, 31; Weiss, Forsythe, Coate & Pease *The United Nations and Changing World Politics* 5th edn (2007).

[12] The superpowers from the start of the Cold War apparently believed that the UN was a potential mechanism for showing favour to States whose allegiance they sought. Consider the U.S. National Security Council's evaluation of control over participation, noted in Wolfrum *Die Internationalisierung Staatsfreier Räumer: die Entwicklung einer internationalen Verwaltung für Antarktis, Weltraum, hohe See und Meeresboden* (1984) 52 n. 105.

[13] Chapter 2 above discusses the first Advisory Opinion; Chapter 1, the second. A third Advisory Opinion on admission was sought during the early 1950s but, in part for the same reasons admission itself was problematic at the time, no further question on the subject was put to the International Court: Pomerance 'Seeking Judicial Legitimation in the Cold War: U.S. Foreign Policy and the World Court, 1948–1962' (1995) 5 *Ind Int'l & Comp LR* 303, 309–12.

[14] Mr Urquia (El Salvador) GAOR 10th sess 555th plen mtg 14 Dec 1955 ¶ 100.

principle of universality,' and thus finally to reject a restrictive application of Article 4, now will be considered.

3.2 *The General Assembly and the Non-admissibility of Spain*

The crisis in the constitution of the UN that was called the 'logjam' well could be characterized as a contest between a view favouring universal admission and a view holding onto a notion of restrictive interpretation of Article 4. The States opposing admission of certain applicants in the first years of the UN Charter did not express their opposition with sufficient consistency however to develop a constitutional interpretation with lasting effect. With respect to certain remaining non-member States, opponents to their admission expressed objections in terms of World War II alliance loyalties. That a State adhered to the aggressors in the war could have been connected naturally enough to the criteria for admission, but only some of the member States advocating against admission made the connection or drew any particular attention to it. More generally, non-admission of former supporters of the Axis was described in terms suggesting that this was a special case having little relevance to future applicants. This was a further instance of the member States declining to build a coherent basis for the implementation of Article 4(1).

The main case of contested admission in which member States scrutinized the World War II loyalties of an applicant was that of Spain. The question of the admission of Spain revisited ground already staked out between the USSR and the western allies. The rationale against admitting the Iberian applicant was essentially the same as that articulated by the Soviets against including Argentina in the Conference on International Organization at San Francisco. Like Argentina, Spain had not been an active member of the alliance against fascism.[15] Spain, in fact, while formally neutral, had been an active, if, by intention, not a highly effective, supporter of the Axis.[16] Spain was considered suspect on this ground.

---

[15] See Polish Communications dated 8 Apr and 9 Apr 1946, reprinted in *UN Ybk* 1946–7 p. 345. Exclusion of Spain from the UN was identified as one of the main goals of the Soviet Union in the General Assembly at the time: Mosely 'Soviet Policy in the United Nations' (1947) 22 *Procs of the Academy of Pol'l Science* 28, 36. It might be postulated that Spain during the war had breached an obligation to deny assistance to the Axis powers – and, thus, that opposition to admitting Spain to the UN was indeed based on constitutional interpretation of the Charter: a State which breaches its international obligations is not a State committed to the purposes and principles of the Charter. However, as one writer said, there lacked 'any general agreement on the substantive rights and duties of third parties to the conflict': Ginsburgs 'The Soviet Union, the Neutrals and International Law in World War II' (1962) 11 *ICLQ* 171, 172.

[16] See Detwiler 'Spain and the Axis During World War II' (1971) 33(1) *Review of Politics* 36, especially the quotation of Churchill's assessment of Spain's role in World War II, id 53. Further

The difference between Spain and Argentina is that in 1946 a constitutional standard existed at least in skeleton form in the plain text of the Charter, so it would have been possible to refer non-admission to the text and in so doing develop the text in the direction of a rigorous vetting of future applicants. The details of what the member States and the Organization had to say about Spain merit consideration, for they contained suggestions as to how the substantive admission criteria might have been implemented.

As with Argentina, the question over Spain first presented itself at San Francisco. The Conference on International Organization in 1945 had expressed 'unanimous moral condemnation' over the role of Spain in the war.[17] The Charter organs of the UN maintained this position in the first session. According to the General Assembly, the government of Spain owed its establishment in the late 1930s to Axis support. This was not the same as objecting to admission of Spain for actual conduct of the Spanish government. It was, instead, to object on the basis of historic facts. This presented the possibility that a State might be refused admission, on the ground of defects which the State could correct only by jettisoning the government of the day: change of policy would not be enough. Perhaps the fascist government of Spain was seen as a lesser included case of the Italian and German governments of World War II, governments the termination of which was a pre-condition for a return to normal relations by those States: nobody would have settled for a 'reformed' Axis government (whatever the word 'reformed' applied to such a government could have meant). Or perhaps the objection to Spanish participation in the UN could be referred to a principle that governments that come to power by unlawful use of force by foreign powers, like territorial changes effected through such means, are not to be recognized. Whatever the rationale, the General Assembly in 1946 scrutinized the political origins of the government of a State. The result of the scrutiny was evident in a provision to invite non-member States to register their treaties with the UN under Article 102 of the Charter. Spain was not invited:

> It is desirable, as a matter of practical convenience, that arrangements should be made for the publication of any treaties or international agreements which non-member States may voluntarily transmit and which have not been included in the treaty series of the League of Nations. These arrangements should not, however, extend to treaties or international agreements transmitted by any non-member State such as Spain, the Government of which has been founded with the support of the Axis powers and does not, in view of its origin, its nature, its record and its

---

to the diplomatic machinations of Spain, see the memoir of diplomat Beaulac *Franco: Silent Ally in World War II* (1986).

[17] *UN Conference on International Organization: Documents,* vol. I p. 10.

close association with the aggressor States, possess qualifications necessary to justify membership in the United Nations under the provisions of the Charter.[18]

If the General Assembly had been looking for a way to apply the Article 4(1) provision that a State, to be admitted, be 'peace-loving,' to apply it in a resolution concerning Article 102 was, to say the least, oblique. It also was dubious as a matter of policy. Treaty registration, of the various fields of activity of the United Nations, is one in which a policy of universal participation is unimpeachable. To make a secret of instruments which establish obligations under public international law is incompatible with rule of law. It also has been said that secret treaties generally destabilize international relations.[19] Treaty registration under Article 102 has little to do with the composition of the government of the State party to the treaty. It instead aims to assure transparency respecting the binding commitments entered into by every State. As much as any UN function, treaty registration would seem better served by universal participation. Be that as it may, the General Assembly here took the position that a State, by its 'origin...nature...record and...association,' might fail to satisfy the criteria for admission. Security Council statements in 1946 also were directed against Spain.[20]

The position soon to emerge was significantly more permissive. The question now to be addressed is on what basis did the member States and the UN establish the more permissive position which eventually prevailed.

3.3 Universality as Legal Requirement?

The historical record shows that the founders of the UN anticipated that the post-World War II international organization, in time, would include most or all

---

[18] GA res 23(I) ('Registration of Treaties and International Agreements'), 10 Feb 1946 pream ¶ 2.

[19] Secret treaties have been identified particularly as a factor leading to the First World War: see e.g. Ponsonby *Democracy and Diplomacy: A Plea for Popular Control of Foreign Policy* (1915). They remained a concern to American policy makers in World War II, when the United Kingdom assured the United States that it had made no secret arrangements respecting territorial adjustment with other States, especially with the Soviet Union: Langer & Gleason *The Undeclared War, 1940–41* 1st edn (1953) 681.

[20] The Security Council took note of the condemnation of Spain at the San Francisco Conference and of subsequent statements by member States. It appointed by SC res 4 (1946), 29 Apr 1946, a subcommittee of five members to examine 'whether the situation in Spain has led to international friction and does endanger international peace and security.' The situation in Spain was removed later that year from the list of matters of which the Security Council was seized: SC res 10 (1946), 4 Nov 1946. The Security Council resolutions did not mention admission. For statements of member States and relevant transactions see *UN Ybk* 1946–7 pp. 345–51.

States. For example, in discussions leading to adoption of the Atlantic Charter on 11 August 1941, the United States and Great Britain considered it important to give assurance that Germany and Italy, after the destruction of their aggressor regimes, would be fully incorporated into the international system of trade and economic development.[21] Churchill's public statement of March 1943 calling for a 'United Nations headed by the three great victorious powers' included the prediction that it would include 'some day all nations.'[22] There was no indication in such statements however as to how long the 'day' would be in coming. Churchill and his contemporaries did not envisage it to be close at hand. The delegates to the Conference on International Organization in 1945 said that universality was 'an ideal toward which it was proper to aim, but which was not practicable to realize at once.'[23] This was a good deal short of calling admission a right of all States or a presumption in UN procedures. Fawcett, in his writing on the (British) Commonwealth, said that the League of Nations, too, was formed with a view eventually to achieving universal membership – but that that end would be approached 'only gradually.'[24] The heads of the UN Specialized Agencies, in 1950 in a joint statement on admission of new members, said, 'We re-affirm the validity of this *principle* of universality.'[25]

To consider the legal basis for universality in the UN, it is necessary first to consider what precisely is meant by the term; how universality fits into the scheme of the UN Charter as a whole; and how universality relates to the Charter principle of sovereign equality. These matters taken together then may shed light on the question whether universal membership in the UN is a requirement of law.

3.3.1   *Universality Defined*

(i) *A UN Principle*
States in formal statements respecting the UN in its early years were clear that universal admission was a principle to guide the Organization – and just as clear that it was by no means a rule requiring automatic admission of particular applicants. Moreover, a cautionary principle was embodied in specific admission criteria, and this presented a counterpoise to universality. According to France,

---

[21] Russell *A History of the United Nations Charter* (1958) 36.
[22] Ibid. 105 quoting Churchill statement as recorded in British Information Services *British Speeches of the Day* vol. I (April 1943) 1–10.
[23] UNCIO *Report of Rapporteur of Committee I/2* Doc 1178 vol. 7 p. 326.
[24] Fawcett *The British Commonwealth in International Law* (1963) 227.
[25] Seventh Report of the Administrative Committee on Coordination to the Economic and Social Council, Doc E/1682, 11 May 1950 pp. 2–3. Emphasis added.

...universality was the ultimate goal to strive towards; but...in no case should the other principles, which were the very foundation of the United Nations, be sacrificed in the desire to attain that goal too rapidly. Article 4 of the Charter provided that membership in the United Nations was open to all peace-loving States which accepted the obligations contained in the Charter and which, in the judgment of the United Nations, were able and willing to carry out those obligations. There could be no doubt about the meaning of that text. Member States were therefore bound to admit only States worthy of collaborating in the great work of the United Nations. Nothing would be more contrary to the spirit of the Charter than to accept every applicant State, almost automatically. Nothing would be more dangerous for the future of the Organization.[26]

France further said, referring to the preparatory work involved in drafting the Charter,

> The concern for selectness, the fear of opening the United Nations to States which were not peace loving and which were unable to fulfil the obligations of the Charter or not willing enough to do so, were clearly expressed on every page of the records of that work. A choice had therefore to be made, and the merits and qualifications of each applicant had to be weighed. That was an obligation and not merely an option.[27]

The United Kingdom took a similar view:

> The United Kingdom Government would gladly see as many properly qualified sovereign States as possible become Members of the United Nations but it could not accept the idea that universality would mean the imposition upon Members of the obligation automatically to admit any State that submitted an application. That could not be done in the light of Article 4 of the Charter, which defined the requirements and the conditions that must be fulfilled before an applicant could be admitted to membership of the United Nations.[28]

And the United States

> regarded the United Nations as a universal Organization, which should ultimately embrace all States in the world...Yet it could not be denied that the concept of absolute universality was not applicable. Each Member was bound to determine that an applicant possessed, as prerequisites to admission, the qualifications set forth in Article 4 of the Charter...To admit an applicant which did not meet those standards was not in accordance with the Charter.[29]

Universality might be an objective of the UN – but it was a rather distant objective and 'absolute universality' was not on the table. Article 4 was accepted as a statement of standards, and these were to be applied to limit admission

---

[26] Mr Montel (France) GAOR 4th sess 251st plen mtg 22 Nov 1949 ¶ 55.
[27] Ibid. ¶ 56.
[28] Sir Alexander Cadogan (United Kingdom) GAOR 4th sess 252nd plen mtg 22 Nov 1949 ¶ 10.
[29] Mr Cooper (USA) ibid. ¶ 44.

to 'properly qualified sovereign States.' The admission process was to be conducted with a view to 'selectness,' even as member States sought to widen the community within the Organization's compass. Article 4, it may be concluded, was intended to temper whatever directive might otherwise be read from the Charter favouring universality.

(ii) *A Measure of Tasks and Potential*

Even if one were to accept the view that universality in some sense trumps Article 4, that alone would not necessarily be tantamount to a legal mandate requiring admission of all States, much less a rule setting out a timetable for the result. It is open to question whether an authoritative definition of 'universal' as a legal term exists. The UN Charter does not define 'universal,' and its only use of the term sheds no particular light on its meaning as applied to international organizations.[30] Insofar as a definition can be gleaned from relevant sources, it falls considerably short of a formula for automatic admission of States to any given organization.

El-Erian at the start of the ILC's consideration of the topic relations between States and international organizations said that a universal organization 'is one that includes in its membership all the States of the world.'[31] As of 1963, at any rate, '[t]his [was] not the case of any past or present international organization yet.'[32] When the International Court in *Barcelona Traction* referred to treaties having a very wide subscription, it referred to 'instruments of a universal or quasi-universal character.'[33] It was necessary to reserve whether the universal instrument in the strict sense of the word existed. The same consideration would apply to international organizations as to international instruments; the expression 'quasi-universal' perhaps could be applied to both. Schwarzenberger preferred the term 'universalist.'[34] Oppenheim talked about organizations 'of potentially universal character.'[35] Several French writers used the similarly general expression

---

[30] Article 1 includes among the Purposes of the United Nations 'To develop friendly relations among nations based on respect for the principle of equal rights and self-determination of peoples, and to take other appropriate measures to strengthen universal peace.' Article 55 on international economic and social co-operation provides that the UN shall promote, *inter alia* 'universal respect for, and observance of, human rights and fundamental freedoms for all without distinction as to race, sex, language, or religion.'

[31] El-Erian First Report ¶ 64, *ILC Ybk* 1963 Vol. 2 p. 167.

[32] Ibid.

[33] ICJ Rep 1970 pp. 3, 32 ¶ 34.

[34] Schwarzenberger *A Manual of International Law* vol. I 4th edn (1960) 227. Quoted El-Erian First Report ¶ 64, *ILC Ybk* 1963 Vol. 2 p. 167.

[35] Oppenheim *International Law: a treatise* vol. I 8th edn (Sir Hersch Lauterpacht ed) (1955) 370. Quoted El-Erian First Report ¶ 64, *ILC Ybk* 1963 Vol. 2 p. 167.

'à avocation universelle.'[36] A 'universal' organization, then, would appear to be one which might in principle include all States, not necessarily one in which all-State membership is an accomplished fact.

The Vienna Convention on the Representation of States in Their Relations with International Organizations of a Universal Character[37] is one of the few international texts to consider the concept of universality in the context of international organizations. It does not however use the term 'universal' to mean that the international organizations to which the term applies must have all States as members. The Convention in Article 1(1) sets out the following definition of an 'international organization of a universal character': 'the United Nations, its specialized agencies, the International Atomic Energy Agency and any similar organization whose membership and responsibilities are on a worldwide scale.' Noteworthy here is that the Convention does not define 'universal' to mean actual inclusion of all States. The definition is, first, by way of example – 'the United Nations, its specialized agencies [and] the International Atomic Energy Agency.' Notably, none of these at the time (1971) included all States. The definition goes on to incorporate a general reference – 'similar organization[s] whose membership and responsibilities are on a worldwide scale.' The operative expression – 'worldwide scale' – is not specific as to the States that must belong for an organization to be 'universal.' It would seem that the member States are not to be restricted to any one region, but that is the extent of the guidance the expression provides. The lack of specificity is apparently purposive. According to the ILC Commentary on draft article 1,[38] 'The question whether an international organization is of universal character depends not only on the actual character of its membership but also on the potential scope of its membership and responsibilities.'[39] Two considerations therefore are relevant when asking whether an organization can properly be called universal: (1) 'the actual character of its membership'; and (2) 'the potential scope of its membership and responsibilities.' The former consideration is one of 'character,' a fairly open-ended concept. The latter is one of *'potential* scope' – which is to say that an organization, to be universal in the sense concerned, need not have a particular scope but, rather, need only have the *potential* for it.

---

[36] El-Erian cites Bastid *Droit des Gens: Principes généreux* (1960) (collected lectures) 329; Rousseau *Droit International Public* (1953) 180; Reuter *Institutions internationales* 3rd edn (1962) 202.

[37] Adopted 14 Mar 1975, A/CONF.67/16; 34 parties; 35 needed: not yet entered into force.

[38] The definition set out in draft article 1(1) differed only slightly from that in Convention Article 1(1) as adopted. The draft article provided, '"international organization of universal character" means an organization whose membership and responsibilities are on a worldwide scale': adopted by the ILC at the 23rd sess 1148th mtg 30 July 1971, published in *ILC Ybk* 1971 vol. II pt one p. 284.

[39] *ILC Ybk* 1971 vol. II pt one p. 285 Comment (4).

Whatever the scope, the potential for its achievement is enough, according to the ILC, to establish that an organization is 'universal.' Moreover, universality of 'scope' refers not only to scope of 'membership' but also to scope of 'responsibilities.' The word 'responsibilities' here means tasks. It follows that an organization, to be universal in the sense described, has global tasks, as much as it has global membership.[40] None of this runs against the grain of a restrictive interpretation of admission criteria in the constitutive instrument. The ILC drafting work had in view the possibility that a 'universal' organization, though 'worldwide,' might not include every State. To say, then, that an organization is universal is not to prescribe a rule requiring admission of all States.

3.3.2   *Universality in the Charter as a Whole*

As suggested by a reading of Article 4(1) and related provisions of the Charter, it is far from clear that universal admission is a requirement of the UN as originally constituted. Article 4(1) sets out conditions or criteria for admission. The International Court of Justice, in developed reasoning in its Advisory Opinion on *Admission,* was clear that these are substantive criteria, and that a member State, in coming to a view as to whether the criteria are satisfied by an applicant, may consider a range of evidence. That an institutional apparatus for dealing with applicant States is defined in Article 4(2) further suggests that admission was not intended to be a mere *pro forma* exercise. The General Assembly, when it called for individual consideration of every candidate State, was consistent with this position.[41]

The Charter, in the architecture of public order it envisages, also is consistent with a restrictive interpretation of admission criteria. Article 2, paragraph 6 provides as follows: 'The Organization shall ensure that States which are not Members of the United Nations act in accordance with these Principles so far as may be necessary for the maintenance of international peace and security.' Two observations may be made with respect to Article 2(6). First, Article 2(6) furnishes a legal basis for a general legislative competence on matters involving peace and security. The competence can be called general, for the reason that it extends to all States, not just those acceding to the terms of the Charter upon

---

[40] Some governments in comments to the ILC preferred the words 'object and purpose' to 'responsibilities,' which would have expressed the connection between scope of membership and the tasks of the universal organization more directly: El-Erian Sixth Report, 2 & 29 Mar, 5, 9 & 26 Apr, 12 & 14 May 1971 ¶ 52, *ILC Ybk* 1971 Vol. 2 Pt One p. 18.

[41] GA res 197B (III), 8 Dec 1948 (calling on the Security Council to 'tak[e] into account the circumstances in each particular case').

admission as members.[42] Second, following from the first observation, the Organization was conceived as existing in a world containing both States admitted to
UN membership and States not admitted. This is the State system in which the
framers of the Charter knew the Organization was to exist, and they made no
provision in the Charter to say when the dualism of members and non-members
would end, or if ever it would. A restrictive interpretation of admission criteria
likely would perpetuate a State system in which some States are UN members
and others not. The scheme in the Charter to maintain peace and security among
States assumes that there are member States and non-member States. The scheme
thus accommodates a restrictive interpretation of admission criteria. It also may
be that the duties of the UN in the field of peace and security further call for
a relatively cautious approach to admission.[43]

3.3.3   *Universality and Sovereign Equality*

Sovereign equality, a principle embedded in the Charter, it might be said furnishes
a legal basis for rejecting a restrictive interpretation of the admission criteria of
Article 4(1). It is true that the UN Charter incorporates the principle of sovereign
equality. Sovereign equality was invoked in the wartime planning that led to the
adoption of the Charter,[44] and '[t]he Organization is based on the principle of
the sovereign equality of all its Members' (Article 2(1)). In some general way,
this might be seen to support treating admission criteria in a liberal fashion so
as to bring about membership of all States. In light of the extensive authority
attributed to the United Nations – especially to the Security Council – and the

---

[42] On the general legislative competence of the UN, see Comment 5 to Draft Art. 1 ('Essential
requirements of a treaty'), Hersch Lauterpacht, Special Rapporteur on the Law of Treaties, 24
Mar 1953: *ILC Ybk* 1953 vol. II p. 98.

[43] Judge Alvarez in his Individual Opinion in the *Admission* case took the view that admission
of States has a relation to the duty of the UN to protect international peace and security.
'Cases may arise,' Judge Alvarez said, 'in which the admission of a State is liable to disturb
the international situation...Consequently, even if the conditions of admission are fulfilled
by an applicant, admission may be refused.' ICJ Rep 1948 pp. 57, 71. States in the advisory
proceedings took a similar view: see, e.g., ICJ Pldgs 1948 p. 82 (Milan Bartoš for Yugoslavia);
ICJ Pldgs 1948 p. 109 (Manfred Lachs for Poland).

[44] E.g., in paragraph 4 of the Moscow Conference Agreement of 1943, in which the Conference
parties stated
> That they recognize the necessity of establishing at the earliest practicable date a general
> international organization, based on the principle of the sovereign equality of all peace-lov-
> ing states, and open to membership by all such states, large and small, for the maintenance
> of international peace and security.

Department of State Release No. 460, 1 Nov 1943, adopted by House Resolution 370, 18 Dec
1943: 78th Cong 1st Sess Doc No. 351 (House docs): War Conference at Moscow: Official
Text of the Moscow-Conference Agreement.

centrality of the Organization to international relations, what meaning could 'sovereign equality' retain, if there emerged two classes of States – one of member States, and one of non-members? There is of course the structural consideration noted above that the Charter plainly envisages the continued existence of non-member States. But sovereign equality is a powerful consideration itself, and one certainly belonging to the Charter scheme. It therefore cannot be ignored as a legal prop to universal admission.

The principle of sovereign equality of States was referred to in international law well before the establishment of the UN.[45] 'No principle of general law,' said Chief Justice Marshall in 1825, 'is more universally acknowledged than the perfect equality of nations. Russia and Geneva have equal rights.'[46] The core of the principle is that no State, as a matter of law, exists in subordination, or supremacy, to another. States have plenary power under international law, meaning that a State may do any of those acts that it is possible for an entity to do under international law.[47] It is a principle with practical consequences, for example with respect to the bilateral character of settlements of territorial and maritime disputes,[48] and it is imprescriptable.[49]

Sovereign equality has been affirmed in authoritative statements. The CSCE Helsinki Final Act (1975) included the following:

> I. *Sovereign equality, respect for the rights inherent in sovereignty*
> The participating States will respect each other's sovereign equality and individuality as well as all the rights inherent in and encompassed by its sovereignty, including in particular the right of every State to juridical equality, to territorial integrity and to freedom and political independence. They will also respect each other's right freely to choose and develop its political, social, economic and cultural systems as well as its right to determine its laws and regulations.

---

[45] See e.g. Hall *A Treatise on International Law* 8th edn (1924) 50–8; Oppenheim *International Law: A Treatise* 1st edn (1905) 161–7; Wheaton *Elements of International Law* 8th edn (1866) 33–4. The classic American treatment is Dickinson *Equality of States in International Law* (1920). See generally Anand 'Sovereign Equality of States in International Law' (1986) 197 *Hag Rec* 9; Klein *Sovereign Equality Among States: The History of an Idea* (1974).

[46] *The Antelope*, 23 U.S. (10 Wheat) 66, 122 (1825).

[47] For consideration of the term 'sovereignty' in this (legal) sense, see Kelsen 'The Principles of Sovereign Equality of States as a Basis for International Organization' (1944) 53 *Yale LJ* 207, 208–10; Crawford *Creation* 2nd edn 32–3; Schermers 'Different Aspects of Sovereignty' in Kreijen ed (2002) 185; Hannum *Sovereignty and Self-Determination: The Accommodation of Conflicting Rights* (1990) 14–6.

[48] *Case Concerning Maritime Delimitation and Territorial Questions between Qatar and Bahrain (Qatar v Bahrain)* Merits, Dissenting Opinion Judge Ad Hoc Torres Bernárdez, ICJ Rep 2001 pp. 40, 420 ¶ 464.

[49] *Fisheries Jurisdiction Case (Spain v Canada)* Jurisdiction, Dissenting Opinion Judge Ad Hoc Torres Bernárdez, ICJ Rep 1998 pp. 432, 635 ¶ 137.

Within the framework of international law, all the participating States have equal rights and duties. They will respect each other's right to define and conduct as it wishes its relations with other States in accordance with international law and in the spirit of the present Declaration. They consider that their frontiers can be changed, in accordance with international law, by peaceful means and by agreement. They also have the right to belong or not to belong to international organizations, to be or not to be a party to bilateral or multilateral treaties including the right to be or not to be a party to treaties of alliance; they also have the right to neutrality.[50]

The statement on sovereign equality in the Helsinki Final Act contains two dimensions: freedom to control internal institutions and practices without outside interference; and freedom to conduct international relations in accordance with the State's own wishes. Included in the latter is the freedom of the State to decide its own relations to international organizations. The General Assembly expressed the principle of sovereign equality in 1970 in the Declaration on Principles of International Law Concerning Friendly Relations and Co-operation Among States in Accordance with the Charter of the United Nations:

All States enjoy sovereign equality. They have equal rights and duties and are equal members of the international community, notwithstanding differences of an economic, social, political or other nature.
In particular, sovereign equality includes the following elements:
(a) States are juridically equal;
(b) Each State enjoys the rights inherent in full sovereignty;
(c) Each State has the duty to respect the personality of other States;
(d) The territorial integrity and political independence of the State are inviolable;
(e) Each State has the right freely to choose and develop its political, social, economic and cultural systems;
(f) Each State has the duty to comply fully and in good faith with its international obligations and to live in peace with other States.[51]

Here, too, sovereign equality relates to rights of domestic jurisdiction and freedom from external coercion.

As reflected in the Friendly Relations Declaration and the Helsinki Final Act, the principle of sovereign equality has gained considerable purchase in modern practice.[52] This observation is supported by the actual shape that States have

---

[50] Conference on Security and Co-operation in Europe, Final Act, Helsinki, 1 Aug 1975, Principle I of the Declaration on Principles Guiding Relations between Participating States: 14 ILM 1292.

[51] *The principle of sovereign equality of States* in Declaration on Principles of International Law Concerning Friendly Relations and Co-operation among States in accordance with the Charter of the United Nations, GA res 2625 (XXV), 24 Oct 1970 (adopted without vote).

[52] Consider also affirmation of the Friendly Relations Declaration in practice and by writers. Upon adoption of the Friendly Relations Declaration, the President of the General Assembly said that the Declaration 'marks the culmination of many years of effort for the progressive development and codification of the concepts from which basic principles of the Charter are

assumed in modern times. States as international legal persons in the last hundred years have become more, not less, homogeneous, in the sense of conforming to a single juridical template. Where various legal qualifications on statehood were accepted, especially before the World Wars – e.g., protectorates,[53] free cities,[54] capitulations[55] – the tendency through the twentieth century was toward homogenization of international actors into States sharing a core of legal characteristics.[56] Thus practice in international law has approximated the principle that States be 'equal members of the international community,' even as States have become more heterogeneous in their legal relations and sociological characteristics.

It seems at least broadly consistent with the sovereign equality of States that the UN should at some stage have come to include all States. The Philippine representative to the UN in 1955, for example, said, 'My Government believes in the universality of the United Nations as a cardinal principle of our Charter . . . [all States] should have a place in our Organization on a basis of sovereign equality.'[57] Hans Kelsen, discussing the October 1943 Moscow Conference at which the Allies took steps toward a post-war United Nations, noted the link between sovereign equality and the constitutive plan of the organization.[58]

---

derived': GAOR 25th sess 1883rd plen mtg 24 Oct 1970 p. 2 ¶ 9. It was not said which of the concepts was the result of progressive development, or which already existed in international law. Robert Rosenstock, Legal Affairs Advisor to the U.S. delegation at the UN at the time, noted disagreement as to whether the Declaration was binding or merely recommendatory: 'The Declaration of Principles of International Law Concerning Friendly Relations: A Survey' (1971) 65 *AJ* 713, 714–15. For a recent comment on sovereign equality, see Lee 'International Law, International Relations Theory, and Preemptive War: The Vitality of Sovereign Equality Today' (2004) 67 *Law & Contemporary Problems* 147, esp. historical review at 150–3.

[53] Crawford *Creation* 2nd edn 282–382; Hannum *Self-Determination* 16–7, 18. See also *Case Concerning Rights of Nationals of the United States of America in Morocco (France/USA)* ICJ Rep 1952 pp. 176, 184–5, 188, 192–3.

[54] Crawford *Creation* 2nd edn 233–44, 447, 505, 522; Hannum *Self-Determination* 17; Méir Ydit *Internationalised Territories: From the 'Free City of Cracow' to the 'Free City of Berlin'* (Leyden: A.W. Sythoff, 1961) 22–4, 27–8, 50–9, 71, 95–108, 153–83, 185–229, 231–71. See also *Consistency of Certain Danzig Legislative Decrees with the Constitution of the Free City* Advisory Opinion, 1935 PCIJ Ser A/B No 65 pp. 49–50; *Treatment of Polish Nationals and Other Persons of Polish Origin or Speech in the Danzig Territory* 1932 PCIJ Ser A/B No 44 pp. 11–19; *Polish Postal Service in Danzig* Advisory Opinion, 1925 PCIJ Ser B No 11 p. 10.

[55] Fidler 'A Kinder, Gentler System of Capitulations? International Law, Structural Adjustment Policies, and the Standard of Liberal, Globalized Civilization' (2000) 35 *Tex ILJ* 387, 389–98, esp. the 19th century treatises cited at 389 n. 8. See also *Case Concerning the Protection of French Nationals and Protected Persons in Egypt (France v Egypt)* Order of 29 March 1950 (Discontinuance) ICJ Rep 1950 p. 28.

[56] *See* Crawford *Creation* 2nd edn 254.

[57] Mr Romulo (Philippines) GAOR 10th sess 555th plen mtg 14 Dec 1955 ¶ 132.

[58] Kelsen 'The Principle of Sovereign Equality of States as a Basis for International Organization' (1944) 53 *Yale LJ* 207.

However, nothing in the principle of sovereign equality as it existed before the UN era said that sovereign equality entailed admission to any particular group or organization of States. It was clear in the 19th century that sovereign equality, though necessary for a system of international law, was not equivalent to a general international law right to participate in international conferences and the like.[59] And 20th century practice did not in so many words modify this position. The General Assembly in the Friendly Relations Declaration of 1970 certainly had the chance to – but it did not. The Helsinki Final Act, in its statement on sovereign equality, addressed the relation between sovereign equality and membership in international organizations. As quoted above, the Final Act said that States have 'the right to belong or not to belong to international organizations.' The Helsinki Final Act would not have been the place to revise the UN constitutional system, yet it is a significant article of State practice and thus may be considered as influencing the legal development of the subject matter it addressed. The statement on sovereign equality and a 'right to belong or not to belong' could perhaps be interpreted as meaning that a State may choose to belong to an organization, as against the wishes of a dissenting constituency. The more natural interpretation, in context, however, is that no State or organization may force another State to belong to an organization. The concern was to prohibit forcible inclusion of a State by an organization like the Warsaw Pact or NATO, not to license the forcible entry by the State into an organization. From general international law and particular practice an inference favouring universal membership may be drawn, but a prescription is not to be found there.

The UN Charter itself draws no direct connection between sovereign equality and admission. Article 2, paragraph 1 of the Charter indicates that the principle of sovereign equality is basic to the Organization. Taken in a general way, this would suggest openness to the broadest possible approach to admission of States. If all States are equal before the law, and the United Nations is to be a mechanism for the development of rule of law, it well may be argued that membership should be universal. However, the exact wording of Article 2(1) is as follows: 'The Organization is based on the principle of the sovereign equality *of all its Members*' [emphasis supplied]. As to what the principle means for States not members of the Organization, or whether it even applies to them, Article 2(1) is silent. The Charter also mentions sovereign equality in connection with the Trusteeship System and, there, too, only specifies its application as among member States. Article 78 stipulates that the Trusteeship System 'shall not apply to territories which have become Members of the United Nations, relationship among which shall be based on respect for the principle of sovereign equality.' The application of the Trusteeship System to a territory entailed considerable

---

[59] Bowett *The Law of International Institutions* 4th edn (1982) 383–4.

qualification of the rights which the territory might exercise at international level. By precluding trusteeship over member States on the basis of sovereign equality – but not over non-members – Article 78 suggests that sovereign equality at least in some sense has a distinct meaning for purposes of the Charter.

Plainly, the Charter leaves existing customary international law and general principles of interpretation intact. Sovereign equality, in general international law, applies to all States, whether or not Article 2(1) or Article 78 re-states that position. The relation of States to one another outside the United Nations however is not the question. What the Charter says about admission is the question. It would require a stretch of interpretation to conclude that the language of Article 2(1) or Article 78 says anything about admission, other than to reflect, perhaps, a general preference for liberal application of admission criteria. Moreover, the Charter provisions which refer to sovereign equality do not involve a rule but rather a principle – and they link the principle to the Organization with the rather vague words 'based on.' The Charter founders knew how to craft prescriptive language with definite effect (consider the executive provisions of Chapter VII); they did not use such language to link the principle of sovereign equality to the substance or procedure of admission.[60]

Whatever sovereign equality in the Charter might mean, it is certainly not a mandate for universal admission. And no other Charter provision comes any closer to conferring such a mandate.[61] The Court in the *Admission* Advisory Opinion said that Article 24 of the Charter, 'owing to the very general nature of its terms, cannot, in the absence of any provision, affect the special rules for admission which emerge from Article 4.' The same must be the case for provisions more general than Article 24.[62] The specific terms respecting admission set out in Article 4 therefore, under the maxim of interpretation *generalia*

---

[60] In this light, it may even be doubted what meaning Article 2(1) has for 'all its Members.' States sometimes have rejected as contrary to the Charter 'the view that States which are admitted to the United Nations belong to different classes of membership.' Mr Menon (India) GAOR 10th sess 556th plen mtg 15 Dec 1955 ¶ 135. The specific Charter provisions conferring the veto on the five permanent members of the Security Council is hard to reconcile however with categorical acceptance of a 'no different classes' position. Alvarez sees the veto right as inconsistent with sovereign equality: *International Organizations as Law-makers* (2005) 70.

[61] It is sometimes said that Article 2(6) gives a legal basis for universality: Ginther 'Article 4' in Simma ed *The Charter of the United Nations: A Commentary* 2nd edn vol. I p. 178 ¶ 1. Article 2(6) provides,

> The Organization shall ensure that states which are not Members of the United Nations act in accordance with these Principles so far as may be necessary for the maintenance of international peace and security.

cf. Russell *United Nations Charter* 358. If universal membership had been the intention here however, this was a rather oblique way of establishing its legal basis.

[62] ICJ Rep 1948 pp. 57, 64.

specialibus non derogant, which certainly applies to the Charter,[63] must be taken as the original position under Charter law.

* * *

In the next Chapter we will give further consideration to how States and the UN itself through practice may have interpreted or changed the Charter as a source of legal rules and as a system of constitutional order. For present purposes it suffices to conclude that the express provisions concerning admission, as well as the overall architecture of the Charter and its main principles, do not furnish any self-evident basis for a legal presumption of the admissibility of all States. It falls then to consider here the grounds in policy that might have impelled the move toward a liberal interpretation of Article 4.

3.4   Universality as Policy Decision

It was by way of an assertion of policy discretion, not by way of implementation of a legal requirement self-evident in the Charter, that the organs of the United Nations acted to displace substantive criteria for admission with the principle of universality. The General Assembly in 1953 established a Committee of Good Offices, with a mandate to

> consult with members of the Security Council with the object of exploring the possibilities of reaching an understanding which would facilitate the admission of new Members in accordance with Article 4 of the Charter.[64]

Though this provision included what might have been a limiting phrase ('in accordance with Article 4 of the Charter'), on inspection it becomes clear that what the General Assembly had in mind was widening membership to universal breadth. In the second preambular paragraph to the resolution establishing the Committee of Good Offices, the General Assembly said that 'universality

---

[63] *Certain Expenses of the United Nations (Article 17, Paragraph 2, of the Charter)* Advisory Opinion, Sep Op Sir Gerald Fitzmaurice, ICJ Rep 1962 pp. 151, 211. And to treaties generally: *SGS Société Générale de Surveillance SA v Islamic Republic of Pakistan* Decision on Objections to Jurisdiction, 6 Aug 2003 (Feliciano, President; Faurès & Thomas, members) 8 ICSID Rep 383, 418 ¶ 65; *The Payment of Certain Serbian Loans Issued in France* 1929 PCIJ Ser A No. 20 p. 30. cf. *Official Records of the United Nations Conference on the Law of Treaties*, Second Session, Summary of records of the plenary meetings and of the meetings of the Committee of the Whole, p. 253, 91st meeting of the Committee of the Whole ¶ 41; and *Case Concerning the Gabčíkovo-Nagymaros Project (Hungary/Slovakia)* ICJ Rep 1997 pp. 7, 76 ¶ 132; and Liberia, Written Statement, IMCO Advisory Proceedings, ICJ Pldgs 1960 p. 66.

[64] GA res 718(VIII), 23 Oct 1953 ¶ 1. On the work of the Committee, see Gross 'Progress Towards Universality of Membership in the United Nations' (1956) 50 *AJ* 781, 796–98.

of membership in the United Nations is subject only to the provisions of the Charter.' The operative words here, it is submitted, are 'universality of membership.' The paragraph as a whole is question-begging, assuming as it does that very little stands in the way of universal membership: the word 'only' implies that 'the provisions of the Charter' are *de minimus* as respects limits on admission to membership. Yet the main question is what limits do the provisions of the Charter actually place on admission to membership? The task of the Committee of Good Offices, in practice, would be to undertake consultations with the member States of the Security Council, with a view to breaking the 'logjam.'[65]

General Assembly resolutions adopted during the two sessions that followed (1953 and 1954) affirmed that a decision was approaching to embed a permissive interpretation of admission criteria in the constitution of the Organization. The Assembly in 1954 noted

> the growing general feeling in favour of the universality of the United Nations, membership in which is open to all peace-loving States which accept the obligations contained in the Charter and, in the judgment of the Organization, are able and willing to carry out those obligations.[66]

The inclusion of words closely tracking those of Article 4 might have suggested that the General Assembly intended to maintain the vitality of substantive admission criteria – but, as in the resolution of the year before, the main sense of the statement was to be found in words pointing presumptively to unrestricted membership – 'in favour of the universality of the United Nations.'

The Secretary-General made clear that admission on as wide a basis as possible indeed was to be the policy of the Organization. The rationale was chiefly political:

> Almost half the countries of Europe are absent from the council tables. It is inevitable that the effectiveness and influence of the United Nations are lessened by this fact, not only as regards the questions of direct concern to Europe, but other problems, too, where the experience of the European peoples would make possible a great contribution towards their solution. This consideration applies also to the peoples in other parts of the world who do not yet have the representation in the United Nations to which their role in world affairs entitles them.[67]

The proposition now is widely accepted that an international organization is necessary that may draw upon 'the experience of [various] peoples.' Inclusion of all States at 'the council tables' is probably indispensable in the interests of

---

[65] See Report of the Committee of Good Offices, 19 Sept 1955, A/2973, GAOR 10th sess Annexes agenda item 21 pp. 1, 2 ¶¶ 6–7.

[66] GA res 817(IX), 23 Nov 1954 pream ¶ 1.

[67] Mr Dag Hammerskjold *Introduction to the Annual Report of the Secretary-General* GAOR 9th sess, supp No. 1, A/2663 (1954) p. xii.

comity and for other purposes, including purposes integral to the UN Charter. The statement that 'their role in world affairs entitles' States to admission, however, has no legal basis; and the ascendance of a policy of universal admission, however much that policy might promote central purposes of the UN – even be indispensable to them – equally would impede other purposes. An assessment of the balance of the policy merits was how the decision was reached by the 1955 session that admission would be open to all.

In similar vein, it was said that certain functions that the United Nations was created to perform require maximum breadth of participation by States. Syria, for example, said,

> The Member States of the United Nations were pledged to maintain international peace and security. How could they honour that pledge if the Organization was not really universal, especially since peace was indivisible? In these circumstances how could they attain other purposes of the United Nations, such as developing friendly relations among nations, achieving international co-operation and being a centre for harmonizing the actions of nations in the attainment of those common ends?[68]

The United Nations indeed serves as co-ordinator of international functions which a particular or regional organization could not perform. The value of a universal organization in this regard was, and remains, perhaps the most convincing argument of policy in favour of a liberal practice with respect to admission.

A further consideration set out in favour of universal admission was that the world had changed significantly since 1945, and new conditions made it desirable to have participation by all States in the UN. Speaking in the Ad Hoc Political Committee shortly before what would prove to be the decisive General Assembly session, Indonesia's representative said,

> [T]he authors of the Charter had drafted Article 4 in 1945, at a time when they were engaged in a struggle to the death with the Axis Powers. They had therefore naturally attributed the label "peace-loving" to themselves. States which had then owed allegiance to the Axis Powers had been deemed not to be peace-loving and by definition unfit to be Members of the United Nations. However, the yardstick then used was no longer serviceable. The world picture had changed radically since 1945.[69]

---

[68] Mr Shukairy (Syria) GAOR 10th sess Ad Hoc Pol Com 28th mtg 5 Dec 1955 ¶ 54.
[69] Mr Sudjarwo (Indonesia) GAOR 10th sess Ad Hoc Pol Com 30th mtg 6 Dec 1955 ¶ 7. See also Mr Urquia (El Salvador) GAOR 10th sess Ad Hoc Pol Com 29th mtg 6 Dec 1955 ¶ 15:
> Although the principle of universality had not prevailed at San Francisco...political developments since then, the advent of the atomic age, and a decade of international tension had demonstrated the necessity of widening United Nations membership. In that connexion Article 4 of the Charter should not be too rigidly interpreted. It had been drafted at the conclusion of the Second World War to prevent the admission of enemy States, a term

This was a noteworthy admission: universality was not part of the Charter as adopted. Conditions arising since 1945 however militated in favour of its inclusion as a principle to guide UN action. The suggestion here was that any restriction under the Charter with respect to admission was a remnant of the World War II alliance. Keeping States out had had the purpose of maintaining unity against certain aggressor States. Defeat of the Axis powers and their increasing re-integration into international relations, if the Indonesian position is to be accepted, in short, rendered Article 4 a dead letter. A fundamental change in circumstances, in this view, required a fundamental change in how the UN applied its provisions for admission. This raises the possibility that, though no legal basis existed at the beginning to require universal admission, subsequent practice, driven by the new circumstances, either re-interpreted or amended the Charter and, so, established a new legal position. The next Chapter, below, will consider the possibility in greater depth.

On 8 December 1955, the General Assembly adopted a further, and pivotal, resolution on admission, noting 'the general sentiment which has been expressed on numerous occasions in favour of the widest possible membership of the United Nations.'[70] This, perhaps, looks like a step back from universality – the phrase 'widest possible membership' being open to the interpretation that membership would be only to the extent 'possible' under the Charter. The interpretation actually taking shape, however, was that membership should be widened until co-extensive with the community of States as a whole. The 8 December 1955 resolution in fact was less than a week before the Council and Assembly would admit a 'package' of sixteen candidate States. This, it is submitted, marked a turning point, after which the substantive criteria of Article 4(1) largely would fall by the wayside, opening the road to universal admission.

Widening admission so as to attain a membership of universal scope was what member States interpreted the recent resolutions to call for. The statement by the representative of the United Kingdom set the tone:

> My Government has never thought of the United Nations as an association of like-minded States, such as an alliance or a coalition. Nor have we thought of the United Nations as a place from which we should exclude countries of whose political and social systems we may not approve. The Charter lays down that, in order to qualify for admission, States must be peace-loving and must be able and willing to carry out the obligations contained in the Charter. We certainly do not interpret this as meaning that we must approve of all the policies of those countries whose applications for membership we are ready to support. It is true that Article 4 of

---

defined in Article 53, paragraph 2. Ten years had elapsed since then and, in view of the changes in the international situation, Article 4 should be applied liberally.

[70] GA res 918(X), 8 Dec 1955 pream ¶ 1. The resolution was adopted 52–2:5 (against: China, Cuba; abstaining: France, Greece, Israel, USA, Belgium).

the Charter lays down specific qualifications for membership. There is, however, nothing which prevents each Member of the United Nations from assaying the qualifications of a candidate with benevolence – and my delegation's attitude will be an attitude of the utmost limit of benevolence.[71]

The United Kingdom statement could be taken as a précis of the future of the Organization. Its origins as an alliance against the aggressor States in World War II was diminished – it was 'never thought of…as an…alliance or a coalition.' Exclusion on the basis of 'political and social systems' was rejected. And the 'specific qualifications for membership' of Article 4 were to be interpreted in an 'attitude of the utmost limit of benevolence.' Representatives of other States spoke to similar effect, even States – e.g., France[72] – that said they were concerned to preserve the substance of the Article 4(1) criteria. These statements are in some contrast to the earlier statements of the same member States, noted above, in which they had upheld a restrictive view of admission. They certainly took liberties in their account of the World War II alliance and the United Nations' origins therein. A deliberate decision of policy had been arrived at, to reverse the earlier, if tentative, acceptance that the substantive criteria in Article 4(1) should be rigorously applied.

The mid-1950s sessions of the UN were the last in which the criteria of Article 4(1) were a main object of debate. A group of eighteen States were seeking admission at the time, and the logjam they caused occasioned discussion in the Security Council and General Assembly about standards for admitting new members. Though this produced an extensive record, it was already clear that circumstances had changed since 1946. Enough consensus had existed in 1946 favouring a strict application of admission criteria that the General Assembly could adopt the resolution rejecting Spain as unsuitable even for treaty registration on grounds of the origins and characteristics of its government. The General Assembly in the 1950s, by contrast, adopted no resolution expressly rejecting an applicant. In fact, no applicant seeking admission at the time ultimately would be denied admission. The eighteen States seeking admission all were admitted – and none subject to the formal disapprobation that the Assembly had directed against Spain in 1946. Delays effected by Security Council veto were with respect

---

[71] Sir Pierson Dixon (United Kingdom) SCOR 10th yr 701st mtg 10 Dec 1955 ¶ 49.
[72] Mr Alphand (France) SCOR 10th yr 701st mtg 10 Dec 1955 ¶ 111:
> We are very anxious that most of the States which have applied for membership should be admitted, but we do not consider that we should sacrifice to this principle and this wish the rules which are explicitly laid down in the Charter.

But also Mr Alphand (France) same paragraph:
> We have always been in favour of the principle of universality which is, implicitly, one of the corner-stones of our Charter.

to two applicant States, Japan and Mongolia.[73] For Japan, this meant a one-year delay only; for Mongolia, admission would be granted in 1961. None of the sixteen applications for admission going to the General Assembly in 1955 faced anywhere near the one-third negative vote required in the General Assembly to defeat an application.

The admissions of 1955–6 did not take place without objection. States in the Security Council and General Assembly put forward arguments against admission of particular applicant States, and, while a political theme runs through much of the debate, States expressed their positions in reference to the substantive admission criteria of the Charter. The arguments merit consideration as a later illustration of how Article 4(1) might have furnished substantive legal standards.

3.5   The Package Deal

For a number of reasons, it was a large group of States that sought admission in the mid-1950s. Some of these, like Libya, had been dependent territories until only a short time before and thus, as yet lacking statehood, had not been eligible to join an inter-State organization.[74] Others, like Spain, Italy, and Japan, had been encumbered by their involvement with, or membership in, the Axis during World War II. Japan's position had become settled only in the early 1950s, after seven years of Allied military occupation.[75] Others, as will be seen below, were caught up in unresolved territorial or other claims of chiefly regional interest. All the applicants felt the effects of the Cold War, then at its height and sometimes manifesting itself in controversies over admission.

---

[73] China (whose seat the Nationalist government on Taiwan held at the time) vetoed Mongolia: SCOR 10th yr 704th mtg 13 Dec 1955 ¶ 54. The USSR vetoed Japan: ibid. ¶ 70; SCOR 10th yr 706th mtg 15 Dec 1955 ¶ 116.

[74] Italy had renounced its possessions in Africa by Article 23(1) of the Treaty of Peace of February 10, 1947: 49 UNTS 3, 139. Libya was placed under joint control of France and the United Kingdom: id Article 23(2). By Annex XI to the Treaty, the Allies agreed to accept the recommendation of the General Assembly as to the final disposition of the former Italian colonies. The General Assembly, by resolution 289A (IV), 21 Nov 1949 ('Question of the disposal of the former Italian colonies') ¶¶ 1–2, recommended the establishment of Libya as an independent State no later than 1 Jan 1952. Libya became independent on 24 Dec 1951: GA res 515(VI), 1 Feb 1952 (adopted 53–0:0, GAOR 7th sess 370th plen mtg 1 Feb 1952 ¶ 202).

[75] On international law aspects, see Ando *Surrender, Occupation, and Private Property in International Law: An Evaluation of U.S. Practice in Japan* (1991). On foreign policy aspects, see Schaller *The American occupation of Japan: the origins of the Cold War in Asia* (1985); Buckley *Occupation diplomacy: Britain, the United States, and Japan, 1945–1952* (1982).

The Security Council in December 1955, without substantive comment, recommended sixteen States for admission as member States of the UN.[76] All sixteen were promptly admitted by resolution of the General Assembly.[77] This was the so-called package deal,[78] reached with a view to clearing the admission logjam of the past decade.

The Security Council however had not recommended admission of Japan or Mongolia. Both also were seeking admission at the time, the latter since 1946.[79] The objections to admission of Japan and Mongolia to be sure were motivated by Cold War considerations of balance in the Assembly, but member States debating the matter expressed their objections in reference to the substantive criteria of Article 4(1). The controversy over admission of Japan and Mongolia therefore suggests the potential of Article 4(1) to function as a legal regulator of membership – as well as suggesting the impediments to its implementation.

Of the sixteen States which did receive Security Council recommendation for admission in 1955, seven occasioned negative votes or abstentions in the General Assembly. The negative votes and abstentions, combined, were not very numerous. These are set out in the Table in Chapter 5 below. They nevertheless are significant, for they make up a large part of a limited practice of objection. As we have seen, the admission question had been occasioning debate in both

---

[76] *Letter dated 14 December 1955 from the President of the Security Council, addressed to the President of the General Assembly,* 14 Dec 1955, A/3099. The States recommended for admission were Albania, Jordan, Ireland, Portugal, Hungary, Italy, Austria, Romania, Bulgaria, Finland, Ceylon, Nepal, Libya, Cambodia, Laos, and Spain.

[77] GA res 995 (X), 14 Dec 1955.

[78] The proposal to admit a 'package' of applicant States at first was supported by some of the States comprising the Special Committee on Admission of New Members: see, e.g., explanatory memorandum submitted by Egypt and the Philippines *Report of the Special Committee on Admission of New Members* 25 June 1953, A/2400 GAOR 8th sess Annexes, agenda item 22 ¶ 9. Writers using the term include Ginther in Simma ed. p. 180 ¶ 10; McWhinney 'The International Court of Justice and International Law-Making: The Judicial Activism/Self-Restraint Antinomy' (2006) 5 *Chinese JIL* 3, 9; Huang 'Taiwan's Status in a Changing World: United Nations Representation and Membership for Taiwan' (2003) 9 *Ann Surv Int'l & Comp L* 55, 73; Chen 'The Meaning of 'States' in the Membership Provisions of the United Nations Charter' (2001) 12 *Ind Int'l & Comp LR* 25, 49–50; Pomerance (1995) 5 *Ind Int'l & Comp LR* 303, 343; Dugard *Recognition and the United Nations* (1987) 57; Cohen (later Higgins) 'The Concept of Statehood in United Nations Practice' (1961) 109 *U Pa LR* 1127 1127, 1142; Hotz 'The United Nations Since 1945: An Appraisal' (1961) *Annals of the American Academy of Political & Social Science* 127, 133. See also *Rep SC* (1954–5) p. 84 ¶ 8.

[79] See *Rep SC* (1952–1955) 86, citing application of Mongolia, 24 June 1946: SCOR Suppl 4, 1st yr 2nd ser Annex 6(3) pp. 17–18.

Council and Assembly since the first session of the United Nations in 1946.[80] Indeed, most of the sessions between the first and the mid-1950s produced busy agendas under the admission item. For present purposes, attention may be drawn to discussions in the Council and the Assembly, in and around the time of the eventual decisions to accept admission of the eighteen applicant States. A few words may be said about the UN debates concerning each contested applicant.

3.5.1 *Japan*

Japan applied for admission shortly after the restoration of self-government that followed the end of military occupation in 1952.[81]

The Security Council on 12 December 1956 voted unanimously to recommend admission of Japan as a member State.[82] Japan was admitted as a member State on 18 December 1956.[83] The vote in the General Assembly was unanimous.[84] The admission of Japan had been sought in the previous session (1955), but entanglement of the question of admission of Japan with admission of Mongolia had derailed the proposal. The Soviet veto, wielded against Japan, apparently had been with a view to forcing admission of both States – or preventing admission of either. The United States Permanent Representative said, 'It is altogether shocking to see this attempt... to link a great nation like Japan with a geographical abstraction like Outer Mongolia in a sordid package deal.'[85] Iran also doubted whether the two applicant States should be 'put... on an equal footing.'[86] Belgium took the view that linking the question of admission of Japan to that of admission of Mongolia was 'unconstitutional, as is clearly apparent from the advisory opinion of the International Court of Justice.'[87] Though there were heated exchanges respecting non-admission of Japan in the 1955 session,[88] the main objecting State – the USSR – did not offer objections

---

[80] See, e.g., GA res 35(I), 19 Nov 1946 ('Question of the re-examination by the Security Council of certain Applications for Admission to Membership in the United Nations'); and the earlier discussion in the Security Council: reviewed *extenso* in *UN Ybk* 1946–7 pp. 413–22.

[81] Application for admission, submitted by Japan: S/2673, 16 June 1952.

[82] SC res 121, 12 Dec 1956. See also Letter dated 12 December 1956 from the President of the Security Council to the President of the General Assembly concerning the application of Japan for admission to membership in the United Nations: GAOR 11th sess Annexes, A/3447, agenda item 25 p. 3.

[83] GA res 1113 (XI), 18 Dec 1956.

[84] GAOR 11th sess 623rd plen mtg 18 Dec 1956 ¶ 4.

[85] Mr Lodge (USA) SCOR 10th yr 708th mtg 21 Dec 1955 ¶ 17.

[86] Mr Abdoh (Iran) ibid. ¶ 52.

[87] Mr Van Langenhove (Belgium) ibid. ¶ 18.

[88] See, e.g., SCOR 10th yr 708th mtg 21 Dec 1955 *passim*.

in terms of the admission criteria of Article 4(1).[89] The lack of expressed legal basis for objection to Japan's admission may be seen to have eroded admission criteria as a legal rule: if admission and non-admission were to be referred solely to the political preferences of member States, then Article 4(1) would begin to look like an afterthought, rather than the constitutional underpinning to UN admission that it was intended to be.

3.5.2   *Mongolia: Admission Deferred*

Mongolia had applied for admission to membership on 24 June 1946.[90] Its admission would be considerably deferred.

The member State most vocally opposed to admission of Mongolia, by contrast to the Soviet Union with respect to Japan, set out a number of Article 4(1) grounds. China said that Mongolia was not a State, but that, even if it were, its conduct undermined its case for admission. Mongolia, according to China, had participated in the aggression against Korea and, before that, had invaded China (in 1947).[91] The Chinese representative warned about 'officiating at the burial of Article 4 of the Charter.'[92] Cuba also expressed the view that the proposed admission of Mongolia (as well as several other States allied with the Soviet Union) would be to disregard Article 4 and to ignore the Advisory Opinion on *Conditions of Admission*.[93] The United States position with respect to Mongolia was that its government was 'not now independent and [its] present subject status constitutes or derives from the violation of treaties and other international engagements.'[94] The United Kingdom doubted whether Mongolia was independent.[95]

---

[89] Japan's UN admission and membership were addressed generally in a report of the Japanese Association of International Law Study Group: *Japan and the United Nations* (1958).

[90] SCOR 1st yr 2nd ser, supp No 4, doc 2/95.

[91] Mr Tsiang (China) GAOR 10th sess 552nd plen mtg 8 Dec 1955 ¶¶ 33–38; SCOR 10th yr 703rd mtg 13 Dec 1955 ¶ 56; SCOR 10th yr 706th mtg 15 Dec 1955 ¶ 56.

[92] Ibid. ¶ 41.

[93] Mr Nuñez Portuondo (Cuba) GAOR 10th sess 552nd plen mtg 8 Dec 1955 ¶¶ 55–56, 67–68. Mr Nuñez Portuondo was particularly concerned to reject the position taken by certain members of the *Ad Hoc* Political Committee (which had been considering the admission problem), that the minority opinion in the *Conditions of Admission* case could be given equal weight to the opinion of the Court: 'Some delegations even maintained a view so absurd that I, in my twenty-five odd years of practice as a lawyer, and at times as a professor of law, had never heard of it, namely, that in a court of law the majority opinion and the minority opinion were of equal value' id ¶ 67.

[94] Mr Lodge (USA) SCOR 10th yr 701st mtg 10 Dec 1955 ¶ 89.

[95] But, making reference to the existence of diplomatic relations between India and Mongolia, the UK decided to vote in favour of Mongolia's admission: Sir Pierson Dixon (United Kingdom) SCOR 10th yr 703rd mtg 13 Dec 1955 ¶ 14.

China set out its position in detail again in 1961. The politics of admission, by that time, had compelled China to accept the Mongolian application. The USSR threatened to block admission of Mauritania a second time if admission of Mongolia was again delayed, and, perhaps, influence was brought to bear on the Republic of China to step aside so as to avert a mini-logjam over the admission of recently independent former colonies. The legal position under Article 4(1) nevertheless was recapitulated, if as a last breath of objection with little hope of finally blocking admission of the applicant. The Chinese permanent representative in 1961 argued that Mongolia had been unlawfully separated from China by Russia in 1911, and, moreover, that the Soviet Union, in 1924, had 'recogniz[ed] that Outer Mongolia is an integral part of the Republic of China.'[96] China also adduced evidence that the Soviet Union had violently suppressed local resistance, including through purges of the Mongolian government.[97] 'The fact is,' the representative of China said, 'that Outer Mongolia is not really independent.'[98] Mongolia also again was alleged to have engaged in aggression against China.[99]

The United States, referring to the *Conditions of Admission* Advisory Opinion, reiterated its opposition to arrangements 'linking the admission of any one applicant with that of another' – but concluded that admission of Mongolia was not such an arrangement.[100] The United Kingdom described its Security Council vote in favour of admission as 'an act of faith that [Mongolia] will accept and abide by these obligations once it has been admitted to the United Nations.'[101] This was a matter of giving Mongolia 'the benefit of the doubt.'[102] To give 'the benefit of the doubt' on an Article 4(1) question indicated that the position by then was becoming entrenched, that every State is presumptively fit for admission.

The General Assembly in 1961 noted that the Security Council on 4 December 1960 had been unable to recommend admission of Mongolia, because one of the permanent members (China) had remained in opposition. The Assembly interposed the following determination:

> [T]he Mongolian People's Republic is a peace-loving State within the meaning of Article 4 of the Charter of the United Nations, ... it is able and willing to carry

---

[96] Mr Tsiang (China) SCOR 16th yr 971st sess 25 Oct 1961 ¶ 25.
[97] Ibid. ¶¶ 30–31.
[98] Ibid. ¶ 33.
[99] Ibid. ¶ 75.
[100] Mr Yost (USA) SCOR 16th yr 971st sess 25 Oct 1961 ¶ 37.
[101] Sir Patrick Dean (United Kingdom) SCOR 16th yr 971st sess 25 Oct 1961 ¶ 51.
[102] Ibid.

out the obligations of the Charter, and…it should, in consequence, be admitted to membership in the United Nations.[103]

Mongolia was admitted as a member State on 27 October 1961.[104]

3.5.3   *Albania*

According to Greece,

> Albania does not fulfil the conditions laid down in Article 4 of the Charter. Albania's conduct and record in international affairs provide ample proof that its Government is neither able nor willing to carry out the obligations laid down in the Charter.[105]

The conduct to which the Greek representative drew the attention of the General Assembly included failing to repatriate Greek children and hostages; and infiltrating agents into Greece with the goal of 'the overthrow of the legal order.'[106] Cuba, referring to concentration camps and forced labour, said that slavery existed in Albania 'as a legal institution.'[107] China objected to admission of Albania on the same terms as it objected to admission of the other East European States with communist governments.[108] It was also objected that Albania at that time existed under a 'subject status' resulting from breach of treaty.[109] Implying that their independence was no more real than that of territories forcibly annexed, China referred to Albania and the other East European candidate States in the same breath as Latvia, Estonia and Lithuania.[110] Such entities in China's view were subsisting under unlawful foreign military occupation, and they therefore could not be received by the UN as States, much less as peace-loving or Charter-compliant States.

---

[103] GA res 1602 (XV), 19 Apr 1961 ¶ 1. The operative language had been that put forward by the Soviet Union: see A/L.336, amendments to A/L.335, 18 Dec 1960, GAOR 15th sess 1960/61, Annexes, Vol. I, agenda item 20, p. 10.

[104] SC res 166, 25 Oct 1961; GA res 1630 (XVI), 27 Oct 1961. See also Letter dated 25 October 1961 from the President of the Security Council to the President of the General Assembly, A/4940, GAOR 16th sess agenda item 92 Annexes p. 1.

[105] Mr Palamas (Greece) GAOR 10th sess 552nd plen mtg 8 Dec 1955 ¶ 17.

[106] Ibid. ¶¶ 18–19; and cf. ¶¶ 122–23. Greece's characterization of the conduct of Albania was not unilateral. The General Assembly had acknowledged the findings of a Commission of Investigation that Albania, Bulgaria, and Yugoslavia were supporting guerrillas carrying out hostilities in Greece against the Greek government: GA res 109(II), 21 Oct 1947 ('Regarding Threats to the Political Independence and Territorial Integrity of Greece') ¶ 3. See also observations of Mr Cooper (USA) GAOR 4th sess 252nd plen mtg 22 Nov 1949 ¶ 48.

[107] Mr Nuñez Portuondo (Cuba) GAOR 10th sess 552nd plen mtg 8 Dec 1955 ¶¶ 73–74.

[108] See below China's remarks.

[109] Mr Lodge (USA) SCOR 10th yr 701st mtg 10 Dec 1955 ¶ 89.

[110] Mr Tsiang (China) ibid. ¶ 46.

The British objections to Albania – though, in the event, these did not lead Britain to use the Security Council veto – were particularly serious. The Corfu Channel incident was relatively fresh in mind, and, despite the award of the International Court,[111] 'the Albanian Government ha[d] so far consistently refused to make any amends for this outrage.'[112] The British objection was not the first of its type. It will be recalled that France in 1946 had referred to Siam's acceptance of pacific dispute settlement as a condition for admission (see Chapter 2 above). If the UN system aims to foster rule of law, then non-compliance with a determination of the International Court, principal judicial organ of the system, is not consistent with the purposes of the Charter, nor would be rejection of pacific settlement *ab initio*.

3.5.4   *Jordan*

Israel, which abstained from voting on admission of Jordan, recorded no substantive reasons for its negative vote at the time the General Assembly voted to accept the application.[113] However, Israel earlier had said in the Ad Hoc Political Committee that Jordan had 'embarked on hostilities against Israel,'[114] a position presumably precluding a judgment that the applicant was peace-loving. Israeli leaders at the time also said that failure to 'respect fundamental human rights within their own territories' presented 'a certain potential risk to international society,' a position applicable to Libya as well.[115]

3.5.5   *Hungary*

As it had alleged against Albania, so did Cuba allege against Hungary that that State maintained slavery as an institution. Religious persecution was also alleged, with reference in particular to the imprisonment of the Cardinal Primate of the Catholic Church in Hungary.[116] China objected to admission of Hungary on the same terms as it objected to admission of the other East European States with communist governments.[117] It also was objected that Hungary at the time existed under a 'subject status' resulting from breach of treaty.[118]

---

[111] *Corfu Channel (United Kingdom v Albania)* (Assessment of the Amount of Compensation) ICJ Rep 1949 p. 244.

[112] Sir Pierson Dixon (UK) SCOR 10th yr 703rd mtg 13 Dec 1955 ¶ 15.

[113] Mr Najar (Israel) GAOR 10th sess 552nd plen mtg 8 Dec 1955 ¶¶ 79–85.

[114] GAOR 4th sess Ad Hoc Pol Comm 27th mtg 2 Nov 1949 p. 144.

[115] Hebrew University of Jerusalem Study Group *Israel and the United Nations* (1956) 177.

[116] Mr Nuñez Portuondo (Cuba) GAOR 10th sess 552nd plen mtg 8 Dec 1955 ¶¶ 75–76. China echoed the Cuban statement about religious freedom in Hungary: Mr Tsiang (China) SCOR 10th yr 703rd mtg 13 Dec 1955 ¶ 53.

[117] See below China's remarks.

[118] Mr Lodge (USA) SCOR 10th yr 701st mtg 10 Dec 1955 ¶ 89.

3.5.6   *Romania*

Cuba made the allegation of slavery also with respect to Romania. China objected to admission of Romania on the same terms as it objected to admission of the other East European States with communist governments.[119] It was also objected that Romania at the time existed under a 'subject status' resulting from breach of treaty[120] and was engaging in hostile acts against a neighbouring State.[121]

3.5.7   *Bulgaria*

As Cuba alleged against several of the East European States, so did it allege that Bulgaria was a slave State. According to China, by admitting Bulgaria, the United Nations 'accepted their captivity, *de facto* and *de jure*,' and China thought it was doubtful whether 'specific reservations and qualifications' made with respect to that admission would prove of any use. The Chinese Permanent Representative said that admission of Bulgaria (and the other three States with communist governments) was 'the evil part of the 'package deal.''[122] It was also objected that Bulgaria at the time existed under a 'subject status' resulting from breach of treaty.[123]

A further objection to admission of Bulgaria related to reparations under the World War II peace treaties. The peace treaties had established obligations on Bulgaria to make reparations to various States, and, it was said, Bulgaria failed to fulfil these. According to Greece, 'The fulfilment by a State of the contractual obligations it has assumed is a touchstone both of its attitude and of its willingness as a Member of the United Nations to carry out the obligations prescribed by the Charter.'[124] It might be said that the matter in issue was a bilateral dispute, and as such would have been addressed more appropriately in negotiations or in judicial or arbitral proceedings between the States concerned. Linkage nonetheless was clear to the Article 4 requirement of willingness and ability to fulfil the obligations incumbent on member States under the Charter. Greece reasoned that the conduct of a State with respect to one set of its obligations under international law predicted its conduct with respect to other obligations.

Bulgaria also was criticized for supporting communist guerrillas in Greece.[125] There was a postscript to Bulgaria's UN admission, for its delay carried an unexpected advantage: Bulgaria's acceptance of the compulsory jurisdiction of the PCIJ could not be invoked under Article 36(5) of the ICJ Statute to

---

[119] See below China's remarks.
[120] Mr Lodge (USA) SCOR 10th yr 701st mtg 10 Dec 1955 ¶ 89.
[121] Mr Cooper (USA) GAOR 4th sess 252nd plen mtg 22 Nov 1949 ¶ 48.
[122] Mr Tsiang (China) GAOR 10th sess 556th plen mtg 15 Dec 1955 ¶¶ 61–2.
[123] Mr Lodge (USA) SCOR 10th yr 701st mtg 10 Dec 1955 ¶ 89.
[124] Mr Palamas (Greece) GAOR 10th sess 552nd plen mtg 8 Dec 1955 ¶ 21.
[125] Mr Cooper (USA) GAOR 4th sess 252nd plen mtg 22 Nov 1949 ¶ 48.

establish compulsory jurisdiction for purposes of proceedings instituted by Israel in 1957. The Court determined that it was decisive that, by the time Bulgaria had been admitted as a member State of the United Nations (and was *ipso facto* a party to the Statute of the ICJ), the PCIJ had ceased to exist. According to the Court, 'it is one thing to preserve an existing undertaking by changing its subject-matter; it is quite another to revive an undertaking which has already been extinguished.'[126] The end of the PCIJ (on 18 April 1946) according to the Court had brought an end to any relevance that Bulgaria's acceptance of compulsory jurisdiction under the former Statute might have had under Article 36(5) of the new Statute – though this position was energetically contested in a joint dissenting opinion.[127] From the position of the Court, a substantive difference thus may be adverted to, as between original membership in the United Nations, and admission under Article 4. This however did not spring from special rights accorded Original Members as such but, instead, was a result contingent on the fact that no State had been admitted to the Organization under Article 4 before 18 April of its first year.[128] If a State party to the PCIJ Statute and not an Original Member had been admitted to the UN before the expiry of the PCIJ, then that State would have been a State admitted pursuant to Article 4 and also a party to the ICJ Statute pursuant to Statute Article 36(5). As it happened, no such category of States came to be.

3.5.8   *Libya*

As it did with respect to Jordan, Israel abstained from voting on admission of Libya.[129] Libya was a 'later adherent to the anti-Israel group.'[130] Israel, in the Ad Hoc Political Committee some days before the admission of the logjam States, already had made clear its attitude toward the Jordanian and Libyan applications:

> The Government of Israel would have no objection to, and would in fact welcome, the admission of most of the eighteen States. It had diplomatic and consular relations with some of them and was linked to many of them by ties of sincere friendship. On the other hand, it could not view favourably the application of the Hashemite Kingdom of the Jordan and had little enthusiasm for that of Libya. [The Israeli] delegation therefore reserved its right to explain its views with regard to those two

---

[126] *Aerial Incident of July 27th, 1955 (Israel v Bulgaria)* (Preliminary Objections) ICJ Rep 1959 pp. 127, 145.

[127] Joint dissenting opinion, Judges Lauterpacht, Koo, and Spender, ICJ Rep 1959 pp. 127, 156 *ff.*

[128] Afghanistan, Iceland, Sweden and Thailand were admitted later in 1946.

[129] Mr Najar (Israel) GAOR 10th sess 552nd plen mtg 8 Dec 1955 ¶¶ 79–85.

[130] *Israel and the United Nations* 188.

applicants in subsequent stages of the admission process. In doing so Israel would be concerned not with its own interests, but with those of the Organization.[131]

Obviously, few if any States took it upon themselves to set out objections in the UN for purely altruistic reasons; most objections to admission related to particular situations concerning the objecting States. Yet it was not at all far-fetched to draw a connection between Article 4 and the interests 'of the Organization.' The Charter provision that sets out the constitution of the Organization – in the literal sense of setting out how the Organization chooses its constituents – would be difficult to isolate from systemic interests. Moreover, where the objection relates to a question of international peace and security, the interests of the whole would seem to be inseparable from the relevant local or regional considerations.

3.5.9   *Spain*

Earlier objection to Spain was discussed above. Mexico continued to object, abstaining from the General Assembly vote by which Spain was admitted to membership. Mexico explained its abstention by reference to the earlier statements determining that Spain was not a suitable candidate for admission, including the declaration of the Conference on International Organization of 25 June 1945 and General Assembly resolutions 39(I) of 12 December 1946 and 114 (II) of 17 November 1947.[132] Spanish membership was a matter with respect to which Mexico proved tenacious.[133]

3.6   *Conclusions*

Statements by certain member States were directed at the 'package deal' as a whole. It was said that the deal had the effect of ignoring objectionable characteristics of the governments of certain candidate States. Cuba, on 8 December 1955, after presentation of the report of the *Ad Hoc* Political Committee, took the position that admission of States with communist governments would be a violation of Article 4. These States, the Cuban representative said,

---

[131] Mr Naiar (Israel) GAOR 10th sess Ad Hoc Pol Com 30th mtg 6 Dec 1955 ¶ 40.

[132] Mr De La Colina (Mexico) GAOR 10th sess 555th plen mtg 14 Dec 1955 ¶ 136.

[133] See Letter dated 28 September 1975 from the representative of Mexico to the Secretary-General, SCOR 30th yr Suppl for July–Sept 1975, S/11831, in which Mexico, invoking Articles 5 and 6, called for the 'Spanish regime [to] be suspended from the exercise of the rights and privileges of its membership.' That is to say, Mexico continued to protest Spanish membership to the final years of the Franco dictatorship.

not only do not fulfil the conditions laid down in Article 4 of the United Nations Charter, but...are States whose Governments do not respect any of the principles of international law. They are States which scoff at international law; which even now are violating the Convention on the Prevention and Punishment of the Crime of Genocide; which do not respect human rights; which still maintain concentration camps by the hundred; which, in brief, are totally opposed to the principles of our Organization.... They are neither peace-loving nor ready fully to comply with the obligations imposed on them by the Charter, and, as we all know, they respect none of the most elementary rights of man or the citizen.[134]

The admission of such States, the Cuban representative went on to say, was to overturn the interpretation of Article 4 set down by the International Court.[135]

France also objected that the legal rules on admission were being ignored or overridden in practice. According to France, the *Ad Hoc* Political Committee had prevented adoption of amendments to a resolution on admission that would have emphasized the operation of the Article 4(1) substantive criteria. The Permanent Representative of France expressed dismay that States in the Committee had rejected legal requirements in favour of a political solution – 'political considerations must override legal principles.'[136] The French representative said France supported 'admission of the greatest possible number of States' – but

> no mater how desirable this result may be, to attempt to achieve it by violating the Charter would...be a mistake fraught with fateful consequences for the United Nations.[137]

By the decision to admit unqualified States, 'the United Nations [had] deliberately chosen between the path of legality and the path of arbitrary action.'[138]

Related to the objection on grounds of arbitrariness was the process consideration that had arisen in the *Admission* Advisory Opinion: linkage of applications would deprive applicants of appropriate consideration. Belgium said that candidate States could not be treated as a package, the 1948 Advisory Opinion having clarified that linking admissions is contrary to Article 4.[139] The United States, in 1953 in the Special Committee on Admission,[140] had voiced concerns in similar terms, saying that the package deal 'represented barter rather than

---

[134] Mr Nuñez Portuondo (Cuba) GAOR 10th sess 552nd plen mtg 8 Dec 1955 ¶¶ 49, 56.

[135] Ibid. ¶¶ 64–8.

[136] Mr Alphand (France) ibid. ¶ 92.

[137] Ibid. ¶¶ 90–91.

[138] Ibid. ¶ 97.

[139] Mr Van Langenhove (Belgium) SCOR 10th yr 702nd mtg 10 Dec 1955 ¶ 29.

[140] Which had been established in the previous session 'to make a detailed study of the question of the admission of States': GA res 620A (VII), 1 Dec 1952 ¶ 2.

an application of Charter principles.'[141] The question of linkage, while one of lawfulness under Article 4, well may be distinct from the question of admission criteria. The two questions are however related: if candidates are treated in groups, it is hard to see how substantive conditions of admission can be considered in the specific circumstances of each candidate. Moreover, if the International Court was right, then conditioning admission of one State upon admission of another would be to breach the Charter, for linkage does not go to any of the criteria of Article 4, paragraph 1, and those criteria are exhaustive. Justification would have to be sought on terms like those suggested by the *Admission* case dissenting judges, who thought that concerns of international security had their own, independent relevance and therefore should be taken in account side by side, or if necessary in addition to, the enumerated criteria. China saw separate voting as a measure 'to salvage a part of Article 4,'[142] which was to imply that package voting would deny even 'part' of the article effect.

As illustrated by the statements of member States objecting to admission of particular candidates, a number of legal positions notable for their relation to the Article 4(1) criteria were taken. The range of positions[143] may be summarized as follows:

(i) The candidate State was in such a condition of political and military subordination to another State that it could not be said to possess the independence requisite to statehood for purposes of international law.

(ii) The candidate State or its government came into being through an unlawful intervention by another State or States.

(iii) The candidate State maintained internal policies which grossly violated fundamental rules of human rights, such as the prohibition against genocide or the prohibition against slavery.

(iv) The candidate State was an aggressor, it having invaded or threatened force against a neighbour.

(v) The candidate State was in default of a bilateral obligation toward an existing member State, and this was not indicative of the required willingness to carry out the obligations of the Charter, among these being the obligation to observe international agreements.

---

[141] *Report of the Special Committee on Admission of New Members* 25 June 1953, A/2400, GAOR 8th sess Annexes agenda item 22 ¶¶ 102–3.

[142] Mr Tsiang (China) SCOR 10th yr 702nd mtg 10 Dec 1955 ¶ 32.

[143] Compare list of grounds for objection to admission in Pomerance 307 n. 8. And see also brief comment on non-admission of Albania, Mongolia, and Transjordan: Günther Jaenicke 'Die Aufnahme neuer Mitglieder in die Organisation der Vereinten Nationen' (1950/51) 13 *ZaöRV* 291, 313.

(vi)   The candidate State failed to act in accordance with the principle of pacific resolution of international disputes, for example by defaulting in an obligation to appear in international proceedings or by refusing to satisfy international judgments.

(vii) A condition that another candidate be admitted in order for the candidate State to be admitted was contrary to the 1948 Advisory Opinion, in particular its holding that every candidate is to be evaluated on its own merits without the attachment of criteria additional to the five contained in Article 4(1) of the Charter.

Chapter 4

Universality Affirmed: The Eclipse of Substantive Admission Criteria

Ten years before the package deal which cleared the logjam of States seeking admission to membership, the General Assembly had disqualified Spain from the UN. The reason was that enemy States had been instrumental in Spain's government coming to power. The rejection of a State from admission thus was a judgment concerning its government. The judgment was that the future conduct of a government could be predicted by reference to its origins and, implicitly, by reference to its present policy. The UN might have reached such a judgment in connection with more than one application for admission, if the criteria for admission had been interpreted to entail a stringent test of every candidate. The admission of eighteen candidates as member States in 1955–6 made clear that the criteria would not be interpreted that way. A significantly more liberal approach prevailed, and the UN thereafter would grant admission with a view to achieving universal membership. The judgment that a candidate had failed to prove its fitness for admission thus turned out to be an artefact of a short episode of UN history, not an indication of a future constitutional approach. States in the General Assembly immediately after the large-scale admissions of 1955–6 expressed their views as to the direction that admission practice by that point had taken. The present Chapter will consider those views and ask what effect the practice of the time had on the admission provisions of the Charter. In turn, this is a way of asking by what process did the Charter come to accommodate the modern, universalist approach to admission.

4.1 Universality under Charter Law: The Views of States after the Package Deal

Member States, in the aftermath of the great debate over admission, acknowledged that the principle of universal membership had been affirmed. Their contemporary statements make at least this much clear. A principle however is not the same thing as a rule. Less clear is the extent to which States had come to take the view that universality had become a rule under the Charter as developed. Contemporary statements by certain State representatives suggested that universality remained a matter of principle, a goal to be sought but not a constitutional stricture. A minority of States said that the development underway already had gone much further: universality, they said, had become, or was on the verge of becoming, a legal presumption embedded through practice in the Charter. This practice and the arguments, such as were put forward in connection with it, merit consideration.

Following the admission in 1955 of the largest group of States up to that time, some whose admission had been long delayed, the tenor of remarks was celebratory. The Yugoslav representative, for example, '[saw] in this historic event a decisive victory on the road towards the universality of the United Nations.'[1] The Permanent Representative of Thailand said that the UN 'now... has become, in effect, a truly worldwide organization.'[2] The Permanent Representative of El Salvador, who it will be recalled doubted whether the Charter contains even the principle of universality, said on 14 December 1955 that this nevertheless was the future of the organization: 'The United Nations,' he said, 'can survive only by one day becoming the Organization of all the States of the world.'[3]

Canada said that admission 'does not mean... the acceptance of any particular form of government or any particular ideology' but, simply, 'that [the] Organization... has now applied, to a greater extent than before, the principle of universality.'[4] The representative of Peru referred to 'the dream... that this Organization of ours should be truly universal.'[5] Diverse States approved the shift toward universal membership signified by the sixteen admissions of 15 December 1955, among them Indonesia,[6] Yemen,[7] Syria,[8] Burma,[9] Lebanon,[10] Liberia,[11]

---

[1] Mr Mates (Yugoslavia) GAOR 10th sess 555th plen mtg 14 Dec 1955 ¶ 94.
[2] Prince Wan Waithayakon (Thailand) ibid. ¶ 114.
[3] Mr Urquia (El Salvador) ibid. ¶ 101.
[4] Mr Martin (Canada) ibid. ¶ 39.
[5] Mr Belaúnde (Peru) ibid. ¶ 58.
[6] Mr Sudjarwo (Indonesia) GAOR 10th sess 556th plen mtg 15 Dec 1955 ¶ 7.
[7] Mr Tarcici (Yemen) ibid. ¶ 29.
[8] Mr Tarazi (Syria) ibid. ¶ 51.
[9] Mr Barrington (Burma) ibid. ¶ 55.
[10] Mr Rizk (Lebanon) ibid. ¶ 91.
[11] Mr Lawrence (Liberia) ibid. ¶ 103.

Afghanistan,[12] Saudi Arabia,[13] Haiti,[14] and Chile.[15] Ambassador Lodge said that the United States was 'overjoyed' at the admission of 'twelve free nations.'[16] The inference to be drawn was that American official sentiment toward the admission of the other four States was less enthusiastic. The United States nevertheless had not stood in the way, and piecemeal reservations in any event did not dampen the prevailing mood. If a general attitude was to be discerned among the member States, it was that universal admission deserved applause. Giving an enthusiastic reception to new member States, however, would have been justified by reference to protocol and, in any case, it says little about the prior decision to grant admission. One must look further, if one seeks an indication of underlying State opinion concerning the development of Charter law.

Certain States did not restrict themselves to generalities. It was said by some that the *Admission* Advisory Opinion and Article 4 not only posed no obstacle to a policy of universal admission but made universal admission a legal requirement. Peru expressed the opinion, in the Special Committee of Good Offices concerning admission of new members, that universal admission follows from Article 4 of the Charter as interpreted by the International Court.[17] (More will be said about the Peruvian position below). It was the view of the Ministry of Foreign Affairs of Mongolia that Mongolia's admission was required under 'the precise provisions of the United Nations Charter concerning membership' and that the veto of its own application for admission (to be repeated in 1956) had been the result of a 'policy of discrimination.'[18] India regretted the veto of Mongolia's application, saying that this was contrary to universality.[19]

The position set out by Iraq was, ostensibly, more developed. According to Iraq,

---

[12] Mr Ludin (Afghanistan) ibid. ¶ 112.

[13] Mr Shalfan (Saudi Arabia) ibid. ¶ 114.

[14] Mr Price-Mars (Haiti) ibid. ¶ 124.

[15] Mr Perez de Arce (Chile) ibid. ¶ 154; Mr Ortega (Chile) GAOR 10th sess 552nd plen mtg 8 Dec 1955 ¶ 129 ('… the principle of universality is essential as the very basis of the international community…'). See also, joining the position that universality is implicit in the Charter, statement of Mr Menon (India) GAOR 10th sess 556th plen mtg 15 Dec 1955 ¶ 133 (regretting veto of Mongolian application).

[16] Mr Lodge (USA) GAOR 10th sess 555th plen mtg 14 Dec 1955 ¶ 106.

[17] Report of the Special Committee on Admission of New Members, 25 June 1953, A/2400, GAOR 8th sess annexes, agenda item 22 ¶ 10.

[18] Telegram dated 13 December 1956 from the Minister for Foreign Affairs of the Mongolian People's Republic addressed to the Secretary-General, S/4954, SCOR 16th yr supp (July, August, September 1961) p. 127. The telegram contained the text of a statement of the Ministry of Foreign Affairs.

[19] Mr Menon (India) GAOR 10th sess 556th plen mtg 15 Dec 1955 ¶ 133.

[T]his Organization should open its doors to all States that wish to enter. There is no doubt that certain norms which the Charter prescribes must be observed, but those norms could not be dealt with in a manner of absolute standards. There is relativity. That relativity is unfortunately inevitable. None of us is perfect; no State that wishes to enter the United Nations is perfect. That is why we must accept the principle of relativity of norms in admitting new Members and in opening the doors to all those who wish to join us.[20]

Iraq admitted that there are 'certain norms which the Charter prescribes' but then, under the rubric of 'relativity,' denied that those 'norms' equate to substantive criteria to control admission. This was to give with one hand and to take away with the other. To be sure, the Iraqi statement above did not go so far as to say that the UN *shall* 'open its doors to all States.' A hortatory 'should' kept the statement from being an assertion of mandatory admission. Iraq nevertheless was plainly against rigorous application of the Article 4(1) criteria. The statement that 'no State…is perfect' is not to be doubted; but it also is beside the point, for the Charter does not say that perfection is the standard for admission. Certain, specified criteria are the standard, and, unlike perfection, these are susceptible to ordinary methods of appreciation by member States. That the UN system contains a procedural mechanism to formalize such methods was seen in Chapter 2, as was seen the development in practice by which the UN and its member States effectively left the mechanism on the sidelines. Declining to implement a Charter provision is one thing; amending or modifying it is another. The question, which the last section of this Chapter will address, is whether the shift in practice to favour universal admission was of such a character as to have amended the constitutive instrument.

The most vigorous attempt at an exegesis of the UN Charter to justify the shift to universal admission was made by Víctor Belaúnde, permanent representative of Peru and chairman of the above-mentioned Committee of Good Offices charged with resolving the admission deadlock.[21] According to the Peruvian permanent representative,

Article 4 has to be interpreted not only in the literal sense but also, and primarily, in accordance with its spirit. Article 4, in substance, lays down the principle of universality, since the only thing that can be opposed to that Article and to the principle of universality is the discretionary and arbitrary judgement of a member of the Security Council; and I have proved that such a judgement is contrary to the Charter, as also to the advisory opinion given by the Court in 1948. But there is a connexion between the principle of universality, inherent in nearly all

---

[20] Mr Al-Jamali (Iraq) GAOR 10th sess 556th plen mtg 15 Dec 1955 ¶ 13.
[21] Dr Víctor A Belaúnde (1883–1966), a senior statesman of his country, was widely published in the subjects of legal theory and Latin American history; and was one of the drafters of the 1933 constitution of Peru: (1967) 2(3) *Latin American Research Review* 229, 230.

the essential articles of the Charter, and the text of Article 4, for now more than ever before there is no country which is not animated not only by a love of peace but also by a horror of war.[22]

The Peruvian statement did not go so far as to declare universal admission a rule, instead describing it as a 'principle,' but the inference to be drawn from the statement in full goes further than that. The statement is clear that a rejection of admission – i.e., a rejection of universality – could be the result only of 'discretionary and arbitrary judgment.' Moreover, it is asserted that 'there is no country which is not animated not only by a love of peace but also by a horror of war.' This begins to suggest that admissibility under Article 4 is not a matter to be proved but, rather, a presumption. More about a putative presumption in favour of admission will be said below.

Ambassador Belaúnde went on to say,

> Treaties that do not regulate interests but create rights and establish rules which may be considered as rules of law must always be interpreted in the light of their objects. Thus if the object of the United Nations is universality, if all the Purposes and Principles of the Charter are universal, then the overriding principle in the interpretation of Article 4 must be universality.[23]

This draws attention to the rule of treaty construction that a provision of a treaty may be interpreted in light of the object and purpose of the treaty. It was noted in Chapter 1 above that distinctions are sometimes drawn between treaties whose purpose mainly is to set out the rights and obligations of particular parties; and treaties whose purpose is to constitute structures of international public order. Object and purpose therefore may differ widely as between different sorts of treaties. This is legally consequential.

Whatever the distinctions and their consequences, however, certain rules of construction apply to treaties generally. The object and purpose of the treaty is not the only point of reference when interpreting the treaty. Nor is it the first. The plain meaning of the language of the treaty is the usual starting point. To reject, as Belaúnde did in the previous extract, that a member of the Security Council has the authority to prevent admission of an applicant to the United Nations is to ignore specific language in the Charter – language, moreover, given an authoritative construction by the International Court in the 1950 *Competence* Advisory Opinion. The position that to exercise a power as it was expressly conferred by the Charter is 'contrary to the Charter' was not a widely held position, and it is difficult to see how to reach such an interpretation without significantly revising the text of the Charter itself.

---

[22] Mr Belaúnde (Peru) GAOR 10th sess 552nd plen mtg 8 Dec 1955 ¶ 150.
[23] Mr Belaúnde (Peru) ibid. ¶ 153.

Argentina's goal before and during the *Competence* advisory proceedings had been to suppress the Security Council veto in matters of admission notwithstanding the assignment of functions to the Council in Article 4, paragraph 2. If the General Assembly had adopted the Argentine draft, then the question put to the Court would have been directed to that end. Few States joined Argentina, and the question in fact put to the Court was not whether the veto was available in admission matters; the question was whether the General Assembly had the authority to admit an applicant in a situation where the Security Council has not reached an affirmative decision recommending admission. The Court of course did not address a question that the General Assembly had not asked. The search nevertheless continued for a way around the veto on questions of admission, a search which may be seen as part of a larger movement by States not members of a superpower bloc to enhance the authority of the General Assembly. Peru in 1955 picked up the brief where Argentina a little earlier had been stymied. The same obstacle remained: the Charter is unambiguous that the Security Council and General Assembly share power over the matter of admission. To avoid this constitutional allocation, the Peruvian representative sought a way to argue around the plain text of paragraph 2. In the Charter itself, none exists, and none was found. What did exist by the end of 1955 that had not at the time of the *Competence* advisory proceedings was a sea change in Security Council practice. A concurrent vote of Council and Assembly remained a requirement, but the substantive criteria for admission had been largely left aside.

An arch-teleological reading of the Charter had been advanced to credit a policy by which the substantive criteria of Article 4(1) soon were to be all but completely by-passed. It would be to reject a canon of construction, to insist that every provision of a treaty be interpreted in all situations in isolation of the spirit of the treaty. Article 31, paragraph 1 of the Vienna Convention on the Law of Treaties of 1969 (VCLT) provides that a treaty 'shall be interpreted in good faith in accordance with the ordinary meaning to be given to the terms of the treaty in their context *and in light of its object and purpose.*'[24] This was consistent with the earlier statement of the International Court in the *Competence* Advisory Opinion:

> [T]he first duty of a tribunal which is called upon to interpret and apply the provisions of a treaty, is to endeavour to give effect to them in their natural and ordinary meaning in the context in which they occur. If the relevant words in

---

[24] Emphasis supplied. Vienna Convention on the Law of Treaties, adopted 23 May 1969, entered into force 27 Jan 1980: 1155 UNTS 331, 340. The interpretative principles contained in Articles 31, 32, and 33 of the 1969 Vienna Convention may not however in all situations apply to the constitutive instrument if Rosenne's view is taken as correct: Rosenne *Developments in the Law of Treaties 1945–1986* (1989) 192.

their natural and ordinary meaning make sense in their context, that is an end of the matter.[25]

The question is how to deal with situations where the ordinary meaning is not the same as the 'object and purpose' or otherwise at variance with an interpretation that might be arrived at by reference to the broader 'context.' International organizations interpret the treaty instruments on which they are based in face of changes in the environment in which they operate. An example illustrates the type of situation in which an interpretation properly may be based on the object and purpose of the treaty.

The International Bank for Reconstruction and Development (IBRD) in the 1980s had to decide how to deal with the phrase 'United States dollars of the weight and fineness in effect on July 1, 1944.' That phrase, appearing in Article II of the IBRD Articles of Agreement, had been the basis for measuring the authorized capital of the Bank; it in turn was based on the gold standard. The International Monetary Fund however later replaced the gold standard with a different method of valuation – the Special Drawing Right (SDR). The Bank decided that the object and purpose of the Agreement would be served by substituting 'SDR' for the clear terms of Article II (the 1944 gold dollar). Amerasinghe identifies this as an example of a defensible application of a teleological interpretation in preference to a literal reading of unambiguous terms in a constitutive instrument. It was arguably proper, because a new situation had arisen, not envisaged when adopting the constitutive instrument – namely, replacement of the gold standard with a new system of valuation.[26] The clear terms of the instrument, referring to the gold standard for purposes of measuring the Bank's authorized capital, made little sense, if applied literally after the gold standard had been replaced. To preserve the sense of Article II of the IBRD Articles, the institution had to draw on the object and purpose of the agreement.

But this was a clear departure from an assumption basic to the instrument at the time it was adopted. It was clear in two respects. First, there could be no doubt that there had been a change: the SDR was not the same as the gold standard. Second, no difficulty was presented in relating the changed circumstance to a particular provision of the instrument: one term simply gave way to its replacement. By contrast, the purported fundamental change relative to admission of States was to a much greater extent a matter of appreciation. And even if agreement obtained that a change had occurred, it still would not have been as clear as in the IBRD case how to relate the change to a specific treaty

---

[25] *Competence of the General Assembly for Admission of a State to the United Nations* Advisory Opinion, ICJ Rep 1950 pp. 4, 8, citing *Polish Postal Service in Danzig* 1925 PCIJ Ser B No. 11 p. 39.

[26] Amerasinghe *International Organizations* 34–5.

provision. So perhaps an assumption had arisen that no State desires war: what of the requirement that the applicant accept other UN principles? Would the purported change in circumstances really have been enough to lead Article 4(1) to drop out of the Charter?

There are other considerations that make it difficult to see how the matter of admissions in the 1950s had undergone such fundamental change as to impel Charter revision. In the first decades of the Charter, there were non-member States at all times. This fact of the environment in which the UN was created did not change. The situation in 1955 in the UN is therefore not analogous to situations in which interpretation was necessary in the face of external change. In 1945 it was plain to the drafters of the Charter that there were, and would continue to be, States not members of the Organization. The inclusion of substantive criteria for admission reflects this point.

Perhaps another basis for the Argentine and Peruvian interpretations can be identified. Reaching an interpretation based on 'object and purpose' of the constitutive instrument may be justified, where the most specific terms of the instrument are not specific enough. A rule may have been set out but the mechanisms for its implementation left unclear; or the rule itself may have been expressed in terms too wide to avoid ambiguity as to the conduct it requires, permits, or proscribes. The principle of effectiveness (*ut res magis valeat quam pereat*) is said to be the basis for resorting to 'object and purpose,' which is to say, the object and purpose of a treaty do not transform its specific terms but, rather, supplement them to assure that they operate.[27] This is especially the case where 'there are lacunae, though in principle interpreting organs have generally deferred, as they should, to the principle of the ordinary meaning.'[28] These are some considerations relevant to judging whether Belaúnde's interpretation of the admission provisions of the Charter was valid.

This much can be said of Belaúnde's interpretation: it addressed a Charter function which Article 4 already specified and which needed no such interpretation to be put into effect. The interpretation, put forward by several States in 1955 and summarized by Belaúnde, in truth had a result almost opposite of that supported by the principle of effectiveness. Reference was made to object and purpose, not to substantiate under-specified provisions, but, rather, to cause the substantive criteria of Article 4(1) virtually to disappear from consideration of candidatures for admission. Ordinary meaning merits deference from other methods of interpretation, and the situation in which object and purpose typically is brought into play – a lacunae in the constitutive instrument – is not the situation with respect to Article 4(1), which, by the Court's analysis in 1948, was

---

[27] Amerasinghe 59.
[28] Ibid.

complete as to the criteria for admission of States to membership. To override the criteria, by reference to general objects and purposes of the Charter, was a doubtful act of interpretation.

Similarly, while one may refer to 'inherent' principles in an instrument to achieve a consistent interpretation, this is not what Belaúnde did. The effect instead was to rewrite, or to overwrite, specific, operative words. As recalled already, within any legal text, there is a hierarchy of interpretation, such that more specific provisions prevail over more general provisions concerning the same subject matter. There was good reason behind the International Court's peremptory language in the *Competence* Advisory Opinion ('an end of the matter'): if the meaning of the text is clear on the face of the 'relevant words' – i.e., the words most specifically relating to the matter in issue – and no consideration of changed circumstances impels a different approach, then nothing further needs to be said. It certainly would not have been necessary to refer to words of much greater generality to find a new meaning for provisions which not only were clear on their own terms, but, on their terms, fit neatly into the architecture of the constitutive instrument as a whole in circumstances not objectively different from those contemplated at the time of the drafting of the instrument. Hierarchy is acknowledged, in a somewhat different sense but with similar result, in VCLT Article 31(3)(b) and Article 32, where subsequent practice[29] and records of the preparatory work of the drafting conference ('*Supplementary means of interpretation*')[30] are given subordinate position in the interpretative scheme. The Peruvian permanent representative's assertion that the principle of universality is 'inherent in nearly all the essential articles of the Charter' implies an extremely powerful brand of inherence – all the more so, in view of the fact that the Charter contains the word 'universal' in only two articles, neither of which says anything about admission to membership,[31] and does not contain the word 'universality' at all. In the end, the assertion is dubious as a legal statement and probably is better taken as an exercise in rhetoric.[32]

---

[29] 1155 UNTS at 340.

[30] Ibid. art. 32: 1155 UNTS at 340:

> Recourse may be had to supplementary means of interpretation, including the preparatory work of the treaty and the circumstances of its conclusion, in order to confirm the meaning resulting from the application of article 31, or to determine the meaning when the interpretation according to article 31:
>
> (a) leaves the meaning ambiguous or obscure; or
>
> (b) leads to a result which is manifestly absurd or unreasonable.

[31] Arts 1 and 55.

[32] The Peruvian representative by turns adopted and eschewed legal language. Several days earlier in the Security Council, Belaúnde had referred to objections to the proposed admission of States as 'dubious and debatable legalism': SCOR 10th yr 701st mtg 10 Dec 1955 ¶ 19.

A pervasive, unwritten principle of universality was not, however, the only consideration adduced in favour of universal admission. The Peruvian representative also referred universal admission to the legal distinction between a State and its government. Belaúnde's remarks in the Security Council several days before the logjam was broken merit quoting at length:

> When we speak of a State – and Article 4 refers to States – we are not referring simply to the government. That would be an error, because in the State there is a transitory and temporary, albeit important element – the Government, and a permanent... element – the nation. When we speak of a State, the emphasis should be on the nation, rather than on the government. Governments pass, but nations remain. Governments make mistakes; they represent the transitory opinions of mortal men hammered out on the perilous anvils of power. The nation represents veneration of the dead and affection for the young, memories of past glories, perhaps repentance for great sins [etc.]...It is the nation, then, with which we are concerned, not the government. Let us not pass judgement on governments. The admission of new Members...does not represent a judgement; it represents the admission of a nation, of a State, and its integration in the community of peoples. It represents a hope, and perhaps an encouragement. In some cases it may represent an act of oblivion, a welcome act if it leads to or strengthens repentance...
>
> This interpretation of Article 4 is a matter of great seriousness. If we lay stress on governments, if we set to work to examine the conduct of governments and ignore the nation, we are making a grievous mistake, for Article 4 refers not to governments but to States...and in the United Nations the word State, with its rich sociological and juridical content, cannot be forgotten in a legalism unworthy of the intellectual and moral stature of the Organization.[33]

When making the plea '[l]et us not pass judgement on governments,' Belaúnde relied on a real distinction under international law. A State for purposes of international law is not the same thing as its government. A few words may be said about this; and Belaúnde's assertion examined that the distinction should have consequences for admission of States to the UN.

A word first may be said about Belaúnde's reference to State and the 'nation' as related concepts, both distinct from the government of a State. Belaúnde referred to the 'sociological...content' of the word 'State,' and spoke in emotionally heightened terms about the 'nation' (e.g., '...memories of past glories, perhaps repentance for great sins...'). This seems to have been for atmospherics; it was unnecessary to sustain the legal point, in itself broadly valid. States are international legal persons, and they are not the same as the governments which represent them. Governments are the mechanisms by which States act in international relations.[34] Governments change with greater frequency than the

---

[33] Mr Belaúnde (Peru) SCOR 10th yr 701st mtg 10 Dec 1955 ¶¶ 27–8.

[34] See Talmon *Recognition of Governments in International Law: With Particular Reference to Governments in Exile* (1998) vii–vii, 115–16, quoting *German Settlers in Poland* 1923 PCIJ Ser B No. 6 p. 22. See also Crawford *Creation* 2nd edn 33–5.

States they represent, and a change of government has significantly fewer legal consequences (at international level) than the disappearance or creation of a State. It even may be said that, once created, a State is presumed to continue its existence as an international legal person.

The presumption of the continuity of a State is one of the most difficult to displace in international law.[35] The persistence of a State as an international legal person is evident, on consideration of cases like Poland between 1939 and 1945 and Somalia since the early 1990s. Whether because of external force or internal disarray, effective government ceased to exist in the national territory, but the State remained. The State also remained, where significant changes occurred in its constitution and territorial limits, such as with the Federation of Malaya (1963 and 1965) and the Soviet Union (1990–91). It is not necessary for present purposes to analyze the juridical logic behind the presumption of continuity of the State. The following may be said by way of summary: it is necessary to fix responsibility for certain acts on a legal person, and, because States remain the chief international legal persons,[36] they remain the chief entities in international law on which responsibility may be fixed. There is only a limited basis in general international law, even in the early 21st century, for treating entities other than States as international legal persons. To be sure, international organizations possess international legal personality, but the vast majority of international organizations are created by States. International organizations also may create international organizations[37] as well as their own subsidiary bodies possessing characteristics of international legal personality (e.g., privileges and immunities

---

[35] See generally Crawford *Creation* 2nd edn chs. 16, 17 (pp. 651–717). The continuity even of the 20th century 'divided States,' though under pressure of their particular circumstances, had to be considered when addressing their international status: see Caty *Le Statut Juridique des États Divisés* (1969) 23–39. On continuity of treaty rights, see Schachter 'State Succession: The Once and Future Law' (1993) 33 *Virg JIL* 253.

[36] Weil 'Le droit international en quête de son identité' (1992) 237 *Hag Rec* (VI) 13, 33, 87–8; van Staden & Vollaard 'The Erosion of State Sovereignty: Towards a Post-territorial World?' in Kreijen ed *State, Sovereignty, and International Governance* (2002) 164, 183–4; Ben Achour 'État, Cultures, et Mondialisation' in Boisson de Chazournes & Gowlland-Debbas eds *Liber Amicorum Georges Abi-Saab* 101, 122; Movsesian 'The Persistent Nation State and the Foreign Sovereign Immunities Act' (1996) 18 *Cardozo L Rev* 1083, 1089–92. Or, if not States, then, perhaps, *a* State: Rabkin *The Case for Sovereignty: Why the World Should Welcome American Independence* (2004) 103.

[37] The Preparatory Commission for the Comprehensive Nuclear Test-Ban, for example, exists to carry out activities contemplated under the Comprehensive Nuclear-Test-Ban Treaty pending entry into force of the Treaty after ratification by the Annex 2 States (pursuant to Art. XIV) – after which time a Conference of the States Parties to the Treaty will be held and a Comprehensive Nuclear Test-Ban Treaty Organization established. It may be a matter of appreciation whether it is the Preparatory Commission or the States which establish the new Organization.

of their personnel),[38] but organizations so created are a small minority, and even there, the constituting organizations themselves will have been created through a constitutive act by States. Where international organizations may confirm or accede to treaties, this, too, is traceable back to States,[39] and the constitutive power of the international organization as treaty-maker well may be limited.[40] Individuals and other non-State actors may be directly subject to international law, but there again the basis is extremely narrow, if it has any firm existence at all, on which individuals and other such actors can be treated as international law subjects without some prior act of State consent, whether direct or through an international organization, itself created by States.[41] Private investors may have the right to institute arbitration against a State under international law, but, where they do, the basis of the right is a treaty between States.[42] Outside the noted exceptions, for the conduct of entities other than States to be subject to international law, the conduct generally still must be referred to one or another State. This is the main ground for the presumption that a State, even absent effective government, continues as an international legal person. Serious problems of responsibility would arise if the presumption of continuity were to be removed. Indeed, where doubts about the identity of a State have subsisted

---

[38] Consider the International Criminal Tribunal for the Former Yugoslavia, established by SC res 827, 25 May 1993; and the Statute of the Tribunal, Art. 30.

[39] Alvarez *International Organizations as Law-makers* (2005) 15–16.

[40] As it is in the 1986 Vienna Convention on the Law of Treaties between States and International Organizations or between International Organizations, adopted 21 March 1986, A/Conf.129/15. The Convention enters into force according to Article 85 on the thirtieth day following the date of deposit of the thirty-fifth ratification – but only ratifications by States count under this provision. The 1986 Vienna Convention has not yet entered into force (as of December 2008), for, though it has forty parties, more than five of them are international organizations.

[41] Leonardo Díaz González made the observation that the procedures by which individuals might practically benefit from rights under international law are similarly contingent:

> [W]hereas States had been the original subjects of international law and were still at the heart of international life,…international organizations, created by the will of States, had international personality at a secondary level. As for individuals, they acquired such personality indirectly through the machinery set up by international organizations, to which individuals had access.

Special Rapporteur's introduction to the Fourth Report on Relations between States and international organizations (A/CN.4/424) ILC 41st sess 2133rd mtg 7 July 1989 ¶ 8 *ILC Ybk* 1989 Vol. I p. 282. Cf. the considerably more conservative view of Guillaume Pambou-Tchivounda in connection with the Preliminary Report of the Special Rapporteur (John Dugard) on Diplomatic Protection: ILC 50th sess 2521st mtg 29 Apr 1998 ¶¶ 19–25 *ILC Ybk* 1998 Vol. I pp. 13–4.

[42] See *Occidental Exploration & Production Co v Republic of Ecuador* [2005] EWCA Civ 1116, [2006] Q.B. 432, 9 Sept 2005 (Mance LJ) ¶ 16. Contrast the classic position in *The Mavrommatis Palestine Concessions Case (Greece v Great Britain)* (1924) PCIJ Rep Ser A Nos. 2, 7, which was pleaded, but rejected, in *Occidental v Ecuador*.

(e.g., Yugoslavia, about which see Chapter 6), problems of responsibility have presented themselves starkly in the judicial setting.

If the State is the main and durable vessel of rights and obligations in international law, then the governments of States are the main, if relatively transitory, agents which take the concrete measures attracting and discharging obligations, acquiring and utilizing rights. The relative importance of States and governments is suggested by the modern practice of recognition. Most States once were in the practice of extending formal recognition not only to the formation of new States but also to changes of government within a State.[43] This is no longer the case. Many States have ceased to issue statements of formal recognition at all in connection with changes of government;[44] others still recognize changes of government but only where some doubt subsists as between rival claimants, such as in a civil war.[45] The modern position is consistent with the essentially municipal significance of changes of government. When a new government is

---

[43] The main case on problems arising from recognition of a government is the *Tinoco Arbitration*, (1924) 18 *AJIL* 147 (Taft CJ, arbitrator).

[44] Lord Carrington's statement of 1980 set out the British policy, which a number of States have followed: 408 HL Debs cols 1121–2, 28 Apr 1980; 983 HC Debs Written Answers cols 227–9, 25 Apr 1980.

[45] For a summary of practice see Talmon *Recognition* 3–14 and accompanying citations. Recognition of governments subsists in those exceptional cases that prove the rule: States may recognize a change of government, where it is contested which claimant to government is the agent of the State for purposes of international relations. The main situation in which recognition continues to be applied to a change of government, then, is that where the change raises questions with implications not restricted to municipal law.

The Restatement (3rd) Foreign Relations Law of the United States § 203 ('Recognition Or Acceptance Of Governments') says

(1) A state is not required to accord formal recognition to the government of another state, but is required to treat as the government of another state a regime that is in effective control of that state, except as set forth in Subsection (2).

(2) A state has an obligation not to recognize or treat a regime as the government of another state if its control has been effected by the threat or use of armed force in violation of the United Nations Charter.

(3) A state is not obligated to maintain diplomatic relations with any other state.'

See also, ibid., Comment a ('Recognition of state and government distinguished') and Reporters' Note 1 ('United States practice as to recognizing governments'), observing that it has been U.S. practice since the 1970s 'to deemphasize and avoid the use of recognition in cases of changes of governments and to concern ourselves [instead] with the question of whether we wish to have diplomatic relations with the new governments.' Quoting [1977] *Digest of US Practice in Int'l L* 19–21. This does not preclude courts from considering related questions. Courts, sometimes, take a position, distinct from that of the political branches of government, when considering entities of ambiguous status between States and governments, for example in questions concerning Palestine/the Palestinian Authority: see, e.g., *Ungar v Palestine Liberation Organization*, 402 F.3d 274, 280–1 (Selya, CJ, 2005).

established in a State, that is a matter for the constitutional law of the State; only exceptionally is it a matter for international law. Other States will be affected directly by the establishment of a new State, for this entails changes of territory and succession to rights and obligations under international law. New legal positions emerge, opposable against existing States, and which those States may oppose against the new State. The arrival of a new government, by contrast, seldom produces such international effects.

Belaúnde to be sure was correct that Article 4 'refers to States.' It is also the case, relative to States at any rate, that governments are 'transitory and temporary.' The part of the Peruvian statement that requires scrutiny is that concerning the relation between States and governments in 'pass[ing] judgement.' It was asserted that the UN 'should not pass judgement on governments.' State and government are indeed distinct legal concepts, the former being an international legal person, and the latter, the agent, chosen through internal constitutional processes, that represents the State in international relations. The distinctness of two legal concepts however does not preclude a very tight connection between them. Indeed, some concepts are kept legally distinct, for the reason that they are functionally so tightly connected. For example, whether a corporation has violated a particular regulation must be referred to actual acts done by individuals or subordinate entities comprising the corporation, yet the distinctness between the corporation and its functional components or persons holding a beneficial interest in it is overcome only in the exceptional case of veil-piercing; the corporation itself in the usual case is the entity that bears liability. It would make nonsense of corporate liability, to say, categorically, that, in judging a corporation, reference cannot be made to the actions of relevant individuals or entities. The legal distinction is even more pronounced as between States and their governments, for States are subjects of international law and governments, generally, are not[46] – and the functional link is at least as integral: a State acts at international level through its government.

The government of a State therefore is the entity, the actual conduct of which is to be examined to judge the State. If a treaty or other international instrument requires judgment as to the character of a State (e.g., 'peace-loving State') or to the State's capacity for action (e.g., 'able and willing to carry out these obligations'), then it is by reference to the character or actions of its government that judgment is to be reached. The same goes for the consistency of conduct with

---

[46] A corporation well may be subject to a different national legal system from its shareholders or component entities (see *Barcelona Traction (Belgium v Spain)* ICJ Rep 1970 p. 3) – but there is no category problem with them being subject to the same national legal system. By contrast, as between States and governments, only the former are by definition legal persons in the international system.

treaties. Treaties bind the State, but whether the State has incurred responsibility under the treaty is judged by reference to the things which the government of the State does or fails to do.[47] The things which the government does or fails to do are the main measure of the State for purposes of international law. The consequences which follow attach to the State as far as concerns international rights and obligations, for it is the State, not the government, which holds rights and obligations under international law. To say that one cannot 'pass judgment on governments' therefore perhaps reflects a valid position in international law – but this would be only in the narrow sense that, if a government carries out an act or policy in violation of international law, the responsibility for the act or policy does not attach to the government as an international law matter. It presumptively could not, for the government is not an international legal person. Responsibility attaches to the State – which the government is in most instances the agent with plenary authority to represent on the international plane. The Permanent Court was clear on this in 1923, and the ILC was as well in 2001: 'States can act only by and through their agents and representatives.'[48] As States act by and through their governments, Belaúnde's argument must in the end be rejected. To decline to evaluate governments is to deny that States themselves can be held responsible under international law.

4.2   *The Charter after Eclipse of the Substantive Criteria*

It has been said that 'the constitutive instrument of an international organization is constantly undergoing a process of adaptation to the needs of society.'[49] It also has been said that '[c]onstitutions of international organizations, being

---

[47] This holds also for the (limited) instances of responsibility of States where actors other than the government of the State are authors of the conduct in question. For example, under Article 5 of the Articles on the Responsibility of States for Internationally Wrongful Acts,

> The conduct of a person or entity which is not an organ of the State...but which is empowered by the law of that State to exercise elements of the governmental authority shall be considered an act of the State under international law, provided the person or entity is acting in that capacity in the particular instance.

For responsibility to attach, the State must empower the other 'person or entity' by its law – which is to say, some governmental organ of the State must reach a decision to that effect. Articles adopted, ILC 53rd session, 9 Aug 2001; reproduced in GA res 56/83, 12 Dec 2001 and A/56/49 (vol. I/Corr.4); and Crawford ed *The International Law Commission's Articles on State Responsibility: Introduction, Text and Commentaries* (2002) 61–73.

[48] *Questions relating to Settlers of German Origin in Poland* Advisory Opinion of 10 Sept 1923, 1923 PCIJ Ser B No. 6 p. 22; Crawford ed *Commentaries* 82 Comment (5) to Art. 2.

[49] Zacklin *The Amendment of the Constitutive Instruments of the United Nations and Specialized Agencies* (1968, reissued with forward by Schermers, 2005) 26. See also ibid. 171–97.

organic instruments, may require change both in the light of experience in the organizations as well as in order to keep pace with developments in international society.'[50] The Charter does not require universal admission on its plain terms. Yet the substantive criteria for admission were implemented in practice only in exceptional cases, and universal admission by the mid-1950s would become the dominant position taken in the Organization. As a matter of the law of the Charter, how is this development to be characterized? Did the practice of the Organization effect an interpretation of the Charter, so as to add to or clarify the terms of Article 4(1)? Or did practice go further than that and in result amend the Charter?

To arrive at an answer, one may consider general international law respecting the interpretation and amendment of the constitutive instruments of international organizations – though general international law has not developed so much that the constitutive instruments of particular organizations do not continue to occupy much of the field when it comes to their own interpretation and amendment. The United Nations is for some purposes to be assimilated with international organizations generally, but for others it must be considered unique. The UN Charter and its implementation in practice therefore must be the main points of reference.

4.2.1   *Practice as Effecting Change in the Constitutive Instrument*[51]

The general law of international organizations is not so extensively developed as to displace the constitutive instrument of each organization as a source of rules and principles to govern the organization. General interpretative rules, as set out in the 1969 Vienna Convention, apply to the constitutive instruments of international organizations, but this is 'without prejudice to any relevant rules of the organization' – the clause of Article 5 of the 1969 Vienna Convention which recalls the relevance of the many constitutive instruments and their par-

---

[50] Amerasinghe 447.

[51] On the interpretation of the constitutive instruments of international organizations, see generally Amerasinghe *Principles of the institutional law of international organisations* 2nd rev edn (2005) 24–66, 447–63; Zacklin (1968, reissued 2005); Schermers & Blokker *International Institutional Law: unity within diversity* 4th rev edn (2003); McDougal, Lasswell & Miller *The Interpretation of International Agreements and World Public Order: Principles of Content and Procedure* (1994); Rosenne *Treaties* 181–258, 353–447. On the relevance of the 'views of Member States' as to the lawfulness of actions taken by an international organization, see Blokker 'Beyond "Dili": On the Powers and Practice of International Organization' in Kreijen et al. eds (2002) 299, 312.

ticularities.[52] A 'without prejudice' clause pertaining to 'any relevant rules of the organization' is included in the 1986 Vienna Convention as well.[53]

Some writers emphasize not only the distinctiveness of each constitutive instrument but say that such instruments comprise a category subject to its own general rules of interpretation, distinct from the rules applicable to other treaties, including other multilateral treaties. Rosenne goes so far as to say that the resemblance of constitutive instruments to multilateral treaties 'is for the most part a superficial one,' the development of the 'law governing the constituent instruments of intergovernmental organizations [being] in process of development along lines peculiar and appropriate to those instruments and their function in the international community.'[54] Thus, when considering the development of a constitutive instrument, it is relevant to ask to what extent the particular terms of the instrument apply as against a general law of treaty interpretation; and, further, which general law of treaty interpretation applies. This is the position with respect to the provisions of the constitutive instrument generally.

Admission to membership in international organizations is especially likely to be referred to the particular constitutive instrument rather than to general law:

> Matters concerning membership depend primarily on the provisions of the constitutions of international organizations and on the practice of each organization. Whether the area concerned is admission to membership, suspension from privileges, termination of membership or the related issue of representation of members, it is not easy to identify general principles relevant to the interpretation of all constituent documents. On the other hand, there may be consistent practices across many organizations in implementing provisions of constitutions that could be usefully studied.[55]

The commentary of the ILC at the time the Commission adopted the draft articles on succession of States in respect to treaties confirms this position. 'International organizations take various forms,' the ILC said, 'and differ considerably in their treatment of membership. In many organizations, membership, other than original membership, is subject to a formal process of admission.'[56]

---

[52] 1155 UNTS 331, 334.

[53] Op. cit.

[54] Rosenne *Treaties* 257. See also ibid. 243. Rosennne here provides an analogue for international law, if not a precise one, to Chief Justice Marshall's advice, '[W]e must never forget that it is a *constitution* we are expounding': *McCulloch v Maryland* 4 Wheat. 316, 407 (1819) [emphasis original].

[55] Amerasinghe 105.

[56] ILC 26th sess 1301st mtg 26 July 1974, Draft articles on succession of States in respect of treaties, Spec Rapp Sir Francis Vallat *ILC Ybk* 1974 Vol. II Pt One p. 177 Comment (2). See also El-Erian's observation that a general definition of 'international organization' does not

The Convention on the Succession of States in Respect of Treaties (1978) as adopted also is relevant in this connection. Article 4 of the Convention 'applies to the effects of a succession of States in respect of: (a) any treaty which is the constituent instrument of an international organization *without prejudice to the rules concerning acquisition of membership*...'[57] The 1978 Convention thus treats the 'rules concerning acquisition of membership' as part of the legal system of the constitutive instrument, such that those rules do not give way to a general law of succession. This further indicates the legal significance of Article 4(1) of the Charter as a legal regulation. A new State does not succeed to membership; it seeks it under the specified terms.

If instead of interpretation, the question is amendment of the constitutive instrument, then general principles of treaty interpretation may be still less relevant. VCLT Article 40 sets out a number of general principles concerning amendment of treaties, but provides in its first paragraph that specific terms concerning mechanisms of amendment contained in the treaty itself prevail ('[u]nless the treaty otherwise provides'). The United Nations Charter, in Article 108, provides the terms for its amendment. According to Article 108,

> Amendments...shall come into force for all Members of the United Nations when they have been adopted by a vote of two-thirds of the members of the General Assembly and ratified in accordance with their respective constitutional processes by two-thirds of the Members of the United Nations, including all the permanent members of the Security Council.

These are terms setting out a formal process of amendment. The process entails a vote by the General Assembly, meaning a decision adopted by that organ; and the permanent members of the Security Council possess the power of veto over proposed amendments. Unlike the amendment provision of the Covenant of the League of Nations, the UN Charter makes amendments so adopted

---

need 'to go into the conditions of admission,' because these are 'regulated by the constitutional instruments of the organization and the resolutions of its competent organs': Sixth Report, Relations between States and International Organizations, 2 & 29 Mar, 5, 9 & 26 Apr, 12 & 14 May 1971 ¶ 51, *ILC Ybk* 1971 Vol. 2 Pt One p. 18.

[57] Emphasis added: 1946 UNTS 4, 7, concluded 23 Aug 1978, entered into force 6 Nov 1996. It further may be noted that the 1978 Convention provides that a succession does not 'as such affect' boundary régimes (Art. 11) or 'other territorial régimes' (Art. 12): 1946 UNTS at 10. Like the relations *inter se* among States in an international organization, such régimes have constitutive effects which concern States in addition to the ones whose boundary, territory – or membership – is directly regulated.

Parties to the 1978 Convention as of July 2008 are Bosnia and Herzegovina, Croatia, Cyprus, Czech Republic, Dominica, Ecuador, Egypt, Estonia, Ethiopia, Iraq, Liberia, Monaco, Macedonia, Montenegro, Saint Vincent and the Grenadines, Serbia, the Seychelles, Slovakia, Slovenia, Tunisia, and Ukraine.

binding 'for all Members'; there is no opt-out or expulsion mechanism to be triggered against a dissenting minority.[58] The formal process of amendment thus has a constitutional aspect, in that dissent does not preserve the prior position. Amendments adopted modify the constitution for all participants. The United Nations certainly could amend its admission provisions by way of the formal provisions for amendment; the OAS, for example, has changed its own admission provisions in that way.[59]

Voting in the organs of an organization under the amendment provisions of the constitutive instrument is not the only process by which member States may effect an amendment to the constitutive instrument. The 1969 Vienna Convention provides in Article 39 as follows:

General rules regarding the amendment of treaties
A treaty may be amended by agreement between the parties. The rules laid down in Part II apply to such an agreement except in so far as the treaty may otherwise provide.

Article 39 thus identifies 'agreement between the parties' as a further process which may effect amendment of a treaty. Like any agreement, such 'agreement between the parties' need not be written. It can be inferred from the conduct of the parties. That is to say, practice of the parties to a treaty may effect amendment of the treaty. 'A consistent practice,' Amerasinghe says, 'could clearly provide cogent evidence of common consent to a change.'[60]

Other writers broadly concur that practice may give rise to amendment – or at least to 'transformation.' According to Zacklin, 'the transformation of the Charter...has exceeded the expectations of the most optimistic delegate at San Francisco and the manner in which this has been accomplished is one of the most important and fascinating aspects of United Nations practice.'[61] A general 'transformation' is not the same as amendment, but Zacklin took the view that practice may significantly re-work the constitutive instrument. For the UN, Zacklin says, this has been for the better:

If, in fact, the Charter had remained as static as the virtual absence of formal amendments might suggest, the United Nations would by now have become an obsolete and totally ineffective institution utterly in the backwater of world events. This has not been the case. In effect, the United Nations has demonstrated a

---

[58] See also Article 6, paragraph 2 of the Convention on the Organisation for Economic Co-operation and Development, whereby abstaining Members are not bound by decisions or recommendations adopted by the organization: adopted 14 Dec 1960, entered into force 30 Sept 1961, 888 UNTS 180, 185.

[59] Bühler *State Succession and Membership in International Organizations* (2001) 23 n. 95.

[60] Amerasinghe 462.

[61] Zacklin 181.

remarkable capacity for adaptability to changing conditions and the Charter has undergone, in the process, a considerable transformation. This transformation has been accomplished, in the main, without recourse to the formal amendment procedures of the Charter.[62]

Zacklin is certainly right that an international organization without 'the means of some change is without the means of its conservation.'[63] The question is, how to characterize the changes observed. It may be that the distinction between interpretation and amendment is too formal to be of use in practice. A less specific word such as 'transformation' or 'modification' perhaps avoids problems of category. Yet how a change is brought about has definite, practical results, not least of all, when considering what mechanisms might be used to retrace the steps of constitutional development back toward an earlier position. More will be said below about the possible legal consequences of the difference between interpretation and amendment.

The effect of practice on the constitutive instrument, as distinct from the formal process of amendment, is given greater emphasis by some writers than others. Rosenne, to an extent that identifies a theory of international organization distinct from that of Amerasinghe or Zacklin, emphasizes the 'established practice of the organization' as relevant to its constitution. The phrase 'established practice of the organization' is that provided in the 1986 Vienna Convention.[64] The same phrase is used in paragraph 4 of draft article 4 on Responsibility of International Organizations (defining 'rules of the organization').[65] According to Article 2(1)(j) of the 1986 Vienna Convention, '"rules of the organization" means, in particular, the constituent instruments, decisions and resolutions adopted in accordance with them, and established practice of the organization.'[66] A number of international organizations have confirmed or acceded to the 1986 Vienna Convention,[67] but the requisite number of States have not ratified for

---

[62] Zacklin 180–1.

[63] *Pace* Burke *Reflections on the revolution in France, and on the proceedings in certain societies in London relative to that event. In a letter intended to have been sent to a gentleman in Paris* (1790) 29.

[64] Op. cit.

[65] ILC Report on the work of its 56th sess, 3 May–4 June and 5 July–6 Aug 2004, GAOR 59th sess Supp no 10: A/59/10 p. 103.

[66] The draft adopted by the ILC under Special Rapporter Paul Reuter included this provision, with the difference that the second element was specified simply as 'relevant decisions and resolutions': adopted 21 July 1982, ILC 34th sess 1750th mtg ¶ 63 *ILC Ybk* 1982 Vol. II Pt Two p. 17.

[67] These are the IAEA, ICAO, International Criminal Police Organization, ILO, IMO, Organisation for the Prohibition of Chemical Weapons, Preparatory Commission for the Comprehensive Nuclear Test-Ban, UNIDO, UPU, WHO, and WIPO. Organizations having signed but not confirmed or acceded are the Council of Europe, FAO, ITU, UNESCO, and World Meteorological Organization.

the Convention to enter into force.[68] It also should be noted, as the ILC did in its Commentary to the 1982 draft, that the 'main purpose' of the Convention is not to regulate 'the status of international organizations, but the regime of treaties to which one or more international organizations are parties.'[69]

Yet the reference to 'established practice' in the 1986 Vienna Convention in Article 2(1)(j) and in other instruments is significant for the constitutional law of organizations. In comments which the ILC received in connection with the responsibility of international organizations, a certain acceptance of 'established practice' as relevant to organizational law is in evidence. The IMF sees 'established practice' as affirming the particularity of each organization's law: the established practice of the organization (together with its treaty and 'decisions of its governing bodies') are the 'only' basis on which the question, e.g., of attribution can be determined.[70] The UN Secretariat commented that 'in connection with peacekeeping operations...principles of international responsibility for the conduct of the force have for the most part been developed in the 50-year practice of the Organization.'[71] The World Health Organization agreed that 'the role of the practice of [the] organization...cannot be ignored and should be given formal status through its inclusion in the concept of "rules of the organization."'[72] It well may be that in the twenty-two years since adoption of the 1986 Vienna Convention, 'established practice' has rooted itself more firmly as part of a general law of constitutional interpretation in international organizations. The question is precisely what its significance is.

The ILC commentary on the 'established practice' provision in the 1982 draft articles leading to the 1986 Convention merits consideration:

> [R]eference is made to *established practice*. This point once again evoked comment from Governments and international organizations. It is true that most international organizations have, after a number of years, a body of practice which forms an integral part of their rules. However, the reference in question is in no way intended to suggest that practice has the same standing in all organizations; on the contrary, each organization has its own characteristics in that respect. Similarly, by referring to "established" practice, the Commission seeks only to rule out uncertain or disputed practice; it is not its wish to freeze practice at a particular moment in an organization's history...[73]

---

[68] See note 41 above.
[69] *ILC Ybk* 1982 Vol. II Pt Two p. 20 Comment (21).
[70] A/CN.4/545 p. 16.
[71] Ibid.
[72] Ibid. See also discussion in Gaja Second Report A/CN.4/541 pp. 10–13 ¶¶ 20–6.
[73] *ILC Ybk* 1982 Vol. II Pt Two p. 21 Comment (25). Citations omitted. See also Comment (11) to draft article 4 on Responsibility of International Organizations, A/59/10 p. 108: 'paragraph 4...gives considerable weight to practice.'

It is hardly surprising that the provision 'evoked comment.' To indicate that the internal law of the organization can develop through the accretion of its own actions suggests the acquisition of a further degree of autonomy by the organization that the constituent States likely will desire to check as against the original compact in which they assigned it certain specified powers and functions. In particular, the constituent States likely will desire to maintain the position that formal processes of amendment are superior to practice in the hierarchy of the organization's internal law-revising rules. The ILC thus recalls that 'the reference... is in no way intended to suggest that practice has the same standing in all organizations...each organization has its own characteristics in that respect.'

The Commentary indicates a further limit on practice as a source of the law of the organization. The word 'established' is 'to rule out uncertain or disputed practice.' This raises the question what makes a practice 'uncertain' or 'disputed.' A range of positions suggests itself, from one in which objection by one State alone prevents practice from crystallizing into a new rule; to one in which clearly contrary practice or numerous objectors are needed. Yet the ILC did not wish 'to freeze practice at a particular moment in an organization's history.' This reflects the tension between a view readier to accept evolutionary processes as a source of change within an organization, and a view which adheres more strictly to the organization's treaty basis and the formal mechanisms established on that basis. The tension does not appear entirely to have been resolved in the ILC's discussions leading to the 1982 draft. It remained at least as late as the drafting work on responsibility of international organizations, when the Organization for the Prohibition of Chemical Weapons asked for clarification as to when 'an alleged practice would be deemed to be an "established practice."'[74]

The significance of practice, Rosenne says, was hinted at in the early 1950s, when the General Assembly resolved to publish the *Répertoire of the Practice of the Security Council* and the *Repertory of the Practice of United Nations Organs*.[75] Rosenne's view that practice has a special significance in the development of international organizations is kindred to Fitzmaurice's theory of the 'emergent purpose,'[76] a theory to which Rosenne expressly refers.[77] It also bears relation to the views of Hersch Lauterpacht and Charles de Visscher, who, though having

---

[74] Comments and observations received from Governments and international organizations 12 May 2005, A/CN.4/556 p. 23.

[75] GA resns 686 (VII), 5 Dec 1952; 796 (VIII), 27 Nov 1953, about which see Rosenne *Treaties* 241–2.

[76] Sir Gerald Fitzmaurice 'The Law and procedure of the International Court of Justice: Treaty Interpretation and Certain Other Treaty Points' (1951) 28 *BY* 8; *The Law and Procedure of the International Court of Justice* vol. I 49, 342 (1986).

[77] E.g. in *Treaties* at 240.

quite different 'philosophical outlook[s] towards international law' both 'treated the constituent instruments of international organizations as a special type of instrument for purposes of interpretation.'[78] Rosenne however would seem to take the view that practice performs more than an interpretative function with respect to the constitutive instrument. Rosenne's view is distinct as well from a position which simply says that practice can amend a constitutive instrument. Rosenne says, instead, that the constitution of an international organization is not the same thing as the treaty establishing the organization in the first place, the constitution being the result of accretions over time generated by practice. The constitutive instrument in this view is not a complete statement of the particular law of the organization it created but, rather, a starting point, to which must be added law-making developments that have followed.[79] This in result is similar to the position which treats practice as a source of interpretation, where interpretation may have an additive effect or gap-filling effect; but it differs, where it conceives of the founding treaty and subsequent practice as components of a wider 'constitution.'

The better view perhaps is that the particular question of interpretation presented will affect the balance to be struck as between treating the constitutive instrument as a normal international agreement and treating it as a special type with its own constitutional properties. The dispute between Nicaragua and the United States in the 1980s, for example, raised a question as to the meaning of the Charter's regulation of threat and use of force. This was a question as between two States, and, so, it might have been said, the character of the Charter as a treaty to which the two States in adversary proceedings are party should not be ignored.[80] Other questions by contrast may go to the management, composition, and functions of the organization as a legal entity; writers have submitted that these are questions involving the distinctive constitutional aspect of the treaty which created the organization. The question with which the present work has been mainly concerned, admission of applicants to the United Nations, is a question of the latter type and therefore would implicate the constitutional aspects of the UN Charter. Yet that observation alone does not provide an answer. Even if one accepts that a constitutional character is to be attributed to the Charter, the question remains what mechanisms of amendment are capable of operating in the circumstances.

---

[78] Ibid. 233 n. 64 citing Lauterpacht *The Development of International Law by the International Court* 267 (1958) and de Visscher *Problèmes d'interprétation judiciaire en droit international public* 140 (1969).

[79] Rosenne *Treaties* 191, 205 (with reference to the drafting work for the Vienna Conventions). And ibid. 232.

[80] Rosenne makes this point and the distinction: *Treaties* 224, citing ICJ Rep 1986 pp. 14, 117 ¶ 225.

The International Law Commission in the drafting work leading to the 1969 Vienna Convention was clear that amendments could arise by way of practice. The ILC in the draft was more explicit about the potential effect of practice than in the text actually adopted. Draft article 38 had indicated that '[a] treaty may be modified by subsequent practice in the application of the treaty establishing the agreement of the parties to modify its provisions.'[81] The ILC Commentary to the draft provision said, *inter alia*, that 'a consistent practice, establishing the common consent of the parties to the application of the treaty in a manner different from that laid down in certain of its provisions may have the effect of modifying the treaty.'[82] It was recalled that Roberto Ago, as President of the Tribunal in the *Air Transport Services Arbitration (USA v France)* (1963), had stated that a 'course of conduct' may be more than a basis for interpretation; it may modify the treaty:

> [A] course of conduct may...be taken into account not merely as a means useful for interpreting the Agreement, but also as something more: that is, as a possible source of subsequent modification, arising out of certain actions or certain attitudes, having a bearing on the judicial situation of the Parties and on the rights that each of them could properly claim.[83]

The Tribunal in *Air Transport Services* was dealing with the effects which an agreement and subsequent practice had on the legal rights and obligations between two States. The constitution of an international organization is not the same as the 'judicial situation' of a bilateral dispute. But, if the more general point stands – that 'certain actions or certain attitudes' can be a 'source of subsequent modification' – then the position that Ago set out in *Air Transport Services* is relevant to Article 4(1) of the Charter.

An initial question is whether such a process of amendment – amendment through practice – applies to the constitutive instrument of a particular international organization with respect to a particular subject falling within the organization's competence – e.g., admission to membership in the UN. The clause in VCLT Article 39 'except in so far as the treaty may otherwise provide' reprises the principle behind VCLT Article 5: if 'relevant rules' contained in the constitutive instrument of an international organization make their own provision, then those rules prevail over the Convention, including the Convention's rules concerning amendment. Some constitutive instruments contain no provi-

---

[81] *ILC Ybk* 1966 Vol. II p. 236.
[82] Ibid. Comment (1).
[83] Decision of 22 Dec 1963 (Ago, President; Reuter and De Vries, Members): 3 ILM 668, 713 (1963). Citing *Temple of Preah Vihear (Cambodia v Thailand)*, ICJ Rep 1962 p. 6, 33: 'Both parties, by their conduct, recognized the line and therefore in effect agreed to regard it as being the frontier line.'

sion concerning formal amendment. The North Atlantic Treaty constituting NATO is an example.[84] The amendment rules of general international law as reflected in the Vienna Convention thus in that instance presumably would not be superseded by the constitutive treaty. Other constitutive instruments, however, do contain provisions concerning formal amendment. Article 108 of the Charter is such a provision. It would seem therefore that the UN's own rules concerning amendment are prior to the general rules. This is not the same as saying that the general rules disappear from the picture altogether. Instead, the general rules play a subsidiary role in controlling amendment under the Charter.

That a treaty containing its own amendment provisions may be affected by practice is suggested when one considers examples of evolving constitutive instruments. The EC Treaties, which contain their own amendment provisions, have been changed by interpretation, and perhaps by practice, though Amerasinghe is doubtful whether the changes to the EC Treaties have amounted to amendments as such.[85] Another case, perhaps clearer, is the Geneva Convention on the Territorial Sea and Contiguous Zone of 1958.[86] Practice, it is said, resulted in amendment of the Convention. Fishing zones had not originally been a category of contiguous zone for purposes of the Convention, but they began in practice to be treated as such and in this way extended the scope of the definition of 'contiguous zone'. Article 30 of the Convention provides for a formal procedure of revision.[87] Therefore, a treaty containing its own amendment provision is susceptible to amendment by way of practice. VCLT Article 39, saying that amendment may be by way of agreement of the parties, thus is an operative principle, even where the treaty contains its own amendment provisions.

It also may be noted that the exception clause of VCLT Article 39 ('except insofar as the treaty may otherwise provide') does not pertain to the main clause ('[a] treaty may be amended by agreement between the parties'). The exception applies to Part II of the Convention and to agreements to amend the treaty, i.e. to the mode and form of the agreements – but not to the prior question whether agreements to amend the treaty may be made. An express negative provision in the treaty forbidding amendment by means other than those formally specified to be sure would prevail, for the parties' intentions are primary. The principle that amendments may derive from the agreement of the parties – and thus from practice – seems otherwise to hold, including

---

[84] 34 UNTS 243, signed 4 Apr 1949, entered into force 24 Aug 1949.
[85] Amerasinghe 462–3.
[86] Convention on the Territorial Sea and the Contiguous Zone, Geneva, 29 Apr 1958, entered into force 10 Sept 1964: 516 UNTS 206.
[87] 516 UNTS at 222–4.

where the instrument contains particular affirmative provisions setting out an amendment mechanism.

Finally, it also should be born in mind that the organs of the United Nations are the first instrumentalities to have authority to interpret the Charter.[88] The Conference on International Organization in 1945 adopted a declaration concerning interpretation, which contained the following paragraph:

> In the course of the operations from day to day of the various organs of the Organization, it is inevitable that each organ will interpret such parts of the Charter as are applicable to its particular functions. This process is inherent in the functioning of any body which operates under an instrument defining its functions and powers. It will be manifested in the functioning of such a body as the General Assembly, the Security Council, or the International Court of Justice. Accordingly, it is not necessary to include in the Charter a provision either authorizing or approving the normal operation of this principle.[89]

Rosenne, among others, has been critical of the position that such a principle should be liberally applied. He calls it 'a precept for legal nihilism.'[90] Yet the Organization has applied the principle, to such an extent that it would be hard to deny its force, even as attempts are made to establish fuller forms of accountability for actions taken on the basis of interpretations so reached. The General Assembly and the Security Council interpret their own powers of amendment, including reaching a view as to whether the practice of the Organization may serve as a mechanism of amendment. The principal organs, acting as if they can amend the Charter through practice, have a certain independent bearing on the question whether amendment of the Charter is possible through that mechanism. Rosenne thought this problematic, and it certainly raises the further question of what agency then exists to review the interpretations that UN organs reach as to their own powers. The absence of a fully satisfactory answer to the question owes to the comparative underdevelopment of a law and process of responsibility for international organizations.

4.2.2   *Interpretation or Amendment?*

(i)   *General Considerations*
Practice, as suggested above, may be a source of amendment of treaties. *A fortiori* interpretation of a treaty also may result from practice. Writers have distinguished interpretation and amendment, and the economy of legal construction well

---

[88] Amerasinghe 25–6.
[89] XII UNCIO 709.
[90] Rosenne *Treaties* 225. And ibid. 227.

may justify treating them as distinct processes. Some basic distinctions between interpretation and amendment may be instanced.

Interpretation, described in general terms, may have one of two results. Interpretation may develop a new position which fills a lacuna in the constitutive instrument. In this situation, the instrument is silent as to some situation facing the organization, and it thus requires such development, lest a sort of *non liquet* prevail resulting in inaction. The other possible result of interpretation is to establish precedence as between two or more positions, where the positions both are permitted under the constitutive instrument but not assigned a hierarchy. Such precedence may go so far as to relegate a permitted alternative position to disuse – the most thorough-going result that might be attributed to a process of interpretation.

An amendment, by contrast, establishes a position which contradicts a position in the constitutive instrument. This may include replacing a position under the instrument with a new position not consistent with the initial one; or negating the initial position without establishing any substitute for it at all.[91] It may be that this latter form of amendment bears similarity to that result of interpretation which leads to the disuse of one among multiple permitted alternative positions. In both situations, practice has led to the disappearance of positions that the instrument had contemplated. It may be that, where the position has disappeared and had been permitted but not required the situation is one of interpretation; whereas, where the position has disappeared and had been required, the situation is one of amendment.

If identifying when an amendment has occurred is approached as a forensic task, then the relevant indication is that the practice in question has resulted in the organization acting contrary to the (existing) law of the instrument.[92] The rule concerning abstentions in Security Council decision-making illustrates the relation.

> [I]f practice...gives rise to an interpretation that contradicts and, therefore, amends the constitution of an institution, because it continues to be adopted as an appropriate interpretation, this is a question which pertains to amendment and not to interpretation as such. But it is not clear that practice that contradicted an express

---

[91] The two situations are the same, if the absence of a position is taken itself to be a position. The assumption here, which does not necessarily obtain in all situations, is that 'position' entails an actual statement in the instrument, not an absence of one. An active definition of 'position' is supported by practice: consider instances of a Court 'declining to take a position' on some or another matter: e.g. *Cotter v Massachusetts Ass'n of Minority Law Enforcement Officers* 219 F.3d 31, 36 (1st Cir 2000 Boudin CJ); *Acierno v Cloutier* 40 F.3d 597, 620 (3rd Cir 1994 Cowen CJ). Logically, in 'not taking a position,' the Court indeed has said *something*, but to distinguish between taking a position and not taking a position is well-established.

[92] Zacklin 173.

text was accepted as of interpretative value. Although the interpretative practice surrounding the voting provisions of Article 27(3) of the UN Charter, for instance, could be regarded as having given rise to an amendment, it has not been and need not be treated as such. A case may be made that the practice of treating an abstention as not giving rise to the absence of an affirmative vote in regard to the votes of the permanent members of the SC is not a contradiction amounting to an amendment of Article 27(3). Had the negative vote of a permanent member been disregarded in the tallying of votes, such a practice would have been in contradiction of the express terms of the Article and its adoption would have amounted to an amendment. The practice in fact adopted resulted in giving the meaning 'not negative' to the term 'affirmative' which is less removed and may be construed as development rather than amendment. Generally, it may be said that practice of interpretative value does not contradict or amend a text as such and thus can be regarded as being based on prior agreement where it is used to interpret a text.[93]

The conclusion reached is that the instances in which practice has affected a constitutive text mostly have resulted in interpretations of the text, not in amendments. It even may be posited, as a principle of construction, that interpretation is the presumptive characterization, so that, absent clear evidence to the contrary, a given instance of constitutional change is to be characterized in that way. Practice, in most cases,

> is used to fill in a gap or take care of an unforeseen situation rather than to contradict a text. Practice has generally been used to help a constitution to evolve where there is ambiguity, vagueness or a gap in the constitutional text, rather than to defy clear prescriptions. It is thus a mechanism for purposeful and agreed evolution.[94]

It nevertheless is admitted that practice may have more radical effect: '[T]here is a presumption that practice clearly contrary to a text cannot negate the text itself.'[95] In the character of all presumptions, this can be displaced or rebutted. The question is by what showing of evidence. At some point, a consistent course of practice contradicting a position in the constitutive text will affect the text. Meaning will not remain static indefinitely in the face of decisions and actions supporting a contradictory position. In the practice of any given organization, however, it may be difficult to say which decisions and actions can effect amendment.

A relevant consideration is that amendment does not take place 'surreptitiously as it were by interpretation.'[96] Creeping or evolutionary amendment,

---

[93] Amerasinghe 54–5.

[94] Ibid. 60.

[95] Ibid. 65. Though this proposition concerns mainly practice relative to adopted resolutions and decisions of organs of an international organization, it applies to the constitutive instrument as well: '[A] practice may not "change" a constitutional provision in the sense of amending it.' ibid. 54.

[96] Ibid. 460.

on this consideration, is not a possibility. Amendment arises from contrary practice, and a given incident of practice is either contrary or it is not, even though time and appreciation may be needed to judge which it is. There is also the matter of consensus and the support of the member States. A measure of whether practice *contra legem* has resulted in amendment well may be the balance between concurrence and dissent within the organization. 'The practice required to modify or amend multilateral treaties, including the constitutions of international organizations,' says Amerasinghe, 'may involve somewhat more stringent requirements than in the case of bilateral treaties. What has to be proved is that the practice reflected an agreement among *all the parties*.'[97] Unanimity of the parties supporting a new position which plainly contradicts the old is perhaps the sure case of amendment by practice. This would appear to have been the situation when INTELSAT, during the process of privatization, elected unanimously to dissolve itself without referring the matter to the express provisions for amendment. Dissolution went forward, against constitutionally mandated waiting periods.[98] Unanimity certainly produces the clear case. The question remains whether in all cases unanimity is required.

(ii) *Article 4(1): Interpreted or Amended?*
With the above general considerations in mind, we may ask whether the package deal of 1955–6 and its associated practice subjected Article 4(1) to development through interpretation – or, instead, put that provision to a process of amendment. To reach even a tentative answer, positions must be established with respect to two prior matters. The first of these is the meaning of the rule under Article 4(1) as it originally existed: it must be established what Article 4(1), as adopted, meant with respect to criteria for admission of States. And, second, it must be established what the position was, after the package deal. If the later position was simply a development built upon the earlier position; or if it filled lacunae in Article 4(1), then the answer to the main question is that practice interpreted relevant provisions of the Charter. If the later position was *contra legem* – if it contradicted the original position as set down in the law of the Charter – then practice is perhaps better characterized as having amended the Charter in the matter of admission of States as new members.

---

[97] Ibid. 463. Emphasis added.
[98] See provision in Art. XVII respecting 90-day period for distribution of draft of proposed amendment (sub ¶ (b)) and further 90-day period before entry into force of amendments so adopted (sub ¶ (e)): Agreement relating to the International Telecommunications Satellite Organization "INTELSAT": 1220 UNTS 21, 45–6, 20 Aug 1971; entered into force 12 Feb 1973. INTELSAT did not wait, and nor did the private equity firms financing its privatization.

Evidence relevant to the original meaning of Article 4(1) includes the text of the Charter; the interpretation placed on it by the ICJ; its drafting history; and the views of States concerning its meaning.

To start with the text itself, one observes that Article 4 has a mandatory sense, and this entails a judgment. The Organization, if it is to admit a candidate to membership, must reach the 'judgment' that the candidate is 'able and willing to carry out [the] obligations [contained in the Charter].' 'Judgment,' as a general term, denotes no particular procedural mechanism; a decision-maker can reach a judgment in various ways. However, the word excludes a purely discretionary approach. The Court said as much in the *Admission* Advisory Opinion as discussed already.[99]

One may make at least two further observations about the judgment required under Article 4. First, States in 1945 certainly knew how to draft treaties under which further States may become party simply by the unilateral act of accession or ratification. Such direct means of establishing admission were available even where provisions were in force limiting which States could become parties, as was the case, for example, under the Convention on the Execution of Foreign Arbitral Awards of 1927. Under Article 7, the Convention is open only to 'those Members of the League of Nations and non-Member States on whose behalf the Protocol of 1923 [on Arbitration Clauses] shall have been ratified.' Article 8 provides that the Convention shall enter into force three months after deposit of ratification by any further eligible State, with no further decision or formality required.[100] Thus a limiting criterion can exist without provision for judgment as to its fulfilment. This is not the approach taken by the States adopting the Charter in 1945.

Second, Article 4 of the UN Charter is clear that the judgment, in the particular context of applications for admission, is to be a judgment reached under a definite institutional mechanism. This then is not an abstract judgment, for the second paragraph of Article 4 allocates competence in considering applications for admission between the Security Council and General Assembly. It is an allocation of competence with actual consequences, as the Court made clear in the 1950 advisory opinion on *Competence*.

It might be said of the substantive criteria in Article 4(1) that these are optional, that one should interpret the absence there of mandatory words such as 'shall' or 'must' as an indication that the relevant UN organs are not obliged to determine that an applicant has satisfied the criteria. However, the Court in the *Admission* advisory opinion referred to the criteria as a legal rule governing

---

[99] See Chapter 2, pp. 29–39, above.
[100] 92 LNTS 301, 307–8, adopted 26 Sept 1927, entered into force 25 July 1929. Montenegro became a party to the 1927 Convention by succession on 23 Oct 2006.

admission, not as optional terms to be applied in some cases at the election of the organs concerned. To treat them as optional would be to cast doubt on their character as a legal regulation. The dissenting judges McNair et al agreed that the five criteria specified in Article 4(1) must be fulfilled; their difference was not with the Court's identification of the criteria as binding. It was instead that they interpreted Article 4(1) as allowing further considerations to be imposed as conditions of admission. Even in the much-diminished form that Article 4(1) has taken in practice, the criterion of statehood is mandatory; entities other than States have not been admitted to the Organization, and, as will be seen in the next Chapter, the chief argument remaining against admission in particular cases has been that the applicant is not a State. The provision of paragraph 1 that the Organization 'is open to' applicants meeting the five criteria there specified means, on its terms, that an applicant (at least) must satisfy the criteria in order to be judged qualified for admission.

Judicial decision and the consistent practice of admitting only States to the United Nations support the interpretation that the substantive terms of Article 4(1) are mandatory. The drafting history of the admission provisions of the Charter also supports the interpretation. A number of proposals were considered at Dumbarton Oaks, when the first drafts were being proposed for a general, post-war international organization. A matter of concern was to define the rules by which the Organization might be extended to include further States, in addition to those likely at the time to accede to the final draft of the constitutive instrument as original members. The views of States on the matter were not uniform. Brazil proposed that the Charter say as follows:

1. The International Organization shall be composed of all sovereign States that now exist or which in the future may exist under their own independent conditions of life.
2. No State may be expelled from the Organization or voluntarily withdraw from it.[101]

The Brazilian proposal amounted to a statement that a State is *ipso facto* a member of the United Nations. To have made membership automatic would have been to exclude any process of admission; and it also would have been to exclude any substantive criteria controlling eligibility for admission.

To have defined the Organization as automatically embracing all States – but to have included no mechanism to determine what 'all States' means – would have side-stepped the problems of appreciation inherent in determining whether an entity constitutes a State. Further matters, such as willingness and ability to carry out obligations entailed elsewhere in the constitutive instrument, simply

---

[101] Doc 2, G/7 (e), pp. 6–7 UNIO vol. 3 pp. 237–8.

would have been left out of the equation. A charter so drafted would have contained little or no analogue, then, to the substantive criteria of Article 4, paragraph 1. It might have been said that the phrase 'all sovereign States that now exist or which in the future may exist under their own independent conditions of life' entails some basic substantive requirement. Statehood, as has been seen, is the core criterion of Article 4(1) – namely, that an entity, to be admitted to membership, must be a State. An instrument based on the Brazilian proposal to be sure would have included the one, residual criterion. It would have lacked any means to determine its fulfilment in a case of doubt. The Brazilian proposal otherwise used words of such breadth as to exclude any further substantive restrictions on admission.

It is in the character of positions reached automatically that they do not involve judgment. Under the position of the Brazilian draft, questions of admission to the UN therefore would not have involved judgment. As noted, no procedural steps were specified for controlling admission of States to membership, and no competence allocated between organs within the organization on questions of admission. There would have been in short no analogue to paragraph 2 of Article 4 either. The absence of procedural mechanisms further illustrates the extent of the difference between this alternative approach to controlling admission to membership and the approach eventually adopted. The Organization, under the rejected proposal, would have consisted of all States, now existing or in the future created, and it would have included them, without any intervening judgment or decision.

The Brazilian position was not isolated. Guatemala, too, proposed that the organization be based on 'absolute universality,' and a number of other Latin American States (though not all of them) expressed a preference for a liberal, rather than a restrictive, approach to membership.[102]

Such free-form provisions on membership were decisively rejected. The relevant paragraph of the Dumbarton Oaks Proposal, as actually adopted, read as follows: 'The General Assembly should be empowered to admit new Members to the Organization upon recommendation of the Security Council.'[103]

Statements interpreting Article 4 in the early years of the Charter tended to confirm that admission was to be controlled with reference to substantive criteria. The Assistant Secretary-General for Legal Affairs said in 1947 that the United Nations 'must be as universal as possible.'[104] This was not a declaration that universality as such was a requirement. The limitation 'as possible' meant to subject a preference in policy to the requirements of the Charter. In any

---

[102] Doc 2, G/7 (f)(I), p. 1 UNIO vol. 3 p. 257.
[103] Doc 1, G/I, p. 4 UNIO vol. 3 p. 5.
[104] SCOR 2nd yr 186th mtg 18 Aug 1947 pp. 2032–3.

event, the statement should not necessarily be taken to have constituted formal advice from the Assistant Secretary-General to the Organization, and by its terms appears to have been more a political observation than an articulation of a legal standard. A proposal around the same time to include reference to the 'principle of universality' in the preambles to certain General Assembly resolutions was rejected in the First Committee.[105] General Assembly resolution 197B (III) contained the phrase '*[h]aving noted* the general sentiment in favour of the universality of the United Nations...'[106] This was the result of an amendment (proposed by Bolivia) which deleted from the original Swedish draft the phrase 'in the light of the principle of universality.'[107] Subsequent General Assembly resolutions, also urging the widest possible admission of candidates, similarly avoided referring to universality as a 'principle.'[108] Even insofar as the Assistant Secretary-General's observation concerning universal membership might have been taken to have had the character of formal legal guidance, the conclusion drawn from it was that universality could at most be described as a *desideratum* and favoured by 'sentiment;' it was not a 'principle.' The distance, then, to establishing universality as a presumption was that much greater.

Certain States at the time of the *Competence* advisory proceedings were prepared to refer to universality as a 'principle,' but there was still support for a considerably more limited view of the meaning of the term under the Charter. According to Venezuela,

> [L]'universalité est, sans doute, l'un des principes essentiels des Nations Unies; mais la lecture de la Charte révèle qu'une telle universalité n'est pas conçue comme principe absolu, ni même comme un fait totalement réalisé. Les Nations Unies penchent vers l'universalité comme un *desideratum*, mais avec les restrictions établies par la même Charte.[109]

To include all States in the Organization, according to Venezuela, then, was a desired goal, but not something yet achieved. Moreover, even as the Organization might strive toward the goal, it had to do so within the 'restrictions established by the...Charter.' Israel held a similar view.[110]

France a little earlier had been clear that the Charter not only did not require universality but had 'deliberately rejected' the idea:

---

[105] GAOR 2nd sess, 1st Comm, p. 579, annex 14a, A/C.1/183.
[106] GA res 197B (III), 8 Dec 1948 pream ¶ 3.
[107] GAOR 3rd sess, Ad Hoc Pol Comm, Annexes p. 9, A/AC.24/17 (Swedish draft); GAOR 3rd sess, Ad Hoc Pol Comm, Annexes, p. 10, A/AC.24/18 (Bolivian amendment).
[108] E.g., GA res 506 A & B (VI), 1 Feb 1952; 718 (VIII), 23 Oct 1953.
[109] ICJ Pldgs 1950 p. 152.
[110] Hebrew University of Jerusalem Study Group *Israel and the United Nations* (1956) 197.

Or, si nous nous plaçons au point de vue du droit positif, c'est-à-dire la *lex lata*, il n'est pas douteux que la Charte de San-Francisco rejette délibérément l'idée de l'universalité. S'il en était autrement, il n'y aurait même pas besoin de l'article 4 de la Charte.[111]

This was to apply the principle of *ut res magis valeat quam pereat* to the admission provisions of the Charter. There 'would have been no reason' to include such provisions, if the position instead was simply that any and all applicants are to be admitted as members. The position to be implemented, then, was the position which gives meaning to Article 4.

The positions which States took with respect to Article 4 are a guide as to its meaning, but the UN system contains in the ICJ a judicial authority which is the main organ competent to give legal interpretations, including interpretations of constitutive instruments of various organizations.[112] The International Court indeed has examined the practice of the United Nations to come to a judgment as to the meaning of certain provisions of the Charter. The analysis adopted in the *Expenses* opinion, in particular, though it does not confirm that practice can act so as to amend the Charter, nevertheless draws observations from the practice of the UN to support an interpretation of Article 17(2) ('The expenses of the Organization shall be borne by the Members as apportioned by the General Assembly').[113] A determination of the Court, under its advisory jurisdiction, would be difficult to ignore without undermining the Court in its role as principal judicial organ of the United Nations system. The position reached in practice under Article 4(1), by which universal admission is treated as a presumption of Charter law, has not, however, been examined by the Court. The Court's two advisory opinions concerning admission under Article 4 examined other questions, and, in any event, they came before the package deal. Universality cannot be said to have been entrenched through judicial action.

The position under Article 4, as originally adopted, thus may be characterized as follows:

---

[111] ICJ Pldgs 1948 p. 71.

[112] The European Commission thought that the phrase 'established practice of the organization,' as an element of the definition of 'rules of the organization' in the draft articles on responsibility of international organizations, should be extended to read 'established practice of the organization, including case law by its courts': ILC 56th sess, Responsibility of international organizations, Comments and observations received from international organizations, 25 June 2004: A/CN.4/545 p. 15.

[113] *Certain Expenses of the United Nations (Article 17, Paragraph 2, of the Charter)* Advisory Opinion of 20 July 1962, ICJ Rep 1962 pp. 151, 157–8. The matter there was straightforward enough, for '[a]ctually, the practice of the Organization is entirely consistent with the plain meaning of the text': ibid. 160.

(i) The United Nations is not a closed organization limited to its Original Members.

(ii) The United Nations is to control admission by limiting it to applicants which fulfil certain specified criteria.

(iii) The Organization is to determine, by reaching a judgment, whether an applicant has fulfilled the criteria.

(iv) The Security Council and General Assembly share competence over the process of judgment.

(v) The allocation of competence in the Charter implies that the Organization is to establish and implement further procedures to enable those principal organs to undertake the evaluations necessary to the process of judgment.

We may compare this position to that reached after the package deal and its associated practice.

The position reached as a result of the package deal and its associated practice may be characterized by reference to the results themselves. Chapter 3 above considered the transactions leading to so many new admissions. The mass entry of States into the UN in 1955–6 does not necessarily in itself however say what happened to the constitutional law of the Charter. The absence of a judicial determination about that practice leaves it all the more unsettled whether it took place within the Charter, in breach of the Charter, or with the effect of changing the Charter. To attempt a legal characterization of that watershed in UN practice, one may turn to the practice of States and to the views of writers.

A number of States said that opening admission to all applicants was the only choice under the Charter. The New Zealand representative, for example, said that 'the criteria set out in Article 4 are not capable of objective demonstration and must therefore be a matter of subjective judgement.'[114] The conclusion drawn from this was that all the then-candidate States should be admitted.[115] New Zealand seemed to say that the Charter as originally adopted, on its plain terms concerning admission, could not be implemented in any procedurally rigorous way. This would imply that to elide the criteria for admission was to acknowledge a fault in the conception of the draft instrument as adopted in 1945.

Other States put the matter differently. The presumption under Article 4(1), they said, had shifted to favour admissibility. This was not to say, as New Zealand had said, that it is futile to attempt to implement Article 4(1). It was, instead, to say that the Charter now had a different meaning from that which followed from its plain text. The former enemy States and other applicants had had the burden

---

[114] Sir Leslie Munro (New Zealand), SCOR 10th yr 701st mtg 10 Dec 1955 ¶ 96.

[115] Ibid. ¶ 97.

after 1945 of proving that they satisfied the Charter criterion that member States be 'peace-loving,' but, by 1953, Egypt and the Philippines, for example, would say that 'States should be considered as peace-loving unless they are actually found by an appropriate organ of the United Nations to be guilty of a threat to the peace, a breach of the peace or an act of aggression.'[116] This explicitly was to shift the burden from the applicant to the UN and thus to presume admissibility. The view of States that the presumption was now one of admissibility was indicated some years later (in 1961) with the admission of Mongolia, the British remarks concerning which have been mentioned already.[117]

In certain States' positions, however, one can discern doubts as to the effectiveness of practice as a mechanism of Charter amendment. A number of States, espousing the view that admission should be universal, did not say that universal admission resulted from a change in Charter law. It was said, instead, that the Charter from the start had permitted admission of all States. An interest in establishing a legal system to govern international society, it was suggested, supported admission, a position perhaps suggesting in turn that support for universal admission is to be found in natural law.[118] Certain member States identified the necessary legal basis within the constitutive instrument itself. The Soviet Union saw the admissions of 14 December 1955 as 'true to its policy of strict compliance with the provisions of the Charter.'[119] Even if it is right to say that universal admission is true to 'strict compliance' with the Charter, it is not necessarily the case that the Charter requires universal admission. The position instead could be that universal admission is one possibility among two or more possibilities, both or all of which are consistent with the Charter. Other States, as already seen, however, believed the Charter left no choice: admission in their view was a requirement, to be implemented in furtherance of a fundamental goal of the Organization.

---

[116] Explanatory memorandum on the admission of new Members (Working document submitted by Egypt and the Philippines), Report of the Special Committee on Admission of New Members, 25 June 1953, A/2400, GAOR 8th sess, Annexes, agenda item 22, Annex 7 ¶ 8. See also Mr Belaúnde (Peru) SCOR 10th yr 701st mtg 10 Dec 1955 ¶¶ 24, 28: '[I]f Article 4 is interpreted in…light [of the *Admission* Advisory Opinion of 1948], it is consistent with universality, because every country should and could be and…must be, peace-loving. It is therefore inconceivable that any State should not be able to carry out its obligations…'

[117] Admission having been 'an act of faith': Sir Patrick Dean (United Kingdom), SCOR 16th year 971st sess 25 Oct 1961 ¶ 51, about which see Chapter 3, p. 90, above.

[118] Soder *Die Vereinten Nationen und die Nichtmitglieder: Zum Problem der Weltstaatenorganisation* (1956) 257–8. Soder generally was concerned with the philosophical underpinnings and historical development of a world organization of States. See his *Die Idee der Völkergemeinschaft: Francisco de Vitoria und die philosophischen Grundlagen des Völkerrecht* (1955).

[119] Mr Kuznetsov (USSR) GAOR 10th sess 555th plen mtg 14 Dec 1955 ¶ 117.

As seen above, the Charter in its original meaning does not permit admission where the applicant fails to fulfil the criteria of Article 4(1). Given the original meaning, to say that the Charter now requires universal admission would be to say that the Charter has been amended. The position, apparently adopted by the USSR, that the Charter *permits* universal admission, does not ostensibly go so far. It would be consistent with the Charter as adopted, if member States were to judge that all applicants to the UN fulfil the criteria of Article 4(1). But the actual fulfilment of the criteria by all applicants seems improbable on the facts of international relations. To say that the Charter permits universal admission therefore is either a statement with little or no possibility of having practical effect; or it is a (slightly) veiled call to amend the Charter. '[W]here a constitutional text clearly places an obligation on an entity, there being no question of gaps or lack of anticipation, an interpretation which permits the entity to avoid that obligation would amount to amendment of the text.'[120]

Not all States shared the views of Russia, Peru, and New Zealand that the Charter permitted universal admission, required universal admission, or simply had to be side-stepped to avoid a conceptual fault. The Dominican Republic said that 'correct application of what we may call the principle of universality' was to be pursued – but that 'wrong application...can lead only to the rebellion...of facts and circumstances.'[121] This was the view preserving the operability of the Article 4(1) criteria as against the preference for wide membership. Some States indeed doubted whether, as a matter of the law of the Charter, the discretion existed to admit all States regardless of their conduct or character. Two Permanent Members of the Security Council, France and China, at the time said that the package deal violated Article 4 and was tantamount to ignoring the International Court. Other States broadly agreed.[122] It was said that the package deal of 1955 was inconsistent with the *Admission* Advisory Opinion, for the International Court had been clear that it would be unlawful for States to condition admission of one State upon admission of another. According to China,

---

[120] Amerasinghe 460.
[121] Mr Diaz Ordoñez (Dominican Republic) GAOR 10th sess 556th plen mtg 15 Dec 1955 ¶ 122.
[122] According to Australia, a 'package deal' was 'contrary to the Charter': Sir Percy Spender (Australia) GAOR 10th sess Ad Hoc Pol Com 28th mtg 5 Dec 1955 ¶ 41. Lebanon said that 'each application for admission should be examined on its own merits': Mr Khouri (Lebanon) ibid. ¶ 67. Honduras characterized the package deal as a political solution, perhaps necessary and even 'honourable,' but 'doubtful' as a matter of Charter law: Mr Carias (Honduras) GAOR 10th sess Ad Hoc Pol Com 30th mtg 6 Dec 1955. cf. Turkey, which saw the package deal as a procedural deviation but not a violation of Charter substance: Mr Menemencioglu (Turkey) GAOR 10th sess Ad Hoc Pol Com 28th mtg 5 Dec 1955 ¶ 84.

The proposal before us puts the thirteen deserving and qualif[ied] applicants in one package with the five undeserving and disqualified applicants. The device of a package is contrary to the opinion of the International Court of Justice. It cannot be otherwise, for admission must be on individual merit. We cannot close our eyes and say: let us admit all. That is against the Charter as interpreted by the International Court of Justice.[123]

To 'admit all' indeed risked erasing the substantive admission criteria of Article 4(1), and it was to deny that each candidate should be judged on its own merits as 'deserving' or 'undeserving.' Objections such as China's showed that certain States recognized that the events then in train held considerable significance for the Charter. The package deal and its associated practice indeed tended to negate the substantive criteria of Article 4(1) – a result which is difficult to characterize other than as tending toward Charter amendment.

Certain provisions of the Charter have been subject to desuetude, most significantly the provisions on the furnishing of armed forces and on the organization and authority of the Military Staff Committee (Articles 43–48).[124] Those provisions were not so much put aside, as never activated in the first place. The transitional security arrangements under Chapter XVII, directed to the circumstances of the Second World War, too, are probably best viewed today as inoperative, though, unlike the provisions of Chapter VII here noted, these did not call for the establishment of any particular institutions and, so, it is not possible to point to any distinct failure of implementation as evidence of their disappearance from the Charter. The present disuse of those provisions must be referred instead to the passing of the wartime circumstances of their adoption. As such, while Articles 43 through 48 might be called dormant rather than deceased, Chapter XVII would seem in effect dead letter.

Neither situation obtains exactly with respect to Article 4. It is certainly not the case that circumstances have so changed that there is no need in the Charter for an admission provision. As recently as June 2006, a State sought (and received) admission,[125] and the possibility exists that further States will come into being. The UN will have to deal with their applications. It might be that a process of desuetude has been at work on Article 4, but, if so, its effect would not embrace all of Article 4. The allocation of competence between the Security Council and General Assembly in paragraph 2 continues to have effect, and no change is envisaged in the institutional mechanism by which the UN admits a new member. Paragraph 1 by contrast has fallen, in part, into disuse: we have

---

[123] Mr Tsiang (China) GAOR 10th sess 552nd plen mtg 8 Dec 1955 ¶ 40. See also Mr Palamas (Greece) ibid. ¶ 10; Mr Nuñez Portuondo (Cuba) ibid. ¶¶ 66–7; and Mr Tsiang's remarks at SCOR 10th yr 703rd mtg 13 Dec 1955 ¶ 26.

[124] See Zacklin 195.

[125] On recent admission practice see Chapter 6, pp. 249–50, below.

seen how the UN largely ceased in practice to apply substantive criteria for admission. Yet to speak as if Article 4(1) has been taken completely out of the picture is to ignore the practice: an applicant that is not a State, or the claimed statehood of which is seriously disputed, still will not be admitted. The United Nations is not a body of non-governmental organizations (even as the role of such organizations in some UN processes has grown).[126] And, where it is not clear that an applicant has articulated a claim to be a State, as has been the case to date with Taiwan, the principal organs have refused, rightly or wrongly, so much as to entertain an application. It would be an exaggeration to say that Article 4(1) has been struck from the Charter. Yet it would ignore the position reached since the 1950s to say that Article 4(1) remains entirely intact. The practice suggests that what remains is its residuum.

Leo Gross commented on the rise of universality, a major constitutional shift in the history of the UN:

> An often recurring theme was the desirability for the United Nations to achieve universality of membership. That it was desirable to aim at this objective was not doubted at the San Francisco Conference. The decision then taken and incorporated in Article 4 of the Charter was, however, in favor of membership open to such states as satisfied certain requirements.[127]

This was implicitly to criticize the United Nations for having put aside 'certain requirements' in a preoccupation with universality of membership. Not all writers stopped at implicit criticism. Jacob Robinson, perhaps influenced by the experience of his native Lithuania, the unlawful annexation of which did not prevent the Soviet Union from having a privileged place at the UN, said that the package deal effectively jettisoned the juridical criteria for admission. 'The admission on an exchange basis of two groups of candidates,' Robinson wrote, 'was carried out without regard to the individual eligibility of each candidate, with the implication that Article 4 was "dead"'.[128] The result was to '[do] away with all elements of Article 4, par. 1.'[129] Eugene Cotran, though referring to a liberal admission practice as 'only reasonable and practical,' apparently agreed that the developments of the mid-to-late 1950s amounted to a side-lining of the Article 4(1) criteria (and, he said, in the case of the seating of the United Arab Republic

---

[126] Treaty-making at the initiative of the General Assembly for example has come to involve intensive participation by non-governmental organizations. Consider the role of NGOs in the Working Group under the Ad Hoc Committee responsible for drafting the United Nations Convention on the Rights of Persons with Disabilities: http://www.un.org/esa/socdev/enable/rights/ahcwg.htm

[127] Gross 'Progress Towards Universality of Membership in the United Nations' (1956) 50 *AJ* 791, 800.

[128] Robinson 'Metamorphosis of the United Nations' (1958) 94 *Hag Rec* 497, 500.

[129] Ibid. 500–1.

without formal decision by the Security Council or General Assembly, even the Article 4(2) procedural mechanisms were left out of the game).[130] Amerasinghe, too, is clear that the package deal was not 'proper' under the Charter, in light of the interpretation of Article 4(1) developed by the Court in the *Admission* Advisory Opinion.[131] Universality was arguably a valid objective of policy; but its attainment entailed the undermining of a basic Charter provision.

It is to be recalled here that some ambiguity exists as to what 'universality,' if carried to its rational conclusion, would mean. Schermers says that '[u]niversality...excludes the possibility of imposing conditions for admission to membership';[132] but also that '[t]he existing universal organizations all have conditions for admitting new Members'![133] It could be that the former statement refers to the logic of the term 'universality' as a general principle of law, and that the latter statement is meant to draw attention to a contradiction between the principle and the constitutive instruments of existing international organizations. If one accepts this reconciliation of the two statements, then they might be seen as calling for amendment of constitutive instruments: the conditions of admission would have to be removed, if the organizations' constitutions were to achieve consistency with their universal aspirations. An authoritative definition of 'universality,' as noted in Chapter 3 above, has yet to be established.

Writers, then, have adopted positions as to the effect of the admission practice of the 1950s. Their analyses carry a certain weight, as a subsidiary guide to the law, but they also underscore a situation which speaks for itself: a large number of States were admitted, seemingly against a Charter system that had been designed to foster substantive evaluation of each application for admission.

The above considerations allow an observation about the effect that the early practice had on the Charter. The practice of the United Nations in the first decade and a half of the Charter did not result merely in an interpretation of particular constitutional provisions that might have required fuller exposition to gain practical effect. The practice did not fill lacunae in the Charter; the Charter already contained a system for controlling admission to membership, institutionally complete (even as it required procedural rules to achieve full implementation). No particular provision of the Charter had required universal membership; yet universal membership was the result. What the Charter did require was an evaluation of each applicant, and a judgment that it fulfilled the substantive criteria of Article 4(1). To decline to evaluate each applicant would

---

[130] Cotran 'Some Legal Aspects of the Formation of the United Arab Republic and the United Arab States' (1959) 8 *ICLQ* 346, 364–5.
[131] Amerasinghe 108.
[132] *International Institutional Law* § 30 p. 22.
[133] Ibid. § 120 p. 81.

have been *contra legem*. The practice of the time therefore indicated a tendency to amend the constitutive instrument.

Some States rejected the abandonment of admission criteria. If it is accepted that practice, in order to amend the constitutive instrument, must not only be consistent, but free from dissent, then it is questionable whether the package deal and its associated practice led to amendment of the Charter. Yet the practice and its results remain. The conclusion is unsatisfactory, that so many States became members of the United Nations by decisions of the Organization that were violations of its constitutional law.

4.2.3   *Entrenchment of Article 4(1) Practice*

From the considerations above, it is difficult to take a categorical view on the legal consequences for the Charter of what here has been called an eclipse of the substantive criteria of Article 4(1). Practice concerning admission of new members, by the period after the package deal, had had at least an interpretative effect on the Charter. The indications from State practice point to the emergence of a presumption of admission, and, it is submitted, this had not been part of the original Charter scheme. The developments of the 1950s and after would be hard to characterize as not having had at least some effect on the adopted terms of the constitutive instrument. It even may be that the practice, by leading to a more total negation of the criteria of Article 4(1), amended the Charter. If that is the position taken, then a further question is presented. If practice has effected an amendment, then what measures would it take to effect a reversion to the earlier position under the Charter? It is a question with practical significance, for situations well may arise in which it is desired to deny or forestall admission of applicants for membership. It would be unacceptable to reject *prima facie* valid applications without reference to a legal standard. It therefore would be practically significant, if a way were found to revert to the earlier, more restrictive position.

The search for a way back to the earlier, more restrictive position requires that we consider the extent to which Article 4(1) practice has entrenched a more liberal position; and it requires that we consider the mechanisms that might be available to reverse such a development. The scenario here to be examined is that in which an amendment was effected by practice, not by the formal procedure set down in the constitutive instrument which, if it had been carried out, would have changed the Charter text. The two paths to amendment, it may be observed at the start, leave two different outward marks. Formal amendment results in the constitutive instrument containing different words than it did before amendment; amendment through practice, while producing a result as if they had been replaced with different words, leaves the words the same. That there is a puzzle starts to be suggested in this light: to speak of reverting to the constitutive instrument as it had been before a change wrought by practice is to speak of going back to language which itself has not been changed. The situation of reversion here posited, then, is in reference to a constant text. The instrument was amended, but by an agreement established through practice, not by putting pen to the letter of the instrument. The details of how such a reversion would work are comparatively uncharted.

An acceptable position, perhaps, is to say that to go from a plain text to a contrary meaning established through practice preserves an option in the future to go back to the text. This would be symmetric with the position in a situation of formal amendment, for, from a formal change of text, it is certainly possible for an organization to retrace its steps: a provision formally amended can be formally amended back to how it was. Even if as a general matter reversion is available regardless of how the amendment was secured in the first place, the question remains however as to what modality would effect the reversion of an amendment which resulted from practice. Would it be enough, simply on one occasion, to act in compliance with the original (constant) text? The text after all remains as evidence of the earlier position and thus might lend a certain support to recent practice consistent with the text but contrary to the earlier, amending practice. Perhaps the text even amplifies the effects of practice consistent with it, so that a smaller scope and shorter duration of practice than changed the meaning of the text would suffice to change it back. Or would the same scope and duration of consistent practice as had been required to establish the unwritten agreement to amend the text be needed to effect the reversion? If the position is taken that practice constituted an agreement to remove the substantive criteria of Article 4(1) from the Charter, then these questions would be relevant to any States seeking to revive a more rigorous evaluation of candidates for admission.

Zacklin sees 'informal processes of constitutional change' as having an 'inherent limitation' – namely, their 'impermanence.' Zacklin writes that '[t]he practice of an organization is basically composed of the will of individual members, whether expressed individually, or collectively through organs, and the practice which brings about a particular development may just as easily bring about a reversal of that development.'[134] This however begs the question of the ease with which one may establish that a given practice has accumulated to the point that it results in legal change. It may not be easy at all. Practice presents difficult questions of degree. How many States must take a position; how definitely must they express the position; for how long and how consistently must they take the position – these are relevant questions. The Permanent Court suggested in *European Commission of the Danube* that a single Romanian statement had

---

[134] Zacklin 197.

an interpretative effect on the instrument there under consideration.[135] The crystallization of an international law rule concerning satellites in earth orbit is sometimes identified as evidence that a single incident may create customary international law.[136] There is also the oft-cited statement of the ICJ in the *North Sea Continental Shelf* cases, in which it was said that 'the passage of only a short period of time is not necessarily, or of itself, a bar to the formation of a new rule of customary international law.'[137] The question in many cases however will be asked whether more than a single incident or brief episode is needed. It is relevant to ask whether the position in question has met with dissent; and, if it has, then so too is it relevant to ask how many States have dissented; how consistently; and for how long. The problems can be particularly acute, when practice is being considered as a motive force behind legal evolution in an organization created at the start by treaty. If practice is excluded altogether, or admitted only in cases of unanimity, then the organization may be unable to adapt to changes in the social environment. However if no standard exists to judge when practice exercises an evolutionary effect on the organization, an equally serious problem arises: the legal relations embodied in the organization may become unintelligible.

In ratifying the 1986 Vienna Convention,[138] Bulgaria declared that it

> considers that the practice of an individual International Organization may be considered as established according to article 2, paragraph 1, sub-paragraph j, *only* when it has been adopted as such by *all* Member States of this Organization.[139]

This is the only reservation recorded to Article 2(1)(j) of the 1986 Convention and, though Germany objected to a Bulgarian reservation with respect to another article of the convention, no objection was lodged against Bulgaria's Article 2(1)(j) reservation by any State. More than one interpretation plausibly may be placed on this practice. It could be that States assume that only a practice participated in or accepted unanimously will establish change in the constitution of an organization, and therefore they view the Bulgarian reservation, superfluous, as requiring neither to be objected to nor joined. It could be that a range of opinion exists among States; and no State participant in the 1986 Convention judged

---

[135] *Jurisdiction of the European Commission of the Danube between Galatz and Braila* Advisory Opinion of 8 Dec 1927, 1927 PCIJ Ser B No. 14 p. 58.

[136] On 'instant' customary international law, see Byers *Custom, Power and the Power of Rules: International relations and customary international law* (1999) 160–1 and works cited ibid. 161 nn. 65, 69. See also Cheng *Studies in International Space Law* (1997) 125–49.

[137] *North Sea Continental Shelf (Federal Republic of Germany/Denmark; Federal Republic of Germany/Netherlands)* ICJ Rep 1969 pp. 3, 43 ¶ 74.

[138] A/CONF.129/15.

[139] Emphasis added. Art. 2(1)(j) it will be recalled includes in the definition of 'rules of the organization' the 'established practice of the organization.'

the reservation to be contrary to the purposes of the convention or objectionable for setting up a special position as between itself and Bulgaria.

But this is to look at the international organization as a network of bilateral relations within a multilateral treaty. The constitutive instrument of an international organization, as suggested above, even if one avoids the more categorical theories of the constitutional character of constitutive instruments, must be admitted to have general effects in public international law. That is to say, at least some of the consequences of the instrument are *erga omnes*. General effects are not to be attributed to the instrument as a matter of presumption, nor are effects relative to particular third parties. The Permanent Court was clear on this, when it considered the legal character of the Gex zone.[140] Third States sometimes will avoid the obligation to respect privileges and immunities of the organization.[141] Yet, at the very least, the constitutive act results in a new international legal person, an entity whose existence certain juridical consequences of which cannot be denied by other international legal persons and against which certain rules can be opposed.[142] Once this much is admitted, the observer may tend to view the organization as having organic characteristics, whatever the treaty characteristics (and these are likely to be significant) it retains. An entity so viewed, as Rosenne would seem to posit, very much has the potential for evolutionary change, even as against some degree of protest or non-participation. If the organization can have legal effects on States and other juridical persons existing outside its constitution, then it would seem capable of having at least equal effects *a fortiori* on those within. The *pacta tertiis* principle certainly applies as between the organization and its members on the one hand and third States on the other; yet the principle does not shield third States from all legal effects arising from the existence of the organization. If the principle thus can be seen as qualified with respect to non-members, then it would be all the more qualified, if it operates at all, as against members dissenting against a new position adopted by majority vote or other process agreed under the constitutive instrument. Such dissenters may not be 'party' to an interpretation or amendment in the sense that they number among those having expressly approved it, but their

---

[140] *Free Zones of Upper Savoy and the District of Gex (France v Switzerland)* 1932 PCIJ Ser A/B No. 46 pp. 146–7.

[141] This was the situation in *Communauté économique des Etats de l'Afrique de l'ouest and others v Bank of Credit and Commerce International* Paris Court of Appeal, judgment of 13 Jan 1993; and *Duhalde v Organización Panamericana de la Salud* Supreme Court of Justice of Argentina, judgement of 31 Aug 1999: cited Gaja First Report A/CN.4/532 p. 11 ¶ 19 n. 56.

[142] Some States and the European Commission take the view that recognition of the international organization is prerequisite to its personality being opposable against a given State. Gaja as Special Rapporteur on responsibility of international organizations refers to this as 'outdated practice': Fifth Report A/CN.4/583, 2 May 2007 p. 5 ¶ 9 n. 7.

prior approval of the relevant decision-making process tempers the application of the general requirement of specific consent. This is the compromise between constitutional development and the autonomy of the member States. An absolute rule of consent is rejected, so as to prevent single members from obstructing development, while members remain free to dissent – by which they may retard the entrenchment of a new position.

To admit that practice may develop the constitution of an organization as against contrary practice in turn is to contemplate gradations of change. Certain instances of practice may meet little or no dissent; others may be subject to a large dissenting minority. Dissent in some instances may persist for a long time; in others it may evaporate over night. The scope of dissent and its duration will calibrate the effect that the practice in question exerts upon the constitutional system. A legal position deriving from a new practice which has the support of only a small majority and is opposed by the rest is less entrenched than a legal position deriving from a long-standing practice enjoying unanimous support. The degree to which practice has entrenched a presumption of universal admission in the constitution of the UN is relevant to a long-term question suggested by the consideration of admission contained in this work: can a more restrictive approach as originally contemplated under the Charter be recovered?

In the time since universality was installed in UN practice, the inclination however has not been to backtrack. Instead, the member States and the Organization have identified as one of their main constitutive projects the completion of the universal vocation of the UN. As will be seen next (Chapter 5), the UN after the logjam would seldom apply more than one, residual criterion of admission – namely, that the applicant, to be admissible, be a State. The actual achievement of universal membership is the subject of Chapter 6.

Chapter 5

Admission after the Package Deal

La notion de l'universalité, êut-elle admise, les cinq conditions de l'article 4 se seraient réduites à une. Il suffirait de justifier de l'existence étatique. On parlerait d'État, sans plus.[1]

5.1 Statehood as the Residual Criterion

The logjam proved to be the last time that a considerable number of contested cases of admission coincided. It proved moreover to be the last breath of the position that Article 4(1) might serve as a substantive control on admission. The Court in the *Admission* Advisory Opinion had been concerned to make clear that States are not to add conditions to admission, for the list set out by the States originally adopting the Charter is complete. In practice States came hardly to apply even the conditions prescribed. After admission of the States comprising the logjam, such controversy as did arise over candidatures for admission concerned mainly the first criterion under Article 4(1), and seldom more than its basic aspect. That is to say, on occasion, doubts were expressed by particular member States as to whether an entity making application for admission in truth constituted a State. It scarcely was asked again whether an applicant for admission was peace-loving; whether it had pledged to fulfil the obligations set out in the Charter; or whether it had the ability or willingness to fulfil them. Objections to an applicant State in effect receded to the narrowest remaining ground under Article 4(1). This well may be seen as the logical result of Belaúnde's more developed argument – the argument that questions of admission should not be decided with reference to the character of a government but, rather, merely with reference to the existence of a candidate State. The few disputes to arise between 1955–6 and the new century concerned mainly

---

[1] Georges Scelle, acting as representative of France, *Admission* advisory proceedings: ICJ Pldgs 1948 p. 71.

this residual criterion. The cases may be treated in two categories: (1) States (or putative States) the territory of which another State claimed as its own; and (2) the so-called divided States.

5.1.1   *Claims to the Territory of a State*

The word 'State' is central in the United Nations Charter, for the Charter opens the Organization to 'States.' The Charter, however, does not define the term. Nor has a definition been formally articulated by any UN resolution or other instrument. Yuen-Li Liang, who served *inter alia* as Director of the UN Codification Division, noted as early as 1951 that a definition of 'State' for purposes of UN membership was a logical necessity.[2] Fifty years later the matter remained unresolved, though not without intervening calls for codification.[3]

Possession of a more or less definite territory frequently is mentioned as a core criterion of statehood.[4] An established State – which for present purposes may be defined as an entity whose statehood is generally accepted – well may continue to exist despite deprivation of territory due to unlawful occupation;[5] and the contours of a State's territory need not be precisely agreed in order for the State to exist as such.[6] However, an entity which has only recently made a claim to independence as a State and which has as yet not won widespread acceptance of the claim or otherwise demonstrated its independent existence may need to make a clearer demonstration that it possesses the effective indicia

---

[2] Liang 'Notes on Legal Questions Concerning the United Nations' (1951) 45 *AJ* 314, 315, 321–6.

[3] See, e.g., Crawford 'Outline of Issues on the Topic of Statehood' Annex 2 to ILC Planning Group: Working Group on the Long-Term Programme of Work, *ILC Ybk* 1996 vol. I(2), reprinted Crawford *Creation* 2nd edn Appendix 4 p. 757.

[4] The source most often cited for a definition of statehood is the Montevideo Convention of 1933 (Convention on the Rights and Duties of States, 26 Dec 1933, 165 LNTS 19); and its element (b) is 'a defined territory.' One should exercise caution however in treating the Convention as authoritative and even in treating its terms as an accurate definition of statehood in international law: Grant 'Defining Statehood: The Montevideo Convention and its Discontents' (1999) 37 *Colum J Trans'l L* 403.

[5] Kuwait in 1990–1 is the main modern example: see, e.g., SC res 661, 6 Aug 1990, ¶ 9, permitting States to assist the 'legitimate Government of Kuwait'; and SC res 662, 9 Aug 1990, calling on States not to recognize the purported annexation of Kuwait by Iraq.

[6] Early questions as to the final definition of the borders of Israel did not prevent consolidation of Israel as a State. The Israel-Jordan Armistice Agreement of 3 Apr 1949 for example treated as provisional its terms relative to the ceasefire lines marking the effective limits of Israeli and Jordanian control: Art. II(2), 42 UNTS 303. The lines differed from those prescribed in GA res 181(II), 29 Nov 1947. Israel was admitted to the United Nations on 11 May 1949 (SC res 69, 4 Mar 1949; GA res 273(III), 11 May 1949), the unsettled frontier having posed no impediment to statehood.

of statehood. Of concern to other States, too, will be whether claims of existing States subsist with respect to the independence-seeking territory, for to treat as a State a territory over which a valid claim subsists well may breach an obligation of non-intervention in internal affairs. A neighbouring State which lays claim to the entire territory of the putative new State thus may present an impediment to the consolidation of statehood. In a number of situations, member States pursued such total claims to the territory of neighbouring entities by seeking to block admission of the entities as member States. Several of these situations involved post-colonial claims over particular territories – though, as will be seen, such claims were not the only considerations adduced by States objecting to admission.

The question of statehood was raised in connection with Mauritania and certain States of the Gulf. In connection with the former, it was argued by Morocco that 'this region of Shengit, called Mauritania, forms, with the rest of Morocco, one single country with clear and precise geographical and historical boundaries.'[7] France, it was said, had disrupted the territorial integrity of Morocco during the period of colonial rule, and it was not for the UN to perpetuate the situation by admitting Mauritania as a member State.[8] Mauritania, in the Moroccan view, was not a State, but, rather, part of Morocco.

With respect to several of the Gulf States, it was argued that these were still under a form of protection by the UK; thus not independent; and thus not States. The deficient criterion in respect of Bahrain, Qatar, and the United Arab Emirates, it was said, then, was that a colonial power as yet had not in truth relinquished control. In the case of Kuwait, however, the main consideration in play, if at times only tacitly, was the claim that Kuwait was in truth part of the territory of Iraq. Adnan Pachachi, as permanent representative for Iraq and appearing on invitation before the Security Council, said that three considerations prevented admission of Kuwait: (1) Kuwait was not a State; (2) Kuwait was 'an integral part of Iraq'; and (3) Kuwait was 'for all practical purposes a British colony.'[9] It will be noted that the second and third points are not so

---

[7] Mr Boucetta (Morocco) SCOR 15th yr 911th mtg 3 Dec 1960 ¶ 194.

[8] Id. ¶¶ 188–211.

[9] Mr Pachachi (Iraq) SCOR 16th yr 984th mtg 30 Nov 1961 p. 5 ¶ 30. See further Iraq's extensive resumé on the question of Kuwaiti independence: ibid. pp. 5–14 ¶¶ 28–69. The Iraqi objections to admission of Kuwait may be compared to those of Morocco to admission of Mauritania, which took place the same year: 'The so-called Republic of Mauritania...is simply a part of Moroccan territory, detached from Morocco by armed force and fraudulently set up as a State in order to serve the sordid aims of colonialism.' Mr Benjelloun (Morocco) SCOR 16th yr 971st mtg 25 Oct 1961 ¶ 238. See also remarks of Mr. Boucetta (also for Morocco), quoted above. It is not surprising that Iraq supported the Moroccan position with respect to Mauritania: 'We regard Mauritania as an integral part of the Kingdom of Morocco. We do not believe that the so-called Islamic Republic of Mauritania meets the first condition

much separate grounds for rejecting admission, as assertions sustaining the first point – itself a legal conclusion which, if it were accepted, indeed would have precluded admission under Article 4(1). The claim that Kuwait had not as yet gained independence from the United Kingdom was actually beside the point, if the wider Iraqi claim were accepted: the removal of the United Kingdom, by Iraq's logic, would not have affirmed Kuwait's independence but, rather, would simply have invited effective 'restoration' of that territory to Iraq.

Rather than picking up all of Iraq's argument, the Soviet Union adhered to the point about relations with the United Kingdom:

> [I]n a situation where there continues in force an agreement between the United Kingdom and the Ruler of Kuwait under which the United Kingdom Government may at any time and under any pretext reintroduce its troops into Kuwait's terri-tory, the status of Kuwait remains essentially unchanged. Kuwait continues in fact to be a vassal, a colony of the United Kingdom.[10]

The Soviets raised the valid (if general) point that an entity which gives up too much effective control without retaining a mechanism to retrieve it well may be sacrificing its statehood. The Soviets however ignored that an extensive array of international relations is perfectly compatible with continued independence. The International Court later acknowledged the breadth of the freedom of a State to enter into military and political agreements with other States.[11] It might be said that a situation such as that which the Soviet Union posited also would raise questions of effective capacity and thus of ability to carry out Charter obligations. The statehood point however would be prior to this, on the terms as expressed.

Mauritania, the United Arab Emirates, Oman, and Kuwait all were in time admitted, and, of these, only Mauritania and Kuwait required more than one attempt. On a second attempt, Kuwait was admitted.[12] Morocco had no vote in the Security Council, but the Soviet Union in 1960 vetoed recommending

---

of membership in the United Nations, and that is, that it is a State.' Mr Kittani (Iraq) SCOR 16th yr 989th mtg 19 Apr 1961 ¶ 52. Guatemala's eventual abstention (see Fig. 1) related to its own claim against Belize. Mauritania's main supporters were newly-independent States in former French colonies in sub-Saharan Africa: see, e.g., remarks of Mr Diop (Senegal) SCOR 16th yr 986th mtg 17 Apr 1961 ¶¶ 29–46.

[10] Mr Zorin (USSR) ibid. ¶ 120.

[11] *Case Concerning Military and Paramilitary Activities in and Against Nicaragua (Nicaragua v United States of America)* Merits, ICJ Rep 1986 pp. 14, 108 ¶ 205.

[12] See Fig 1. Facts adduced by the USSR to support its change of view respecting Kuwaiti independence included (1) withdrawal of UK military personnel; (2) Kuwaiti contributions to inter-Arab development projects; (3) relinquishment by the Anglo-American oil company, Kuwait Oil, of its concession in Kuwait; and (4) recognition of Kuwait as a State by some eighty States: SCOR 18th yr 1034th mtg 7 May 1963 p. 16 ¶¶ 82–5.

admission of Mauritania, apparently in retaliation for western opposition to the Mongolian candidacy.[13] Mauritania was admitted in 1961.[14]

Bangladesh similarly on its first application was rejected, only to be admitted somewhat later. In explaining its veto of the first proposal to recommend admission, China indicated that the armed intervention by India in support of Bangladesh's secession from Pakistan cast doubt on whether the secessionist entity was in truth independent. The Chinese permanent representative also raised concerns about 'the principles of the Charter.'[15] He referred to two in particular. One was that India had failed to implement resolutions of the Security Council and General Assembly calling for pacific settlement of the crisis. This presupposed a degree of Indian control over the situation in Bangladesh and thus might be said to repeat in other terms that Bangladesh was not an independent State. Exceptionally, however, China also referred to the conduct of Bangladesh, not its status, and made reference to general international legal obligations: Bangladesh had threatened to subject Pakistani prisoners of war to criminal trial, which according to China would have been a breach of international law.[16] This then was one of the few later instances in which a State objected to admission of a candidate by pleading the fuller terms of Article 4(1).

Another such instance was a United States veto in 1976 against admission of Viet Nam. An earlier veto (in 1975) had been in response to East Bloc rejection of the application of the Republic of Korea (South Korea). Insofar as the United States had linked the two cases, that veto prompted other States to draw attention to the *Admission* advisory opinion.[17] The 1976 veto is more interesting for present purposes. Setting out grounds for rejecting admission of Viet Nam, the United States referred to the final criterion of Article 4(1) – willingness to fulfil the purposes and principles of the Charter:

> The United States has voted against the application for membership in the United Nations by the Socialist Republic of Viet Nam, not because we doubt that the Socialist Republic of Viet Nam is able to carry out the obligations of the United Nations Charter but rather, because the United States has serious doubts about the willingness of Viet Nam to do so. It is this lack of demonstrated will which leads the United States to conclude that the Socialist Republic of Viet Nam does not meet the standards established by Article 4 of the Charter.[18]

---

[13] SCOR 15th yr 911th mtg 3 Dec 1960 ¶ 246.
[14] SCOR 16th yr 971st mtg 25 Oct 1961 ¶ 228.
[15] Mr Huang Hua (China) SCOR 27th yr 1660th mtg 25 Aug 1972 p. 7 ¶ 73, p. 9 ¶ 82.
[16] Mr Huang Hua (China) SCOR 27th yr 1658th mtg 10 Aug 1972, pp. 7–8 ¶¶ 77–87; SCOR 27th yr 1660th mtg 25 Aug 1972 pp. 7–9 ¶¶ 72–83.
[17] See Chapter 2, p. 41 n. 36, above.
[18] Mr Scranton (USA) SCOR 31st yr 1972nd mtg 15 Nov 1976 pp. 13–4 ¶ 122.

Specific concerns were that the candidate State was delaying the release of remaining U.S. servicemen detained in Viet Nam; failing to permit determination of the fate of U.S. servicemen missing in action; and, generally, violating the human rights of its own citizens.[19] Like the Chinese veto of Bangladesh, the later United States veto of Viet Nam was concerned with the treatment of military personnel at the conclusion of an armed conflict. International humanitarian law thus was entering into considerations set out as part of the admission agenda. The United States went a step further than China, by also invoking expressly an obligation to observe human rights as part of one of the substantive criteria of Article 4(1). It thus was well before the controversy over the States constituting the Human Rights Commission in the early 2000s[20] that the United States objected to a State's UN participation on grounds of a deficient record in human rights.

Yet in both the Chinese objections to admission of Bangladesh and the American objections to admission of Viet Nam, an underlying problem of status remained. Bangladesh had asserted its independence by seceding from Pakistan – arguably, the only instance in the UN era in which a new State was created by a unilateral process as against the earnest opposition and without the express consent of the incumbent State. It was hardly surprising that some States, for a time, doubted its statehood. And in Viet Nam, which up until the Paris Peace Accords of 1973 had been a major military theatre for the United States, the main object of American intervention had been to protect the Republic of Viet Nam (South Viet Nam) as against the (implicit) claim of the Democratic Republic (North Viet Nam). The matter could not plausibly have been put as one of lack of independence in the sense that was expressed with respect to some of the cases noted above, such as the Gulf States maintaining political and military ties to the United Kingdom under treaty. No party doubted that there was at least one independent Viet Nam. The dispute was whether it was the North, the South, or both that were in truth independent. Unification brought an end to the effective existence of a second government in the contested territories, but unification took place by such measures as to arouse further controversy. The objection which led the United States to reject the UN candidature of Viet Nam was that the government in Hanoi did not have authority to represent at international level the territory over which it had secured control after the fall of Saigon on 30 April 1975, a unification carried out by force and in clear

---

[19] Ibid. p. 14 ¶¶ 123–4.

[20] See Task Force on the United Nations *The Imperative for Action, An Update of the Report of the Task Force on American Interests and UN Reform* Gingrich & Mitchell, chairmen (2005) 7. See also Luck 'Prospects for Reform: Principal Organs' in Weiss & Daws eds *Oxford Handbook of the United Nations* (2007) 653, 667; Müller ed *Reforming the United Nations* 38–9; and works cited in Scannella & Splinter (2007) 7 *Hum Rts LR* 41, 42 nn 2 & 3.

violation of the Peace Agreement.[21] Implicit in the objection to the unified Viet Nam's UN admission was that the government had asserted control unlawfully over what in truth was a separate State. The objections to Mauritania and Kuwait were rooted in the claim that those territories belonged to another State and thus in truth were *not* separate States; but in neither of these cases was the claimant able to convert its claim by force into an effective factual situation. North Viet Nam succeeded where the others had failed.

The unified Viet Nam was, in time, admitted as a member State.[22] It was not, of course, the only case where two regimes existed in a territory over which a claim (or claims) subsisted to (re)unify the State. The situation with respect to the other three 'divided States' – Germany, Korea, and China – now may be considered for the particular issues concerning admission they have presented.

5.1.2   *The 'Divided States'*

Claims like Iraq's to Kuwait and Morocco's to Mauritania are distinguishable from another situation in the second half of the 20th century – that of the so-called 'divided States.' In the former situations, there was no general agreement that the claimant and the territory it claimed ever had constituted a single State. By contrast, if 'divided States' are a distinct legal institution at all,[23] their distinctness lies in consensus that there is (or at some point was) a single State in the territory controlled by two competing governments. With respect to Viet Nam, owing to the political and legal confusion which surrounded the winding down of the French colonial administration, there is some doubt whether there had existed a single independent State of Viet Nam before the two separate territorial authorities emerged – for which reason (*inter alia*) Viet Nam merited separate treatment above.[24] Moreover, so far, Viet Nam has been the only instance of a putative 'divided State' in which unification was achieved by force. The cases of Germany, Korea, and China each now will be taken in turn.

---

[21] See in particular ¶¶ 9 and 15: *Keesing's* 1973, 25781A.

[22] See Fig 1. On the controversies over admission of the Germanies, Koreas, Viet Nams, and China, see Crawford *Creation* 2nd edn 181–2 and accompanying notes.

[23] Crawford doubts their unity as a legal category: *Creation* 2nd edn p. 478.

[24] Though the Security Council votes suggested a preponderance of opinion in favour of the Republic of Viet Nam claim: application by South Viet Nam for membership in 1952 was defeated only by the Soviet veto: SCOR 7th yr 603rd mtg 19 Sept 1952 (10–1:0); and in 1952 again attracted a large majority of affirmative votes: SCOR 10th yr 704th mtg 13 Dec 1955 (9–1:1). By contrast, application by North Viet Nam in 1952 was defeated heavily: SCOR 7th yr 603rd mtg 19 Sept 1952 (1–10:0), and a Soviet proposal in 1956 for dual admission failed: GAOR 11th sess Spec Pol Comm 22nd mtg ¶ 52.

(i) *Germany*

Two separate governments were established in Germany following World War II, one governing the American, British, and French zones in the West; the other governing the Soviet zone in the East. Over the ensuing years, the situation of a divided Germany crystallized into two separate States – the Federal Republic of Germany (FRG) and the German Democratic Republic (GDR).[25] The relevant transactions have been studied at length, and they are the subject of significant State practice.[26] The matter which interests us for present purposes is the admission of the two German States to the United Nations.

There was no immediate move to obtain UN membership by the FRG or by the GDR after their establishment in 1949. However, by the 1960s, the matter of representation in international organizations had grown in concern. The GDR in particular sought to consolidate its position, as against claims by the Western Allies and the FRG that the creation of a separate governing authority under USSR auspices in the East was unlawful in view, *inter alia*, of the Quadripartite commitments of 1945 and of subsisting rights and obligations of a pre-1945 unified German State.[27] The Security Council and General Assembly received an application for membership by the GDR in a communication from Bulgaria in 1966.[28]

No action would be taken with respect to the 1966 GDR application. States at the time set out views as to its merits.

Cuba and Czechoslovakia said that the GDR had a record of furthering the principles and purposes of the UN.[29] It was a 'democratic, peace-loving State.'[30] Mongolia said that the GDR was 'a sovereign State which consistently pursues a peace-loving foreign policy fully in accordance with the purposes and principles

---

[25] The position of the FRG as a State appears to have been established not later than 1955 (possibly earlier); the position of the GDR was perhaps slower in solidifying. For the relevant conventional and other practice, as well as citations to the main works, see Crawford *Creation* 2nd edn 454–9.

[26] Ibid.

[27] The main arguments are summarized ibid. 456–7.

[28] SCOR 21st yr supp Jan–March, S/7192; supp July–Sept, S/7508; GAOR 21st sess, Annexes, agenda item 20, A/6283 and A/6443, 28 Feb 1966.

[29] Letter dated 8 March 1966 from the Chargé d'Affairs *ad interim* of Cuba addressed to the President of the Security Council, S/7185 ('...proved by its international record that it is a State which will carry out to the full the obligations it would assume on joining the United Nations...'); Letter dated 17 March 1966 from the Permanent Representative of Czechoslovakia to the President of the Security Council: S/7210 p. 1 ('...absolute devotion...to peaceful foreign policy and its faithfulness toward international obligations').

[30] Letter dated 11 March 1966 from the Permanent Representative of Hungary to the President of the Security Council: S/7195 p. 2.

of the United Nations Charter.'[31] Romania referred to the Article 4(1) criteria almost verbatim.[32] It also was said that the GDR had helped attain 'the extermination of Nazism'[33] and the 'eradication of colonialism.'[34]

A further observation by Czechoslovakia in support of the application was that the GDR already had established relations with 'a whole number of other international organizations.'[35] Poland developed the point somewhat further. According to Poland, the GDR had 'diplomatic, consular and official trade relations' with many States. It was party to 'many' international agreements. And it had established co-operation with 'numerous international organizations of inter-governmental character.'[36] These observations seem to have had the purpose of reinforcing a broader point: the GDR, as its sponsors needed to establish for purposes of admission under Article 4(1), was indeed a State. Evidence of integration in the global system of inter-State relations was equated to statehood, and such evidence certainly pointed toward statehood, where the incidents of integration were such that only a State could be party to them. The problem for the GDR was that a merely partial consolidation of international status would not suffice to attain the main objectives of policy, among which was gaining UN admission. The GDR's status would have to have consolidated to the point where no significant caucus of third States would deny that the GDR was a State – and, in particular, where no permanent member of the Security Council would object to its admission. A measure of progress toward this point could be taken with reference to States' diplomacy, treaty-making, judicial proceedings, and voting decisions relative to the GDR. The GDR and its allies in several statements at the time considered the relevant practice, while simultaneously attempting to build upon it.

Nearly all the East Bloc States adopting positions in support of the GDR application referred to its status as a 'sovereign State.' Czechoslovakia, for example, said that the GDR 'is a free, independent State that enjoys all rights emanating from the sovereign equality of States, and whose Government is a legitimate representative of the people of the German Democratic Republic, effectively exercising all the attributes stemming from the sovereign power over its territory.' Hungary also referred to East German democracy; Mongolia to

---

[31] Letter dated 9 March 1966 from the Permanent Representative of Mongolia Addressed to the President of the Security Council: S/7190 p. 1.

[32] S/7199.

[33] Letter dated 8 March 1966 from the Chargé d'Affairs *ad interim* of Cuba addressed to the President of the Security Council: S/7185.

[34] Ukraine: S/7314 p. 1.

[35] Czechoslovakia: S/7210 pp. 2–3.

[36] Letter dated 15 March 1966 from the Permanent Representative of Poland addressed to the President of the Security Council: S/7204 p. 1.

East Germany's democratic transformation. The references to democracy well may be dismissed as posturing, as against the better claims of the western powers. They nevertheless may be noteworthy, not relative to the character of the East German government but relative to the development of at least minimum standards of municipal government as part of international law.[37]

At the same time, the larger concern was to establish that the GDR, on whatever governmental basis, had consolidated itself as an independent State. The Soviet Union said the following:

> The existence of two German States is an irrefutable fact and it certainly needs no sanctioning by any outside elements. Regardless of the differences between their social and economic systems and their foreign policies, each of these States is a subject of international law and a legal successor of the Germany that was.[38]

To identify both German States as legal successors was to reject assertions of continuity between the Federal Republic and the old unified German State. It also was to say, in close connection with this point, that East Germany was not the result of an act of unilateral secession from Germany but, instead, the product of a process of separate consolidation similar to that creating West Germany. It followed from the Soviet position that 'arguments about the alleged right of the Federal Republic of Germany to represent the population not only of the Federal Republic itself but also of the German Democratic Republic' were 'groundless and absurd.'[39] The basis for the GDR application for admission to the UN was that 'two independent States have been formed and are developing in the territory of the former Reich.'[40] As much as other arguments were made in support of the GDR application, the central argument was put in terms of the one remaining operative criterion of Article 4(1): the applicant must be a State.

Several States referred to universality as a goal of the United Nations and said that admission of the GDR would be a step toward realizing the goal.[41] The formulations on this point however were not free-standing arguments in favour of GDR admission. They indeed may be seen as question-begging, for the UN was to be the universal organization of States – and the very objection to admission set out by the western States was that the GDR was not a State.

---

[37] Writers since have produced an extensive literature on the emergence of a democratic rule or principle in international law. See e.g. works cited below this Chapter, p. 157 n. 49.

[38] Letter Dated 20 April 1966 from the Acting Permanent Representative of the USSR Addressed to the President of the Security Council: S/7259 p. 2.

[39] S/7259 p. 3.

[40] Ibid.

[41] Mongolia: S/7190 p. 3; Poland: S/7204 p. 2; Note Verbale dated 11 March 1966 from the Permanent Mission of Romania Addressed to the Secretary-General, S/7199; USSR, S/7184 p. 1; Note Verbale dated 20 May 1966 from the Permanent Mission of the Ukrainian Soviet Socialist Republic Addressed to the Secretary-General, S/7314.

Even if it elided the main point in dispute at the time, to articulate universality as a ground for admission was to illustrate the depth to which the concept had taken root in State practice since 1945. As for the GDR's case for admission, the point would be carried (or not) on the strength of other arguments.

The GDR's sponsors also argued that it was in the interest of international peace and security that the GDR be admitted. States supporting the GDR application argued that admission of the GDR, together with admission of the FRG, would stabilize international relations in Central Europe and, thus, promote peace and security generally. The function of the United Nations as principal guarantor of international peace and security, the GDR's sponsors posited, could not be separated from the process of admission to the Organization. According to Czechoslovakia, admission of the GDR would promote 'a normalization of relations in the region of Central Europe.' Dual admission of the two German States would 'bring about more favourable conditions for efforts directed to their co-operation and peaceful reunification.' Only a 'recognition of the situation established in Europe as a result of the defeat of [...] German fascism' could permanently safeguard peace, admission of the GDR to the UN amounting to such recognition.[42] Hungary said that admission of the GDR would be 'a most beneficial step in promoting European peace and lessening tension throughout the world.'[43] Poland said that admission would promote peace in Europe.[44]

The USSR carried the main brief on peace and security considerations (as it did for East German admission generally). According to the Soviet statement at the time,

> The German Democratic Republic occupies an important place in the system of international relations and is a serious factor for peace in Europe. As we know, it was on the European continent that wars broke out, in 1914 and 1939, which spread far beyond the bounds of Europe and brought millions of people of various nations to destruction. Even today, one of the most important requirements of international life is to strengthen European security. Consequently the United Nations cannot fail to be concerned in solving this problem and in averting the possibility of new complications and conflicts.
>
> The present situation, in which certain large countries in Central Europe are not represented in the United Nations, in itself reduces the effectiveness of the Organization.[45]

---

[42] Czechoslovakia: S/7210 pp. 2–3.
[43] Letter dated 11 March 1966 from the Permanent Representative of Hungary to the President of the Security Council, S/7195 p. 2.
[44] Poland: S/7204 p. 1.
[45] Letter Dated 7 March 1966 from the Permanent Representative of the Union of Soviet Socialist Republics addressed to the President of the Security Council: S/7184 p. 1.

As a sort of lesser included case, the USSR said that normalization of inter-German relations also would facilitate eventual re-unification,[46] though Soviet leaders were highly conditional about re-unification as a particular goal; they spoke of re-unification, but only on terms assuring permanent neutralization of the resultant single State. It is noteworthy that the USSR, in this connection, did not speak in terms of legal obligations, but instead with reference to policy imperatives – e.g. 'a serious factor for peace' and 'important requirements of international life.' The USSR position nevertheless drew a connection between admission of an applicant as a member State and the UN's function as guarantor of international peace and security: a ground for admitting an applicant, according to the USSR's representations concerning East Germany, was that it would support the UN in the peace and security function.[47]

Did this practice mean that considerations of peace and security were to be added to the criteria for admission of an applicant to membership? One must recall the distinction here between Article 4(1) criteria *per se* and factors going to the existence of one or another criterion. If the statements of the States supporting the GDR application on considerations of peace and security are to be taken as an expression of *opinio juris*, then the effects of admission on peace and security might count among the factors relevant to the criteria for admission to the UN. Individual and dissenting opinions in the *Admission* case accepted such factors and did not see them raising special problems. In the view of the Court, for such factors to be admissible, they would have to relate to one of the five criteria set out in Article 4(1); requiring a State to satisfy additional criteria would be *ultra vires* according to the Court. Relating diverse factors to the five Charter criteria however is permissible – and it hardly requires intellectual gymnastics to do so. Factors of peace and security relate naturally to one or more of the criteria set out under Article 4(1). It is an obligation under the Charter that a State act to support peace and security (or at least refrain from acting against the same). This plausibly could be connected to the Article 4(1) conditions of admission.

The three western powers argued against admission of the GDR. They said, '[T]he Government of the Federal Republic of Germany is the only Government entitled to speak on behalf of the German people in international affairs. It is, furthermore, the only authority in Germany resulting from free elections.' To this statement, the powers added the following points: (1) The GDR had

---

[46] S/7184 p. 2.
[47] Writers also connected German legal questions to security: see e.g. Zieger 'Deutsche Einheit und Europäische Integration' in Zieger, Meissner & Blumenwitz eds *Deutschland als Ganzes: Rechtliche und Historische Überlegungen: anlasslich des 70. Geburtstages von Herbert Czaja* (1985) 11–26.

been denied recognition by the 'great majority of the world community'; (2) the GDR had not been admitted to any UN specialized agency; and (3) the GDR was ineligible for admission under Article 4, which opens the UN only to States.[48] It is noteworthy that the three powers drew an express connection here to Article 4 only on the matter of statehood. Allusion in their statement to democracy ('the only authority in Germany resulting from free elections') may hold general interest, as a proto-development in the field of 'entitlement to democratic governance.'[49] Its connection, if any, to the criteria for admission is obscure, and the western powers, in their statement against the GDR candidacy, made no express reference to such connection.[50] The tenuousness of the democratic criterion equally may be observed with respect to East Bloc pleadings on behalf of the GDR.

The admission of the two German States was entwined with legal questions, some of definite character – e.g., status of the eastern borders[51] – but others of a faintly metaphysical tinge – e.g., the fate of 'Germany-as-a-Whole.'[52] As the admission of the two German States brought about membership of the last of the 'enemy States,' the question also arose as to the continued effect, if any, of the enemy States provisions of the Charter. Articles 53 and 107, it was said, must from that point forward have ceased to be operative Charter provisions. Implicit in this may be an idea that admission certifies the 'peace-loving' character of a State; and, thus, in the special case of the former Axis States, admission would remove the formal disability which the enemy States provisions had attached to them. The Soviet position was that the Four Powers retained the right to intervene in German affairs.[53]

---

[48] Letter dated 16 March 1966 from the Representatives of France, the United Kingdom, and the United States Addressed to the President of the Security Council: S/7207.

[49] See e.g. Franck 'Legitimacy and the democratic entitlement' in Fox & Roth eds *Democratic Governance and International Law* (2000) 25; Crawford 'Democracy and the body of international law' ibid. 91; Murphy 'Democratic legitimacy and the recognition of States' ibid. 123; Salmon 'Internal Aspects of the Right to Self-Determination: Towards a Democratic Legitimacy Principle?' in Tomuschat ed *Modern Law of Self-Determination* (1993) 253; Thornberry 'The Democratic or Internal Aspect of Self-Determination with Some Remarks on Federalism' ibid. 101.

[50] The three-power statement referred also to the 'principle of self-determination,' in violation of which a State may not be created. It could be that the reference to democracy, obliquely, related to statehood through this connection: lacking democratic institutions, the GDR could not, perhaps, have carried out the self-determination act necessary to establish its statehood.

[51] See Gelberg 'The Warsaw Treaty of 1970 and the Western Boundary of Poland' (1982) 76 *AJ* 119, 126–8.

[52] See Crawford *Creation* 2nd edn 458–9.

[53] Kewenig 'Sonderprobleme einer Deutschen Mitgliedschaft in den Vereinten Nationen' in Scheuner & Lindemann eds *Die Vereinten Nationen und die Mitarbeit der Bundesrepublik Deutschland* (1973) 307, 316–7.

The resolution of these questions was not facilitated by the extreme political forces in play along the Cold War's most sensitive frontier, nor did the questions disappear in 1973 upon dual UN admission. The decision to admit both the Federal Republic of Germany and the German Democratic Republic to membership nevertheless brought a degree of clarity to the matter of the status of the two entities. Up to the 1970s, the legal personality of the German States and its practical consequences were disputed at diplomatic level and sometimes in national courts.[54] Upon admission of the FRG and GDR to the UN, doubts lingered as to the theoretical basis for two separate German States and, especially, their relation both to vestiges of the past, unified German State and to whatever future unified State might emerge. Contemporaries saw themselves justified in setting aside the doubts however, in view of the risks which excluding the Germanies entailed. The member States reached a decision that the UN system had to include States which lay at the centre of the economics and politics of Europe – and which hosted the largest concentration of opposing military forces on earth.

The admission of the two German States as member States of the United Nations was treated, to an extent unusual in the practice, as implicating international peace and security.

A tempering of political positions in the early 1970s made possible the conclusion of a number of inter-German agreements and agreements respecting the eastern border of Germany,[55] which, in turn, established the basis for dual admission of the German States. The two States made applications contemporaneously. According to the Minister of Foreign Affairs of the German Democratic Republic

> The German Democratic Republic is aware of the fact that the United Nations emerged in the wake of the sacrificial struggle of the peoples of the anti-Hitler coalition against German fascism and its allies in the Second World War. The foremost aim, as proclaimed in its Charter, is to prevent new aggression and to save mankind from the scourge of war.[56]

The statement holds some interest, in view of the position taken by the GDR that it was not to be held accountable for crimes committed by Germany during World War II. The position, though having legal corollaries in the field of international responsibility, seems to have been chiefly political. The GDR statement issued

---

[54] *Carl Zeiss Stiftung v Rayner & Keeler Ltd* [1967] AC 853; 43 ILR 23.

[55] About which see Gelberg (1982) 76 *AJ* 119. See also Delbrück (and works reviewed) (1990) 84 *AJ* 817.

[56] Letters dated 12 June 1973 from the Minister for Foreign Affairs of the German Democratic Republic to the Secretary-General and from the Chairman of the Council of Ministers of the German Democratic Republic to the Secretary-General: A/9069.

in connection with the UN application perhaps could be taken as moderating the position that East Germany's social restructuring had expunged a history with which West Germany was required still to come to terms. Recitations about World War II however were commonplace in East Bloc State documents. One should be cautious about attributing special significance to any given instance of such practice. The Federal Republic of Germany, for its part, communicated its application in a *pro forma* text.[57] The German States were admitted as member States of the United Nations on 18 September 1973.[58]

Soviet proposals in the 1950s to admit North and South Korea and North and South Viet Nam in single resolutions, as noted above, had been rejected. The dual admission of the German States suggests that a change in attitude had occurred with regard to dual admission as a procedural mechanism. Rosenne suggests that the package deal of 1955–6 'facilitated' dual admission.[59] As a matter of procedural precedent, this may be correct, though dual admission in the German case was perhaps specially related to concern over peace and security. Insofar as dual admission in the German case was accepted for reasons of peace and security, dual admission may be seen as vindicating Judge Alvarez's individual opinion in the *Admission* case.[60]

The heightened concern over the systemic implications of admission also may be taken as an example of the larger concern over the international relations of Germany. It was understood, within Germany and without, that the fate of the State that had been the principal aggressor in World War II merited consideration on special terms. The treaty arrangements that later would effectuate unification of Germany in 1990 again illustrated the sensitivity of questions of status, including, especially, of the eastern frontiers; it is an unusual formula

---

[57] Letter dated 13 June 1973 from the Minister of Foreign Affairs of the Federal Republic of Germany to the Secretary-General: A/9070. See also Letter dated 13 June 1973 from the Minister of Foreign Affairs of the Federal Republic of Germany to the Secretary-General, setting out the FRG's acceptance of rights and obligations under UN Charter as applicable to Berlin (West): A/9071–S/10950. Keeping with the standard formula for application of treaties of the FRG to the western sectors of Berlin, this excepted matters of security and status; and was in accordance with a specific authorization given by the Allied Kommandantura.

[58] For the FRG application, see Letter dated 13 June 1973 from the Minister for Foreign Affairs of the Federal Republic of Germany to the Secretary-General: A/9070–S/10949. For the GDR application, see Letter dated 12 June 1973 from the Minister for Foreign Affairs of the German Democratic Republic to the Secretary-General; Letter of 12 June 1973 from the Chairman of the Council of Ministers of the German Democratic Republic to the Secretary-General: A/9069–S/10945. The Security Council in SC res 335, 22 June 1973 recommended admission of both States. The General Assembly action granting the FRG and GDR admission was GA res 3050 (XXVIII), 18 Sept 1973.

[59] *Treaties* 229 n. 58.

[60] See Chapter 2, p. 37, above.

by which the Four Powers, even a half century after the defeat of the *Reich*, maintain what Jochen Frowein calls a '*droit de regard*' over the external borders of the German State.[61] The 1990 treaty arrangements were revisiting questions considered in the early 1970s in connection with UN admission.

(ii) *Korea*

The World War II Allies, by the Cairo Declaration of 1 December 1943, agreed *inter alia* that the Japanese protectorate over Korea would be liquidated upon final defeat of the Axis power of the East.[62] An arrangement of convenience provided that Japanese forces north of the 38th parallel would surrender to the USSR and those south of the parallel to the United States. The arrangement however, after the surrender, was used by the USSR to establish a separate, socialist government in the North. The General Assembly by resolution 122 (II) of 14 November 1947 established a Temporary Commission on Korea, and a large majority of Assembly members accepted this as the lawful basis for the government of Korea as a whole. Elections were held under the auspices of the Temporary Commission. The USSR and its local allies prevented polling in the North. The result of the elections were recognized as establishing an all-Korea government of international standing to represent the Korean State.[63] Article 2(a) of the Peace Treaty with Japan also apparently acknowledged the independence of a single Korea.[64] Nevertheless, the USSR sought separate admission to the UN in 1949 for the entity it supported in the North – fashioned the People's Democratic Republic of Korea. USSR draft resolutions to refer North Korea to the Committee on Admissions were rejected by large majorities.[65] The Republic of Korea, when sponsored for admission, was put to a full Security Council vote, but the USSR repeatedly used the veto to block admission.[66]

The USSR proposed in the Special Political Committee in 1957 that North and South Korea be simultaneously admitted as member States. The proposal was rejected, 35 to 1.[67]

Over time, the position of the Soviet-sponsored entity in the North of the peninsula crystallized, and third States conceded its separate politico-legal existence. This, together with a relaxation of attitudes after the collapse of the USSR, paved

---

[61] Frowein 'The Reunification of Germany' (1992) 86 *AJ* 152, 155.

[62] (1944) 38 *AJ Supp* 8.

[63] GA res 195 (III), 12 Dec 1948.

[64] 136 UNTS 45.

[65] SCOR 4th yr 410th mtg 16 Feb 1949 (2–8:1); SCOR 12th yr 790th mtg 9 Sept 1957 (1–9:1).

[66] See Fig 1, below, and accompanying note on the Soviet vetoes.

[67] There were also 35 abstentions: GAOR 11th sess Spec Pol Comm 22nd mtg 30 Jan 1957 ¶ 52.

the way for the admission of both North Korea and the Republic of Korea to the UN in 1991. Following the unusual case of the dual admission of the FRG and GDR, the two Koreas were recommended for admission simultaneously in a single Security Council resolution and granted admission simultaneously in a single General Assembly resolution. It was implied at the time that dual admission would promote peace on the peninsula.[68] This recalled the approach taken earlier with the two German States. There, too, as seen above, it had been said that UN membership performs a peace and security function, which may be a consideration favouring admission in face of certain objections.

(iii) *Conclusion*

At a level of generality, it can be said that, with divided States, there were a variety of subsisting claims that cast doubt on the claim of one or both entities to be admitted to membership. Continuity of the State-as-a-whole was one claim. Unlawfulness of the government in one or the other part of the divided territory was another (though this was closely related to the former, for a source of legal infirmity was said to be the violation of the territorial integrity of a unit that had a right to exist as a whole). Yet admission, after a period of contestation, was granted to both parts of Germany and both parts of Korea. This further suggests the force that had gathered in support of universality: even where questions existed as to statehood, entities were being granted admission to the United Nations. This is not to say that admission of the German States or North and South Korea was wrong on grounds of policy. As noted above, States said in support of admission of the two Germanies that their participation in the UN would have beneficial effects on international relations. Whatever the merits of admitting the divided States viewed with respect to their own interests and to the international relations interests implicated, their admission is significant as part of a larger train of developments under Article 4(1). Apart from the case of China and Taiwan, which continues to exist outside clear categories, the divided States were admitted to membership, and this further entrenched the position that the UN is a universal organization to which any State seeking membership is to be admitted. The erosion of the substantive criteria as a limiting rule was continuing apace.

Issues of statehood have been contentious in respect of two further cases, both unresolved in the early 21st century and both implicating UN processes. Taiwan and Kosovo have salient characteristics that distinguish them from one another, but they share two: they both are subject to controversial claims related to statehood; and they both exist outside the membership of the United Nations. Since the establishment of separate authorities in mainland China and Taiwan in

---

[68] SC res 702, 8 Aug 1991; GA res 46/1, 17 Sept 1991.

1949, difficulties have arisen concerning Chinese representation in international organizations including, especially, in the UN. The China-Taiwan situation merits separate treatment from the divided States – both for its unusual characteristics and for the failure, to date, to find a resolution to the matter, such as by way of voluntary unification or dual admission. Kosovo has never been a UN member State, nor has it (yet) sought to be admitted. However, Kosovo already produced a significant collision of political positions following NATO intervention in 1999, and with the declaration of independence of 17 February 2008[69] questions of statehood came to the fore: the General Assembly's advisory request to the International Court later that year was the first ever to call in direct terms for an opinion as to the lawfulness of the creation of a State.[70] The adoption of the request and its support by two Permanent Members of the Security Council[71] makes clear that a Kosovar application for admission, should such application be made, would face concerted challenge.

Taiwan and Kosovo now will be considered in turn.

5.1.3   *Taiwan*

(i) *Introductory*

The immediate aftermath of the revolutionary change of government in China in 1949 presented an anomalous situation in the UN. Two governments maintained rival claims to be the government of one China, and the government which the revolution had effectively banished to Taiwan retained China's representation in the Organization, including as a permanent member of the Security Council, with the power of veto over critical decisions, including decisions on admission to membership. The situation was (and may still be) assimilable to that of a divided State, for both sides once maintained vigorously that there is only one China, and, even after the political shifts connected with the rise of the Democratic Progressive Party in Taiwan after the mid-1980s (and its more recent decline in fortune), Taiwan itself had yet formally to declare itself an independent State. It will be recalled that the claim to be a State is closely associated with, if not

---

[69] 'Kosovo MPs proclaim independence' 18 Feb 2008: http://news.bbc.co.uk/2/hi/europe/7249034 .stm about which see Schaller 'Die Sezession des Kosovo und der völkerrechtliche Status der internationalen Präsenz (2008) 46 AdV 131.

[70] The General Assembly, by GA res 63/3, 8 Oct 2008 (77–6:74), requested that the ICJ 'render an advisory opinion on the following question: Is the unilateral declaration of independence by the Provisional Institutions of Self-Government of Kosovo in accordance with international law?'

[71] Russia and China voted in favour of GA res 63/3: see GA/10764, 8 Oct 2008, Annex. The 'nay' votes were Albania, Marshall Islands, Federated States of Micronesia, Nauru, Palau, and the United States.

a criterion of, statehood itself.[72] The authorities of China and Taiwan do not doubt that independence would be a significant step, in light of the entrenched positions. The most serious difference well may be the one between China, which maintains that Taiwan's relations to the mainland are simply a matter of municipal law and thus may be addressed by China with force if it wishes, and much of the rest of the international community, which maintains that the division between the two territories has a certain international status, if only for the (limited) purpose of the regulation of the use of force. More will be said below about the international status of what some have characterized as the divided State of China.[73] As with other status disputes, however, the analytically more useful approach may be to describe the actual incidents of the relation as it exists and has changed over time.

Toward that end, first to be considered here are steps taken in the UN with respect to the problem of China's representation.

(ii) *Resolution 2758(XXVI): A Question of Credentials*

The anomaly of the exclusion of representatives of the People's Republic of China from the UN subsisted as long as the balance of member States permitted it. The General Assembly by resolution 2758 (XXVI) of 25 October 1971 ('Restoration of the Lawful Rights of the People's Republic of China in the United Nations') addressed the matter of PRC representation, but the steps there adopted were themselves problematic and must be taken mainly as reflecting a new political balance rather than an acceptable final settlement. By resolution 2758, the Assembly decided

> to restore all its rights to the People's Republic of China and to recognize the representatives of its Government as the only legitimate representatives of China to the United Nations, and to expel forthwith the representatives of Chiang Kai-shek from the place which they unlawfully occupy at the United Nations and in all the organizations related to it.

Resolution 2758 invites a number of observations.

The first concerns the constitutional basis for the resolution. This was a resolution concerning credentials, not membership. The difference is significant, for membership is a matter to be determined under Article 4 and is the threshold to the State's relations with the Organization. An applicant may be admitted, or denied admission; and, if the Security Council and General Assembly act to adopt the former disposition, the State from the date of the General Assembly's

---

[72] A position suggested in the *Restatement (Third)*, § 201 Comment f, noting Taiwan by way of example.

[73] Crawford says it fits a standard description of 'divided State' but that the description is of little analytic value: *Creation* 2nd edn 477.

affirmative decision to admit, is a member State. The determination under Article 4 concerns the State and, when affirmative, establishes rights and obligations on the State. By contrast, decisions concerning credentials relate to the identity of the representatives having authority to appear in the various organs of the UN on behalf of a State. A credentials decision, in the usual course of proceedings by which it is adopted, says nothing about the State, other than to verify (or not) a certain relation between the State and persons presenting themselves as its representatives.

The relevant Charter provision is as follows:

Composition
Article 9
1. The General Assembly shall consist of all the Members of the United Nations.
2. Each Member shall have not more than five representatives in the General Assembly.

The determination of the credentials of States' delegations takes place at the beginning of each General Assembly session. A Credentials Committee is appointed, and it reports under Rule 28 of the Rules of Procedure to confirm the credentials of the delegations appearing for the session. The Committee has nine members, which the General Assembly appoints on motion of the President.[74] The General Assembly, then, dealt with the matter of Taiwan under Article 9 of the Charter, the article on which the credentials procedures of the Organization are based. One might ask exactly how the rather general statement in Article 9 of the Charter has developed into a power of appreciation in the hands of the General Assembly to determine the validity of the claim by a particular government to represent a State, a matter which may involve difficult factual and legal questions. A view which writers have expressed is that the General Assembly 'has continuously availed itself of this competence so… it can now be considered legally established.'[75] This would be a case of practice within the Organization substantiating under-specified provisions of the Charter. The view presents no problem, where the consideration of credentials presents no problem. It may be less satisfactory, where a decision concerning credentials has significant negative consequences.

States in the General Assembly, referring to credentials procedures, attempted to address the question of China representation immediately after the establishment of the People's Republic in 1949. Positions expressed by States with respect to China credentials suggest a degree of doubt over the legal basis of measures

---

[74] See generally Magiera 'Article 9' in Simma ed *Commentary* 2nd edn 247, 252–3.
[75] Ibid. 253, citing Ciobanu 'Credentials of Delegations and Representation of Member States at the United Nations' (1976) 25 *ICLQ* 351, 368.

adopted. India in 1950 proposed a General Assembly resolution to give a seat to the PRC delegation.[76] This was to move the matter from the Credentials Committee to the Assembly, which was to suggest that it was not a matter for disposal under procedural rules but, rather, one to be dealt with by the relevant principal organ.[77] A certain proximity to Charter principles may be inferred: States appear to have doubted that the matter remains simply procedural where the authority of competing, effective governments is at issue.

The USSR in the 1950 session proposed draft resolutions to expel the 'Nationalists' and replace them with representatives from the mainland.[78] The Soviet drafts were rejected. Instead, the General Assembly adopted resolution 490 (V), establishing a special committee 'to consider the question of Chinese representation.'[79] The representatives from Taiwan were seated pending the Special Committee's report.[80] The Special Committee, when it reported, gave no recommendation.[81] GA resolution 800 (VIII) decided 'to postpone for the duration of its eighth regular session in the current year consideration of all proposals to exclude the representatives of the Government of the Republic of China and to seat representatives of the Central People's Government of the People's Republic of China.'[82] States raised objections to the credentials of the representatives of the Republic of China in successive sessions, but the matter was repeatedly deferred by General Assembly resolution. The delegates from Taiwan continued to represent the Republic of China.[83] Certain States, including, India, Yugoslavia, Iran, and Mexico, criticized this procedure, on grounds, variously, that the Credentials Committee exists for the purpose of reaching such decisions, so that to put the matter to the General Committee and the Assembly was 'an illegal process, bad precedent and a violation of the principles of judicial examination upon which

---

[76] GAOR 5th sess 277th plen mtg 19 Sept 1950 ¶ 8.

[77] According to Sir Benegal N Rau (India), 'This is a question which has been engaging the attention of various organs of the United Nations for the last eight or nine months without receiving a final answer, and it is not to be expected that the Credentials Committee would be able to answer it...the General Assembly should deal with the matter at once': GAOR 5th sess 277th plen mtg 19 Sept 1950 ¶¶ 11–12.

[78] A/1369, 19 Sept 1950 (proposing to expel KMT representatives); A/1370, 19 Sept 1950 (proposing to seat PRC representatives). See also A/1365, 1 Sept 1950 ('Question of the Representation of China in the United Nations'); and PRC communications of 26 Aug 1950, 18 Sept 1950, A/1364 and A/1364 add 1.

[79] GA res 490 (V), 19 Sept 1950.

[80] GAOR 5th sess 277th plen mtg 19 Sept 1950 ¶¶ 176–86.

[81] A/1923.

[82] GA res 800 (VIII), 15 Sept 1953.

[83] See *Rep UN* (1945–54) p. 253 ¶ 43 n. 30; ibid. (1954–5) p. 112 ¶¶ 14–6; ibid. (1955–9) p. 9 ¶ 16.

the Credentials Committee was based.'[84] One can detect here a certain change-ability of preference between Assembly and Credentials Committee as locus of decision-making; India, for example, variably had said that both had exclusive competence over the matter.

The contest carried on through the 1950s and 1960s, between the United States and other States supporting continued representation of China by the Taiwan government on the one hand and those supporting the seating of the PRC representatives on the other. Australia, Colombia, Italy, Japan and the United States in 1961 introduced a draft resolution to the General Assembly to characterize the question of representation of China as an 'important question' for purposes of Article 18 and thus requiring a two-thirds majority for a dispositive decision.[85] This measure served to reinforce a weakening position in the General Assembly as against the increasing number of non-aligned States not disposed to support the Taiwan authorities' continued participation in the UN. The General Assembly adopted resolutions in the ensuing sessions to similar effect.[86] States seeking to replace the Taiwan delegates with mainland China delegates brought challenges in the Credentials Committee over the same period, calling for rejection of Republic of China credentials. Such attempts failed through the 1970 session,[87] but the balance of membership was shifting against Taiwan. GA resolution 2758 in 1971, quoted above, ended Taiwan's representation.

(iii) *One China, One Membership*
From 1971, then, Taiwan has had no UN representation. It was suggested at the time resolution 2758 was adopted that the UN should not exclude Taiwan. The United States proposed adding as a supplementary agenda item the topic of 'the representation of China in the United Nations.' The explanatory memorandum which the United States submitted with the proposal stated as follows:

> 1. In dealing with the problem of the representation of China, the United Nations should take cognizance of the existence of both the People's Republic of China and the Republic of China and reflect that incontestable reality in the manner by which it makes provision for China's representation. In so doing the United Nations should not be required to take a position on the respective conflicting claims of the People's Republic of China or the Republic of China pending a peaceful resolution of the matter as called for by the Charter.

---

[84] *Rep UN* (1954–55) p. 112 ¶ 14 (objection by India).
[85] GA res 1668 (XVI), 15 Dec 1961.
[86] GA resns 2025 (XX), 17 Nov 1965; 2159 (XXI), 29 Nov 1966; 2271 (XXII), 28 Nov 1967; 2389 (XXIII), 19 Nov 1968; 2500 (XXIV), 12 Nov 1969; 2642 (XXV), 20 Nov 1970.
[87] First Report of the Credentials Committee, 26 Oct 1970: GAOR 25th sess Annexes agenda item 3 A/8142 ¶¶ 6, 9 (proposed rejection of Republic of China credentials not adopted, 5–2:1).

2. Thus the People's Republic of China should be represented and at the same time provision should be made that the Republic of China is not deprived of its representation. If it is to succeed in its peace-keeping role and in advancing the well-being of mankind, the United Nations should deal with the question of the representation of China in a just and realistic manner.[88]

No new agenda item on China was accepted however, and the UN would adopt no measure to ameliorate the anomaly of unrepresented Taiwan – a territory which through the 1970s and 1980s underwent significant growth as a commercial power – growth which, until the 1990s, arguably made it a more important element in the international economy than the still-emergent China of the day.

It may be noted that, as before and after resolution 2758, there was a net conservation of Chinese representatives in the Organization. The General Assembly in one stroke threw out Taipei representatives, to replace them with representatives from Beijing. The decision concerned credentials – that is to say, it was a decision as to which between two competing governments is the properly credentialed agent to represent a State in the United Nations. The substance of the decision was to recognize the credentials of the government in Beijing to represent China; and to reject those of the government in Taipei. The language adopted, with its reference to 'representatives of Chiang Kai-shek' and its characterization of the presence of delegates from Taiwan in the UN as unlawful may appear to reflect a strong line on the outstanding questions between China and Taiwan, but, in truth, the resolution avoided more than it answered. First, it avoided in language and in effect any implication that the General Assembly was deciding to admit an applicant; there was neither an application nor a Security Council recommendation, both of which are required for the General Assembly to decide to admit an applicant as a member State. Nor was any member State suspended or expelled. That, too, would have required concurring principal organ decisions, as well as a draft proposal under Charter Article 5 or 6. The UN in 1971 instead changed its appreciation of the claims by rival governments to represent China, so representation changed; but continuity of a single State of China was presumed. In a certain, and hardly insignificant, sense, this was to concur with both sides in the dispute, for neither the government in Beijing nor the government in Taipei at the time had so much as suggested that two States now existed in the areas they administered.

Resolution 2758 did not answer, but in fact drew all the more attention to, the question of representation of the inhabitants of China and Taiwan. It certainly

---

[88] Letter dated 17 August 1971 from the Permanent Representative of the United States of America to the United Nations addressed to the Secretary-General: A/8442. The U.S. Permanent Representative at the time was George HW Bush.

had been an anomaly that the authorities having effective control over a territory in which only a small fraction was found of the total number of inhabitants of China and Taiwan had been the authorities carrying out the UN representation of China. But the result after the change of representation was just as anomalous in quality, even if there had been some degree of quantitative correction. The authorities having effective control over the larger number of inhabitants from then forward would represent China, but another group of inhabitants, those in Taiwan, would have effectively no representation in the Organization. That the dispute between the two governments continued, sometimes to the verge of armed hostilities, deprives of much credibility a claim by the People's Republic that the UN interests of 'Taiwan compatriots' were handled post-GA resolution 2758 by the China representatives.

Ostensibly, however, as the General Assembly treated the matter, it presented no question of the territorial scope of the government whose representatives, after resolution 2758, would represent China. In this sense, the General Assembly's action, again, accorded with the position of the Taipei government as much as with that in Beijing. Neither, at the time, gave any indication that the 'government of China' had rights over anything less than the territory of China (the Taipei government even from time to time had suggested that it had more, or at least that that territory, properly defined, included more than others recognized).[89] This underlying concurrence, for many years irreducible, has been a source of difficulty when attempting to characterize the dispute in precise legal terms.

The parties' sometimes-shared espousal of the identity of one China notwithstanding, practice gives evidence that, at least for certain purposes, international law treats China and Taiwan as separate territories. The practice will be considered shortly below. First, a word may be said about how the UN credentials process has treated questions of the scope of territorial jurisdiction.

(iv) *Limiting the Territorial Scope of Credentials*
In general, decisions respecting the credentials of representatives do not specify the territory or population over which the sending government has lawful authority. Verifying credentials has proceeded, in other words, on an unexpressed assumption that no doubt exists as to the geographic limits of the State. The controversy over representation in the UN of Taiwan and China, therefore, tended

---

[89] The Nationalist Party was slow in particular to withdraw the claim that China included Mongolia: Green 'China and Mongolia: Recurring Trends and Prospects for Change' (1986) 26 *Asian Survey* 1337, 1343. On the treaty relations of Russia and China relative to Mongolia (which may be identified as the starting point of the modern separation of Mongolia from China) see Elleman 'Secret Sino-Soviet Negotiations on Outer Mongolia, 1918–1925' (1993–4) 66 *Pacific Affairs* 539. See also Charney & Prescott 'Resolving Cross-Strait Relations between China and Taiwan' (2000) 94 *AJ* 453, 456, 461.

to submerge itself in the agreed terms of the two sides: both the government in Taipei and the government in Beijing concurred (at least until the 1990s or early 21st century) that there is a single territory of China. And the change of credentials in 1971 did not contradict the competing governments' position on territory, for they both said that the territory in question was the territory of the one State of China. This tended to remove from consideration matters of self-determination which otherwise may have been relevant.

Cases have arisen, if rarely, when decisions on the credentials of representatives in the UN have involved disputes as to the scope of the territory of a State. The main example was that of Portugal in relation to its colonies. Portugal had asserted that the overseas territories over which it acted as administering power belonged to the metropolitan territory of Portugal. In other words, Angola, Mozambique, and its other possessions Portugal treated as constitutionally indistinct from Portugal itself, and, moreover, insisted that this position have international consequences. One such consequence would have been that representatives whose credentials the UN approved as representatives of Portugal also would represent in the UN the inhabitants of the colonial territories. The General Assembly was clear to deny that consequence. By resolution 3181 (XXVIII),[90] the General Assembly accepted the credentials of the Portuguese delegation but 'on the clear understanding' that they did not represent the colonies. The attachment of such a condition (or 'understanding') to a credentials resolution was unusual. It shows however that the General Assembly could formulate a credentials resolution on such terms as to deny certain representatives the authority to represent certain territory in the Organization. The General Assembly did not formulate resolution 2758 on such terms.

The salient difference was that the Portuguese colonies were understood by the UN, if not by Portugal at the time, to be separate Non-Self-Governing Territories, and as such they possessed the right to exercise self-determination by establishing themselves as independent States.[91] Somewhat earlier Tanzania had proposed attaching a similar reservation to the acceptance of the credentials of Nigeria

---

[90] GA res 3181 (XXVIII), 17 Dec 1973.

[91] According to the ICJ, '[T]he subsequent development of international law in regard to non-self-governing territories, as enshrined in the Charter of the United Nations, made the principle of self-determination applicable to all of them': *The Legal Consequences for States of the Continued Presence of South Africa in Namibia (South West Africa) notwithstanding Security Council Resolution 276 (1970)* Advisory Opinion ICJ Rep 1971 pp. 16, 31 ¶ 52. *See also Western Sahara* Advisory Opinion ICJ Rep 1975 pp. 12, 32 ¶ 55; *Legal Consequences of the Construction of a Wall in the Occupied Palestinian Territory* Advisory Opinion ICJ Rep. 2004 pp. 136, 171–2 ¶ 88. For other territories by contrast the principle does not necessarily equate to a right to independence: *Reference re Secession of Quebec* [1998] 2 SCR 217 ¶¶ 122, 126, 127–30.

as respected Biafra.[92] The federal government was seeking at the time to restore effective control by force of arms (and other means) to Biafra, a province that had declared independence from Nigeria. Biafra was not a Non-Self-Governing Territory for purposes of Chapter XI of the Charter, and so self-determination, though applicable as a matter of relations within Nigeria, did not give Biafra the right automatically to elect independence. Nor did self-determination apply in that special Charter sense with respect to Taiwan. Taiwan can be distinguished even further, because, unlike Biafra or the independence-seeking colonies in Africa, Taiwan itself had never taken a position to the contrary. Their own insistence that the government in Taipei was the government of China provided the opening for China and was a cause of future complications for Taiwan. An earlier claim of separate status, clearly espoused, would have given rise to its own problems, including what doubtless would have been strenuous objections by the PRC. A benefit that would have accrued from articulating such a claim at an earlier date is that the removal of Taiwan representatives through the credentials procedure would have been considerably more questionable.

The establishment of Taiwan as an independent State, if that were to have occurred on unambiguous terms, would have considerably strengthened Taiwan's position with respect to UN admission. Indeed, it would have made admission a presumption. As suggested earlier in this Chapter, the establishment of universality under the UN Charter reduced the criteria for admission to membership under Article 4(1) to a minimal, residual criterion. Statehood has remained the one requirement of admission. The definition of 'State' however has remained a problem in international law, and to say that States may apply and be admitted as UN members is unambiguous only in the cases where statehood itself is not in doubt. The close cases can be intractable. It would not serve here to re-examine the question of statehood in international law. For present purposes, we may consider instead the particular developments concerning Taiwan's status, with a view to judging the extent to which China and Taiwan are to be treated as distinct territories under international law, and for what purposes. This we may do with reference to the particular incidents of the international relations of the territories concerned. World War II is the usual starting point, though earlier relations, too, may be relevant.

(v) *Status of Taiwan: Early Signs of Consolidation*
A degree of ambiguity exists as to the legal consequences for Taiwan of the agreements associated with the termination of hostilities in the Far East in 1945.[93]

---

[92] Report of the Credentials Committee, 20 Dec 1968: GAOR 23rd sess Annexes agenda item 3 A/7228 ¶ 22.

[93] See Crawford *Creation* 2nd edn 198–200.

Nevertheless publicists have been clear that Taiwan 'had had an international life entirely separate from that of China' before the war.[94] Apart from that rather general description, how exactly to categorize their relation, however, is not clear. That they possessed 'separate international lives' gives rise to the possibility that China and Taiwan, 1945–9, were components of an attempted union which, in the event, failed to consolidate itself.[95] It might be presumed that the failure of a short-lived union would have resulted in a reversion to the earlier separate international status; the separate status of Taiwan, for example, as of 1949, had not been subject very long to the attempt to submerge it through a process of association. Other failed attempts at union – e.g., Senegal and Mali – were not taken to prevent the separate entities from establishing independent statehood. The fact however that the continuing authority in Taiwan was the government that had attempted to effectuate the putative union in 1945 – and, moreover, had not given up its claim to govern the whole – would considerably cloud the issue.[96] That both sides rejected independence as a settlement to the civil war probably restricts the conclusions that can be drawn from a failure of union, even assuming that union had been the arrangement attempted.

Subsequent treaty practice, too, has been considered for guidance as to the international status of the territory in question. The PRC and Indonesia in 1955 entered into a Treaty on Dual Nationality. The treaty established rules under which certain persons of Indonesian origin in China were to elect either Chinese nationality or Indonesian nationality. Individuals who did not elect one or the other were subject to default provisions (Article 5). The default provisions, with reference to criteria of parentage, were to result in the assignment of one or the other nationality. There was no third position. However, it seems that 'a number of people of Indonesian origin at that time would have preferred to become citizens of Taiwan and, rather than become citizens of China, had opted for statelessness.'[97] The situation would suggest that at least the default provisions, if not the treaty as a whole, did not apply in Taiwan. More recent

---

[94] Mr Ramangasoavina ILC 26th sess 1284th mtg 25 June 1974 ¶ 29: discussion on the topic Succession of States in respect of treaties, *ILC Ybk* 1974 vol. I p. 188.

[95] Ibid.

[96] Aside from the visible manifestations of Republic of China power in Taiwan – it was RoC forces which oversaw the armistice there with Japan – the Republic declared the integration of Taiwan with China for treaty purposes. According to the Republic of China, from 25 October 1945, 'the date on which Taiwan was restored to the Republic of China,' the Berne Convention of 1886 (to which Japan had become a party during the time it was responsible for Taiwan) 'ceased to be effective' on the island: *Le Droit d'Auteur* 1961 pp. 27–8; ibid. 1932 p. 40.

[97] Mr Kusuma-Atmadja ILC 47th sess 2390th mtg 26 May 1995 ¶ 45: discussion on the topic State succession and its impact on the nationality of natural and legal persons, *ILC Ybk* 1995 Vol. I p. 73.

practice, some of which will be noted shortly, confirms that Taiwan is a separate territory for purposes of treaties.

During the controversy in the 1950s over seizure of foreign vessels on the high seas by Republic of China naval forces, statements were recorded in the International Law Commission reflecting the protests of certain States. Observations of the Government of Poland included the statement that '[f]oreign men-of-war assisted by airplanes forced to stop Polish ships maintaining peaceful commercial communication with the Chinese People's Republic.'[98] A brief remark about the Polish statement is in order. The word 'foreign' logically in this context would mean of a flag other than Poland's or the PRC's. It also implies a State, as one refers to a vessel, person etc as 'foreign' when it has the nationality of a State other than one's own or of the parties to a particular treaty relation (though 'third State' would have been the more natural form of words). The State character of the Republic of China on Taiwan further was apparently assumed in the reference to the offending vessels as 'warships'[99] and 'men-of-war.' The Polish government could have made qualifying statements to the effect that this protest in no way acknowledged Taiwan to have a status separate from China; it also could have referred to the offending vessels in terms which avoided denoting that these were vessels of the armed forces of a State. Instead, Poland used the language here noted. Early signs of acceptance, if tacit, can be seen in this that the two sides of the civil war in China were settling in their respective territorial spheres and giving rise to separate international legal persons, at least for certain purposes.

If what one seeks however is evidence of the consolidation of Taiwan as a separate State, the practice was at best equivocal. The statements of States and international organizations that Taiwan is not a separate State by contrast have been clear. A particular problem which has arisen as a result is that organizations, membership in which is taken to imply statehood, have denied Taiwan access to membership or other forms of participation. This has included organizations with an essentially technical mission, as well as the UN and other political organizations. Some questions relating to participation arising after the credentials decision in General Assembly resolution 2758 now briefly may be considered.

(vi) *Original Membership: a Basis for Special Rights?*
The exclusion of Taiwan from the UN system raises questions about the consequences of original membership. An examination of the practice might suggest

---

[98] *ILC Ybk* 1955 Vol. II p. 1 ¶ 9: Observations of the Government of Poland concerning freedom of navigation on the high seas, transmitted by Mr Jan Balicki.

[99] Ibid. ¶ 12 p. 2: 'Polish merchant ships were stopped by warships and brought to the island of Taiwan.'

that a presumption attaches to the membership of the Original Members of the UN, in addition to the usual presumption of continuity. The main case in point is the re-appearance of Syria in the General Assembly on 13 October 1961 after several years of 'submergence' in the United Arab Republic. This however the UN effectuated without clearly articulating a legal basis.[100] The case was little followed, in precise detail probably not at all. When the United States withdrew from the International Labour Organization and later sought to return; and when the United Kingdom and Germany did the same in respect of UNESCO, these States, though original members of the organs in question, had to apply anew.[101] Moreover, Syria and Egypt were both, separately, Original Members under Charter Article 3, and no objection was raised to the settlement adopted. Any relevance to China and Taiwan is extremely qualified.[102]

One situation in which original membership may have mattered was that of Taiwan's participation in the Asian Development Bank (ADB). The Republic of China had been an original member of the ADB. There was no question of its expulsion, withdrawal or suspension. However, with little articulated reason, it has continued as a member following accession of the PRC in 1986. These transactions merit a brief word.

The ADB was established in Manila in 1965 by treaty among its original members.[103] The Republic of China (Taiwan) was an original member. A Memorandum of Understanding between the ADB and PRC established the admission of the PRC.[104] Taiwan, however, continued as a member (though under a modified name). Article 3, paragraph 1 of the Agreement Establishing the Asian Development Bank provides that membership in the Bank

> shall be open to: (i) members and associate members of the United Nations Economic Commission for Asia and the Far East; and (ii) other regional countries and non-regional developed countries which are members of the United Nations or any of its specialized agencies.

Paragraph 3 makes provision for 'associate' membership of entities 'not responsible for the conduct of their international relations.' The associate membership of such an entity is established upon application presented by the Member

---

[100] About which see Young 'The State of Syria: New or Old?' (1962) 56 *AJ* 484.

[101] Amerasinghe 105–6.

[102] It has been said that a recommendation by the Security Council to the General Assembly to admit an applicant also apparently can survive certain shifts in the underlying situation – e.g., dissolution of a federation, between the time the Security Council recommends admission and the General Assembly admits: Young (1962) 56 *AJ* 484, 485–6 n. 11. Practice however suggests otherwise, i.e. that admission requires separate Security Council recommendation for both applicants. See Chapter 1, pp. 19–20, above.

[103] Signed 4 Dec 1965, entered into force 22 Aug 1966: 571 UNTS 124.

[104] Quoted Crawford *Creation* 2nd edn 203–4.

responsible for its international relations; and by the application, that Member undertakes to be 'responsible for all obligations that may be incurred by the applicant by reason of admission to membership in the Bank.'[105] Taiwan made no application for membership under paragraph 1; nor did any Member State apply on its behalf under paragraph 3. Taiwan was already a Member. Nor was any step taken to transform Taiwan to associate member status. The Agreement in any case contains no provision whereby a Member could be so transformed. The question, then, is to explain Taiwan's continued participation in the ADB following admission of China.

One possibility is that original membership entails special rights. This would find support in the treatment of Syria in the UN after its 're-emergence' from the United Arab Republic. But the cases running the other way (ILO, UNESCO, etc.) tend to weaken that practice as a source of interpretation of other constitutive instruments. To be sure, the original members in the contrary cases had ceased to participate in the organizations in question, so they are perhaps less instructive for the case of Taiwan whose participation in the ADB has been continuous.

Another possibility is that the member States reached a special accommodation under the ADB Agreement, the Agreement in effect having been interpreted with the consent of the members and by their (unobjected) practice. The depository information maintained by the UN for the ADB Agreement includes the following note:

> The Republic of China signed and ratified the Agreement on 4 December 1965 and 22 September 1966, respectively. Upon the admission of the People's Republic of China on 10 March 1986, the Republic of China, representing the Island of Taiwan, was re-designated as "Taipei, China" and continues its membership under that designation.

The expression 'Taipei, China' however is not included on the list of parties maintained by the depository. (Nor is it included in the sublist of associate members). The note here quoted on the Republic of China and the People's Republic of China perhaps is not to be attributed legal consequences, but it is interesting to observe that the participation of the PRC in the Bank is described as having been established by way of 'admission'; and the PRC is listed as a 'member'; and Taiwan 'continues its membership.' To suggest continuity between the Republic of China and 'Taipei, China' is to suggest that there has been no formal relegation of Taiwan to associate status or to some provisional, reduced membership. Membership, as far as one can tell, comes only in those degrees specified in the Agreement. Both Taiwan and the PRC are members; but only one China is included on the membership list.

---

[105] 571 UNTS at 137.

One of the few conclusions that can be confidently reached in respect of this practice is that the establishment of PRC representation was not by way of a credentialing process. It was instead a matter of admitting a State as a new Member. Inclusion of the PRC thus did not involve displacement of Taiwan. But that brings the matter back to its main area of ambiguity. All the while, from the loss by Taiwan in the early 1970s of its representation in the UN system, until the admission of China as a member of the ADB in 1986, the original Chinese member continued as a member. The constitutional requirement of UN membership under the ADB Agreement did not preclude Taiwan from continued ADB membership. Perhaps membership in the ADB once established does not lapse for reason of later loss of qualifying characteristics. The constitutive instrument does not say anything about the effect of later loss of UN membership.

Or it could be that the relevant consideration is that 'China' was all along a UN member. Both the Taipei and Beijing authorities would agree, after all, that China has, since 1945, at all times been a UN member. And, as noted earlier, the change of representation in 1971 did not effect the expulsion of any UN member State. The admission of China in 1986, then, perhaps could be interpreted as the ADB conferring a second membership on one State. The expedient adopted to palliate the Soviet Union in 1945 might be precedent, for, at that time, nobody thought that Ukraine, Belorussia, and the USSR were three States. It was agreed that there was only one. It was by special arrangement that there were three Soviet UN memberships. The ADB Agreement does not in so many words prohibit one State from holding two Memberships. It could be that acceptance of concurrent memberships by China and Taiwan is the result of an informal process of interpretation of the ADB Agreement, by which such an arrangement of dual membership has now been established. The ADB, on the plain terms of its constitutive instrument, is not open to entities which are neither participants in the UN system nor vouched for by a member State. Unless the view is taken that the matter of dual participation is purely an *ad hoc* response without regard to the constitutive instrument, the simultaneous China and Taiwan memberships can only be explained by one or another legal construction.

(vii) *Taiwan's Applications for Admission*
By contrast, in the UN itself no such legal construction has been accepted to allow Taiwan representation – much less a direct approach admitting Taiwan as a member State. UN member States which still recognize Taiwan as the Republic of China have made requests for the inclusion of a Taiwan/Republic of China agenda item in sessions of the General Assembly since 1992. The requests in all instances have been rejected. Explanatory memoranda submitted in connection with the requests set out grounds for establishing Taiwan/Republic of China representation in the UN. In 1998, for example, the member States promoting

the agenda item said that '[p]arallel representation in the United Nations by the two sides of a divided nation poses no barrier to unification; indeed, it can be conducive not only to unification but also to regional security and world peace.'[106] The Soviet bloc States had made a similar argument with respect to peace and security when they had advocated admission of East Germany. Taiwan's advocates noted the German and Korean cases as precedent.[107]

In advance of the sixty-second General Assembly session in 2007, member States which recognize Taiwan as the Republic of China again proposed that Taiwan be admitted as a member State. The General Committee recommended that the General Assembly not include Taiwan membership on the agenda for the session.[108] Secretary-General Ban Ki-moon referred to the proposed item as 'unreceivable,' so it was not included as part either of the General Assembly or Security Council agenda. The Secretary-General referred to GA resolution 2758 (XXVI).[109] Saint Vincent and the Grenadines referred to the exclusion of the Taiwan item as 'a direct attack on the Charter.' Palau said that the Secretary-General had intruded on matters of legal interpretation. It was further proposed (and the proposal not taken up) to 'urg[e] the Security Council to process Taiwan's membership application pursuant to rules 59 and 60 of the provisional rules of procedure of the Security Council and Article 4 of the Charter.'[110]

The question might be presented whether it falls within the authority of the Secretary-General to reject an application for admission as 'unreceivable.' To vest interpretation of the Rules of Procedure in the UN officers who manage the organs in which the rules are executed could be taken as a manifestation of the maxim *ejus est interpretari legum cujus est condere*: those who make the rules are the ones best positioned to interpret them. Yet a problem is presented of accountability, indeed of rule of law under the internal law of the Organization, if such a maxim is applied without a mechanism of review. Michael Wood, speak-

---

[106] Letter dated 8 July 1998 from the representatives of Burkina Faso, El Salvador, the Gambia, Grenada, Liberia, Nicaragua, São Tomé and Principe, Saint Vincent and the Grenadines, Senegal, Swaziland and Solomon Islands to the United Nations addressed to the Secretary-General: A/53/145, Annex ¶ 5.

[107] Ibid. The argument about divided States was not repeated however in more recent submissions, e.g., that in 2006: see Letter dated 10 August 2006 from the representatives of Belize, Burkina Faso, El Salvador, the Gambia, Honduras, Malawi, the Marshall Islands, Nauru, Nicaragua, Palau, Saint Kitts and Nevis, Saint Vincent and the Grenadines, São Tomé and Principe, Solomon Islands, Swaziland and Tuvalu to the United Nations addressed to the Secretary-General, with annexed Explanatory memorandum ('Question of the representation and participation of the 23 million people of Taiwan in the United Nations'): A/61/194.

[108] GA/10617, 21 Sept 2007. Compare to the proposed (and, again, rejected) agenda item in 2008, which concerned only participation in the specialized agencies: A/63/250, 17 Sept 2008, ¶ 60. This reflects, perhaps, a more general shift of emphasis from membership to participation.

[109] GA/10617.

[110] Ibid.

ing from experience in the United Nations, has said that the wide scope given to the principal officers of the Organization to interpret the rules is well-established. This would seem particularly to be the case with respect to applications for admission to membership. According to Wood, 'The formal circulation of a membership application may involve the exercise of political discretion on the part of the Secretary-General, and in delicate cases he is likely to consult those most concerned before taking action.'[111] The application of Macedonia for admission to membership had occasioned 'informal consultations' by the President of the Security Council.[112] Apparently in consequence of the (unpublished) results of those consultations, the Macedonian application was delayed.[113] Wood does not say what the basis in the Charter or the Rules of Procedure is for delaying an application on grounds of 'receivability.' There can be little doubt that wide scope is necessary, lest the proceedings of the principal organs be brought to a standstill. The question is to define the limits. The application of Macedonia was delayed significantly; but it was not delayed indefinitely. Other instances in which the Secretariat has exercised its discretion on a matter of admission, e.g. with respect to the United Arab Republic,[114] the result has been to expedite, rather than to delay, participation of the State in UN affairs. It would seem, when a matter important to the constitution of the Organization arises, and a UN officer deals with the matter in more or less summary fashion by way of a unilateral statement unaccompanied by legal reasoning and with the result that the right of a community is arguably infringed, that recourse should be available to some form of review. Admission to membership is certainly an important matter. This seems self-evident in light of the character of an international organization as an entity comprised of member States. The specific assertion that admission is a procedural matter in any case would be inconsistent with the *Competence* Advisory Opinion.

One possibility is that controversial interpretations by an officer of the Organization be put to a vote of the General Assembly. This was done both in the several sessions (1970–4) when the Hambro Formula prevailed (thus preserving South Africa's representation), and after the re-interpretation by General Assembly President Abdelaziz Bouteflika.[115] This is not to say that the result of a General Assembly decision concerning credentials will not attract controversy on its substance. The Hambro Formula itself met with criticism by States, as

---

[111] Wood 'Participation of Former Yugoslav States in the United Nations and in Multilateral Treaties' (1997) 1 *Max Planck Ybk UN Law* 231, 237.

[112] Ibid. 238.

[113] On the Macedonian controversy, see Chapter 6, pp. 203–13, below.

[114] Cotran 'Some Legal Aspects of the Formation of the United Arab Republic and the United Arab States' (1959) 8 *ICLQ* 346, 364–5.

[115] GAOR 29th sess 2281st plen mtg 12 Nov 1974. About which see critical comment by Gross (1983) 77 *AJ* 569.

did its rescinding. If the transaction by which the General Assembly excluded *Apartheid* South Africa raised legal doubts, then, *a fortiori*, the same might be said about the Secretary-General's measure in 2007 finding the application of democratic Taiwan 'unreceivable.'

Outside the UN, the picture is far less categorical. Taiwan, as noted above, is denied access to organizations where access would imply its complete separation from China, but, apparently as a consequence of the original membership of the Republic of China in the ADB, Taiwan continues to participate in that organization. To give a full picture of the situation, one would have to consider relations between Taiwan and the myriad organizations in which it participates. Particular instances have been noted above. Others have been noted and analyzed in depth elsewhere.[116] A problem that has particularly complicated the Taiwan case, also as noted above, is that Taiwan, to date, has not made a clear declaration of independence. Avoiding such a measure continues to be explicable by reference to political and economic considerations. The considerations are significant, and, if anything, they have grown as the economic and political position of China relative to Taiwan, and relative to Taiwan's various formal and informal supporters, has strengthened.

Yet, in the face of these problems, it is hard to deny that a significant consolidation of Taiwan's position has taken place. The obvious loss of diplomatic position is noteworthy. It was once the case that most States recognized Taiwan as the Republic of China, carried on diplomatic relations with the government in Taipei, and declined to deal with the authorities in Beijing. This is no longer the case; only a small handful of very small and mostly very poor States now recognize Taiwan as the Republic of China. Recognition, however, does not create the State; and even less does statehood depend on the extent and intensity of formal diplomatic relations. A more significant consideration than the diminishing roster of States recognizing Taiwan as China is the growing body of parliamentary and other State declarations acknowledging the relevance of international law to the Taiwan-China difference. Relevant examples may be briefly instanced.

(viii) *Status Redux: Erosion and Consolidation*
Taiwan's status as a separate entity has been consolidated by both internal and external developments. The establishment of multiparty democratic elections and institutions of representative government is frequently noted. Adherence to international standards further establishes Taiwan's relations on an international

---

[116] See esp. Serdy 'Bringing Taiwan into the International Fisheries Fold: the legal personality of a fishing entity' (2004) 75 *BY* 183. And respecting the ADB, see Crawford *Creation* 2nd edn 203–4.

plane. For example, international investment disputes involving the Taiwan government are comparatively rare, notwithstanding Taiwan's significant integration into the international economy, including in the role of host to foreign direct investment: Taiwanese municipal practice is generally consistent with fair and equitable treatment and other international standards.[117] The consistency of Taiwan's international policies with UN goals, such as furthering development in economically disadvantaged States, also is noteworthy. An active international aide program is maintained, the Taiwan government reporting considerable outlays in foreign assistance.[118]

States have welcomed the process of Taiwan's consolidation and called for its further development through the inclusion of Taiwan in international organizations. A United States and Taiwan Resolution was adopted in 1994 by the U.S. Senate, in which the Senate observed that 'recognizing separate governments in the former West Germany and the former East Germany' did not prevent re-unification; and gave its sense that 'the President, acting through the United States Permanent Representative to the United Nations, should encourage the United Nations to permit representatives of Taiwan to participate fully in the activities of the United Nations and its specialized agencies.'[119] This was similar to the position of Taiwan's advocates in the UN: dual admission did not get in the way of eventual unification of divided Germany. A 2000 resolution of the U.S. Congress stated that it was the 'sense of Congress that...Taiwan and its 23,000,000 people deserve appropriate meaningful participation in the United Nations and other international organizations.'[120] A House and Senate joint resolution in 2004 authorized the Secretary of State to endorse and obtain observer

---

[117] The Taiwan-Thailand BIT, for example, contains a fair and equitable treatment provision (Art. 4(1)) and provides for arbitral jurisdiction for disputes between investors and host State (Art. 10): Agreement between the Thailand Trade and Economic Office in Taipei and the Taipei Economic and Trade Office in Thailand for the Promotion and Protection of Investments, signed and entered into force 30 Apr 1996. To be sure, as a major capital exporter, Taiwan is at least as likely to be the sending as the receiving country, and so conclusions about Taiwan's legal system drawn from practice under its BITs are to be qualified accordingly. UNCTAD lists the following States as having entered into BITs with Taiwan: Costa Rica, Dominican Republic, El Salvador, Guatemala, India, Macedonia, Malaysia, Nicaragua, Nigeria, Panama, Paraguay, Philippines, Singapore, Thailand, and Viet Nam. Notably, not all of these are States recognizing the Taiwan authorities as the government of China. A survey of recent arbitral awards discloses no practice under these agreements.

[118] See website of Taiwan's International Cooperation and Development Fund: http://www.icdf .org.tw/english/index.asp It will be recalled that the USSR referred to Kuwait's contributions to international development as relevant when considering the fitness of Kuwait for admission: SCOR 18th yr 1034th mtg 7 May 1963 p. 16 ¶¶ 82–5.

[119] Senate res 148, 10 June 1994 ¶ 1.

[120] H Con Res 390, 106th Cong 2nd sess 24 Jan 2000.

status for Taiwan in the World Health Assembly.[121] Taiwan participation in the WHA was also supported by parliamentarians in the Parliamentary Assembly of the Council of Europe[122] and by the European Parliament.[123]

The European Parliament in a resolution adopted in 2006 'calls for a better representation of Taiwan in international organizations and reiterates its call on the [European] Commission and the Member States to support Taiwan's application for observer status in the World Health Organization.'[124] By the same resolution, the European Parliament said that the PRC anti-secession law of 2005 'does not comply with international law.'[125] This was apparently in light of the threat of force contained in the anti-secession law.[126] The resolution said that 'any arrangement between China and Taiwan can only be achieved on a mutually acceptable basis.' The European Parliament also

---

[121] S 2092 § b(1) 108th Cong 2nd sess 20 Jan 2004.

[122] Proposed motion in the Parliamentary Assembly of the Council of Europe by Mr Leibrecht & others, 30 Jan 2007, Doc 11165 ('Making Taiwan a partner in global health by granting Taiwan observer status at the World Health Assembly'). The motion noted that the U.S. Congress, European Parliament, and the Belgian and Canadian national parliaments had adopted supporting resolutions: ibid. ¶ 8.

   States not members of the UN may be admitted to the WHO by a simple majority vote of the WHA: WHO Constitution, Art. 6. Observer status is available to non-governmental organizations: Art. 18(h). Neither Art. 6 nor Art. 18(h) would appear relevant to Taiwan.

   Art. 8 of the WHO Constitution establishes a class of Associate Members. Associate Members apparently need not be States. The class consists in territories 'which are not responsible for the conduct of their international relations' and on behalf of which a Member State or 'other Authority having responsibility for their international relations' has made application. The expression 'other Authority having responsibility...' would seem to have referred originally to States acting under Trusteeship agreements; or to the Trusteeship Council itself. Later, the expression could have included the United Nations Transitional Authority for Namibia. Assuming a certain mutability in such terms, an argument might be made that the Taiwan Government could act as an 'other Authority' and, under Article 8, make application for Taiwan. The matter is wholly speculative in light of the politics of the WHA. Consider the statements of the PRC and other States in the Assembly: PRC WHA 58th sess, 16–26 May 2005, Summary of Records, General Committee, First Mtg, WHA58/2005/Rec/3, p. 5; Cuba WHA 58th sess, 16–26 May 2005, Summary of Records, General Committee, First Mtg, WHA58/2005/Rec/3, p. 6; Mexico, ibid. p. 9; Mauritania, ibid. p. 11. To similar effect see Russian Federation, ibid. p. 7; Indonesia, ibid. p. 9; Tanzania, ibid. p. 10; Belarus, ibid. p. 11; Burundi, ibid. p. 12; Kazakhstan, ibid. p. 13; and Statement by Ambassador Masood Khan, Permanent Representative of Pakistan at the Plenary of the 59th Session of the World Health Assembly on the 'Question of Taiwan,' Geneva, 22 May 2006.

[123] OJ C 047 E, 27 Feb 2003 pp. 606–7.

[124] European Parliament resolution on relations between the EU, China and Taiwan and security in the Far East: OJ 157E, 6 July 2006 pp. 471–3 ¶ 9.

[125] Ibid. ¶ 5.

[126] For which see Anti-Secession Law, Art. VIII: reprinted Xinhua News Agency 14 Mar 2005.

expresses the view that the future of cross-Straits relations will depend on both sides' willingness to demonstrate flexibility; supports Taiwan's achievements as regards the establishment of a fully-fledged democratic system, social pluralism, and respect for human rights and the rule of law, and takes the view that the will and approval of the 23 million people in Taiwan must be respected and taken into account with a view to a hopefully peaceful solution between the parties.[127]

The resolution does not indicate a 'people *of* Taiwan,' but instead people *in* Taiwan – a form of words avoiding a direct statement that the right to self-determination applies with respect to Taiwan in the external aspect of the right. The resolution otherwise would seem to suggest that certain incidents of self-determination are nevertheless relevant. In particular, any settlement of the governmental arrangements in Taiwan and China must be in a framework respecting the 'will and approval' of the people in Taiwan. This is broadly consistent with the requirement under the second principle of the Friendly Relations Declaration that 'States shall settle their international disputes by peaceful means in such a manner that international peace and security and justice are not endangered.'[128] The specification of 'international disputes' and disputes between 'States' casts doubt however on whether that principle is the main legal basis of the European Parliament statement: to say that the Friendly Relations Declaration is the basis would be to say that both sides are States.

The statement that China's anti-secession law is not consistent with international law is particularly significant. It is difficult to reconcile the statement with a categorical position that Taiwan falls under China's domestic jurisdiction and therefore may be disposed of without regard to at least certain minimum international standards. Even if the statement reserves the question of how precisely Taiwan's international status is to be characterized, it takes a clear position as to the legal character of the division between the two territories: it says that the dividing line is an international law line for purposes of the prohibition against use or threat of force. It will be recalled that the first principle in the Friendly Relations Declaration reiterates the prohibition against threat or use of force against the territorial integrity or political independence 'of any State.'[129] The People's Republic of China would say that the phrase 'of any State' excludes Taiwan from the principle as stated. The principle however also prohibits threat or use of force 'in any other manner inconsistent with the purposes of the United Nations.' This element of the prohibition well may cover use of force in a situation such as that between Taiwan and China, in which the economic, political,

---

[127] OJ 157E, 6 July 2006 resolution op. cit., ¶ 4.
[128] GA res 2625 (XXV) ('Declaration on Principles of International Law concerning Friendly Relations and Co-operation among States in accordance with the Charter of the United Nations'), 24 Oct 1970, Annex.
[129] Ibid.

and human costs of armed conflict would be very high and, arguably, would extend beyond the territory and populations immediately in question.[130] Under the first principle, the Declaration further makes clear that the prohibition against threat or use of force is not to be taken as restricted to narrow circumstances but, instead, is to be applied broadly. '[E]xisting international boundaries' are identified as inviolable. So too are 'international lines of demarcation, such as armistice lines, established by or pursuant to an international agreement to which [the State] is a party or which it is otherwise bound to respect.' There is no formal 'international agreement' which clearly and specifically concerns the ceasefire line between the warring parties of the Chinese civil war. Yet it would ignore a long period of largely consistent practice to say that neither side is 'otherwise bound to respect' the status quo as it has come to exist. Writers, too, have taken the position that the dividing line between Taiwan and China has a certain relevance to international law.[131]

The European Union has entered into trade agreements with Taiwan since the latter's accession in the WTO under the title 'Chinese Taipei (Taiwan).'[132] The Council of Europe also has addressed Taiwan's international relations in further statements. The Parliamentary Assembly of the Council of Europe 'welcom[ed]' Taiwan's membership in the WTO.[133] A proposed motion in the Parliamentary Assembly in January 2007 was put forward for 'Making Taiwan a partner in global health by granting Taiwan observer status at the World Health Assembly.'[134] It was noted that the United States Congress, European Parliament, and the national parliaments of Belgium and Canada also supported Taiwanese participation in the WHA.[135] These transactions involving other States tend to indicate an acceptance that, at least for the purposes they serve, Taiwan has an international legal identity.

Consolidation of status also may be detected in the policies of the government of Taiwan. As noted, Taiwanese internal politics shifted in the 1980s. This led in November 1997 to the defeat of the Nationalist Party in local elections and

---

[130] A similar 'inconsistent with' phrase is included in Article 1 of the Definition of Aggression: 'Aggression is the use of armed force by a State against the sovereignty, territorial integrity or political independence of another State, or in any other manner inconsistent with the Charter of the United Nations...': GA res 3314(XXIX), 14 Dec 1974, Annex.

[131] See works cited Stürchler *The Threat of Force in International Law* (2007) 244 n. 159 and Stürchler's own observations, ibid. 124–5.

[132] E.g. Agreement in the form of an Exchange of Letters between the European Community and the Separate Customs Territory of Taiwan, Penghu, Kinmen and Matsu: OJ L 90, signed 30 March 2006; entered into force 26 June 2006.

[133] PA res 1269 (2002), 23 Jan 2002 ¶ 7.

[134] Proposed PA motion by Mr Leibrecht and others, Doc 11165, 30 Jan 2007.

[135] PA res 1269 ¶ 8.

the establishment in government of the Democratic Progressive Party.[136] There followed a shift in international policy. The government in Taipei had maintained since 1949, as a legal position, that it had authority over the whole of China and was not the government of a separate State. The position after 1997 was not to abandon the old position immediately – nor has it been, to date, to issue a unilateral declaration of independence. However, the public rhetoric of the government in Taipei had shifted toward emphasizing the status of Taiwan *qua* Taiwan. The practice has been documented extensively.[137] Two competing referenda were held on 22 March 2008, one asking whether Taiwan should seek UN admission under that name, another asking whether Taiwan should seek 'to return' to the UN under one or another title.[138] Neither referendum attracted the percentage of voters needed to establish its effectiveness under Taiwan's referendum law. An affirmative and effective vote favouring the title 'Taiwan,' perhaps, would have further consolidated the position of Taiwan as a self-determination unit. A referendum resulting in a declaration of independence would have had definite consequences. Independence was not part of the terms of either proposed referendum however. Other formal measures short of such a declaration are unlikely to have as much legal consequence as the practice demonstrating Taiwan's self-government, democratization, etc.

Nevertheless, the conclusions to be drawn from the evidence, owing to the unusual aspects of China-Taiwan relations, are less clear than in other situations. Even where the subject matter of a dispute is comparatively routine, the standards concerning the period of time necessary for a proposition to crystallize into a rule of customary international law are notoriously imprecise.[139] The dispute concerning Taiwan entails problems of category: China takes it to be a matter of domestic jurisdiction; Taiwan, a matter with certain international aspects. The parties, then, differ as to whether the processes of customary international law are even in play. The practice here however is difficult to dismiss as having no consolidating effect, including consolidating the position that the matter is not in all its dimensions restricted to a single national legal system.

Writers have described the situation of China and Taiwan as 'unique' or '*sui generis*' – and with good reason. Bailey and Daws say that '[t]he Chinese case was unique not because it involved a revolutionary change of government but

---

[136] Copper 48.

[137] For example, remarks of the President of Taiwan during the observance of National Day on 10 Oct 2007 contained over a dozen references to 'Taiwan' – and none to 'Republic of China.'

[138] Government Information Office of the Republic of China (2008), Referendum Proposals, 22 Mar 2008 Presidential Election and Referendums – PRESS KIT Fact Sheet No. 6.

[139] *North Sea Continental Shelf Cases (Federal Republic of Germany/Denmark; Federal Republic of Germany/Netherlands)* ICJ Rep 1969 pp. 3, 43 ¶ 74.

because it was the first in which two rival governments existed.'[140] Yet the particularity of the problem is not described completely even by the observation that there have been 'rival governments.' As Bailey and Daws themselves point out, there have been other controversies over the authority of certain delegates to represent particular States. To be sure, the cases are not numerous, the main examples which the writers note having been those of Hungary in 1956, the Congo (Leopoldville) in 1960 and Kampuchea in 1979.[141] What distinguished the case of Chinese representation is the shear period of time over which rival governments existed. To say something 'exists' means that it exists for a period of time; but the other instances of 'existing' rival governments have been short-lived, one or the other rival not having lasted long against the claim of the other, which by relatively rapid steps proved itself to be superior in terms of effectiveness, lawfulness or both. And the success of one rival's claim in most of the few other examples has been complete: the other claimant, if it is left any institutional manifestation at all, is left little or no territory on which to display its effects. The singularity of the case of China and Taiwan, then, is that there have been two rival governments, now having existed both a long time, and both exercising the normal incidents of municipal government in considerable territories over considerable populations. The duration and intensity of the relevant practice at a certain point raises a question as to what purpose it serves to refer to the situation as one of rival governments in a single State.

The answer, one side says, is clear enough. Maintaining the position that one State only exists in the relevant territorial sphere serves to maintain peace and security, for a claim of independence would trigger use of force as against what one of the claimants would characterize as an unlawful secession. This may be seen to invert the arguments set out – and accepted – in the cases of Germany and Korea. The position there was taken, as seen above, that the interests of peace and security required a plain acknowledgment that separate authorities had consolidated themselves on either side of a dividing line as effectively independent States. Dual admission to the United Nations of both sides in both Germany and Korea was not interpreted as foreclosing an eventual unification. Its main effect, instead, was said to be to incorporate competing parties more thoroughly into the international system. The response that the one-State position preserves peace and security also tends to be question begging, for it implies an

---

[140] Bailey & Daws *The Procedure of the UN Security Council* 3rd edn (1998) 182.

[141] Writers also have mentioned Yemen in 1962, Haiti in 1992, Zaire in 1993, and Afghanistan between 1996 and 2001, though the distinction may be blurred between (i) the cases where rival governments are competing for effective control and (ii) the cases where there is only one claimant but States doubt it merits being treated as the government with authority to represent the State. See Magiera 'Article 9' in Simma ed *Commentary* 2nd edn 247, 253–4.

assumption that use of force as against Taiwan is an inevitable outcome of an independence declaration.

The statements of the various parliamentary bodies reserve what may be the main question: they do not say whether Taiwan is a separate State. What these and other international statements do say is that the separation between Taiwan and China cannot be assimilated completely under claims of domestic jurisdiction and, probably, the Taiwan Strait therefore contains a frontier regulated, for at least certain purposes, by international law. The one purpose for which it is so regulated, it would seem judging by national and international statements, is use and threat of force. A shared position in the practice adverted to above is that, whatever settlement is reached of the difference concerning Taiwan, it must be a pacific settlement, and use or threat of force is to be excluded as a mechanism of policy in the matter.

The record of State practice from the 1990s through the first decade of the 2000s suggests the following points:

(i)   Reaching a pacific settlement of differences between the authorities in the PRC and the authorities in Taiwan is an international interest.

(ii)   Formal acceptance of Taiwan as a State, whether by its admission as a State to an international organization, or by express recognition, under present circumstances is not compatible with the prior international interest in reaching a pacific settlement of differences between the authorities in the PRC and the authorities in Taiwan.

(iii)   Participation of Taiwan in multilateral bodies is extensive, continues to grow, and may be established on such terms as to maintain compatibility with the above-stated international interest.

(iv)   As a matter of policy, Taiwan merits greater access to multilateral institutions; and Taiwanese participation should be supported particularly in multilateral institutions having competence over matters which are addressed best through universal participation, such as health and disease control, climate change and the environment.

(v)   Bilateral relations between States and Taiwan, especially in the fields of trade promotion and investment protection, are extensive and have not been prevented by the outstanding questions of status.

(vi)   The inhabitants of Taiwan have a legal interest in determining the destiny of the territory of Taiwan, and this interest, though it does not at this time equate to a right of unilateral disposition over all matters, entails a right to a negotiated settlement of differences with China.

(vii)   Rule of law, democratic institutions, and human rights are considerably consolidated in Taiwan.

(viii) The international law prohibition against use or threat of force applies as between China and Taiwan, and this position does not require any defini-

tive prior position as to the international status of the territory of Taiwan
or its eventual relation to China.

5.1.4   *Kosovo*

In an era in which universality is an established principle of the United Nations,
universal membership has become one of the main reasons for the Organization.
The UN serves as a general forum in which States may participate as equals
under international law and within institutional processes developed under the
Charter. As a universal organization, the UN also serves to define and advance
international law, for the UN has acted as the centre both of codification and
progressive development that States in 1945 said they hoped it would become.
To exclude an applicant may be to undermine the UN's most important function – to act as a universal organization. To an extent not seen for a number
of years, however, entities displaying considerable effectiveness over defined territories and claiming at least some form of separate status have remained outside
the United Nations. The case of Taiwan has been discussed already. The case of
Kosovo presents a second example.

At the time the present work went to press, Kosovo had not yet made an
application for admission to membership. Nor had the parties principally concerned with the Balkan situation yet reached consensus as to the final status of
Kosovo. Indeed, the division of opinion carries over to the overall membership,
as reflected by the sharp division in the General Assembly vote by which the
advisory request on Kosovar independence was adopted on 8 October 2008.[142]
The local administration in Kosovo and some of its international sponsors take
the position that independence is the most suitable final status. Indeed, this is the
position of the *main* international sponsors of Kosovo and a position which
the United States in particular pursues as a matter of importance. The United
States, the United Kingdom, Germany, France, and Italy recognized Kosovo as
an independent State on 18 February 2008,[143] the day following the territory's
declaration of independence from Serbia. A complete separation from Serbia
remains unacceptable to Serbia and to Russia.[144] A candidature for admission of

---

[142] GA res 63/3, 8 Oct 2008 (77–6:74).
[143] Reynolds 'Kosovo: To Recognise or not to recognise?' 18 Feb 2008, BBC World; Statement
by Secretary Condoleezza Rice, 18 Feb 2008: U.S. Dep't State doc 2008/117. Spain, Cyprus,
and Romania – States with separatist minorities – declined to recognize, as did China. Taiwan
congratulated the Kosovars, a measure which drew criticism from China. Orakhelashvili takes
a critical view of Kosovar statehood: 'Statehood, Recognition and the United Nations System:
A Unilateral Declaration of Independence in Kosovo' (2008) 12 *Max Planck Ybk UN Law* 1.
[144] See Jeremić 'One Nation, Indivisible' *New York Times* 27 Feb 2008. Jeremić, Foreign Minister
of Serbia, adduces international law grounds against the separation of Kosovo from Serbia, in
particular that it (i) 'imposes' a solution accepted only by a small segment of the international

Kosovo, after the unilateral declaration of independence, would in all likelihood attract Security Council veto, assuming that the matter reached the Council. The prior question would be whether such an application would be sent to the Council at all. Considering that France, the United Kingdom, and the United States have given Kosovo significant material and moral support, a Kosovar candidature would not be the project solely of a small handful of States possessing little political leverage. It would be a major initiative of the Atlantic alliance. Notwithstanding the Charter principle of sovereign equality, the institutional processes of the UN do not exist in isolation from politics. The 'receivability' of a Taiwanese candidature could be rejected with little incident, an action carried out behind the scenes. It is far from clear that a candidature of Kosovo would not give rise to considerably greater friction. The advisory request draws another UN principal organ into the matter; an eventual ICJ advisory opinion on Kosovo is no more likely to settle the matter than the other main advisory opinions that involved the Court in self-determination problems led to their settlement either.

If Taiwan's 2007 application is the precedent, then Kosovo and its sponsors would seem to face two choices. They could risk a serious dispute within the UN as to the operation of admission procedures; or Kosovo could decline to seek admission. Both choices present significant problems. Making an application, with the express or tacit support of the European Union and United States in opposition to Serbia, Russia and, probably, China, presents the possibility of a constitutional crisis. The political influence of the opponents of Kosovar independence presumably would be brought to bear not just in Security Council proceedings but, so to speak, in the lobbies, where the chief officers of the Organization have proved effective already at cutting off an application before it is added as a formal agenda item. But this has worked in the past where the sponsors of an application (Taiwan's) were hardly able to make weight against the opponents. The balance in a Kosovar application would be much more nearly matched. The question of the authority of officers like the Secretary-General and the President of the Security Council to control access to the formal procedures of admission then would become much more concrete. In a situation where two rival groups of powerful States took opposite views as to the 'receivability' of the application for admission, it well may not be enough to refer vaguely to inherent powers or the exigencies of institutional management. A constitutional crisis

---

community; (ii) transforms self-determination into a right to independence; (iii) promotes partition as a solution to ethnic conflict; and (iv) breaches SC res 1244, 10 June 1999. See also statements to the press by Dmitry Medvedev (at the time First Deputy Prime Minister of Russia and candidate for President of the Russian Federation): AP wires 'Russia's Medvedev warns Kosovo's independence could set Europe ablaze' 27 Feb 2008.

could be forced by the question, and such a crisis would seem difficult to resolve as against entrenched positions. Recourse would be available, as always, to the Legal Counsel. Perhaps the controversy would invite discussion in the pending advisory proceedings of the Court; there has never been senior authority on the role of the Secretariat over applications for admission, but consistent with its jurisprudence the Court is unlikely to stray from the question in the advisory request narrowly construed. Perhaps the matter would be resolved, by permitting the application to go forward. In any event, to send a Kosovar application to the Security Council would present the same problem that a Taiwanese application would entail – namely, the negative vote of at least one permanent member.

This leads to the second possible course of action. Kosovo could decline to seek admission. Declining to seek admission, which would mean that Kosovo exists as a non-member, however would erode the principle of universality. It has been a theme of this work that the move by the UN to a presumption that all States should be admitted was of constitutional significance. A setback today against universality would come at a time in the history of the Organization when its universal constituency indeed is one of its main justifications.

For the applicant State itself, existence as a State excluded from the UN would be problematic, though not insuperably so. States before the package deal of 1955–6 existed as non-members. Other States waited a long time before seeking admission (see Chapter 6 below). Non-membership has not been fatal to States in the past; if its international sponsors remain committed to Kosovo politically, Kosovo could exist as a non-member, too, without incurring unacceptable direct cost to itself. The cost to the UN however would be measured in the erosion of its mission as universal organization. Exclusion of an independent Kosovo and exclusion of other possible independent States, such as Taiwan after a declaration of independence, would qualify universality. And this would be to qualify universality by excluding applicants whose participation arguably is to be desired on other terms. Including the likes of Taiwan in international organization would not be merely to fulfil the purpose of universal inclusion for its own sake; Taiwan as member State would further other purposes of the Charter as well – promoting rule of law, human rights, economic development, etc. The same would go for an independent Kosovo, all the more so in light of its origins as a remedy for gross violations of fundamental rights by the existing territorial State. The risk is large that excluding such applicants would damage the credibility of the United Nations. It would be all the larger, in the eyes of those who view China and Russia, the main objectors to admission, as less exemplars of UN principles than Taiwan and Kosovo.

The ultimate purpose of the UN, as conceived during World War II, was to prevent repetition of a general collapse of international public order. A showdown over Taiwan, Kosovo, or both would risk exacerbating the tensions that exist between Russia and China on the one hand and the established democracies on the other. This would not cause a general collapse, but it certainly would diminish the capacity for coordinated international action to meet common objectives. Advocates of Kosovo and Taiwan say that the democratic polities should make clear sooner than later that they are committed to promoting their main principles at global level. Those who counsel caution argue that increased friction imposes unacceptable costs and that accommodation is a strategy for integrating non-democratic States gradually into the international system. Whether States choose to promote or to reject the statehood of democratically-constituted entities, the following may be said: the consolidation of statehood by entities located at the fault lines of international relations implicates the criteria and procedures for admission to the UN; and a divergence as to how to receive applications by such entities following unilateral declarations of independence could lead to a crisis in the principal organs recalling that of the first decade of the Organization.

5.2 Contested Admission as the Exceptional Case

Yet, overall, after the package deal of 1955–6, admission of States to the UN has scarcely been an arena for dispute. Contested positions were rare, and, other than the cases of the divided States, most of what disputes did arise over admission between the mid-1950s and the early 1990s were short-lived. Indeed, the number of cases is small in which even so much as a dissenting vote was cast in the Security Council or General Assembly on a question of admission. The United States once vetoed the application of Angola and then abstained from the votes by which Angola shortly after was admitted.[145] Guatemala voted against admission of Belize, on grounds similar to those which had led to objection against admission of Kuwait and Mauritania.[146] The dissenting votes on the Gulf States are noted in Figure 1. At the time the present work went to press, China was the last State to have cast a vote other than an affirmative vote on a question of admission. The applicant was Nauru, one of the remaining States to recognize Taiwan as the Republic of China, and China abstained in the Security Council, urging Nauru to 'strictly comply with resolutions of the United Nations, including General Assembly resolution 2758.'[147] As resolution

---

[145] The United States referred to Angola's reliance on Cuba for military support. See Mr. Scranton (for the USA): SCOR 31st yr 1973rd mtg 19 Nov 1976 p. 26 ¶¶ 265–70.

[146] Statehood was questioned, too, in connection with Belize. Guatemala claimed that Belize was not a self-determination unit entitled to statehood, but, rather, Guatemalan territory unlawfully, or, at any rate, unfairly, broken off from Guatemala by a colonizing Britain. For the Guatemalan argument, see GAOR 36th sess 13th plen mtg 25 Sept 1981 pp. 229–32 ¶¶ 2–33.

[147] Mr Shen Guofang (China) SCOR 54th yr 4017th mtg 25 June 1999 p. 2 cols 1, 2. PRC Security Council practice generally follows the Chinese position that Taiwan's international diplomacy has no legal basis. China also acts secondarily to discourage Taiwan's diplomatic

2758 concerned credentials – a procedural matter related mainly to the house-keeping of the General Assembly – it is not immediately clear on the terms of China's statement how the objection to Nauru's admission relates to Article 4. The underlying Chinese position was that recognition of the authorities in Taipei as the government of China entails unfriendliness toward China and thus may cast doubt on fitness under Article 4(1). The abstention must count as one of the 'far flung derivates'[148] of the one-China policy.

Even in the exceptional cases in which a request for admission was denied, admission was granted in due course – and, in most of those cases, after only short delay. In light of the admission of over a hundred States as members of the United Nations since 1945, it is striking that none ultimately has been rejected; of the total number of States admitted, the number of General Assembly decisions occasioning dissent have been very few; and dissent to admission, as a percentage of total votes cast in the Assembly, has been miniscule.[149]

As seen above, States voting against the majority on questions of admission set out reasons in the contemporaneous debates of the Security Council or General Assembly. Evidence of the reasoning behind negative votes nevertheless is scarce, as there have been few contested applications, and even in the controversial instances not all objecting States set out their reasons in a formal explanation of vote. The responsible organ of the UN provides even less indication of the reasoning behind particular decisions on admission. The Security Council, in its reports respecting admission, as noted in Chapter 2, typically has recorded little or no substantive deliberation on the question whether particular applicants satisfy the Article 4(1) criteria. The UN lacks a functioning procedure to evaluate the claim that an applicant satisfies the criteria of Article 4(1) – even though the claim is implicit whenever an application is made for admission. As seen above, by the time of the package deal, the substantive criteria themselves had started to recede to the margins of UN practice.

---

supporters. Thus the PRC vetoed draft resolutions to send military observers to Guatemala in 1997 and to extend UNPREDEP in Macedonia in 1999: Coicaud *Beyond the National Interest* 227 n. 75.

[148] Eitel's phrase: 'The UN Security Council and its Future Contribution in the Field of International Law. What may we expect?' (2000) 4 *Max Planck Ybk UN Law* 53, 56.

[149] Of approximately 18,000 votes cast in the General Assembly on recommendations to admit applicants as new members, twenty-six have been negative – that is to say, approximately 0.144 %.

Table   UN admission and dissenting votes (1955–1999)

State	Security Council action	General Assembly action
Albania	Admission recommended: SCOR 10th yr 705th mtg 14 Dec 1955 ¶ 29 8–0:3[150] *Abstaining*: Belgium, China, USA	Admitted: GA res 995 (X), 14 Dec 1955 48–3:5 *Against*: Cuba, Greece, China *Abstaining*: Dominican Republic, Netherlands, Philippines, USA, Belgium, Paraguay[151] GAOR 10th sess 555th mtg 14 Dec 1955 ¶ 7
Jordan	Admission recommended: SCOR 10th yr 705th mtg 14 Dec 1955 ¶ 30 Unanimous	Admitted: GA res 995 (X), 14 Dec 1955 55–0:1 *Abstaining*: Israel GAOR 10th sess 555th mtg 14 Dec 1955 ¶ 8
Hungary	Admission recommended: SCOR 10th yr 705th mtg 14 Dec 1955 ¶ 33 9–0:2 *Abstaining*: China, USA	Admitted: GA res 995 (X), 14 Dec 1955 49–2:5 *Against*: China, Cuba *Abstaining*: Greece, Netherlands, Philippines, USA, Dominican Republic, Paraguay GAOR 10th sess 555th mtg 14 Dec 1955 ¶ 11

---

[150] The Security Council, due to Soviet vetoes, the day before had rejected a draft resolution of Brazil and New Zealand: SCOR 10th yr 704th mtg 13 Dec 1955 ¶ 74. On 14 December, the Council voted on a new draft resolution (proposed by the USSR), separate votes being taken as to the inclusion of the name of each candidate State: SCOR 10th yr 705th mtg 14 Dec 1955 ¶¶ 11–47. The main change had been the removal of the Republic of Korea and Republic of Viet Nam from the proposed draft – thus securing Soviet consent: see statement of Mr Tsiang (China), SCOR 10 yr 705th mtg 14 Dec 1955 ¶ 57.

[151] Paraguay was absent from the Assembly on 14 December 1955, and its vote therefore was not counted in the Official Record for the 555th meeting. It asked at the 556th meeting on 15 December that its abstentions with regard to four States be recorded: GAOR 10th sess 556th mtg 15 Dec 1955 ¶ 5.

Table (*cont.*)

State	Security Council action	General Assembly action
Romania	Admission recommended: SCOR 10th yr 705th mtg 14 Dec 1955 ¶ 36 9–0:2 *Abstaining*: China, USA	Admitted: GA res 995 (X), 14 Dec 1955 49–2:5 *Against*: China, Cuba *Abstaining*: Netherlands, Philippines, USA, Dominican Republic, Greece, Paraguay GAOR 10th sess 555th mtg 14 Dec 1955 ¶ 14
Bulgaria	Admission recommended: SCOR 10th yr 705th mtg 14 Dec 1955 ¶ 37 9–0:2 *Abstaining*: China, USA	Admitted: GA res 995 (X), 14 Dec 1955 50–2:5 *Against*: China, Cuba *Abstaining*: Dominican Republic, Greece, Netherlands, Philippines, USA, Paraguay GAOR 10th sess 555th mtg 14 Dec 1955 ¶ 15
Libya	Admission recommended: SCOR 10th yr 705th mtg 1 Dec 1955 ¶ 41 Unanimous	Admitted: GA res 56–0:1 *Abstaining*: Israel GAOR 10th sess 555th mtg 14 Dec 1955 ¶ 19
Spain	Admission recommended: SCOR 10th yr 705th mtg 14 Dec 1955 ¶ 44 10–0:1 *Abstaining*: Belgium	Admitted: GA res 995 (X), 14 Dec 1955 55–0:2 *Abstaining*: Belgium, Mexico GAOR 10th sess 555th mtg 14 Dec 1955 ¶ 22

Table (*cont.*)

State	Security Council action	General Assembly action
Japan (1955)	Votes on draft resolution to recommend admission (draft rejected): SCOR 10th year 704th mtg 13 Dec 1955 ¶ 70 10–1:0 SCOR 10th year 706th mtg 15 Dec 1955 ¶ 116 10–1:0 *Against*: USSR	
Japan (1956)	Admission recommended: SCOR 11th yr 756th mtg 12 Dec 1956 ¶ 48 Unanimous	Admitted: GA res 1113 (XI), 18 Dec 1956
Mongolia[152]	Admission recommended: SCOR 16th yr 971st mtg 25 Oct 1961 ¶ 70 9–0:1 *Abstaining*: USA. China did not take part in the voting.	Admitted: GA res 1630 (XVI), 27 Oct 1961 Adopted by acclamation: GAOR 16th sess 1043rd plen mtg 17 Oct 1961 ¶ 38. China did not take part in the voting: ibid. ¶ 37.
Mauritania (1960)	Vote on draft resolution to recommend admission (draft rejected): SCOR 15th yr 911th mtg 3 Dec 1960 ¶ 246 8–2:1 *Against*: Poland, USSR *Abstaining*: Ceylon	

---

[152] Draft resolutions in the Security Council to recommend admission of Mongolia had been rejected between 1946 and 1961: SCOR 1st yr, 57th mtg 29 Aug 1946 (6–3:2); 2nd yr 186th mtg 18 Aug 1947 (3–3:5); 4th yr 445th mtg 15 Sept 1949 (2–2:7) & (4–2:4); 7th yr 573rd mtg 6 Feb 1952 (2–6:3); 7th yr 597th mtg 8 Sept 1952 (2–5:4); 10th yr 704th mtg 13 Dec 1955 (8–1:2); 10th yr 706th mtg 15 Dec 1955 (1–0:10); 11th yr 756th mtg 12 Dec 1956 (4–2:5); 12th yr 790th mtg 9 Sept 1957 (2–5:4).

Table (*cont.*)

State	Security Council action	General Assembly action
Mauritania (1961)	Admission recommended: SCOR 16th yr 971st mtg 25 Oct 1961 ¶ 228 9–1:1 *Against*: United Arab Republic *Abstaining*: USSR	Admitted: GA res 1631 (XVI), 27 Oct 1961 GAOR 16th sess 1043rd plen mtg 27 Oct 1961 ¶ 195 68–13:20 *Against*: Yemen, Cuba, Guinea, Iraq, Jordan, Lebanon, Libya, Mali, Morocco, Saudi Arabia, Sudan, Syria, United Arab Republic *Abstaining*: Yugoslavia, Afghanistan, Albania, Bulgaria, Byelorussia, Cambodia, Congo (Leopoldville), Czechoslovakia, Ghana, Guatemala, Hungary, India, Indonesia, Mongolian People's Republic, Nepal, Pakistan, Poland, Romania, Ukraine, USSR
Kuwait (1961)	Vote on draft resolution to recommend admission (draft rejected): SCOR 16th yr 985th mtg 30 Nov 1961 p. 9 ¶ 43 10–1:0 *Against*: USSR	
Algeria	Admission recommended: SCOR 17th yr 1020th mtg 4 Oct 1962 p. 71 10–0:1 Abstaining: China	Admitted: GA res 1754 (XVII) 8 Oct 1962

Table (*cont.*)

State	Security Council action	General Assembly action
Kuwait (1963)	Admission recommended: SCOR 18th yr 1034th mtg 7 May 1963 pp. 18–9 ¶¶ 99–100	Admitted: GA res 1872 (S-IV), 14 May 1963
Oman	Admission recommended: SC res 299, 30 Sept 1971	Admitted: GA res 2754 (XXVI), 7 Oct 1971 117–1:2 *Against*: South Yemen *Abstaining*: Saudi Arabia, Cuba GAOR 26th sess 1957th plen mtg
Qatar	Admission recommended: SC res 297, 15 Sept 1971 Adopted unanimously	Admitted: GA 2753 (XXVI), 21 Sept 1971 126–1:0 *Against*: South Yemen[153] GAOR 26th sess 1934th plen mtg p. 36
United Arab Emirates	Admission recommended: SC res 304, 8 Dec 1971	Admitted: GA res 2794 (XXVI), 9 Dec 1971 93–1:0 *Against*: South Yemen GAOR 26th sess 2007th plen mtg

---

[153] South Yemen had indicated at the same plenary meeting that it would vote against the admission of Bahrain as well on the same grounds ('pseudo-independence which perpetuates indirect colonial influence and internal suppression'). However, South Yemen did not vote, instead noting to the Secretariat that it 'had intended to vote against.'

Table (*cont.*)

State	Security Council action	General Assembly action
Bangladesh (1972)	Vote on draft resolution to recommend admission (draft rejected): SCOR 27th yr 1660th mtg 25 Aug 1972 p. 10 ¶ 85 11–1:3 *Against*: China *Abstaining*: Guinea, Somalia, Sudan	
Bangladesh (1974)	Admission recommended: SC res 351, 10 June 1974	GA res 3203 (XXIX), 17 Sept 1974
Republic of Korea (South) (1975)	Vote on draft resolution to recommend admission (draft rejected):[154] SCOR 30th yr 1834th mtg 6 Aug 1975 p. 2 ¶ 5 7–6:2 *In favor*: Costa Rica, France, Italy, Japan, Sweden, UK, USA *Against*: Byelorussia, China, Iraq, Mauritania, USSR, Tanzania *Abstaining*: Guyana, Cameroon	
Republic of Korea (South)	Admission recommended: SC res 702, Aug 8, 1991	Admitted: GA res 46/1, 17 Sept 1991
Democratic Republic of Korea (North) (1991)		

---

[154] See the earlier USSR vetoes of the Republic of Korea: SCOR 4th yr 423rd mtg 8 Apr 1949 (9–1:0); SCOR 10th yr 704th mtg 13 Dec 1955 (9–1:1); SCOR 12th yr 790th mtg 9 Sept 1957 (10–1:0). The 1955 abstention was New Zealand's.

Table (*cont.*)

State	Security Council action	General Assembly action
Democratic Republic of Viet Nam (North)	Vote on draft resolution to recommend admission (draft rejected):	
Republic of South Viet Nam (post-capitulation of Saigon government) (1975)	SCOR 30th yr 1836th mtg 11 Aug 1975 p. 12 ¶ 105 13–1:1 *Against*: USA[155] *Abstaining*: Costa Rica SCOR 30th yr 1846th mtg 30 Sept 1975 p. 6 ¶¶ 41–2 14–1:0 *Against*: USA	
Democratic Republic of Viet Nam (1976)	Vote on draft resolution to recommend admission (draft rejected): SCOR 31st yr 1972nd mtg 15 Nov 1976 p. 13 ¶ 119 14–1:0 *Against*: USA	
Democratic Republic of Viet Nam (1977)	Admission recommended: SC res 413, 20 July 1977	Admitted: GA res 32/2, 20 Sept 1977
Angola (June 1976)	Vote on draft resolution to recommend admission (draft rejected): SCOR 31st yr 1932nd mtg 23 June 1976 pp. 23–4 ¶ 208 13–1:0 *Against*: USA	

---

[155] When casting its veto, the United States stated, '[W]e would have and we will have nothing to do with selective universality, a principle which in practice admits only new members acceptable to totalitarian States': SCOR 30th yr 1836th mtg 11 Aug 1975 p. 13 ¶ 114. See the earlier USSR veto of the Republic (South) of Viet Nam: SCOR 10th yr 704th mtg 13 Dec 1955 ¶ 52. New Zealand abstained; the other member States of the Security Council voted in favour.

Table (*cont.*)

State	Security Council action	General Assembly action
Angola (November 1976)	Admission recommended: SC res 397, 22 Nov 1976, 31st yr 1974th mtg	Admitted: GA res 31/44, 1 Dec 1976
	13–0:1	116–0:1
	Abstaining: USA	*Abstaining*: USA
		GAOR 31st sess 84th plen mtg
Belize	Admission recommended: SC res 491, 23 Sept 1981	Admitted: GA res 36/3, 25 Sept 1981 144–1:0
		Against: Guatemala[156]
Nauru	Admission recommended: SC res 1249, 25 June 1999, 54th yr 4017th mtg	Admitted: GA res 54/2, 14 Sept 1999
	14–0:1	
	Abstaining: China	

The record of contested admissions presents a question: Why did the substantive criteria for admission, after the first decade of the Charter, all but disappear from practice? One explanation may be that the politics of the era made it difficult to engage in substantive, factual evaluations of candidature. That the mutual suspicion of Cold War adversaries may have stunted the fuller development of Article 4(1) was clear from the beginning. Molotov, when objecting to inclusion of Argentina in the Conference at San Francisco, suggested 'that the Soviet as well as other delegations be given a chance to acquaint themselves at length with the facts and to satisfy themselves that the situation in Argentina has really improved.'[157] This might have invited promulgation of a procedural device analogous to the *descente sur les lieux* for which Article 66 of the Rules of Court of the ICJ provides. Western States saw Molotov's suggestion as a formula for intractable debate. If States were to 'acquaint themselves at length with the facts' in future cases, the basis for delay would be nearly limitless, for grounds

---

[156] Notice, above, that Guatemala in 1961 abstained from voting for admission of Mauritania, perhaps a gesture of solidarity with Morocco over territorial claims against neighbouring ex-colonial territories.

[157] 5th Plenary Session 30 Apr 1945, Verbatim Minutes, Doc 42/ P/10, *UN Conference on International Organization: Documents* vol. I p. 346.

for dispute often are extensive. The Soviet invitation to evaluate the facts of Argentina's case foreshadowed the guidance on fact-finding in the *Admission* case where the International Court said that a wide scope of considerations may go to each State's decision as to whether a particular Article 4(1) criterion has been fulfilled. But it also may have raised the suspicion that States would put substantive admission criteria to dilatory ends.

It was inevitable that decisions on admission seldom, if ever, would be taken on 'strictly legal' grounds, whatever the expression 'strictly legal' in this, or any, context might mean. Like any decision, an admission decision was bound to be taken with a view to various interests of the decision-maker. No more could an admission decision be taken on 'strictly legal' grounds than could executing a purchase-and-sale agreement on a house, formalizing a last will and testament, or obtaining the relevant consents to a corporate merger. There seldom, if ever, lacks some underlying functional object behind the use of a legal mechanism. The legal mechanism furnished under Article 4 surely could not be impervious to politics. The commencement of the Cold War, however, brought with it a degree of politicization so acute that the member States perhaps concluded that substantive admission criteria would have to be put aside, if East-West animosities were not to suspend membership in the United Nations in a deepfreeze. To observe that the Cold War obstacles to fuller implementation of the criteria now are gone hardly precludes that other factors still may get in the way. It may be ventured that other, political factors, as yet, have not presented themselves as starkly, even as a small number of specific cases may occasion international difference.

Other factors, however, were in play beside those stemming from Cold War politics. As set out in the Chapters above, submergence of the substantive criteria for admission equally may be traced to a deliberate decision to develop the UN into a universal organization. The member States came to the view that universal membership was a valid objective in itself. Supporting this view was the proposition that universal participation of States in the UN would lead to full implementation of the purposes of the Charter. Whether universality has served all purposes that the founding States envisaged for the UN is a question to which we will turn later.

Chapter 6

Universality Achieved: Micro-States, Neutral States, and the Residue of Empires

Daniel Patrick Moynihan, as United States Permanent Representative, said in the Security Council in 1975 that achieving universal membership in the UN was to be pursued as a goal of international policy: 'The United Nations should be as near as possible to universal membership. As new nations are formed, they should be seen as having a presumed right to membership, given their fealty to the Charter.'[1] This was to repeat what senior diplomats had said before, insofar as they had articulated a principle favouring universal membership, but it also espoused the bolder assertions which held that universality is prescribed under Charter law. More than a mere principle, universality, it now was said, is a presumption. The States seeking admission in the early Charter years had had the task of securing it. For the States comprising the logjam, admission had been significantly delayed, and their candidacies had been subject to extensive debate. A 'presumed right to membership' was not the accepted position in the early Charter years.[2] By the 1970s, it was. A requirement of 'fealty to the Charter' perhaps remained. Under a presumption of admission, however, it is doubtful what effect such a requirement would have in practice. Whether or not a 'presumed right to membership' can be deduced from the Charter, a presumption that every new State is to be a UN member State eventually took hold. The effect of the presumption in practice would be realized in the thirty years following Moynihan's words.

The march toward universal membership has been described elsewhere.[3] It became something like a custom to applaud each successive admission of a State to the United Nations as indicating that universality was that much closer to

---

[1] SCOR 30th yr 1836th mtg 11 Aug 1975 ¶ 116.
[2] Recall the rapporteur's summary from UNCIO (1945); and the Administrative Committee Report to ECOSOC (1950): Chapter 3, p. 70 nn. 23, 25, above.
[3] E.g. Dugard *Recognition* 76–8; Claude *Swords into Plowshares* 4th edn (1984) 83–100.

realization. For example, with respect to Senegal and Mali (1960) it was said that their admissions reflected 'the support of the United Nations as a whole for the universality of this Organization.'[4] With respect to Guinea-Bissau, Bangladesh, and Grenada (1974), it was said that '[t]he admission of these countries...is a further step towards the implementation of the cherished principle of universality enshrined in the Charter.'[5] In the period 1966 to 1969, during which Barbados, Botswana, Guyana, Lesotho, Democratic Yemen, Equatorial Guinea, Mauritius and Swaziland were admitted to membership, no fewer than seventy references were made to universality in the General Assembly.[6] The logjam of the period 1945 to 1955–6 was not to be repeated.

A number of States emerging from the final phase of decolonization nevertheless were not immediately admitted to the United Nations. The difference was that the various small colonial territories that became States in the final decades of the 20th century did not in all cases seek admission immediately. Their period of statehood outside the UN was by their own delay in application, not by delay of an affirmative decision in the Security Council or General Assembly. There remained Switzerland, the European neutral, which had declined to apply on grounds of its position in regional public law. Three tiny principalities and one micro-republic in Europe also existed, for a time, for various reasons, without being members; and special considerations were presented in connection with the membership of certain States emerging from the dissolutions of the Socialist Federal Republic of Yugoslavia (SFRY) and the Union of Soviet Socialist Republics (USSR). It now falls to consider these diverse, final cases, resolution of which led to the very near establishment of actual universality of membership in the United Nations.

6.1   *Independence of States in the 1990s*[7]

The dissolution of socialist federations in Europe in the early 1990s led to the establishment of independence of a large number of States. Several of these – the Baltic States of Latvia, Lithuania, and Estonia – sometimes have argued that they were not new States but, rather, States which were 'restored' or which 're-emerged.' Ukraine and Belarus were in the peculiar position of having been original members of the UN, despite it having been clear that, from 1945 to 1991, they had not been States. A number of others, such as the Czech Republic

---

[4] Mr Pazhwak (Afghanistan) GAOR 25th sess 876th plen mtg 28 Sept 1960 ¶ 128.
[5] Mr Hussein (Somalia) GAOR 29th sess 2233rd plen mtg 17 Sept 1974 p. 62.
[6] *Rep UN* (1966–9) p. 97 ¶ 10 n. 8.
[7] See generally Roger O'Keefe 'The Admission to the United Nations of the Ex-Soviet and Ex-Yugoslav States' (2001) 1 *Baltic YBIL* 167.

and Slovakia, were admitted as members through the normal procedures with no special questions arising as to the process by which they had attained independence. The most difficult cases arose out of the dissolution of the SFRY. A number of the new States and their admission to the Organization merit consideration.

6.1.1   Macedonia[8]

The peculiar case of the contested denomination of independent Macedonia seized the UN for some time. It also led to proceedings by the European Commission against Greece in the European Court of Justice[9] and by Macedonia against Greece in the International Court of Justice.[10] The situation, briefly, was as follows.

Macedonia, a constituent republic of the SFRY, declared independence in September 1991.[11] This was part of the dissolution of the SFRY which would result in the establishment of a number of new States. By Article 49 of the Macedonian Constitution,

> The Republic shall safeguard the status and rights of citizens of neighbouring countries who are of Macedonian origin and of Macedonian expatriots, shall assist their cultural development and shall promote relations with them.
> The Republic shall safeguard the cultural, economic and social rights of citizens of the Republic abroad.[12]

Greece took these provisions, together with the name 'Macedonia,' to imply a territorial claim against Greece. The area around Thessalonica, it was said, was the main target of the claim.

International law has no general prohibition against territorial claims by one State against another. The provision of mechanisms for the pacific resolution of such claims is a purpose of international law. A question may arise, however, as to the lawfulness of the particular modality by which a State expresses a territorial claim. The prohibition against threat of force is basic to modern law. It

---

[8] See Janev 'Legal Aspects of the Use of a Provisional Name for Macedonia in the United Nations System' (1999) 93 *AJ* 155; Wood 'Participation of Former Yugoslav States in the United Nations and in Multilateral Treaties' (1997) 1 *Max Planck Ybk UN Law* 231, 238 *et seq*; Craven 'What's in a Name? The Former Yugoslav Republic of Macedonia and Issues of Statehood' (1995) 16 *Australian YBIL* 199; Pazartzis 'La reconnaissance d'"une ex-République Yougoslave": La question de l'ancienne République Yougoslave de Macédoine (ARYM)' (1995) 41 *AFDI* 281. See also O'Keefe 1 *Baltic YBIL* at 177–9.

[9] *Commission of the European Communities v Hellenic Republic*, Case C-120/94R, Rec 1994 p. I-03037 (denial of Art. 186 interim measures); Case-120/94, 1996 Rec p. I-01513 (removal from the register).

[10] *Dispute Concerning the Implementation of Article 11, Paragraph 1 of the Interim Accord of 13 September 1995*: Application of Macedonia to the International Court of Justice, 13 Nov 2008.

[11] *Commission v Hellenic Republic* (denial of Art. 186 interim measures) ¶ 6.

[12] Ibid., ¶ 7.

entails fuller specification of what forms of expression amount to a threat; as the law stands such fuller specification is still awaited. Plain cases of threat are easily characterized; less clear is the legal consequence to be attached, if any is to be attached at all, to situations of implied threat. Here the subjective element is problematic. Rules and principles restricting hostile propaganda, perhaps, furnish a degree of guidance.[13] The guidance so far however at most is in only general terms, and the cases developing the rules and principles are few. In such circumstances, each further case tends to be referred to its own particularities.

Greece objected to the name 'Macedonia,' and this led the European States to require that Macedonia adopt certain constitutional amendments as a condition for recognizing Macedonia as an independent State.[14] The amendments were duly adopted and provided, *inter alia*, that Macedonia 'has no territorial ambitions;' and that its borders may not be changed unless in compliance with 'goodwill and generally recognized international norms.' The amendments also provided that Macedonia 'shall not interfere with the sovereign rights of other States nor in their internal affairs.'[15] The Arbitration Commission of the Conference on Peace in Yugoslavia (Badinter Commission) adopted Opinion No 6 on 11 January 1992, in which it determined, *inter alia*, that 'the Republic of Macedonia has…renounced all territorial claims of any kind in unambiguous statements binding in international law' and that the name 'Macedonia' therefore 'cannot…imply any territorial claim against another State.'[16] This determination

---

[13] The International Covenant on Civil and Political Rights, Art. 20, ¶ 1, provides, 'Any propaganda for war shall be prohibited by law': adopted 19 Dec 1966; entered into force 23 March 1976, 999 UNTS 171, 178, about which see Kearney *The Prohibition of Propaganda for War in International Law* (2007) 81–132; Joseph, Schultz & Castan *The International Covenant on Civil and Political Rights: Cases, Materials and Commentary* 2nd edn (2004) 544–67 (though mostly concerning ¶ 2). The Friendly Relations Declaration, under Principle 1, states, 'In accordance with the purposes and principles of the United Nations, States have the duty to refrain from propaganda for wars of aggression': GA res 2625 (XXV), 24 Oct 1970, Annex. cf on incitement or instigation as considered by the UN international criminal tribunals, Schabas *The UN International Criminal Tribunals: The Former Yugoslavia, Rwanda and Sierra Leone* (2006) 181–3, 217, 299–301; Mettraux *International Crimes and the* Ad Hoc *Tribunals* (2005) 227, 254–7, 280–2.

[14] See Council of the European Communities, Declaration on Yugoslavia issued by the Extraordinary Ministerial Meeting in Brussels on European Political Cooperation, 16 Dec 1991: (1992) 31 ILM 1485 (reprinted from European Political Cooperation Press Release P. 129/91).

[15] The ECJ set the text out in full in *Commission v Hellenic Republic* (denial of Art. 186 interim measures) ¶ 7. Kearney notes the provisions in Macedonian law prohibiting propaganda for war, though does not say anything about their relevance to Greece's complaint: Kearney *Propaganda* 139, 153.

[16] Opinion No 6 ('On the Recognition of the Socialist Republic of Macedonia by the European Community and its Member States') (1992) 31 ILM 1507, 1511.

did not put an end to the matter, and recognition by the European States was delayed for some time.[17]

Admission to the United Nations also was delayed. Macedonia made application in July 1992. In its application, Macedonia noted the municipal process by which 'the will of the citizens for a sovereign and independent State of Macedonia was confirmed.'[18] When admission eventually took place, it was on unusual terms. The Security Council, in contrast to the purely formal statements adopted in most recommendations to admit applicants as members, in resolution 817 of 7 April 1993 recommended that

> the State whose application is contained in document S/25147 be admitted to membership in the United Nations, this State being provisionally referred to for all purposes within the United Nations as 'the former Yugoslav Republic of Macedonia' pending settlement of the difference that has arisen over the name of the State.[19]

The Security Council, in resolution 817, took note of letters received from Greece and Macedonia respecting the situation.[20] It also noted 'that a difference has arisen over the name of the State' and that the difference 'needs to be resolved in the interest of the maintenance of peaceful and good-neighbourly relations in the region.' The General Assembly, by acclamation, decided thereafter to admit Macedonia as the 181st member State, 'this State being provisionally referred to for all purposes within the United Nations as "the former Yugoslav Republic of Macedonia" pending settlement of the difference that has arisen over the name of the state.'[21]

Macedonia, with reference to the draft text that soon would be adopted as Security Council resolution 817, expressed 'disappointment that it has not proved possible... to adopt the standard straightforward resolution on admission.' Macedonia further stated that it 'will in no circumstances be prepared to accept the "former Yugoslav Republic of Macedonia" as the name of the country. We refuse to be associated in any way with the present connotation of the term "Yugoslavia." '[22] The question has been put whether this was an attempt by

---

[17] The European transactions concerning recognition are related in *Commission v Hellenic Republic* (denial of Art. 186 interim measures) ¶¶ 15–26.
[18] Letter dated 30 July 1992 from the President of the Republic of Macedonia addressed to the Secretary-General, Annex: S/25147.
[19] SC res 817, 7 Apr 1993, adopted without vote: S/PV.3196, pp. 2–3.
[20] Letter dated 24 March 1993 from the President of the Government of the Republic of Macedonia addressed to the President of the Security Council: S/25541, Annex; Letter dated 5 April 1993 from the Government of the Republic of Macedonia addressed to the President of the Security Council: S/25542, Annex; Letter dated 6 April 1993 from the Permanent Representative of Greece to the United Nations addressed to the President of the Security Council: S/25543, Annex.
[21] GA res 47/225, 8 Apr 1993: A/47/PV.98 p. 6.
[22] S/25541 Annex.

Macedonia to make a reservation as to its admission to the United Nations. A reservation would have been highly problematic, as the Charter makes no provision for reservations and rests on the position that the rights and obligations of the member States are *inter pares* as set out in the Charter. The better view however is that Macedonia's statement was not inconsistent with the provisions of resolution 817, which were closely drafted so as to avoid giving the State in question any particular name at all. By not saying exactly what the name of the applicant State is, the Council avoided proposing a definitive settlement of the 'difference.' It also avoided imposing a name on the applicant State.[23] To this extent, then, the measure taken with respect to Macedonia's name did not go as far as earlier cases, in which international pressure had compelled a State formally and definitively to adopt a name other than that which the State itself had proposed.[24]

What the Security Council did say is that its function as principal guarantor of international peace and security bears on the process of admitting an applicant as a member State. The controversy over Macedonia's name 'need[ed] to be resolved,' and its resolution had to be 'in the interest of the maintenance of peaceful and good-neighbourly relations.' The concrete measure taken was to require that Macedonia's participation in the UN be under a special form of words – 'the former Yugoslav Republic of Macedonia.' The nameplate for the Macedonian representative would bear the acronym 'FYROM,' and in diplomatic correspondence and other documents in which reference was made to the State, so too would it be called FYROM. For purposes of alphabetization in the General Assembly, Macedonia was seated next to Thailand; the leading 'the' in 'the FYROM' being taken to constitute part of the expression by which Macedonia was to be referred to.[25]

This is not to say that the language of protest and reservation in Macedonia's statements respecting resolution 817 was directed to no purpose. There is the political purpose of expressing 'disappointment' at the unusual outcome of Macedonia's admission proceedings. President Gligorov, addressing the General Assembly on the occasion of the admission of his State, maintained the optimistic tone typical of such occasions and did not mention disappointments – but did say the name 'Macedonia' (without the objected apparatus) some seventeen times in a speech of fewer than 1000 words.[26] Detectable too in Macedonia's statements, perhaps, is a concern to make emphatic its separation from the FRY. The refusal 'to be associated in any way with the present connotation of the term

---

[23] A point which Michael Wood makes: (1997) 1 *Max Planck Ybk UN Law* 231, 239.
[24] For examples see Pazartzis (1995) 41 *AFDI* 281, 286 n. 24.
[25] (1997) 1 *Max Planck Ybk UN Law* 231, 240.
[26] A/47/PV.98 pp. 17–21, 8 Apr 1993.

"Yugoslavia"' leaves no doubt, if any remained, that Macedonia had established its independence from a State with which formal association in the 1990s might have had adverse consequences for purposes of international responsibility. The Security Council acknowledged this point, the President of the Council saying on the day resolution 817 was adopted,

> The Council is clear in the resolution that has just been adopted [that] "the former Yugoslav Republic" carries no implication whatsoever that the State concerned has any connection with the Federal Republic of Yugoslavia (Serbia and Montenegro). It merely reflects the historic fact that the State recommended for admission to the United Nations in the present resolution was in the past a republic of the former Socialist Federal Republic of Yugoslavia.[27]

That the term 'Yugoslav' in 'FYROM' relates to 'historic' and not legal considerations thus was made perfectly clear.

Greece, for its part, characterized resolution 817 as forming 'an integral and indivisible package' of three requirements. These were (i) settlement of the difference over the name of the applicant State; (ii) adoption of 'appropriate confidence-building measures'; and (iii) 'admitting the new state to the United Nations under a provisional name.' Greece said that the confidence-building measures must, *inter alia*, aim at securing legal and political guarantees that Macedonia 'harbours no territorial claims against Greece'; 'cessation of all hostile propaganda'; and 'termination of the use of Greek symbols – such as the sun of Vergina.' Greece 'underlin[ed]' that

> the hoisting and flying at the United Nations of the flag bearing the Sun of Vergina would result in great damage to the efforts undertaken by the Co-Chairman of the Steering Committee of the International Conference on the Former Yugoslavia and render more difficult, if not defeat, a solution.[28]

The point about the flag was characterized as 'of paramount importance to the Greek people.' A word may be said about the third of the items which Greece said comprised the integral package of Security Council resolution 817.

Greece said that 'admitting [Macedonia]...under a provisional name' was a requirement under resolution 817. As suggested, however, it is hard to distil from the language of the resolution a requirement as to the 'name' of the State being admitted. The Security Council in formulating resolution 817, as already observed, was meticulous in avoiding a definitive statement as to Macedonia's name. The expression 'the former Yugoslavia Republic of Macedonia' was not identified as a 'name' but simply as the phrase to which Macedonia would be

---

[27] S/PV.3196, 7 Apr 1993; distributed as S/25545.
[28] S/25543, Annex.

'referred' upon its admission to the UN. The third item set out by Greece did not reflect a requirement actually included in resolution 817.

Greece in February 1994 adopted a trade embargo against Macedonia. This gave rise to the European Court proceedings mentioned above.[29] The embargo was eventually brought to an end by agreement between the two States.[30] Article 7 of the agreement prohibits hostile propaganda in any form.[31] The matter of the flag was resolved in October 1995, after Macedonia changed the national design.[32] Most States continued for a time to use the designation FYROM. The United States stated on 4 November 2004 that from then onward it would refer to Macedonia, not FYROM.[33] A number of other States apparently also have chosen to refer to the State by its name, Macedonia.[34]

The question of the name of the State continues to be raised, in connection, for example, with discussions over accession of Macedonia to the North Atlantic Treaty. In that context, the question would have to be referred to Article 10 of the Treaty, which requires the unanimous agreement of existing members, if they are to invite further European States to become members of NATO,[35] but Article 11 of the 1995 Interim Accord has been pleaded (by Macedonia) as relevant as well. While in welcome contrast to Bosnia and Croatia little violence attended the accession of Macedonia to independence, the question of its name has subsisted as an irritant for some time.

The position has been taken that no legal basis existed for the provisions of Security Council resolution 817 concerning nomenclature. Igor Janev said that the resolution is '[c]ontrary to the usual wording of Security Council resolutions recommending admission of a State.' In Janev's view, the adoption of a provisional title for the new member State 'served as additional conditions that [Macedonia] was required to satisfy so as to gain admission to the United

---

[29] See *Commission v Hellenic Republic* (denial of Art. 186 interim measures) ¶¶ 27–35.

[30] Interim Accord and Memorandum on Practical Measures Related to the Interim Accord (Greece-FYROM), 13 Sept 1995: 34 ILM 1461.

[31] 34 ILM 1461, 1469.

[32] Wood (1997) 1 *Max Planck Ybk UN Law* 231, 240. The new flag was hoisted at UN Headquarters on 21 October 1995: Pazartzis (1995) 41 *AFDI* 281, 297 n. 88.

[33] 'Diplomatic and Consular Relations: U.S. Relations with Republic of Macedonia' (2005) 99 *AJ* 254.

[34] The Macedonian Government says that, as of November 2007, some 120 States in their diplomatic relations with the State refer to it as Macedonia: Mr Lazar Elenovski, Minister of Defense, Republic of Macedonia, public remarks at the U.S. Institute of Peace, 5 Nov 2007.

[35] The North Atlantic Treaty provides as follows:

'**Article 10**

The Parties may, by unanimous agreement, invite any other European State in a position to further the principles of this Treaty and to contribute to the security of the North Atlantic area to accede to this Treaty...'

34 UNTS 243, 248, signed 4 Apr 1949, entered into force 24 Aug 1949.

Nations.'[36] This was objectionable, Janev argues, under Article 4(1) of the Charter and in view of the interpretation of Article 4(1) set out in the Advisory Opinion on *Conditions of Admission*; the International Court had been clear that only the five criteria set out in Article 4(1) may serve as conditions for admission of an applicant to membership; the terms of resolution 817 amounted to an 'additional condition[].' Janev identifies two elements in resolution 817 in particular as inconsistent 'conditions' of admission: (1) the provisional designation (FYROM); and (2) an obligation to negotiate on the 'difference' respecting the name of the State.

Central to the objection is how these elements are characterized. If they are 'conditions' of admission, additional to the five conditions set out in Article 4(1), then indeed a problem arises of consistency with the 1948 Advisory Opinion. It may be submitted, however, that how the elements are characterized is a close question. The Court certainly meant to prevent the addition of conditions not contained in the Charter, but that was not the Court's only concern. The Court also was concerned not to impinge on the internal functions of each member State involved in reaching the determination of how to cast a vote under Article 4. While the conditions of admission were narrowly defined and five in number, the considerations that might go to determining the fulfilment (or otherwise) of each condition were emphasized to be extremely wide-ranging and not subject to external control. These are each State's 'reasons, which enter into a mental process.' Moreover, the Court was 'not called upon either to define the meaning and scope of the conditions on which admission is made dependent, or to specify the elements which may serve in a concrete case to verify the existence of the requisite conditions.'[37] The question, raised by the theory that resolution 817 imposed an additional 'condition,' is whether the elements contained in the resolution constitute 'conditions' or, instead, permissible 'reasons' or 'considerations' that go to one or more of the conditions. Hersch Lauterpacht went so far as to say that a State could argue 'not very plausibly, but not necessarily in bad faith' that linking a vote on admission to admission of another applicant falls under one of the Article 4(1) conditions. The elasticity of the conditions, Lauterpacht said, was central to the Court's interpretation.[38] This was a point brought out at the time as well in the individual opinions. As between a characterization that they are impermissible, additive conditions and one that they are permissible considerations going to one of the Charter conditions, it is not altogether clear which better applies to the elements in resolution 817.

---

[36] Janev 93 *AJ* at 158.
[37] ICJ Rep 1948 pp. 57, 60; and Chapter 2, pp. 29 ff., above for discussion.
[38] Hersch Lauterpacht *The Development of International Law by the International Court* (1958) 149.

Where two divergent interpretations are presented, each arguable on its merits, the better interpretation, all else being equal, is that which has the greater consistency with established and accepted legal positions. A particular incident of this general principle is that decisions of the Security Council are not presumed to be inconsistent with the Charter and with its associated law (i.e., as developed under the advisory jurisdiction of the Court). Janev nevertheless concludes that Security Council resolution 817 set 'unusual...extraneous conditions on admission, having "no legal basis."'[39] It is far from clear however that these were additional 'conditions.' To interpret them instead as valid considerations that go to the Article 4(1) conditions has the virtue of greater constitutional economy.

Janev also objects that there seems to have been a forward-looking element in resolution 817 – that the 'conditions' imposed 'transcend the act of admission in time.'[40] This would be to say that the Security Council required certain future conduct from the applicant as a condition of admission. It is doubtful, however, that a requirement of future conduct would undermine the resolution's lawfulness. Article 4(1) on its terms and as developed in the Rules of Procedure requires a State to undertake to 'accept the obligations contained in the...Charter.' As noted in Chapter 2, the undertaking, as communicated, is a formal instrument, registered as such. Any undertaking implies future conduct. If it did not, then the obligation entailed by the undertaking, not just in the context of applications for admission to the UN but in treaties and other binding statements generally, would have little or no meaning. To agree to certain terms is to promise certain future conduct. It would be odd to say that a promise to abide by the Charter contains no future element.

The real problem, it may be submitted, is not resolution 817 but, rather, UN practice since 1955–6. The significance of resolution 817 is to cast that practice in stark light. The Security Council when dealing with membership applications very much approximated just the formalistic position that Janev takes to be a requirement under the Charter: the statements of the Security Council, in the overwhelming majority of accepted applications, have been indeed no more than blank recitations, accepting prior *pro forma* undertakings by the applicant as sufficient evidence of the fulfilment of the substantive criteria of Article 4(1). If Janev's point is that Security Council resolution 817 was inconsistent with the way Article 4(1) had been implemented over some forty years in practice, then the point is fair on its terms. The more general observation however may be the more telling: Article 4(1) allows – even requires – a more rigorous evaluation of applicants than in practice has typically been carried out.

---

[39] Janev 93 *AJ* at 158.
[40] Ibid.

It also has been argued that to choose its name is an inalienable right of a State, the right being a manifestation of municipal jurisdiction.[41] It is unclear what peremptory norm would prevent a State from agreeing to a name chosen by another. But there is a more central objection. To say that the choice of name is strictly a municipal matter is to beg the question. The assertion of Greece was that the choice of name was *not* strictly a matter concerning the internal affairs of Macedonia but was, instead, a threat.[42] There can be little doubt that, if a State were overtly to threaten force against a neighbour in pursuit of a territorial or other aim, in the absence of a consideration of self-defense, then that would be an unlawful act.[43] The problematic case is where the act or statement is not clearly a threat. Nikolas Stürchler in an extensive study of the problem notes that international law indeed has attained clarity on a definition of threat of force with respect to certain core situations. These involve a threat to use military means to attain a stated objective.[44] The difficulty is with the less certain situations. Two questions, it is submitted, in truth lay at the heart of the difference over the name of Macedonia: (i) Was Greece's appreciation accurate, that the chosen name implied a threat? And (ii) did that appreciation merit deference by the Security Council?

It will be noted that the European Council, meeting informally in March 1994, had indicated that 'the threat of war or serious internal disturbance affecting the maintenance of law and order relied on by the Greek authorities to justify the

---

[41] Janev 93 *AJ* at 159–60. cf Craven, who assimilates the choice of name to 'choice of a political, economic, social and cultural system': (1995) 16 *Austral YBIL* 199, 234 quoting ICJ Rep 1986 pp. 14, 108 ¶ 205. '[T]he subject of the dispute between Greece and Macedonia,' Craven writes, 'clearly relates to an issue which, as a matter of sovereignty, should fall exclusively within the discretion of Macedonia itself': 16 *Austral YBIL* at 234.

[42] Carrying the factual part of the brief for Greece, see Poulakidas 'Macedonia: Far More than a Name to Greece' (1995) 18 *Hastings Int'l & Comp L Rev* 397.

[43] Cf. Pazartzis, who says as follows:
'[I]l n'existe pas en droit international de règles rassemblant le <<copyright>> et conférant en quelque sorte aux Etats un droit aux caractéristiques de leur identité. Toutefois, l'on s'accorde en droit international sur le fait que la souveraineté ne confère pas à l'Etat des pouvoirs et des droits illimités, surtout lorsque ses relations avec les autres Etats sont mises en cause. En l'occurrence, la question s'est posée de savoir si, en monopolisant un nom qui définit une region plus vaste que celle incluse dans les confines d'un Etat ou en adoptant des symboles d'un autre Etat considère comme lui appartenant, et créant par là une confusion, un Etat ne se conduirait pas ainsi de manière incompatible avec les principes de bonne foi et de bon voisinage. Pour certains, la violation de ces principes constituerait un abus de droit.'
[References omitted] (1995) 41 *AFDI* 281, 287–8.

[44] Stürchler *The Threat of Force in International Law* (2007) 252–75.

[embargo] had not been established.'[45] The findings of a regional organization actively seized of a matter would seem to merit consideration, if not deference, from the United Nations. This is perhaps especially the case, where the matter in issue involves a local factual situation that the regional organization has the faculties to appreciate. The European Council there had not however made a formal determination that the situation relative to Macedonia did not constitute a threat to security; and the relevant meeting in any case took place after the Security Council had voted to recommend Macedonia's admission.

Findings or informal statements of the European Council aside, it was clear that stability in the Balkans was not to be lightly presumed. The situation in Macedonia in particular aroused concern in international organizations, including the UN, which from 1992 onward maintained a presence in the country as part of the larger mission to prevent further conflict in the peninsula.[46] This was at Macedonia's invitation,[47] an act which admitted, it would seem, that some form of international oversight was desirable, if not necessary. Officials in governments in other States of the region were clear that the international presence contributed to stability.[48] Disturbances involving the Albanian ethnic group in Macedonia in 2001 might be taken as evidence that concern over stability was not purely subjective.[49] If to carry out obligations under the Charter involves existing as a State which contributes to, or, at a minimum does not disturb, international peace and stability, then, it might be argued, grounds existed for asking whether Macedonia had been able to carry out those obligations.

---

[45] *Commission v Hellenic Republic* (denial of Art. 186 interim measures) ¶ 35.

[46] This began with the mandate of UNPROFOR in FYROM: SC res 795, 11 Dec 1992; and later acquired a separate title in that country (United Nations Preventive Deployment – UNPREDEP): SC res 983, 31 March 1995.

[47] SC res 795, 11 Dec 1992 was adopted upon consideration of 'the request by the Government in the former Yugoslav Republic of Macedonia for a United Nations presence in the former Yugoslav Republic of Macedonia': pream ¶ 5.

[48] E.g. Bashkurti 'Political Dynamics Within the Balkans: The Cases of Bosnia & Herzegovina, Macedonia, Bulgaria, Serbia, and Montenegro' (2005) 80 *Chicago-Kent L Rev* 49, 50–1. Bashkurti at the time was Deputy Foreign Minister of Albania.

[49] For background to adoption of the Ohrid Framework Agreement, 13 Aug 2001, and the role of the UN presence nationally and regionally, see Brunnbauer 'The Implementation of the Ohrid Agreement: Ethnic Macedonian Resentments' 1/2002 *J on Ethnopolitics and Minority Issues in Europe;* Popetrevski & Latifi 'The Ohrid Framework Agreement Negotiations,' June 2004, occasional paper on theme *The 2001 Conflict in FYROM – Reflections,* Conflict Studies Research Centre (available at www.defac.ac.uk/colleges/csrc/document-listings/balkan/csrc_mpf-2004–07–22/04(15)-Chap3–JP.pdf/); Ludlow 'Preventive Peacekeeping in Macedonia: An Assessment of UN Good Offices Diplomacy' 2003 *Brigham Young L Rev* 761, 783–88. Respecting preventative measures generally (before 2000), see Ackermann *Making Peace Prevail – Preventing Violent Conflict in Macedonia* (2000); Ostrowski, 'Preventive Deployment of Troops as Preventive Measures: Macedonia and Beyond' (1998) 30 *NYU J Int'l L & Pol* 793.

And, yet, fifteen years later, it would be wrong to ignore the many steps taken by Macedonia in the fields of rule of law, democracy, and minority rights,[50] or, whatever the vicissitudes in between, the record of peaceful co-existence which Macedonia has established in the region. The unusual formula in Security Council resolution 817, it may be submitted, in connection with the function of the Council under Article 4(1) served a purpose in its time. Encumbrances put in place to deal with transitory situations however should not themselves become permanent.

The expedient of adopting a title for purposes of international organization membership which purposively, if rather convolutedly, avoids implications contrary to the legal or political position of a protesting State is not unique to Macedonia. As the UN required the use of the title FYROM to assuage concern that the name Macedonia implied an improper claim against Greece, so certain international organizations have adopted various titles for Taiwan, in deference to China.[51] The positions sought to be protected in the two cases are different, but not without common ground. Greece said that the name Macedonia implied a claim by that State to annex part of the territory of Greece. China says that the name Taiwan, implying as it might the independence of that territory, in turn would take territory away from China and put at risk the unity of the country as a whole. The Greek position was that the objected name might aggrandize an admittedly independent State at Greece's expense; the Chinese position is that the objected name might create a new State at China's expense. The positions thus differ, but both are argued by reference to the right of a State to preserve its territorial integrity. If an applicant in truth were to make a claim against the territory of a State which, by the mode of its expression suggested readiness to resort to non-pacific and non-negotiated measures, such claim would raise serious questions under Article 4(1), not least of all whether the applicant is peace-loving and willing to carry out the obligations of the Charter. As suggested above, however, it may be asked in a controversy over denomination whether the name preferred by the entity in question in truth entails the threat that the protesting State claims. The question may be addressed in each case with reference both to the protesting State's appreciation and to authoritative determinations reached elsewhere. These will relate to the regional environment generally, as well as to local and bilateral considerations.

---

[50] Some of these earlier were noted by Acevska 'The Republic of Macedonia: An Atypical Balkan Country' (1997) 20 *Ford ILJ* 1521, 1523–4.

[51] See Chapter 5, pp. 174, 182, above.

6.1.2   *Other States in the Former Yugoslavia*

(i) *Yugoslavia: Extinction, Continuity, or Improvisation?*
The Socialist Federal Republic of Yugoslavia was an Original Member of the United Nations as defined in Article 3 of the Charter. The turbulent end of the SFRY[52] gave rise to certain issues of membership, and the manner in which the principal organs of the United Nations dealt with these issues tended for a time to confuse rather than to clarify them. Judge Kooijmans in a Separate Opinion in the *Case Concerning Legality of Use of Force (Yugoslavia v Belgium)* said,

> The dossier on the controversy with regard to the Federal Republic of Yugoslavia's continuation of the international personality of the Socialist Federal Republic of Yugoslavia is full of legal snags. The decisions taken by the appropriate United Nations bodies are without precedent and raise a number of as yet unsolved questions. Neither should it be forgotten, however, that these decisions have been taken by the organs which according to the Charter have the exclusive authority in questions of membership. Their decisions therefore, cannot easily be overlooked or ignored, even if the interpretations given to them by the member States which have participated in the decision-making process are widely divergent.[53]

This is an accurate, if general, précis of the problem of Yugoslav membership in the UN in the 1990s. As will now be seen, the two organs with 'exclusive authority in questions of membership' adopted decisions respecting the problem of membership, but neither on their terms nor in their subsequent interpretation did the decisions adopted establish a clear position.

Yugoslavia took the position that it continued the international legal personality of the SFRY. The continuation of SFRY membership in international organizations, including the UN, would have followed from this. Yugoslavia in 1992 notified to the UN a Declaration of its parliamentary bodies concerning matters relating to international status and participation in the UN. Paragraph 1 of the Declaration said as follows

> The Federal Republic of Yugoslavia, continuing the State, international legal and political personality of the Socialist Federal Republic of Yugoslavia, shall strictly

---

[52] For extensive citations to legal writers (up to 1997), see Wood (1997) 1 *Max Planck Ybk UN Law* 231, 231–2 n. 1. For political background, see Silber & Little *Yugoslavia: Death of a Nation* rev ed (1997); Woodward *Balkan Tragedy: Chaos and Dissolution After the Cold War* (1995). See also Weller 'The International Response to the Dissolution of the Socialist Federal Republic of Yugoslavia' (1992) 86 *AJ* 569. Respecting Bosnia and Herzegovina, see Simms *Unfinest Hour: Britain and the Destruction of Bosnia* (2001). For views of Yugoslav participants, see works reviewed by Ramet 'Views From Inside: Memoirs concerning the Yugoslav Breakup and War' (2002) 61 *Slavic Review* 558.

[53] *Case Concerning Legality of Use of Force (Yugoslavia v Belgium)* Sep Op Judge Kooijmans ICJ Rep 1999 pp. 124, 178 ¶ 21.

abide by all the commitments that the Socialist Federal Republic of Yugoslavia assumed internationally.

At the same time, it is ready to fully respect the rights and interests of the Yugoslav Republics which declared independence. The recognition of the newly formed states will follow after all the outstanding questions negotiated within the Conference on Yugoslavia have been settled.[54]

The Declaration further said that Yugoslavia pledged 'not to obstruct' the other republics from joining the UN and the specialized agencies. National minority rights would be respected,[55] and Yugoslavia would build 'confidence and understanding with its neighbours proceeding from the principle of good-neighbourliness.'[56]

The Security Council however said that 'the claim by the Federal Republic of Yugoslavia (Serbia and Montenegro) to continue automatically the membership of the former Socialist Federal Republic of Yugoslavia in the United Nations has not been generally accepted.'[57] This was a credible statement in light of the rejection by a significant number of States of Yugoslavia's claim to continuity.[58]

In particular, the new States which had emerged in the territory of the former SFRY rejected, *inter alia*, Yugoslavia's claim to continue the old State. They were consistent in this position. According to Bosnia and Herzegovina, Croatia, Macedonia and Slovenia,

> All States that have emerged from the dissolution of the former Socialist Federal Republic of Yugoslavia, which has ceased to exist, are equal successor States. The Federal Republic of Yugoslavia (Serbia and Montenegro) also has to follow the procedure for admission of new Member States to the United Nations, which would enable the Organization to make its judgment on whether the conditions set out in Article 4 of the Charter of the United Nations are met.[59]

The reference to the 'judgment' of the Organization and the 'conditions set out in Article 4' perhaps was mere formula. In light however of the conduct of

---

[54] Letter dated 17 April 1992 from the Chargé d'Affaires ad interim of the Permanent Mission of Yugoslavia to the United Nations addressed to the President of the Security Council, Annex, Declaration adopted on 27 April 1992 at the joint session of the Assembly of the Socialist Federal Republic of Yugoslavia, the National Assembly of the Republic of Serbia and the Assembly of the Republic of Montenegro: S/23877–A/46/915.

[55] Ibid., ¶ 5.

[56] Ibid., ¶ 6.

[57] SC res 757, 30 May 1992.

[58] The USA, among others, rejected the continuity position as well. For references to statements by these and other States rejecting the continuity position, see *UN Ybk* 1992 p. 138. See also statements of Mr Hohenfellner (Austria) and Mr Erdös (Hungary): S/PV.3116 p. 16, 19 Sept 1992.

[59] Letter dated 28 October 1996 from the Permanent Representatives of Bosnia and Herzegovina, Croatia, the Former Yugoslav Republic of Macedonia and Slovenia to the United Nations addressed to the Secretary-General: A/51/564–S/1996/885.

Yugoslavia at the time, it may be asked whether the other successor States had it in view that a fresh FRY application might not receive immediate recommendation. Bosnia and Croatia instituted proceedings against Yugoslavia in the International Court under the Convention for the Prevention and Punishment of the Crime of Genocide in 1993 and 1999 respectively.[60] Further suggestions can be detected that certain States were considering the possibility of challenging a Yugoslav application on the terms of Article 4(1)'s substantive criteria. The United States, for example, which by veto could block the requisite Security Council recommendation, said that it would support UN admission for Yugoslavia only when 'Serbia and Montenegro meet the criteria in the United Nations Charter, that is, the Federal Republic of Yugoslavia must show that it is a peace-loving State.'[61] The Yugoslav continuity position would have avoided, among other problems, the pitfall of a membership application.

The Security Council, having to deal with the competing positions, adopted resolution 777 on 19 September 1992. In one matter, resolution 777 was clear enough: It '[c]onsider[ed] that the state formerly known as the Socialist Federal Republic of Yugoslavia has ceased to exist.'[62] The implications which followed from that consideration would turn out to be less clear. The resolution provided that 'the Federal Republic of Yugoslavia (Serbia and Montenegro) cannot continue automatically the membership of the former Socialist Federal Republic of Yugoslavia in the United Nations.' It 'recommend[ed] to the General Assembly that it decide that the Federal Republic of Yugoslavia (Serbia and Montenegro) should apply for membership in the United Nations and that it shall not participate in the work of the General Assembly.'[63]

The General Assembly in resolution 47/1 of 22 September 1992 followed the Security Council position broadly, though without reiterating that the SFRY had ceased to exist. The Assembly considered

> that the Federal Republic of Yugoslavia (Serbia and Montenegro) cannot continue *automatically* the membership of the former Socialist Federal Republic of Yugoslavia in the United Nations; and therefore decides that the Federal Republic of Yugoslavia (Serbia and Montenegro) should apply for membership in the United Nations and that it shall not participate in the work of the General Assembly.[64]

---

[60] Bosnia on 20 March 1993: *Application of the Convention on the Prevention and Punishment of the Crime of Genocide (Bosnia and Herzegovina v Yugoslavia (Serbia and Montenegro))* (Request for Provisional Measures), Order of 8 Apr 1993, ICJ Rep 1993 pp. 3, 4–5; Croatia on 2 July 1999: *Application of the Convention on the Prevention and Punishment of the Crime of Genocide (Croatia v Yugoslavia)*, Order of 14 Sept 1999, ICJ Rep 1999 pp. 1014, 1015.

[61] Ms Albright (USA): S/PV.3204 p. 7, 28 Apr 1993.

[62] SC res 777, 19 Sept 1992 pream ¶ 2.

[63] Ibid., ¶ 1: S/PV.3116 p. 11 (12–0:3, China, India and Zimbabwe abstaining).

[64] GA res 47/1, 22 Sept 1992: A/47/PV.7 p. 186 (127–6:26, Kenya, Swaziland, Tanzania, Yugoslavia, Zambia and Zimbabwe against; Angola, Bahamas, Botswana, Brazil, Burundi, Cameroon,

These determinations influenced the disposition of organs outside the UN system, where Yugoslavia's participation was curtailed as well.[65]

An initial question raised by the resolutions is the legal basis for the position that Yugoslavia had ceased to exist. Though only the Security Council resolution stated it explicitly, the position underlay both resolutions. An early authoritative statement of the position was made within the European peace process, specifically by the legal advisory body. The European Arbitration Commission had been clear that Yugoslavia was no more. The Commission said in Opinion No 1 of 29 November 1991 that 'the Socialist Federal Republic of Yugoslavia is in the process of dissolution.'[66] The Commission said in Opinion No 8 of 4 July 1992 that a federal State 'is seriously compromised when a majority of [its constituent] entities, embracing a greater part of the territory and population, constitute themselves as sovereign States with the result that federal authority may no longer be effectively exercised.'[67] The Commission determined, after considering, *inter alia*, the admission of Croatia, Slovenia, and Bosnia as UN members, that the SFRY 'no longer exists.'[68]

The Security Council had extended at least a degree of endorsement to the European framework which had been established to deal with the situation in the former SFRY, including, it would seem, to the arbitration organ.[69] A certain regard by the Security Council to the opinions adopted by that organ might be seen to have followed. A general interest to promote the legal regulation of potentially destabilizing problems of status also would have been a factor favouring Security Council support for, if not deference to, the Commission. Indeed, the Security Council seemingly adopted Opinion No 8 of the Commission, when it determined that Yugoslavia 'cannot continue automatically the membership' of the former SFRY in the UN and said that the SFRY 'ceased to exist.'[70]

The Opinions of the Commission have been scrutinized and found wanting by a number of writers.[71] The problem in the case of the Federal Republic of

---

China, Côte d'Ivoire, Cuba, Ghana, Guyana, India, Iraq, Jamaica, Lebanon, Lesotho, Mexico, Mozambique, Myanmar, Namibia, Papua New Guinea, Sri Lanka, Togo, Uganda, Viet Nam and Zaire abstaining).

[65] Crawford *Creation* 2nd edn 709 n. 48.

[66] 92 ILR 162, 162–3.

[67] Opinion No 8, 4 July 1992: reprinted (1992) 31 ILM 1521.

[68] Ibid., 92 ILR 199, 201, 202/

[69] SC res 713, 25 Sept 1991, establishing the arms embargo against Yugoslavia, 'commended' the EC for 'convening…a Conference on Yugoslavia, including the mechanisms set forth within it' and indicated support for 'the smooth functioning of the process instituted within the framework of the Conference on Yugoslavia.'

[70] SC res 777, 19 Sept 1992, preamble.

[71] For a range of views, see Stahn 'The Agreement on Succession Issues of the Former Socialist Federal Republic of Yugoslavia' (2002) 96 *AJ* 379; Radan 'Post-Secession International Borders: A Critical Analysis of the Opinions of the Badinter Arbitration Commission' (2000) 24 *Melbourne*

Yugoslavia, however, was not so much some infirmity in the determination that the old SFRY had ceased to exist but, rather, the way in which the principal organs of the United Nations interpreted and implemented that determination. If Yugoslavia was no more, then a clear path existed to deal with the situation: the resultant successor States, including the Federal Republic of Yugoslavia, were not member States of the UN, and each was free to apply for membership in the usual way. The problem is that the Security Council and General Assembly were not entirely clear what Yugoslavia's position in the Organization from that point onward was. In their ambiguity, the two principal organs failed to declare a clean break as regarded Yugoslavia's membership. The ambiguity, as against prior determinations, tended to kindle Yugoslav hopes that the UN might give further support to the position that the situation was one of State continuity.[72] And, yet, by turns, the Council and Assembly also asserted the validity of the position that the situation instead was one of State extinction. This in brief was how the UN contributed to the legal confusion attending the fate of Yugoslavia.

Member States by no means uniformly supported the approach being taken with respect to Yugoslav membership. Statements made upon adoption of Security Council resolution 777 and General Assembly resolution 47/1 reflected a range of opinion.

A number of States observed that the resolutions, though not formally adopted under either Article 5 or Article 6, nevertheless had effects that could be likened to suspension or expulsion. A question, it was said, thus arose as to the constitutional basis for the measures taken. According to India,

> There are specific provisions in the Charter regarding membership in the Organization...The draft resolution...does not conform to either Article 5 or Article 6 of the Charter, the only two Articles that deal with the issue which the draft resolution is attempting to address.

Univ LR 50; Rich 'Recognition of States: The Collapse of Yugoslavia and the Soviet Union' (1993) 4 *EJIL* 36; Türk 'Recognition of States: A Comment' (1993) 4 *EJIL* 66; Pellet 'The Opinions of the Badinter Arbitration Committee: A Second Breath for the Self-determination of Peoples' (1992) 3 *EJIL* 178.

[72] See e.g. position set out in *Case Concerning Legality of Use of Force (Yugoslavia v Belgium)* Dis Op Judge *ad hoc* Kreča ICJ Rep 1999 pp. 124, 229–30 ¶ 8.2:

> [T]he Federal Republic of Yugoslavia's membership in the Organization can be continued but not automatically. True, the resolution does not elaborate how that can be achieved but, if we interpret it systematically and together with Security Council resolutions 757 and 777, we will come to the conclusion that the Federal Republic of Yugoslavia's membership in the Organization can be continued in case such a request is "generally accepted".

The Security Council...is competent to recommend either suspension or expulsion of a State. Nowhere in the Charter has the Security Council been given the authority to recommend to the General Assembly that a country's participation in the Assembly be withdrawn or suspended.[73]

China, which together with India and Zimbabwe had abstained from the vote adopting Security Council resolution 777, said, by contrast, that 'the resolution...does not mean the expulsion of Yugoslavia from the United Nations.'[74] This might have been seen as an attempt, in the margins of the resolution itself, to characterize its terms so as to pre-empt a less charitable interpretation. Such interpretation was forthcoming. Kenya, for example, said that the measure to be adopted 'would be tantamount to either the suspension of a Member State...as provided for in Article 5...or...expulsion...as provided for in Article 6.'[75] It is doubted, however, whether there ever has been, or could be, an implied suspension or expulsion from the UN.[76] Zimbabwe said that the measures against South Africa (when its participation in the General Assembly had been blocked through credentialing procedure), were less severe than those now being taken against the FRY – a relation, Zimbabwe suggested, inexplicable in view of the relative gravity of the misconduct in question.[77] Zimbabwe, as victim and more recently author of misconduct, perhaps had special insight for making such comparisons.

A number of States expressed concern as to the legal basis for the resolutions. This related both to the general matter of separation of powers between Council and Assembly (a recurring theme in statements of Non-Aligned States and others not holding permanent Security Council seats); and the specific matter of Articles 5 and 6. Ghana, speaking during the General Assembly proceedings prior to adoption of General Assembly resolution 47/1, said that the Security Council does not have competence under the Charter to recommend the cessation of a State's participation in the General Assembly.[78] Mexico said, after adoption of General Assembly resolution 47/1, that 'the text of the resolution contains nothing that would indicate its basis in law...it finds no support in Article 4, 5 or 6 of the Charter.'[79] Guyana expressed 'great concern about the lack of a clear legal basis for the resolution.' 'Standing as it does against the background

---

[73] Mr Gharekhan (India) S/PV.3116 p. 7, 19 Sept 1992.
[74] Mr Li Daoyu (China) S/PV.3116 p. 14.
[75] Mr Adala (Kenya) A/47/PV.7 p. 167. See also statement of Mr Mwaanga (Zambia) A/47/PV.7 p. 173; Mr Nyakyi (Tanzania) A/47/PV.7, p. 176.
[76] Amerasinghe 117.
[77] Mr Mumbengegwi (Zimbabwe) A/47/PV.7 pp. 164–5.
[78] Mr Ibn Chambas (Ghana) A/47/PV.7 p. 161, 22 Sept 1992.
[79] Mr Montaño (Mexico) A/47/PV.7 p. 188.

of Articles 5 and 6 of the Charter,' Guyana added, 'this important measure should have been…appropriately clothed with legal argument.'[80] Tanzania regretted that the member States had not considered referring the question of Yugoslavia's status to the International Court.[81]

A position that 'does not conform to either Article 5 or Article 6' but which includes some of the practical effects of measures under those articles well may raise questions as to its legal basis. It is no surprise that several member States expressed concern over the absence of formal legal advice at the time. In view of the doubt, the question might be asked, would it not have been more straightforward to expel Yugoslavia? Expulsion, like suspension, after all, has the virtue of a clear basis in the Charter, as well as a clear result. A logical problem however would have presented itself in the circumstances: if in truth the SFRY had ceased to exist (and that position itself had been authoritatively determined), then the SFRY simply could not have been an object of further action of any type under the membership provisions of the Charter. As it had become unsafe in Major Strasser's estimation for Victor Laszlo to stay in Casablanca and equally unsafe for him to leave, so had it become in view of the measures adopted dubious to talk of Yugoslavia staying in the UN; equally dubious to talk of it being expelled.[82] The better position may be that Yugoslav membership by operation of law had lapsed,[83] and, as a matter of convenience and in the interest of comity, Yugoslav representatives were permitted to linger at the UN, albeit under indeterminate rights, during a period when the Organization was endeavouring to achieve a negotiated settlement of on-going Balkan wars.

The spring following adoption of Security Council resolution 777 and General Assembly resolution 47/1, the Security Council recommended that the General Assembly, 'further to the decisions taken in resolution 47/1,' decide that the FRY 'shall not participate in the work of the Economic and Social Council.'[84]

From a strictly political standpoint, the problem appears to have been that the member States, including the Permanent Members of the Security Council, did not agree what balance should be struck between sustaining negotiations

---

[80] Mr Insanally (Guyana) A/47/PV.7 pp. 194–5.

[81] Mr Nyakyi (Tanzania) A/47/PV.7 p. 177. See also statement of Ms Mair (Jamaica) noting lack of 'authoritative legal opinion' on the matters in issue: A/47/PV.7 p. 193.

[82] Epstein, Epstein & Koch *Casablanca* (1942) pp. 80, 94–5: http://www.imsdb.com cf. *Case Concerning Legality of Use of Force (Yugoslavia v Belgium)* Sep Op Judge Oda ICJ Rep 1999 pp. 124, 145 ¶ 3.

[83] Amerasinghe leans in this direction, suggesting that the extinction of a member State results in termination of membership without formal action under the constitutive instrument: Amerasinghe 117.

[84] SC res 821, 28 Apr 1993 ¶ 1, S/PV.3204 pp. 3–5 (13–0:2, China and Russian Federation abstaining).

with the FRY on the one hand and sending a signal of disapprobation on the other. Formal expulsion from the Organization would have been the limit of measures under the membership provisions of the Charter. If expelled, however, the FRY, the thinking went, would have rejected the negotiation process altogether. France, for example, called Security Council resolution 777 'a pragmatic approach' under which the FRY could continue to engage in 'dialogue in Geneva, within the framework of the implementation of the London Conference; in the field, in the light of the need for the cooperation of all the parties with the United Nations Protection Force; and of course here in New York.'[85] Russia was clear that the FRY 'should [not] be excluded, formally or de facto, from membership in the United Nations,' and, like France, viewed continued participation as aiding the peace process.[86] Botswana did not support General Assembly resolution 47/1 but broadly concurred with France and Russia that it was better to preserve contact between the UN and Yugoslavia: 'Yugoslavia,' Botswana's representative said,

> should be kept tightly in the clutches of the United Nations Charter by virtue of its membership of the Organization. It deserves no breathing space on the sidelines, where, rightly or wrongly feeling wronged and persecuted, it can be more troublesome than it has been so far.[87]

A State or other entity need not be a UN member to participate in a negotiation process co-ordinated by the UN,[88] but member States evidently clung to the hope that something would be gained by stopping short of a clear break.

---

[85] Mr Merimee (France) S/PV.3116 p. 12. See also statement of Mr Montaño (Mexico) A/47/PV.7 p. 188 (relative to maintaining UNPROFOR and the London Conference framework).

[86] Mr Vorontsov (Russian Federation) S/PV.3116 pp. 4–5.

[87] Mr Legwaila (Botswana) A/47/PV.7, pp. 169–70, 22 Sept 1992. cf statement of Mr Sardenberg (Brazil) A/47/PV.7 p. 190.

[88] The Republika Srpska during the Dayton negotiations and the Turkish Republic of Northern Cyprus repeatedly since its formation are salient examples. Certain insurgent groups also have participated in negotiations under a UN framework, e.g. the Frente Farabundo Martí para la Liberación Nacional (FMLN), which concluded an Agreement on Human Rights with the Salvadorian Government, about which see Zegveld *Accountability of Armed Opposition Groups in International Law* (2002) 16–7, 49–51. There was also the appearance of non-State entities (Hyderabad is the main case) before the Security Council under Article 35(2) – particularly convincing proof that participation is not conclusive as to statehood. In none of these cases was the entity accepted as a State, and its presence in negotiations did not in itself lead to general legal consequences – though parties might plead consequences from it. Yugoslavia, referring to the Croat, Muslim, and Serb political formations in Bosnia and Herzegovina, said that '[t]he leaders of these State entities are recognized by the United Nations and the European Community as equal participants at the Geneva negotiations which began on 27 July 1993': Rodoljub Etinski (Agent for the FRY) Written Observations of the Federal Republic of Yugoslavia (*Genocide* case) 9 Aug 1993 p. 8 ¶ 8. The point was to argue that participation demonstrated those 'entities' to

The situation as it thus stood gave rise to significant problems concerning succession to rights and obligations of Yugoslavia, not least of all problems related to jurisdiction under the Statute of the International Court. These problems in turn complicated the legal proceedings arising out of the situation in the former SFRY. The International Court adopted contradictory positions[89] for which it was sharply criticized;[90] and the problems of UN membership acquired a sort of afterlife in cases before the International Criminal Tribunal for the Former Yugoslavia.[91] More will be said in the final Chapter below about membership and participation in ICJ proceedings.

In the background to the transactions at the UN was the conduct of the Federal Republic of Yugoslavia in the civil wars in Croatia and Bosnia. Yugoslavia was seen to be a causal agent behind violence in both countries, and the risk was apprehended that Yugoslavia might foment further strife elsewhere in the former territory of the SFRY. Writers have disagreed as to the effect the civil wars had on the legal position of Yugoslavia. Schermers and Blokker say that Yugoslavia's position on continuity with the SFRY was rejected 'perhaps because it was considered the main party responsible for the outbreak of war in the territory of

---

be States – and thus Bosnia and Herzegovina, as against their statehood, could not itself be a State. The ICJ, while declining to address what effect non-recognition by the FRY might have had, did not accept the conclusion sought to be reached: ICJ Rep 1996 pp. 595, 611, 613 ¶¶ 19, 26. The FRY's mistake was to assume that only States can negotiate.

[89] Compare *Application for Revision of the Judgment of 11 July 1996 in the Case Concerning Application of the Convention on the Prevention and Punishment of the Crime of Genocide (Bosnia and Herzegovina v Yugoslavia)* (Preliminary Objections) Judgment of 3 Feb 2003 ICJ Rep 2003 pp. 7, 31–2 ¶¶ 70–2; and *NATO cases* (Preliminary Objections) Judgment of 15 Dec 2004 ICJ Rep 2004 pp. 279, 308–10 ¶¶ 74–9 esp ¶ 79. From the former decision, it well may be inferred that there are only admitted States – a considerable further support to the universality of the UN. The 2004 judgment declined jurisdiction on grounds that Yugoslavia was *not* a member. The best analysis is Crawford *Creation* 2nd edn 707–14.

[90] See esp. Joint Declaration of Vice-President Ranjeva, and Judges Guillaume, Higgins, Kooijmans, Al-Khasawneh, Buergenthal and Elaraby: ICJ Rep 2004 pp. 279, 330–4.

[91] Kerr *The International Criminal Tribunal for the Former Yugoslavia. An exercise in law, politics, and diplomacy* (2004) 185–9; Akande 'The Jurisdiction of the International Criminal Courts over Nationals of Non-Parties: Legal Basis and Limits' (2003) 1 *J Int'l Crim Justice* 618, 628–31. Akande says that, 'whilst some of the membership rights of a state (e.g., voting rights) may be taken from a member of the organization, a state is either a member or it is not. It cannot be a member for certain purposes but not for others.' In light of the practice of including Taiwan for various purposes in certain organizations, it may be asked whether this is too categorical. See also the discussion in the *NATO cases* about the three distinct positions taken by different parts of the UN system with respect to the relationship between Yugoslavia and the UN in the 1990s. One may infer from this that an entity may be a member of the UN for some purposes (e.g., responsibility to meet annual financial assessments) but not for others (e.g., voting in the General Assembly): *Case Concerning Legality of Use of Force (Serbia and Montenegro v Belgium)* Preliminary Objections, Judgment of 15 Dec 2004, ICJ Rep 2004 pp. 279, 305–7 ¶¶ 65–70.

the former Yugoslavia.'[92] Michael Wood calls Yugoslavia's involvement in the regional wars 'legally irrelevant.' The difference of view merits consideration.

Practice has established that unlawful use of force well may undermine the claim of an entity to constitute a State. The unlawfulness of the military measures taken by the sponsoring State was a central consideration when other States rejected the purported creation of Manchukuo; and later of the Turkish Republic of Northern Cyprus. Breaches of certain other peremptory norms of international law likewise have frustrated attempts to establish new States – e.g., in Rhodesia and the South African 'Homelands.' Plainly, a claim by an occupying authority to have established a new State as against the subsisting claims of the State whose territory is occupied, even where occupation itself is under colour of law, is problematic. Yugoslavia's claim was the opposite: continuity does not concern creation of a new State but, rather, it is to assert that there has been no change in legal personality as between an earlier and a later point in time. Also, to be sure, its breach of a peremptory norm does not result in a State, the continuous existence of which is undisputed, ceasing to be a State. But, where continuity is disputed, whether there has existed a single State during the relevant period is the very matter in issue. In a close case between continuity and succession, credible evidence that the claimant has breached a basic rule (e.g., the prohibition against use of force, prohibition against genocide) may be relevant, even as the evidence, on its own, does not defeat the claim of continuity. In the least, the views of States that are targets of aggression by the claimant will be given some consideration in reaching a general judgment as to the continuity claim.

Assuming that Yugoslavia in the 1990s was indeed a new State, Yugoslavia's involvement in the wars most certainly was not irrelevant under a strict reading of the Charter with respect to admission of new members. The main question, for present purposes, is whether Yugoslavia's involvement in the Balkan civil wars actually entered into consideration under Article 4(1) or related Charter provisions. The UN, in response to the situation in the territory of the former SFRY, clearly aimed to subject Yugoslavia's participation to qualification in some way. The problem was a failure to adopt a form of qualification that fit within established Charter categories.[93] As James Crawford has suggested, the focus in the General Assembly on the apparatus of membership (seats, name-plates, flags etc) suggested 'that the problem here was more like one of representation or

---

[92] *International Institutional Law* 3rd edn (1995) 76, quoted at Wood (1997) 1 *Max Planck Ybk UN Law* 231, 244 n. 33. cf. Lloyd 'Succession, Secession, and State Membership in the United Nations' (1994) 26 *NYU J Int'l L & Pol* 761, 783.

[93] See Blum's criticism: Blum 'Was Yugoslavia a Member of the United Nations in the Years 1992–2000?' (2007) 101 *AJ* 800, 818.

credentials than of the existence of the entity in question as a State.'[94] Doubt as to the statehood of the Yugoslav entity does not seem to have been the problem. The problem was the conduct of the State.

It will be recalled that statehood is not the only criterion for membership set out in Article 4(1), even as, in practice, it may have come to be the one, residual criterion applied in actual membership questions. The confused, even contradictory, positions adopted with respect to participation of the FRY in the 1990s perhaps were the outward sign of a subterranean effort to apply more rigorously the other substantive admission criteria. If intervention in civil wars of neighbouring States is not relevant to the criterion of being 'peace-loving' or of having the willingness to carry out Charter obligations, then it would seem that scarcely any actual situation would be relevant to an Article 4(1) criterion. That a more definite position could not be set out in respect of Yugoslav membership perhaps reflects the uncertainties which remained, as to the exact scope of Yugoslav responsibility for events in the Balkan civil wars. Yet that there were serious questions about Yugoslav conduct could not be denied. Even *in extremis*, then, perhaps the only remaining criterion is statehood.

Yugoslavia itself did not definitively abandon its claim to continue the SFRY – and did not, accordingly, apply for admission – until a point in time at which active Yugoslav involvement in the civil wars had ceased. The FRY application, when finally it was made, thus did not serve directly to test the operability of the other Article 4(1) criteria. That the application did wait until activity had ceased in the military theatre itself however suggests that Yugoslavia had been seriously concerned that an application earlier might have been rejected. Statements by member States with Security Council veto power in particular may have been interpreted as cause for concern. The statement of the United States Permanent Representative was noted above. In full, Permanent Representative Albright said

> The United States will support the application of the Federal Republic of Yugoslavia for membership in this Organization when – and only when – Serbia and Montenegro meet the criteria in the United Nations Charter, that is, the Federal Republic of Yugoslavia must show that it is a peace-loving State and demonstrate its willingness to comply fully with Chapter VII resolutions of the Security Council.[95]

A similar, if slightly less emphatic, statement had been made upon adoption of Security Council resolution 777.[96] On adoption of General Assembly resolution 47/1, the UK Permanent Representative, Sir David Hannay, said,

---

[94] Crawford *Creation* 2nd edn 709.
[95] Ms Albright (USA) S/PV.3204 p. 7, 28 Apr 1993. Wood says that the FRY wished to avoid a new application, among other reasons, because it 'might well have been unsuccessful': (1997) 1 *Max Planck Ybk UN Law* 231, 243.
[96] Mr Watson (USA) S/PV.3116 p. 13, 19 Sept 1992.

If and when an application is submitted by the Federal Republic of Yugoslavia (Serbia and Montenegro) it would likewise be considered in accordance with the Charter. The conditions for admission to membership set out in Article 4 of the Charter are clear: the applicant must be a peace-loving State; it must accept the obligations contained in the Charter; and it must, in the judgment of the Organization, be able and willing to carry out these obligations.[97]

The Hungarian representative put it more bluntly. Though he qualified his observation as being on 'political terms,' the Hungarian representative said that 'the primary responsibility for the bloody events that have been laying waste the territory of the former Yugoslavia for a year and a half must undeniably be borne by the authorities in Belgrade.'[98]

The positions here taken, apart from implying that Yugoslavia had legal responsibility or at least should have been held politically accountable for violence in the former territory of the SFRY, suggest the significance of controls on admission to membership generally: admission is not an incidental function of the international organization, nor one that presumptively yields to other obligations. This is consistent with the position under the 1978 Vienna Convention on the Succession of States in respect of Treaties. Article 4 of the Convention contains a 'without prejudice' clause respecting, *inter alia*, 'the rules concerning acquisition of membership.'[99] Even where rights and obligations under treaties of the predecessor State by operation of the law codified in the 1978 Convention may continue (or not),[100] membership, in principle, is to be considered according to the constitutive instrument. In short, where the constitutive instrument requires a fresh look, the régime of succession does not intervene. The warning, scarcely concealed in the statements noted above, was that, under a fresh look, the FRY well may have failed to satisfy the Charter's own rules.

The difficulties surrounding Yugoslav membership suggest a wider point as well. The State remains the principal holder of rights and obligations under international law.[101] It follows that to cast the identity of a State in doubt is to present significant problems in fixing international responsibility for conduct for which no other international legal person in the circumstances can plausibly be held responsible: if there is no State, and no other actor can be held to account, then the conduct in question goes undeterred and any parties whom it may have injured unrepaired. The International Court at first, by maintaining

---

[97] Sir David Hannay (United Kingdom) A/47/PV.7 pp. 142–3, 22 Sept 1992.

[98] Mr Erdös (Hungary) A/47/PV.7 p. 182.

[99] Vienna Convention on the Succession of States in Respect of Treaties, adopted 23 Aug 1978; entered into force 6 Nov 1996: 1946 UNTS 4, 7.

[100] On the problems which arose with respect to Yugoslavia's participation in various multilateral treaties, see Craven 'The *Genocide* Case, the Law of Treaties and State Succession' (1997) 68 *BY* 127; Wood (1997) 1 *Max Planck Ybk UN Law* 231, 251–6.

[101] See Chapter 4, pp. 109–11, above.

a 'studied neutrality,'[102] found its way to holding that at least certain breaches of international law in the civil wars of the early 1990s could be attached to Yugoslavia.[103] This was more satisfactory than judging that no actor could be held responsible, but side-stepping the question of Yugoslavia's identity had a cost if one values clarity in jurisprudence. It would be a far reach to say that the Court's holdings on jurisdiction, standing, and opposability in the Yugoslav cases were among its clearest. A definitive position from the United Nations as a whole relative to the identity of Yugoslavia might have opened a more direct path for the Court. The most direct path for the UN as a whole on the matter of Yugoslavia's identity would have been to call early on for a new application to membership and, even if this had failed, the option still would have been open to have included Yugoslavia as a non-member State in the processes of the Court.

The UN Legal Counsel had advised in 1992 that 'admission to the United Nations of a new Yugoslavia under Article 4 of the Charter [would] terminate the situation created by resolution 47/1.'[104] The Federal Republic of Yugoslavia eventually accepted that it was not a continuation of the SFRY,[105] which set the legal groundwork for its own application.[106] The Security Council recommended admission, and the General Assembly admitted the FRY on 1 November 2000.[107]

(ii) *Slovenia, Croatia, and Bosnia and Herzegovina*

Three of the States emerging out of the disintegration of the SFRY were admitted to the UN on 22 May 1992.[108] The independence of Slovenia, Croatia, and Bosnia and Herzegovina already had been recognized by the United States and most of the States of Europe.[109]

---

[102] Crawford *Creation* 2nd edn 711.

[103] *Application of the Convention on the Prevention and Punishment of the Crime of Genocide (Bosnia and Herzegovina v Serbia and Montenegro)* Judgment of 26 Feb 2007 ¶¶ 377–458.

[104] Letter dated 29 September 1992 from the Under-Secretary General, the Legal Counsel, addressed to the Permanent Representatives of Bosnia and Herzegovina and Croatia to the United Nations: A/47/485, Annex.

[105] Letter dated 27 Oct 2000 from President of the FRY to the Secretary-General, A/55/528, S/2000/1043; Agreement on Succession Issues, 29 June 2001: (2002) 41 ILM 3.

[106] Ibid.

[107] SC res 1326, 31 Oct 2000; GA res 55/12, 1 Nov 2000.

[108] Slovenia: SC res 754, 18 May 1992, GA res 46/236, 22 May 1992; Croatia: SC res 753, 18 May 1992, GA res 46/238, 22 May 1992; Bosnia and Herzegovina: SC res 755, 20 May 1992, GA res 46/237, 22 May.

[109] Grant *Recognition* 149–98.

Michael Wood sees the admission of Slovenia, Croatia, and Bosnia and Herze-govina as having given rise to '[n]o special problems.'[110] The process of admission indeed followed the usual procedure, and the associated UN statements took a standard form of words.[111] For Bosnia and Herzegovina however UN membership well may have had more constitutive relevance than it is received as having for States generally.[112] There was from the start a need to consolidate the new State as against serious disruptions of municipal public order and external threat. The later international settlement of the Bosnian civil war and the new government structures established pursuant to the settlement have continued to exist under international guarantee.[113] The integration of Bosnia and Herzegovina into inter-national organization thus has had more than the usual significance, even as its main incident – UN admission – was accomplished in the usual way.

6.1.3   States in the Former USSR

(i) *Introductory*

Political changes in the USSR led to significant re-organization of government in the late 1980s and, eventually, to separation of fourteen Union Republics from Russia. The question had been presented to the United Nations before, how to deal with the emergence of a new State from the territory of an exist-ing member. The main case was the separation of Pakistan from India in 1947. The First Committee requested advice from the Sixth Committee at the time as to the legal consequences. The question put (by Argentina) was, 'What are the legal rules to which, in the future, a State or States entering into international life through the division of a Member State of the United Nations should be subject?'[114] Law drafting projects later would consider in significantly greater

---

[110] (1997) 1 *Max Planck YBK UN Law* 231, 236.

[111] For Croatia see Report of the Committee on the Admission of New Members Concerning the Application of Croatia for Admission to the United Nations, S/23935, 15 May 1992; and SCOR 47th yr 3076th mtg 18 May 1992, adopting Committee recommendation without vote. For Slovenia see Report of the Committee on the Admission of New Members Con-cerning the Application of Slovenia for Admission to the United Nations, S/23936, 15 May 1992; and SCOR 47th yr 3077th mtg 15 May 1992, adopting Committee recommendation without vote. For Bosnia and Herzegovina see Report of the Committee on the Admission of New Members Concerning the Application of Bosnia and Herzegovina for Admission to the United Nations, S/23974, 20 May 1992; SCOR 47th yr 3078th and 3079th mtgs 20 May 1992, adopting Committee recommendation without vote.

[112] Cf. O'Keefe (2001) 1 *Baltic YBIL* 167, 175.

[113] About which see Grant 'Internationally Guaranteed Constitutive Order: Cyprus and Bosnia as Predicates for a New Nontraditional Actor' (1998) 8 *J Trans L & Pol'y* 1.

[114] Letter of the President of the General Assembly dated 26 September 1947, A/C.6/145, GAOR 2nd sess, 6th Comm, pp. 304–5, annex 6.

detail the general matter of the emergence of new States, with a view especially to setting out rules to govern succession to treaties.[115] The Sixth (Legal) Committee in 1947, in answering the question at hand, concerned itself chiefly with the question of membership in the Organization, so the answer given is directly relevant for present purposes. According to the Sixth Committee,

> 1. [A]s a general rule, it is in conformity with legal principles to presume that a State which is a Member of the Organization of the United Nations does not cease to be a Member simply because its Constitution or its frontier have been subjected to changes, and that the extinction of the State as a legal personality recognized in the international order must be shown before its rights and obligations can be considered thereby to have ceased to exist...
> 2. [W]hen a new State is created, whatever may be the territory and the populations which it comprises and whether or not they formed part of a State Member of the United Nations, it cannot under the system of the Charter claim the status of a Member of the United Nations unless it has been formally admitted as such in conformity with the provisions of the Charter.[116]

The continuity of States, as noted in Chapter 4 above, is a presumption in international law. The link between statehood and membership in the United Nations, which has been the subject of extensive comment,[117] would seem to support the position that membership, too, like statehood itself, is subject to a presumption of continuity. As the Sixth Committee advised, 'simply because its Constitution or its frontier' have changed does not mean that a State's legal personality has come to an end – an observation which the Committee connected directly to membership. Membership, too, the Committee said continues through constitutional and territorial change. Creation of a new State, for example from the territory of an existing member State, by contrast, does not have the effect of carrying over to the new State the membership of the State from which it separated. Membership must be sought anew, and by the new State on its own account.

(ii) *The Agreed End of Soviet Power*
The position with respect to Pakistan and India set out in the first years of the Charter at least broadly applied in the 1990s with respect to the separation of territory from the USSR.[118] Russia would continue the legal personality of

---

[115] See esp. Arts 16–29, Vienna Convention on Succession of States in Respect of Treaties, adopted 22 Aug 1978, entered into force, 6 Nov 1996: 1946 UNTS 3, 9–18.

[116] Letter of the Chairman of the Sixth (Legal) Committee addressed to the Chairman of the First Committee, dated 8 October 1947: A/C.1/212, GAOR 2nd sess, 1st Comm pp. 582–3, annex 14g.

[117] See, e.g., Dugard *Recognition and the United Nations* (1987).

[118] A position suggested by Scharf 'Musical Chairs: The Dissolution of States and Membership in the United Nations' (1995) 28 *Cornell ILJ* 29, 50–1.

the USSR, including the various incidents thereof. The other Union Republics established their independence as new States. These measures were not the result of the operation of law alone. They were regulated by specific agreements among the parties concerned. A significant step in the independence of the various Union Republics was the express consent of Russia to the separation. Russia acknowledged the independence of the Baltic States of Latvia, Lithuania, and Estonia in August/September 1991. For the rest, a general framework was fashioned to establish the independence of new States, the consent of Russia thereto, and a political basis for their future relations. The other Union Republics, except Georgia, entered into an agreement in December 1991 establishing the Commonwealth of Independent States, to which Russia too is a party, and by which their independence was established and the end of the USSR as a political formation ratified. The Minsk Agreement and its Alma Ata Protocol constitute the legal mechanism by which ten Union Republics and Russia achieved the orderly separation of the former from the latter. The details of the arrangements ending the Soviet Union may be related briefly.

Russia, Belarus and Ukraine entered into the Minsk Agreement on 8 December 1991. Article 1 of the Minsk Agreement establishes a Commonwealth of Independent States (CIS).[119] Article 11 terminated the application of Soviet law in the participating States' territories from the time of signature.[120] Article 14 terminated the activities of all former USSR organs in the participating States' territories.[121] By Article 13 of the Minsk Agreement, the agreement 'is open for accession by all States members of the former Union of Soviet Socialist Republics, and also by other States sharing the purposes and principles of [the] Agreement.'[122]

A Declaration by the Heads of State of the Republic of Belarus, the RSFSR and Ukraine accompanied the Minsk Agreement. The Declaration '[n]ot[ed] . . . that the de facto process of withdrawal of republics from the Union of Soviet Socialist Republics and the formation of independent States has become a reality.'[123]

Another eight former Union Republics joined the three States parties to the Minsk Agreement in adopting a Protocol to that agreement at Alma Ata on 21 December 1991.[124] The Alma Ata Protocol provides that Azerbaijan, Armenia, Belarus, Kazakhstan, Kyrgyzstan, Moldova, the Russian Federation, Tajikistan, Turkmenistan, Uzbekistan, and Ukraine 'shall constitute the Commonwealth of Independent States.' The Protocol thus extended the Minsk Agreement to eight

---

[119] (1992) 31 ILM 138.
[120] Ibid., 145.
[121] Ibid., 146.
[122] Ibid., 146.
[123] Ibid., 142.
[124] (1992) 31 ILM 147: reprinted from A/47/60–S/23329, 30 Dec 1991.

States in addition to the three original parties.[125] In a Declaration adopted the same day at Alma Ata, the eleven parties stated, *inter alia*, that the CIS 'is neither a State nor a supra-State entity.'[126] Several further instruments were adopted on 21 December 1991 at Alma Ata, including instruments respecting command-and-control of nuclear weapons and the dismantling of Soviet public organs.

A Decision by the Council of Heads of State of the CIS also was adopted. In the Decision, the CIS member States stated that they intend 'to discharge the obligations under the Charter of the United Nations and to participate in the work of that Organization as full Members.'[127] In the second preambular paragraph of the Decision, they bore in mind 'that the Republic of Belarus, the Union of Soviet Socialist Republics and Ukraine were founder Members of the United Nations.' The first of two operative paragraphs of the Decision stated, 'The States of the Commonwealth support Russia's continuance of membership of the Union of Soviet Socialist Republics in the United Nations, including permanent membership of the Security Council, and other international organizations.'[128] This stood in significant contrast to the objections raised against the claim of Yugoslavia to exist as a continuation of the SFRY. The parties most directly concerned, in the Yugoslav case, rejected the claim. The parties most directly concerned, in the Russian case, accepted and 'support[ed]' it.

Article 14 of the Minsk Agreement establishing the CIS had designated Minsk the location of the Commonwealth's coordinating organs.[129] The CIS member States a year later adopted a CIS Charter. Article 7 of the CIS Charter defines as 'original members' those States which signed the Minsk Agreement and the Alma Ata Protocol. Article 7 of the CIS Charter, adopting the position set out in Article 13 of the Minsk Agreement noted above, provides that the CIS is open to 'any state sharing the purposes and the principles of the Commonwealth and assuming the obligations under the present Charter.'[130] Article 7 requires the agreement of all CIS members for the admission of a new member. Article 8 provides for associate membership and observer status. A member State may terminate its own membership (Article 9). The Commonwealth may adopt '[m]easures, acknowledged by [...] international law' against a member State for violation of the CIS Charter or for 'systematic non-fulfilment of its obligations' under CIS agreements or CIS decisions (Article 10).[131]

---

[125] Ibid., 147.

[126] 1st operative ¶: ibid., 148.

[127] Ibid., 151.

[128] Ibid., 151.

[129] (1992) 31 ILM 138, 146.

[130] Adopted at Minsk, 22 Jan 1993, entered into force 22 Jan 1994: 1819 UNTS 57, 61.

[131] 1819 UNTS 57, 62. On establishment of the Commonwealth of Independent States, see Yakemtchouk 'La Communauté des États Indépendants CEI' (1995) 41 *AFDI* 245.

The CIS member States, less Ukraine and Turkmenistan, established an Economic Union by treaty on 24 September 1993. Ukraine and Turkmenistan were at first associate members, Turkmenistan later joining as a full member. Georgia, the one former Union Republic not to have joined the CIS arrangements in December 1991, became a party to the Economic Union treaty in October 1993.[132] Georgia eventually became a full member but withdrew during the hostilities of August 2008.

The States emerging out of the former Soviet Union, with the exception of the Baltic States, thus established a multilateral treaty framework which, among other purposes, served to affirm the independence of those States and to support the continued UN membership of the three former USSR Union Republics which had been original members of the Organization. Particular issues arising out of the UN membership of those and the other former Union Republics now may be considered.

(iii) *The Baltic States*

Latvia, Lithuania, and Estonia established their effective independence from the Soviet Union somewhat earlier than the other Union Republics emerging as States in the early 1990s.[133] Each of the three States received assurances directly from Russia and from the USSR providing for their separation.[134] The status of Russia and the USSR was yet fully to be clarified, so the two broadly affirming Baltic independence helped remove uncertainty which might otherwise have arisen. The State Council of the Soviet Union recognized the three as independent States on 6 September 1991.[135] This sets the Baltic States apart from the other Union Republics, in that the other republics established their independence in a multilateral treaty framework consisting of the Minsk and Alma Ata instruments, as noted above.

A question presented by Latvia, Lithuania, and Estonia has been whether the independence which they established in the 1990s can be seen as a continuation of the independence of the three Baltic States established during the Russian Civil War and maintained until unlawful annexation by the USSR in 1940 (if not later). If Baltic independence can be seen as such, then a further question is what the practical incidents of that continuity might be.[136] Writers, some

---

[132] For a summary of these transactions and the purposes of the Economic Union, see Khabarov 'Introductory Note' (1995) 34 ILM 1298–1301.

[133] See Kharad 'La reconnaissance internationale des Etats baltes' (1992) 96 *RGDIP* 843.

[134] E.g. Lithuania by a Treaty on the Fundamentals of Interstate Relations between Lithuania and Russia, 29 July 1991: see Kalimas 'Legal Issues on the Continuity of the Republic of Lithuania' (2001) 1 *Baltic YBIL* 1, 14–5.

[135] Noted without citation by Ginther 'Article 4' in Simma *Charter of the United Nations: A Commentary* 2nd edn (2002) 177, 192.

[136] The widest surveys in English are Ziemele *State Continuity and Nationality: Baltic States and Russia: Past, Present and Future as Defined by International Law* (2005); Mälksoo *Illegal*

of them from the Baltic States, have argued the position of continuity.[137] The Baltic governments have for their part stated that their States are continuations of the pre-1940 independent Baltic States.[138] The period of submergence in the Soviet Union nevertheless was long, and the position that these were successor States also has been taken.[139] Some States acted on the assumption that the Baltic States in the 1990s were new States but had come into existence against a background of certain links to a pre-1940 personality.[140] In any event, the Baltic States in their earlier iteration had not exercised effective independence at the time of the adoption of the UN Charter. Even if the position is accepted that all of the pre-1940 rights of the then-independent Baltic States continued in the post-1990 Baltic States, UN membership could not, *ratio temporis*, have numbered among those rights. The Baltic States in September 1991 were admitted as member States in the normal way.[141]

(iv) *Ukraine and Belarus: Union Republics as Original Members*
Ukraine and Belarus, in 1945, were Union Republics of the Union of Soviet Socialist Republics. That is to say, as a matter of the constitutional law of the USSR, these were municipal components of the Soviet federation – with the usual consequences that such status entails under international law. The entities comprising a federation, while sometimes carrying out certain incidents of international relations on their own, do not possess international legal personality separate from the States of which they are part.[142] This position is reflected, for example, in Article 4 of the Articles on State Responsibility, where conduct of such subordinate entities is attributed to the State, not to the subordinate entities.[143] It therefore was anomalous that Ukraine and Belarus were accepted as Original

---

Annexation and State Continuity: the Case of the Incorporation of the Baltic States by the USSR (2003).

[137] See e.g. Kalimas op. cit.

[138] For a summary of relevant practice of Latvia, see Jākobsone 'Latvia: The Claim for Independence' (2001) 1 *Baltic YBIL* 233, 241–2; of Lithuania, see Jakštonytė & Cvelich 'Constitutional and International Documents Concerning the International Legal Status of Lithuania' ibid., 301, 301–2; of Estonia, see Salulaid 'Restoration of the Effect of Estonian International Treaties' ibid., 225.

[139] E.g. by the Russian Federation.

[140] This perhaps best describes the United States position: Grant 'United States Practice Relating to the Baltic States, 1940–2000' (2001) 1 *Baltic YBIL* 23, 49–55, 93–98.

[141] Estonia, SC res 709, 12 Sept 1991, GA res 46/4, 17 Sept 1991; Latvia, SC res 710, 12 Sept 1991, GA res 46/5, 17 Sept 1991; Lithuania, SC res 711, 12 Sept 1991, GA res 46/6, 17 Sept 1991.

[142] Crawford *Creation* 2nd edn 483–9. See also works cited Chapter 2, pp. 26–7 n. above.

[143] About which see Commentary ¶¶ (9), (10), Crawford ed *The International Law Commission's Articles on State Responsibility: Introduction, Text and Commentaries* (2002) 97–8.

Member States of the United Nations. The bargains involved in the arrangement were mentioned in Chapter 2. The consequence of the original membership of Ukraine and Belarus, as far as concerns developments in the 1990s, was that those Union Republics of the USSR, upon attaining independence in 1991, were treated as continuing UN membership already in effect. The CIS heads of State, in the Decision adopted on 21 December 1991 at Alma Ata, as noted above, bore in mind that Ukraine and Belarus were Original Members of the UN.[144] No application or act of admission therefore was required for either Belarus or Ukraine. It is difficult to draw any general principle from this practice, except, perhaps, that improvised solutions adopted to meet political circumstances in some instances have long-term legal and institutional effects.

(v) *Georgia*

The former Soviet Socialist Republic of Georgia, after establishing its independence from the USSR, went for a time before being admitted as a UN member State. Georgia held a referendum in which a large majority of the electorate endorsed independence. The declaration of independence was adopted on 9 April 1991.[145] The government of Zviad Gamsakhurdia however was not secure as against internal opponents. An armed attack on parliament on 22 December 1991 set events in train which would lead to Gamsakhurdia's forcible removal from power and the establishment, on 2 January 1992, of a military council in place of the elected government.[146] The election that had established the former government itself, however, had been subject to question, in light of serious irregularities in the polling process. The new, unelected governing authority appointed as its head Eduard Shevardnadze, the former foreign minister of the USSR. Shevardnadze's official position was confirmed by a national election on 11 October 1992. The government of Georgia, for approximately the first year and a half of Georgian independence, thus lacked a clear democratic basis. Complicating the situation further were separatist movements in Georgia and associated armed conflict.[147]

Whereas the three Baltic States had been admitted to the Organization on 17 September 1991; and the other non-Russian ex-Union Republics on 2 March 1992, admission of Georgia was (somewhat) delayed. First, Georgia itself delayed applying: its application was transmitted to the Secretary-General in letters from the President and the First Deputy Minister for Foreign Affairs

---

[144] (1992) 31 ILM at 151.
[145] Suny *The Making of the Georgian Nation* 2nd edn (1994) 326.
[146] Ibid., 328.
[147] Ibid., 328–32.

dated 6 May 1992.[148] Then it was two months before the Security Council voted to recommend admission.[149] The General Assembly admitted Georgia as the 179th member State on 31 July 1992.[150] Admission of the other former USSR republics had awaited affirmation that their separation had the consent of the USSR/Russian Federation. Consent was established by Russo-Soviet declarations in connection with each of the Baltic States; the instruments adopted at Minsk and Alma Ata established the legal basis for separation of the other republics. The delay in admitting Georgia may be attributed to doubts which presented themselves with respect to the Georgian government. The government was not the result of democratic decisions freely taken by the Georgian people; it had lost control over parts of the national territory; and violence between competing factions cast in doubt what hold the government had on affairs in Georgia generally. Considerations such as these had not been grounds in the past for delaying admission of a State to membership in the United Nations, so the possibility is presented either that (i) international law was undergoing development toward substantiation of rules concerning either effective government or democracy or both; or (ii) participation in the Minsk and Alma Ata framework was instrumental to satisfying the criterion of independent statehood, and, so, it was because Georgia had not entered that framework in December 1991 that UN admission was delayed.

Roger O'Keefe says that the criteria for admission under Article 4(1), in the cases of Moldova and Georgia, in view of the disruptions then occurring in their national territory, 'were appreciably indulged.'[151] The central governments at the time indeed lacked effective control over significant parts of the State territory. In Moldova, a 'Dnestr Soviet Republic' had sought to separate and remain part of the USSR;[152] in Georgia, South Ossetian and Abkhazian separatists denied the central government effective control over their provinces.[153] Georgia's admission,

---

[148] Circulated on 18 June 1992: A/46/938 – S/24116.

[149] SC res 763, 6 July 1992 (adopted without vote).

[150] GA res 46/241, 31 July 1992.

[151] O'Keefe (2001) 1 *Baltic YBIL* 167, 175.

[152] See the European Court of Human Rights' summary of events in Transdniestria: *Ilaşcu & Othrs v Moldova and Russia*, ECHR, Judgment of 8 July 2004, application no 48787/99 ¶¶ 28–66.

[153] The situations in Abkhazia and South Ossetia have been the subject of reports of a number of UN organs. See e.g. the précis in *Report of the Representative of the Secretary-General on the Human Rights of Internally Displaced Persons* (Walter Kälin), ECOSOC Commission on Human Rights, 24 March 2006: E/CN.4/2206/71/Add.7 pp. 5–6 ¶¶ 6–9. See also relative to Abkhazia Statements of the President of the Security Council: e.g. Note on measures toward a comprehensive political settlement of the conflict in Abkhazia, Georgia: S/24542, 10 Sept 1992; Note on the situation in Georgia: S/24637, 8 Oct 1992; Note on the situation in Abkhazia: S/25198, 29 Jan 1993. In August 2008, the long-running unrest in Abkhazia and

as noted, was somewhat delayed, but, otherwise, the Committee on Admission of New Members treated the application of Georgia as unexceptional. Moldova was admitted at the same time as the other CIS members. The eventual consent of the USSR to the separation of these States may be taken as completing the process of Moldova's and Georgia's establishment as States and their engagement with international organization. This may be seen as a reprise of earlier admission practice in connection with certain States in the 1960s (e.g., Congo) where, similarly, the absence of secure government in the national territory otherwise may have raised doubts under Article 4(1).

(vi) *Other Territories of the USSR*
The other States to accede to independence in the former territory of the USSR as noted above did so through a process of consent, their separation taking place on agreed terms. Certain assurances were obtained respecting the control and disposition of nuclear, chemical, and biological weapons; and succession to arms control agreements was established. No particular problems of admission to membership presented themselves.[154]

The Russian Federation, consistent with the 1947 advice of the Sixth Committee, continued the legal personality of the USSR and, thus, continued as an original member and Permanent Member of the Security Council. The change of name from 'Union of Soviet Socialist Republics' to 'Russian Federation' was notified by Russia to the Secretary-General in the following terms:

> I have the honour to inform you that the membership of the Union of Soviet Socialist Republics in the United Nations, including the Security Council, and in all other organs and organizations of the United Nations system is continued, with the support of the States of the Commonwealth of Independent States, by the Russian Federation (the RSFSR). In this connection, please, use in the United

---

South Ossetia considerably escalated. Russia deployed military forces in South Ossetia and other parts of Georgia following an attempt by the government of Georgia to re-establish central authority in the province. Russia on 26 August 2008 recognized South Ossetia and Abkhazia as independent States. The North Atlantic Council by a statement adopted 27 August 2008 condemned the recognition as 'violat[ing]' the many UN Security Council resolutions [Russia] has endorsed regarding Georgia's territorial integrity, and is inconsistent with the fundamental OSCE principles on which stability in Europe is based': http://www.nato.int/docu/pr/2008/p08–108e.html. No request for inclusion of South Ossetia or Abkhazia on the agenda for admission of new members to the UN had yet been made as of December 2008.

154 Armenia by SC res 735, 29 Jan 1992, GA res 46/227, 2 March 1992; Azerbaijan, SC res 742, 14 Feb 1992, GA res 46/230, 2 March 1992; Kazakhstan, SC res 732, 23 Jan 1992, GA res 46/224, 2 March 1992; Kyrgyzstan, SC res 736, 29 Jan 1992, GA res 46/225, 2 March 1992; Moldova, SC res 739, 5 Feb 1992, GA res 46/223, 2 March 1992; Tajikistan, SC res 738, 29 Jan 1992, GA res 46/228, 2 March 1992; Turkmenistan, SC res 741, 7 Feb 1992, GA res 46/229, 2 March 1992; Uzbekistan, SC res 737, 29 Jan 1992, GA res 464/226, 2 March 1992.

Nations the name "The Russian Federation" in the place of the name "The Union of Soviet Socialist Republics."

The Russian Federation remains responsible in full for all the rights and obligations of the USSR under the UN Charter, including the financial obligations.

Please, accept this letter as constituting credentials to represent the Russian Federation in the UN organs for all those currently possessing the credentials of the representatives of the USSR to the UN.[155]

The Minsk Agreement adopted several weeks before had stated in its preamble that 'the Union of Soviet Socialist Republics as a subject of international law and a geopolitical reality no longer exists.'[156] This statement would give rise to some confusion. The 'geopolitical reality' of the USSR certainly had changed, but, as the parties' own position eventually demonstrated, any legal change was not such as to break the continuity between Russia and the defunct Soviet Union for purposes of international law. In view of the particular purposes for which the statement itself was adopted, reliance on the statement by some writers to support a general position that Russia and the USSR were different States for international law purposes is mistaken. The earlier statement in the CIS framework instruments that the Soviet Union had ceased to exist 'as a subject of international law' was a political measure adopted to clarify that USSR instrumentalities would no longer operate in the territory of the other former Union Republics; and, of keen importance, to build confidence that no USSR body would oppose the separation of Union Republics from Russia and their establishment as independent States.[157] The intention was implicit in this to avoid confusion and violence the likes of which attended dissolution of the SFRY. If the statement to the effect that the USSR had been subject to extinction nevertheless is taken as having been intended to produce legal consequences, then the best view is that that statement was superseded by later characterizations, these in turn supported by largely consistent practice, at least with respect to Russia's membership in the UN.[158]

---

[155] Letter from Boris Yeltsin, President of the Russian Soviet Socialist Republic, to Javier Pérez de Cuellar, Secretary-General of the United Nations, as quoted in Scharf (1995) 28 *Cornell ILJ* 29, 46 n. 92. Original citation: ST/LEG/SER.E/18 (Vol. I), Ch. I.2, n. 9, 24 Dec 1991.

[156] (1992) 31 ILM 138, 143: reprinted from A/46/771, 13 Dec 1991.

[157] Though Lukashuk apparently saw the relation between the legal and political aspects differently: (1992) *86 ASIL Proc* 1, 23. cf Blum, who, apparently on the strength of the extinction statement in the CIS instruments, takes the (minority) view that the case for continuity between the SFRY and FRY was stronger than that for USSR/Russia: 'UN Membership of the "New" Yugoslavia: Continuity or Break?' (1992) 86 *AJ* 830, 832–3.

[158] Which by no means is to say that the matter of the identity of the Russian Federation was clear for all purposes. Questions of continuity and succession in the transition between USSR and Russian Federation led to an extensive literature reflecting the controversial points: see e.g. Dronova 'The Division of State Property in the Case of State Succession in the Former

It is not recorded whether Chechnya, the one territory to attempt to secede from Russia in the 1990s, took steps to apply for UN admission.[159]

6.1.4   *Czech and Slovak Republics*

Czechoslovakia, by way of voluntary dissolution, ceased to exist at the end of 1992.[160] Two new States resulted from this, and the Czech Republic and Slovakia were admitted as member States.[161] The United Nations notes, as an historical matter, that 'Czechoslovakia was an original Member of the United Nations from 24 October 1945.'[162] No State has continued the original membership of Czechoslovakia.

The Czech and Slovak cases in their contrast to others again suggest, if obliquely, the connection between UN membership and statehood. The instances in the 1990s in which the emergence of new States had been straightforward

---

Soviet Union' in Eiseman & Koskenniemi eds *State Succession: Codification Tested Against the Facts* (2000) 781; Bokor-Szegö 'Questions of State Identity and State Succession in Eastern and Central Europe' in Mrak ed *Succession of States* (1999) 95; Craven 'The Problem of State Succession and Identity Under International Law' (1998) 9 *EJIL* 142; Koskenniemi 'The Present State of Research Carried Out by the English-Speaking Section of the Centre for Studies and Research' in Eiseman & Koskenniemi eds *State Succession: Codification Tested Against the Facts* (1996) 98; Warbrick 'Recognition of States: Recent European Practice' in Evans ed *Aspects of Statehood and Institutionalism in Contemporary Europe* (1996) 9; Scharf (1995) 28 *Cornell ILJ* 29; Juillard 'The External Debt of the Former Soviet Union: Succession or Continuation?' in Burdeau & Stern eds *Dissolution, Continuation et Succession en Europe de l'Est: succession d'états et relations économiques internationales* (1994) 67; Shaw 'State Succession Revisited' (1994) 34 *Finn YBIL* 5; Williams 'The Treaty Obligations of the Successor States of the Former Soviet Union, Yugoslavia, and Czechoslovakia: Do They Continue in Force?' (1994) 23 *Denver JIL & Pol'y* 1; Müllerson 'The Continuity and Succession of States, by Reference to the Former USSR and Yugoslavia' (1993) 42 *ICLQ* 473; Rich 'Recognition of States: The Collapse of Yugoslavia and the Soviet Union' (1993) 4 *EJIL* 36; Symposium 'State Succession in the Former Soviet Union and in Eastern Europe' (1993) 33 *Virg JIL* 253; Blum 'The Soviet Union's Seat at the United Nations' (1992) 3 *EJIL* 354; Koskenniemi & Lehto 'La succession d'Etats dans l'ex URSS, en ce qui concerne particulièrement les relations avec la Finlande' (1992) 38 *AFDI* 905.

[159] On the limited international relations of Chechnya, see Grant 'Afghanistan Recognizes Chechnya' (2000) 15 *Am U ILR* 869–894.

[160] See Letter dated 10 December 1992 from the Permanent Representative of the Czech and Slovak Federal Republic to the United Nations addressed to the Secretary-General, noting the decision taken by the Federal Assembly on 25 Nov 1992 to dissolve the CSFR with effect from 31 Dec 1992; and communicating the intention that two new States would apply for admission thereafter: A/47/774.

[161] The Czech Republic was recommended for admission in SC res 801, 8 Jan 1993; the General Assembly voting to admit in GA res 47/221, 19 Jan 1993. Slovakia was recommended for admission in SC res 800, 8 Jan 1993; the General Assembly voting to admit in GA res 47/222, 19 Jan 1993.

[162] See list of Members: http://www.un.org/members/list.shtml

were the instances in which admission to the UN had been straightforward as well. Where controversy and doubt arose, they related both to State creation and to UN admission.

6.2   *Very Small Island States*

A number of States which gained independence in the 1960s and 1970s did not immediately seek admission. These were the small island States of the Pacific. Kiribati, Nauru, Tonga, and Tuvalu established their independence in 1979, 1968, 1970, and 1978 respectively.[163] They were admitted as UN member States in 1999 and 2000.[164] The four thus were States for extended periods (and had participated in regional organizations) before being admitted as member States of the United Nations. Concern that they lacked the financial resources necessary to participate in the United Nations had been a consideration leading the very small island States to refrain from seeking admission. The benefits of admission eventually were seen to outweigh the costs. One of the main benefits for very small States is that belonging to a universal forum allows them to maintain contacts to many States at a small fraction of what it would cost to maintain a worldwide diplomatic apparatus. The admission of the four remaining Pacific island States added to the approximately forty Small Island Developing States (SIDS) which already were members. The Security Council at the time took 'great satisfaction' in the applicant States' commitment to 'uphold the purposes and principles of the Charter...and to fulfil all the obligations contained therein.'[165]

The SIDS are one of a number of coalitions that 'under-represented' member States have established to promote common interests in various international organizations. An early step toward establishing their agenda was a Programme of Action for the Sustainable Development of Small Island Developing States, adopted at Bridgetown, Barbados in 1994[166] and joined to a contemporane-

---

[163] Crawford *Creation* 2nd edn 737–8.

[164] Kiribati: A/53/1004 (25 June 1999 Security Council communication recommending admission), GA res 54/1, 14 September 1999; Nauru: A/53/1005 (June 25 1999 Security Council communication recommending admission), GA res 54/2, September 14, 1999; Tonga: A/53/1029 (28 June 1999 Security Council communication recommending admission), GA res 54/3, 14 September 1999. Tuvalu was recommended for admission in SC res 1290, 17 Feb 2000 and admitted by GA res 55/1, 5 Sept 2000.

[165] E.g. Presidential Statement on Admission of the Republic of Kiribati to the United Nations, 29 June 1999: S/PRST/1999/18; Presidential Statement on Admission of Nauru to the United Nations, 29 June 1999: S/PRST/1999/19; Presidential Statement on Admission of the Kingdom of Tonga to the United Nations, 28 July 1999: S/PRST/1999/23.

[166] *Report of the Global Conference on Sustainable Development of Small Island Developing States*, Bridgetown, 25 Apr–6 May 1994: A/Conf.167/9 and Corr.1 and 2.

ous Barbados Declaration.[167] By establishing a coalition the small island States increased their prominence in international organization. There ensued, among other statements, a Secretary-General's report on establishing a development strategy for SIDS.[168] Various international concerns enter into that strategy. The effects of trade liberalization are among the SIDS's main international concerns. Very small territories with under-diversified economies, most SIDS depend to a high degree on commerce with and investment from other States. They are little insulated against wider trends – e.g., fluctuation in commodity prices, competition from other developing countries. Even a single investment dispute over a hotel-building project may have macro-economic consequences for a Small Island Developing State.[169] The General Assembly in 1994 recognized SIDS as a category requiring special consideration in the Uruguay Round of trade negotiations.[170]

SIDS also may face problems in connection with global warming. Their economies are vulnerable to changes in maritime climate, and, if sea levels were to rise considerably, a number of such States would be deprived of national territory.[171] One may consider scenarios in which certain SIDS are deprived of territory altogether, a sort of environmental attack recalling instances in which a foreign invader displaced the lawful government of a State – but having total effect and little possibility of reversal. This might present unusual questions as to the continuity of a State's rights to the Exclusive Economic Zone[172] and, perhaps, as to international responsibility for the loss.

The UN Framework Convention on Climate Change (UNFCCC) has acknowledged that global warming presents certain problems to SIDS,[173] including the threat of rising sea levels.[174] SIDS have taken steps to promote their interests under UNFCCC.[175] They also have acted within the Human Rights Council. The

---

[167] Ibid., annex I.

[168] *Report of the Secretary-General: A development strategy for island developing countries*: A/49/227 and Add.1 and 2, 18 July 1994.

[169] Consider *Asian Village Antigua Ltd v Government of Antigua and Barbuda* UNCITRAL Arb, Award of 28 Sept 2007 (Crawford, Sole Arbitrator) (unpublished).

[170] GA res 49/100, 19 Dec 1994 pream ¶ 4. Noting the position of SIDS in the WTO see Sonia Rolland 'Developing Country Coalitions at the WTO: In Search of Legal Support' (2007) 48 *Harv ILJ* 483, 499, 502, 510, 513.

[171] See Mills & Hancock *Small Island States in Indian and Atlantic Oceans: Vulnerability to Climate Change and Strategies for Adaptation* (2005).

[172] Grant 'States Newly Admitted to the United Nations: Some Implications' (2000) 39 *Colum J Trans'l L* 177, 191–2.

[173] See Climate Change Secretariat (UNFCCC) *Climate Change: Small Island Developing States* (Bonn: UNFCCC, 2005).

[174] Ibid., 13–23.

[175] For a diagram of SIDS and the negotiating groups of UNFCCC to which they belong, see ibid., 3.

Maldives put forward a draft resolution in the 7th Council session, and this was adopted on 28 March 2008. The Human Rights Council, by the resolution, recognizes 'that the world's poor are especially vulnerable to the effects of climate change, in particular those concentrated in high-risk areas.'[176] The Council requested the Office of the High Commissioner for Human Rights to conduct 'a detailed analytical study of the relationship between climate change and human rights.'[177]

Writers have noted SIDS as a category of States and the measures they have taken to promote shared interests, especially in the environmental field.[178] Though they have not established a separate international organization, the SIDS's coordination as a group within the UN suggests the value generally in coordination among States sharing certain values and objectives.

6.3 *The European Micro-States*

So-called 'micro-States'[179] in Europe are another group of very small States, admission of which to the United Nations was delayed for a time. Liechtenstein sought admission to the League of Nations but was rejected. This was not on grounds that Liechtenstein was too small to be a State. Diminutiveness does not appear to have precluded statehood at the time, and it certainly does not now. Instead, it was doubted that Liechtenstein had the effective capacity to satisfy the obligations incumbent on a League member.[180] Other European

---

[176] A/HRC/7/L.21 ('Human rights and climate change'), 20 March 2008 pream ¶ 8.

[177] Ibid., ¶ 1.

[178] E.g. Bluemel 'Unraveling the Global Warming Regime Complex: Competitive Entropy in the Regulation of the Global Public Good' (2007) 155 *U Penn L Rev* 1981, 1988 n. 18; Gillespie 'Small Island States in the Face of Climatic Change' (2004) 22 *UCLA J Env L & Pol'y* 107; Gillespie & Burns eds *Climate Change in the South Pacific: Impacts and Responses in Australia, New Zealand and Small Island States* (1999). On SIDS in international law generally see Slade 'The Making of International Law: The Role of Small Island States' (2003) 17 *Temple Int'l & Comp LJ* 531.

[179] The legally distinct aspect of micro-States, if any, derives not from their diminutiveness per se, but, rather, from possible legal consequences of the practical measures, especially in the field of treaty relations with larger neighbours, which the micro-States have taken in pursuit of physical security, economic development, diplomatic relations, etc. Yet this, too, is not so much referable to any general legal category as to the specific incidents of each State's treaty and other relations. See Grant 'Micro-States' *Max Planck Encyclopaedia of Public International Law* (2008) [forthcoming].

[180] Duursma *Fragmentation and the International Relations of Micro-States. Self-determination and Statehood* (1996) 170–74. See also remarks of Roberto Ago: *ILC Ybk* 1971 vol. 1 p. 6 ¶ 38.

micro-States apparently did not seek admission to the earlier general organization in earnest.[181]

Perhaps judging from the practice of the League that the new international organization would not welcome them either, the European micro-States immediately after 1945 appear not to have pursued UN membership with particular interest. The first steps toward participation, some time later, were to seek observer status, which, in several cases, the UN allowed.[182] Liechtenstein had informal talks in the 1960s on the subject of membership,[183] but no application is recorded. The European micro-States would exist for nearly half a century as non-members.

This by no means was to repeat the earlier logjam of 1945–56. The delays in admission of numerous States in the first decade of the Charter was as against the formally expressed will of those States to gain admission. Candidatures, such as that of Mongolia, were on the table and remained so for a long time. They were rejected in Security Council proceedings. Grounds were adduced for rejecting them. Failure to satisfy the criteria of Article 4 was a main ground. The last States to exist as a group for any significant time outside the UN by contrast were delayed admission because they themselves delayed application, and objections to their admission were not objections grounded on doubt as to their status as States, much less as to their character as peace-loving. The main problem, anticipated by existing member States and, it would seem, moreover, in the councils of the micro-States themselves, was that the Article 4 criterion of ability to meet the obligations of the Charter might be unattainable for States with minimal resources. A further problem – not one related directly to Article 4 but identified by member States concerned to maintain an effective international organization – was that the UN would not be able to function with a membership roll very much larger than a hundred or so States.

A number of proposals were considered in the 1960s and early 1970s with a view to accommodating the wish of the micro-States for greater representation in the international arena while preserving something of the economy of an inter-State organization that was said to be under strain from rapid increase in numbers. Two in particular merit a brief word.

---

[181] Monaco and San Marino, too, apparently had applied, but they withdrew the applications before the League adopted a formal decision: Dugard *Recognition and the United Nations* (1987) 70. Andorra does not appear to have applied.

[182] San Marino for example participated as an *ad hoc* observer in the General Assembly 6th session (1951) and was a permanent observer from March 1987: Duursma 254. Monaco opened a permanent observer mission in 1956: ibid., 303.

[183] Duursma 195.

One proposal was that the status of permanent observer missions to the UN be formalized, with criteria and procedures for the missions set out in detail. The Secretary-General in 1967, acknowledging that 'a suggestion of this nature involves considerable political difficulties,' set out considerations favouring a systematic approach to the representation of very small States in the UN.[184] The Organization needed a 'clear directive as to the policy to be followed,' if observer status were to provide a general solution to the problem of micro-State representation.[185] If such a directive had been adopted, it would have provided a mechanism for the micro-States to participate in the Organization without being admitted and incurring the full costs of membership.[186] The UN indeed has welcomed permanent observer missions. The Vatican City continues to use this mechanism to maintain contact to the UN, and Switzerland used it for the long period between the founding of the UN and its admission as a member State. However, permanent observer missions have not been accepted by other States as a long-term alternative to admission. The micro-States used it only as a sort of half-way house, pending admission as member States.[187] Switzerland objected to extending permanent observer status to a large number of very small States, on the ground, apparently, that doing so would have devalued Switzerland's own participation.[188] The concept attracted interest in the 1960s and early 1970s but was never institutionalized as a means for securing the representation of more than a few States for significant periods of time.[189]

---

[184] Introduction to the Annual Report of the Secretary-General on the Work of the Organization, 15 Sept 1967, GAOR 22nd ses Supp no 1A, A/6701 Add.1 ¶ 165.

[185] Ibid., ¶ 168.

[186] *ILC Ybk* 1970 vol. II pp. 7–8, Relations between States and International Organizations, art. 52, 'Functions of permanent observer missions,' Commentary, ¶ 4. See also *ILC Ybk* 1971 vol. II pt 1 p. 94, art. 54, 'Accreditation to two or more international organizations or assignment to two or more permanent observer missions,' Observations of the Government of Finland.

[187] Among the States which have maintained permanent observer missions are Switzerland (1948–2002), Austria (1949–55), Italy (1949–55), Republic of Korea (South) (1949–91), Finland (1952–5), Japan (1952–5), Federal Republic of Germany (1952–73), Republic of Viet Nam (South) (1952–76), Spain (1953–5), Monaco (1956–93), Bangladesh (1972–4), German Democratic Republic (1972–3), Democratic People's Republic of Korea (North) (1973–91), Guinea-Bissau (1974), Democratic Republic of Viet Nam (North) (1975–7). The Holy See has had an observer mission since 1964. For information to 1975, see Jay *United Nations Observer Status: An Accumulation of Contemporary Documents* (1976).

[188] Gunter 'Switzerland and the United Nations' (1976) 30 *Int'l Org* 129, 141. Further observer missions have been listed on the United Nations web pages.

[189] On permanent observer status generally, see Mower 'Observer Countries: Quasi Members of the United Nations' (1966) 20 *Int'l Org* 266. The continued use of observer status for most of the UN era and the more or less established pattern that it early achieved and since has followed may justify referring to it as an institution of the UN system. However, clear criteria for conferring the status were not set, and the lack of institutional clarity has been cause for

Another proposal for accommodating States of diminutive size (both newly created and ancient) was that they be admitted as member States but under special arrangements of multiple representation. Under such arrangements, which were proposed but never adopted, one General Assembly vote would be given to each of several groups of very small States, the members of each group apparently to decide how to cast the group's vote through consensus or other decision-making procedure. It was envisaged that each micro-State would join one or another of several such groups. Multiple representation was proposed in the International Law Commission during discussion of the topic of relations between States and international organizations.[190] Problems with multiple representation may have been presented under Charter law. In particular, one may ask whether it would have been consistent with UN Charter Article 18(1), under which each member of the General Assembly 'shall have one vote.' As multiple representation was not put into effect, it was not determined whether it would have been acceptable to the very small States. Political objections well may have prevented its acceptance even if the Charter had permitted it.

A Security Council Committee of Experts was established in August 1969 to give detailed consideration to the micro-State question, including proposals for possible modified forms of UN participation. The Committee issued one interim report on questions arising from 'the emergence of a growing number of independent States, very small in area and population and lacking human and economic resources.'[191] The Committee did not meet after June 1970, and the proposals noted above, which the United States and United Kingdom had promoted, were put aside, partly, it is said, on the unreported advice of the UN Legal Counsel.[192]

---

dispute, especially respecting national liberation movements and the like – e.g., respecting the PLO: *United States of America* v *Palestine Liberation Organization*, 695 F. Supp. 1456 (S.D.N.Y., 1988, Palmieri, DJ); *Applicability of the Obligation to Arbitrate under Section 21 of the United Nations Headquarters Agreement of 26 June 1947* ICJ Rep 1988 p. 12. See further Thomas 'When the Guests Move In: Permanent Observers to the United Nations Gain the Right to Establish Permanent Missions in the United States' 78 *Ca L Rev* 197 (1990). The present work has not been directly concerned with the question of participation by non-State entities, though this might be treated as a membership question as well: see Alger 'Widening Participation' in Weiss & Daws eds *Oxford Handbook* 701–15. On the use of observer status by divided States, see Caty *États Divisés* 209–13.

[190] ILC 23rd sess 1106th mtg 25 May 1971 Mr Sette Câmara ¶ 67 *ILC Ybk* 1971 vol. I p. 128. Multiple representation was not novel to diplomacy more generally, it having been adopted by States in connection with their participation in diplomatic conferences since the 19th century: ibid., Mr Bartoš ¶¶ 61–2 pp. 127–8.

[191] SCOR 25th yr Supp Apr-June 1970 p. 210, S/9836, 15 June 1970.

[192] Bailey & Daws *The Procedure of the UN Security Council* 3rd edn (1998) 352. See also the detailed discussion of early UN treatment of the 'micro-State question' in Duursma 134–42.

The existence of the micro-States for a time as non-members did not present the same anomaly as the non-membership, for example, of Japan or Spain, major States with long histories of participation at the centre of international relations. Nor was non-membership of the micro-States a central concern on the UN agenda. The resolution of the 'micro-State problem,' if ever it really had been a problem, was to admit micro-States on the normal terms. The European micro-States were admitted as UN member States in the early 1990s. This was preceded in some cases by admission to functional organizations.[193] The Vatican City, territorial seat of the Holy See, remains the one generally recognized State not to have sought admission to the United Nations. As noted above, the Vatican maintains a permanent observer mission to the General Assembly.[194]

A presumption of universal admission, whatever doubts may be entertained as to its basis in the Charter, became entrenched in United Nations practice in the period after resolution of the pre-1955–6 logjam. Once it was a presumption that any State seeking admission will be granted admission, the path was open to universal membership in the Organization. Delay in admission of some of the micro-States was a late, minor echo of more rigorous application of the Article 4(1) admission criteria. The echo faded away with admission of the European micro-States in the early 1990s. Membership in the UN in the ensuing decade achieved near-universal scope.

The admission of the small Pacific islands States has already been mentioned. The most conspicuous absence from membership in the Organization thereafter was that of Switzerland.

6.4   *Switzerland*

The ages-long European neutral,[195] the Swiss Confederation had taken a view that the obligations entailed by its special international position were extensive. There followed from this a highly conservative view as to what forms Switzerland's

---

[193] San Marino, for example, before being admitted to the UN, was admitted to UNESCO, the WHO, and the ILO: Duursma 238–42.

[194] About the participation of the Vatican and Holy See in various international organizations, see Duursma 374–419.

[195] Switzerland could trace its neutrality to the late medieval period. The modern crystallization of Swiss neutrality as a status in the public law of Europe can be situated with the 1815 Vienna settlement. The literature on Swiss neutrality is extensive, especially in the German language. See, e.g., Diez 'UNO-Beitritt und Neutralitäts-erklärung' in Dutoit & Grisel eds *Recueil de Travaux Offerts à M Georges Perrin* (1984) 77; Haug 'Die allfällige Mitgliedschaft der Schweiz in den Vereinten Nationen und das Internationale Komitee Roten Kreuzes' in Diez, Monnier, Müller, Reimann & Wildhaber eds *Festschrift für Rudolf Bindschedler zum 65.Geburtstag* (1980) 511; Schindler 'Die Lehre von den Vorwirkungen der Neutralität' ibid., 563, 568–72.

participation in international organization might take. It would be misleading to call this a policy of disengagement, for Switzerland had been host State of the second headquarters of the United Nations (at Geneva),[196] belonged to most of the specialized agencies,[197] and maintained an active diplomacy of global scope.[198] Switzerland also participated in international peace-keeping missions – more actively than most member States.[199] However, the Swiss view of political international organizations, and of the United Nations in particular, was that membership is not consistent with neutrality. On the initial Swiss reading of the UN Charter, the instrument is a mutual defense pact, and Switzerland eschews military alliances. The obligation under Charter Article 25 to 'accept and carry out the decisions of the Security Council in accordance with the present Charter' in particular was objectionable, because a Chapter VII enforcement action might require a member State to deploy troops outside its territory in situations where the State itself is not under armed attack. Humanitarian relief missions were not the problem; Switzerland participated (and continues to participate) actively in that field. The problem instead was that situations might arise in which armed action is required other than for humanitarian purposes. Such an obligation, in the traditional Swiss view, would not be consistent with the pre-existing obligations entailed by Swiss neutrality.

A similar view had been expressed in Sweden and Austria, other major European neutral States, when the matter of their applications for UN admission had come up. The relation between neutrality and UN admission drew the attention of eminent jurists.[200] Neutrality, however, did not long delay admission. Both States sought, and were granted, admission in the 1950s – in Austria's case, shortly after the State Treaty was adopted settling questions of its post-war status.[201] The question arises, why Switzerland interpreted neutrality to impede

---

[196] The League of Nations had left a substantial physical plant, and it seemed sensible for the new organization to use it: Gunter 'Switzerland and the United Nations' (1976) 30 *Int'l Org* 129, 138–40.

[197] For a list see Gunter 30 *Int'l Org* at 143 n. 47.

[198] For example, Switzerland routinely served (and continues to serve) as the protecting power representing the interests of States in third States with which they do not maintain diplomatic relations – e.g., the interests of the United States in Cuba and Iran: Probst *'Good Offices' in the Light of Swiss International Practice and Experience* (1989) 114–7.

[199] Gunter 30 *Int'l Org* at 144–6.

[200] E.g. Kunz and Verdross: Kunz 'Austria's Permanent Neutrality' (1956) 50 *AJ* 418, 423–4; Verdross 'Austria's Permanent Neutrality and the United Nations Organization' (1956) 50 *AJ* 61.

[201] Which is to say that Austria was admitted practically as early as possible. Before adoption of the State Treaty, it might have been doubted whether Austria was independent in the usual sense; the precise date of Austria's 'reappearance' is subject to appreciation: Crawford *Creation* 2nd edn 669–70. On the neutrality question and Austrian admission, see further Amerasinghe 108–9.

application to the UN for so long. This may be answered by contrasting neutrality as it was generally conceived, and the Swiss conception of a State clothed in a special public law status.

Declaration of neutrality by a State in most instances was seen as a unilateral act, done by the State of its own volition. There resulted from the declaration certain obligations on the State making it. These in particular concerned avoiding preference as between belligerent States, restricting use of the national armed forces to self-defense (and then only on the national territory), and endeavouring to prevent belligerent States from entering the national territory.[202] But the obligations had to be considered with reference to the unilateral and discretionary character of the declaration giving rise to them. It was not for other States to establish neutral status on the State; the status resulted from a decision taken by the State itself. As respected interpretation of the incidents of neutrality in particular situations, the neutral State was bound to be sure by the rules of customary international law defining neutral rights and obligations, but the establishment of neutrality in the first place resulted from a decision by the neutral State. While neutrality, once established, affected the relations of the State to other States, and general international law provided the rules for interpreting what neutrality might mean in particular situations, neutrality derived from the decision of that State on its own, not from decisions reached elsewhere.

The Swiss position was different. According to Switzerland, Swiss neutrality was part of the public law of Europe. It was not simply a result of Swiss declarations, however consistently Switzerland may have asserted its neutrality over the centuries. Neutrality in Switzerland's case arose from a multilateral process of decision involving the States of Europe.[203] The Concert of Europe as a whole, from 1815, had adopted the position that Switzerland was to be a permanently

---

[202] Oppenheim *Treatise* 5th edn Hersch Lauterpacht ed vol. 2, 539–48; Hall *Treatise* 8th edn 708–54; Wheaton *Elements* 8th edn 412–537.

[203] This was the widely accepted position. The Law Officers of the Crown expressed the position thus: (1) That the Neutrality of Switzerland was established and guaranteed on the ground of the general interest of Europe, quite independently of Switzerland herself, or of Sardinia; and by an Instrument to which they were not originally parties...(3) That Sardinia and Switzerland, which were not parties to the Treaty (which first established and guaranteed the Neutrality of Switzerland in the "general interest") cannot by agreement "inter se" made for their separate interest, as opposed to the general interest of Europe, retain to themselves any optional or "facultative" power of actually de-neutralizing, or of permitting the de-neutralization either of any portion of Switzerland (proper) or of any portion of the Territory in question.

Opinion of 18 May 1859, reprinted in McNair *Law of Treaties: British Practice and Opinions* (1938) 314. The multilateral origins of Swiss neutrality are considered in Vagts 'Switzerland, International Law and World War II' (1997) 91 *AJ* 466. See also Spiropoulos's observation about the *erga omnes* character of obligations arising from Swiss neutrality: ILC 7th sess 306th mtg 7 June 1955 ¶ 17 *ILC Ybk* 1955 p. 138.

neutral State, and the position was received as a main element of the European legal order. Neutrality thus was not a status resulting simply by the election of Switzerland itself. It certainly could not be abridged by Swiss decision alone. On this ground, Switzerland's application for UN admission was not the same as Sweden's or Austria's.

The view of Swiss neutrality as special and preclusive of particular forms of international engagement was not however held by all Swiss authorities, and it varied over time. Switzerland at the beginning of the UN era had considered, but then retracted, measures to become a member State. The view crystallized thereafter that Switzerland should not be a UN member State. The view did not turn out to be immutable. Swiss government legal advisers eventually said that neutrality does not preclude admission. The Swiss Federal Council and Federal Assembly carried out studies in the early 1970s, and, informed by expert opinion, these concluded that it was consistent with Switzerland's special international position to seek admission to the UN.[204] The march toward universal membership by then well underway was referred to as a relevant factor. The Report of the Federal Council said that universal membership would make Switzerland's admission legally safer: 'The closer the United Nations comes to universality, the harder it will be to conceive of situations in which the United Nations would stand in opposition to non-member States.'[205] This did not answer how Switzerland would reconcile the expansive view of the obligations of neutrality with enforcement measures against a *member* State. The point however was clear enough. The Swiss government by the 1970s did not see UN membership as antithetical to Switzerland's special international status.

Arguments of policy also seem to have persuaded Swiss leaders to seek admission – for example, the interest of Switzerland not to be left out of law codification projects undertaken in the Sixth Committee.[206] And, as of the early 1970s at any rate, the Cold War had rendered the collective security provisions of Chapter VII essentially inoperative. Absent superpower agreement, the Security Council could not adopt the resolutions that would have put those provisions into operation in actual cases of threat to the peace, breach of the peace, or act of aggression. This situation seems to have assuaged concerns of Swiss policy makers.[207]

Chapter VII, however, famously, had a rebirth at the end of the Cold War.[208] The Security Council, at least for a time in the early 1990s, appeared likely to act

---

[204] These are cited and discussed by Gunter: 30 *Int'l Org* at 130 n. 4.

[205] Report of the Federal Council to the Federal Assembly Concerning Switzerland's Relations with the United Nations, 17 Nov 1971 p. 11: quoted, Gunter at 150.

[206] Gunter at 151–2.

[207] Gunter at 150–1.

[208] It has been referred to, for example, as a 'new era dawning': Freudenschuß 'Collective Security' in Cede & Sucharipa eds (2001) 73, 78. It was called at the time 'the dawn of a new era': Mr Kanju (Jamaica) A/47/PV.7 p. 36, 22 Sept 1992.

more vigorously. The Gulf War resolutions indicated the expected development.[209] If the Security Council continued to adopt such resolutions, then member States would find themselves more frequently obliged to act under Chapter VII than they had during the Cold War. This in turn, perhaps, refreshed neutralist concern that UN membership would entail incompatible alliance obligations.

And the traditional view of neutrality was a resilient feature of public sentiment. Swiss voters, if not Swiss governments and their advisors, viewed neutrality as having a very wide breadth. Apparently, it was not seen as a narrow legal point but rather as an institution sweeping into the category of prohibited relations an extensive array of conduct viewed by most States as routine. Neither the near-desuetude of Chapter VII nor official assurances immediately prevailed over public scepticism. An attempt by the Swiss government to seek admission to the Organization was blocked in referendum in 1986.[210]

Public opinion in Switzerland, as elsewhere, of course, is not static. The Swiss public eventually had a change of view toward the UN and toward international relations more generally.[211] The one-time refusal by many Swiss citizens to allow their government to seek UN admission gave way to readiness to take that step toward formalizing an engagement that already long had been underway. The political environment having become more hospitable to the Organization, the government put the matter of application for admission once again to the people of Switzerland. The people voted for application. Switzerland applied. The impediment in the way of Swiss UN membership had consisted in hesitancy by the State to make application more than in hesitancy by the UN to grant admission. Switzerland delayed application because of neutrality; the small island States because of financial considerations. In all of these cases, delay resulted from the States' own decision to delay application, not from objections in the UN.

In its application, Switzerland stated as follows:

> The Federal Parliament and Federal Council are responsible for taking the necessary measures to safeguard the neutrality of the country. Switzerland is a neutral State whose status is enshrined in international law. The United Nations recognizes that the neutrality of a Member State does not affect the fulfilment of its obligations under the Charter and contributes to the achievement of the purposes of the United Nations.
>
> As a Member of the United Nations, Switzerland will remain neutral.[212]

---

[209] E.g. SC resns 678, 29 Nov 1990; 687, 3 Apr 1991.

[210] Mockli 'The Long Road to Membership: Switzerland and the United Nations' in Gabriel & Fischer eds *Swiss Foreign Policy, 1945–2002* (2003) 46. A proposal to establish a standing Swiss military contingent for UN service was rejected in referendum in 1994: ibid., 64.

[211] Church *The Politics and Government of Switzerland* (2004) 205–23.

[212] Letter dated 20 June 2002 from the President and the Chancellor of the Swiss Confederation on behalf of the Swiss Federal Council addressed to the Secretary-General: S/2002/801–A/56/1009, Annex.

The application also noted the referendum of 3 March 2002 by which 'the people and cantons' authorized application. The degree of specificity as to municipal process in this application is unusual, most applicants saying little about the relation between their own constitutional requirements and UN application. Reference to the municipal process seems to be associated with situations where some question might otherwise be raised as to the validity of an application.[213] Switzerland in its application alluded once more to the international law origin of neutral status, and restated the position that membership does not derogate the status. The extent and detail of this application distinguishes it from the *pro forma* notes which most applicants seeking admission have submitted. The Swiss application concludes with a formulation of the standard acceptance of Charter obligations and preparedness to carry them out – but adds to the formulation the words '[o]n the basis of the above.' The question might be raised whether such language is an attempt to reserve a position under the Charter, but in practice it has been ratified as an acceptable incident of the process of admission of the neutral State.[214]

The Security Council on 24 July 2002 recommended Switzerland for admission.[215] The General Assembly on 10 September 2002 admitted Switzerland as the 190th member State.[216]

6.5   Conclusion

In the same session that Switzerland was admitted, the General Assembly admitted Timor-Leste as the 191st member State.[217] Montenegro, one of the republics of the remaining Yugoslav federation (which since 2003 had gone by the title 'Republic of Serbia and Montenegro'),[218] held a referendum on 21 May 2006 in which a majority of those voting chose independence.[219] Montenegro declared

---

[213] Recall the applications of Senegal and Mali after dissolution of the Federation of Mali: about which see Chapter 1, pp. 19–20 above; and the assurances given by Montenegro as to the process by which it attained independence.

[214] But consider the divergent ways writers have characterized Switzerland's membership in the League: Rosenne *Treaties* 220 n. 45.

[215] A/57/259; SC res 1426 (2002), 24 July 2002.

[216] GA res 57/1, 10 Sept 2002.

[217] A/57/258, SC res 1414 (2002), 23 May 2002; GA res 57/3, 27 Sept 2002.

[218] The constitutional amendments which included the change of name entered into force on 4 Feb 2003: *UN Ybk* 2003 pp. 411–2. For a summary of the changes of name from 1992 to 2000, see *Case Concerning Legality of Use of Force (Serbia and Montenegro v Belgium)* Preliminary Objections, Judgment of 15 Dec 2004, ICJ Rep 2004 p. 279, 291 ¶ 25.

[219] *Report submitted by the Republic of Montenegro pursuant to Article 25, paragraph 1 of the Framework Convention for the Protection of National Minorities*, 25 July 2007: CoE Doc ACFC/SR(2007)002.

independence, effective from 3 June 2006.[220] Admission to the UN was almost immediate.[221] The permanent representative of Albania said at the time, '[w]ith the admission of this new peace-loving State...the goal of universality moves closer to its ultimate attainment.'[222] What more needed to be done would have to be left for the Albanian permanent representative to say. Putting to one side the problematic situations of Kosovo and Taiwan, certain other entities proximate to States,[223] and the special case of the Vatican City and Holy See, the United Nations from the early 2000s has been the universal organization of States.

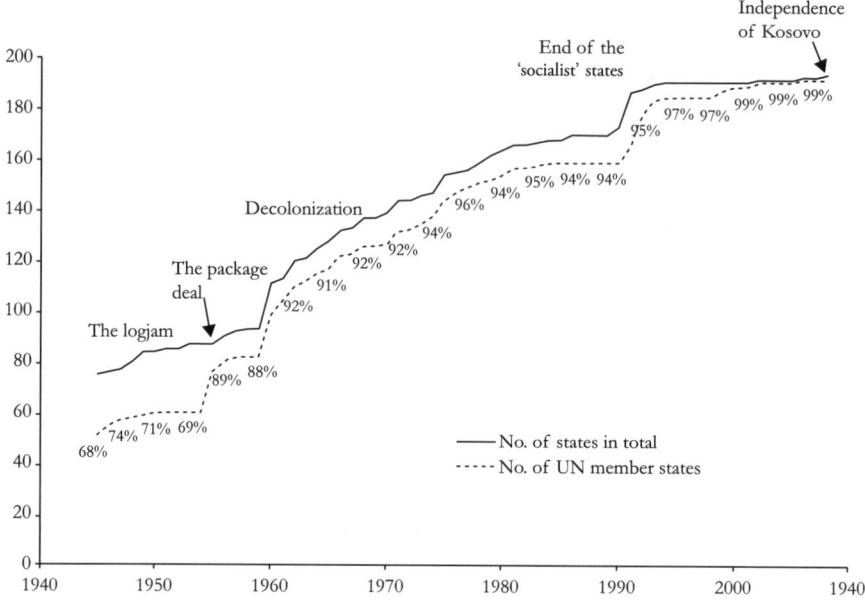

Figure 2: Creation of States and Admission of States (1945–2008)*

* Adapted and updated from Figure 1, Crawford *Creation* 2nd edn p. 187. cf UN membership chart in Bailey & Daws 3rd edn p. 349.

---

[220] On the internal processes leading to Montenegro's independence, see Cazala 'L'Accession du Monténégro à l'Indépendance' (2006) 52 *AFDI* 160, 164–72.

[221] A/60/902, SC res 1691 (2006), 22 June 2006; GA res 60/264, 28 June 2006. Other international organizations admitted the new State forthwith: Cazala 52 *AFDI* at 175–6.

[222] GAOR 60th sess 91st plen mtg 28 June 2006.

[223] The main examples of entities proximate to States but not (yet) member States of the UN are the Cook Islands and Niue. The two are States in free association with New Zealand. Both are participants in the 1949 Geneva Conventions, which does apparently make those instruments the example of a universal treaty.

Chapter 7

Consequences of Admission

As seen in the Chapters above, admission to the United Nations ceased to require that the applicant fulfill the substantive criteria set out in Charter Article 4 – save one. The exceptional criterion has been statehood: even as its conduct or the character of its internal institutions will not be scrutinized as part of the admission process, to be admitted the applicant still must be a State. This has made it possible in practice that nearly all entities that are States are UN members. The non-members today are entities which have not sought admission – the main example in 2008 was the Vatican City; have been subject to dispute as to their status – e.g., Kosovo and Taiwan; or as yet remain associated with another State by way of ties that it is acknowledged they are free to sever – e.g., the Cook Islands and Niue. Admission to the UN, then, or at least a presumption of admissibility attaching to States that seek it, would seem to be a modern incident of statehood in international law. Yet by no means is admission a *criterion* of statehood; a State remains a State whether or not it is a UN member. Creation of the State is not an effect of admission.

Admission is so closely bound now to statehood that it is natural nevertheless to look for some special aspect in the relation. This final Chapter starts by considering the relation between admission and statehood. We then turn to other effects that universal membership may have, both on legal relations and on the politics of international relations.

7.1 *Legal Consequences of Admission as a Member State*

The most obvious consequence of admission to the United Nations is that the State, upon admission, becomes a member of the United Nations. As we saw in Chapter 2, membership is automatic upon the vote of the General Assembly to admit an applicant as a member State; no further municipal or international step is required. Membership entails financial obligations to the Organization; it entails certain, at least minimal, rights of participation in UN organs. The rights of participation can be generalized however only so far. The Charter expressly elevates the rights of the Permanent Five members of the Security Council above the rest in that principal organ, so it is not accurate to say that States have an absolutely equal right to participate in UN processes. The level field of rights in the General Assembly may be referred to the principle of sovereign equality; the more restricted membership in specialized organs like the Human Rights Council reflects various functional considerations.

To give substance to the rather general observation that admission confers membership, we have to ask, then, what legal consequences follow from membership. We may consider possible legal consequences under five rubrics: (i) the general international law concerning the creation of States; (ii) international responsibility; (iii) standing in the International Court of Justice; (iv) rights of participation in other UN processes; and (v) a presumption of continuity in international legal relations, manifested in the UN by continuity of membership.

7.1.1   *Statehood and UN Membership*

The admission of a State to the United Nations does not create the State. This point has been made elsewhere. For example, the International Court could say that '[t]here is no doubt that Serbia and Montenegro is a State for the purposes of Article 34, paragraph 1, of the Statute' – before it said whether that State was a member of the United Nations and thus a Party to the Statute by virtue of Article 35(1).[1] It follows from earlier practice as well: States existed before there was a United Nations. And it follows even more closely from the logic of the Charter: to be admitted, the applicant must already be a State.

Moreover, the rights and obligations of a State under general international law clearly do not begin with admission. It is central to an understanding of international law as guarantor of basic public order that any particular formal status – such as membership in an international organization – cannot be the prerequisite to protection from the use or threat of force: a State does not acquire license to use force at international level simply by denying the status of the target of its contemplated aggression. Admission of a State as a member of the United Nations is therefore clearly not the act creating the obligation to refrain from threat or use of force against the territorial integrity of the State. Nor is continued membership a requirement for continued statehood. Sean Murphy notes that suspension from an organization – from the OAS for example – by no means calls into question the existence of the State suspended.[2]

---

[1] *Case Concerning Legality of Use of Force (Serbia and Montenegro v Belgium)* Preliminary Objections, Judgment of 15 Dec 2004, ICJ Rep 2004 pp. 279, 298–9 ¶ 46.

[2] Murphy 'Democratic legitimacy and the recognition of States and governments' in Fox & Roth eds *Democratic Governance and International Law* (2000) 123, 129.

Yet the relation between statehood and membership in the United Nations is significant. The requirement under Charter Article 4(1) that, to be admitted, the applicant be a State forges a link between the UN and statehood. It means that admission, in the least, is a certification by the Organization as to the status of the entity.[3] Given its role as chief organized expression of international society[4] and the (continued) position of States as the main components of that society, the Organization is more than a passive observer as to matters of statehood. The move toward universality, as discussed in the Chapters above, tends to increase the significance of the relation between membership and statehood. If the States of the world and the UN were to form an identity, then that in itself would be significant.

The link between the UN and statehood is noted in international instruments as well. Rule 2 of the Rules of Procedure and Evidence of the International Criminal Tribunal for the former Yugoslavia lists three categories of entities which are States for purposes of the Rules. The first category is 'a State Member or non-Member of the United Nations.'[5] Again, it is clear that membership in the United Nations is not a prerequisite to statehood, nor does admission constitute the State – but it is natural enough to relate statehood to UN membership. Why else define the category 'State' by reference to membership at all? That a drafter would clarify that the category is not limited to UN membership reflects the tendency to think of UN membership and statehood as coterminous.

The International Court of Justice in the case which Bosnia and Herzegovina instituted against Yugoslavia under the Genocide Convention was not concerned with whether UN membership and statehood are the same thing, but the Court was indeed concerned with whether the applicant was a State. Yugoslavia had argued that the Bosnian declaration of independence was unlawful and thus Bosnia was not a State:

> The Federal Republic of Yugoslavia contests the legitimacy of the Applicant... [The] secession of the "Republic of Bosnia-Herzegovina" [was] carried out in contravention of the Constitution of this former Yugoslav Republic, as well as the rules of international law.[6]

The Court rejected the Yugoslav position: Bosnia was a State. The main evidence to which the Court referred for this conclusion was the admission of Bosnia to the UN by the 'bodies competent under the Charter' for that decision:

---

[3] Dixon *Textbook on International Law* 3rd edn (1996) 99.
[4] More about which see below this Chapter, pp. 277 ff.
[5] As revised: IT/32/Rev.40, 12 July 2007.
[6] Rodoljub Etinski (Agent for the FRY) Written Observations of the Federal Republic of Yugoslavia (*Genocide* case) 9 Aug 1993 p. 6 ¶ 6. See also ibid., Annex 1 p. 16, setting out international opinion that recognition of Bosnia was 'premature.'

The Court notes that Bosnia and Herzegovina became a Member of the United Nations following the decisions adopted on 22 May 1992 by the Security Council and the General Assembly, bodies competent under the Charter. Article XI of the Genocide Convention opens it to 'any Member of the United Nations'; from the time of its admission to the Organization, Bosnia and Herzegovina could thus become a party to the Convention. Hence the circumstances of its accession to independence are of little consequence.

To be sure, like any holding of the Court, this was specific to the dispute in question. The statement is striking nevertheless for what it says about UN admission and statehood: admission is conclusive as to statehood, including in the face of an objection relative to the 'circumstances of [a State's] accession to independence.' Admission of Bosnia to the UN cleared up the question about how Bosnia became a State. Moreover, once admitted, a State will not be deprived any legal right, at least within the UN system and within conventional systems established with the UN as their reference point, that hinges on its status as a State. The Genocide Convention, among other instruments, defines the scope of participation by reference to UN membership.

To posit a relation between statehood and UN membership is not controversial at least at a level of generality. The Organization after all is open to 'all other peace-loving *states.*' Writers routinely note a connection between UN membership and statehood.[7] Martin Dixon says that UN membership 'will now entail a presumption of statehood which it would be very difficult to dislodge.'[8] Rosenne, too, would seem to characterize admission as confirming the statehood of the admitted applicant. A confirmatory effect arises from admission, because an obligation attaches to the existing members to accept the constitutive decisions that the organization reaches. Rosenne says as follows:

> The admission to membership is...the consequence of the combination of the application and the favourable determination of the competent organ or organs, and upon its effectuation the State becomes a member of the organization on the same footing as all other existing members. It follows that the unilateral application to be admitted as a member has some affinity with the unilateral act by which a State expresses its consent to be bound by an existing treaty open to it. This gives partial effect to the principle *ex consensus advenit vinculum.* It would indeed be accurate to state that the application corresponds to the treaty element which, as seen, underlies the constituent instrument of every international organization, even one formally established by an instrument which is not a treaty within the meaning of the Vienna Conventions. But there the similarity ends, for the application is only the first stage in the process of admission, which is completed by the

---

[7] E.g., Reisman, Arsanjani, Wiessner & Westerman *International Law in Contemporary Perspective* (2004) 230–1; Shaw *International Law* 5th edn (2003) 180–1; Weston, Falk & Charlesworth *International Law and World Order: A Problem-Oriented Coursebook* 3rd edn (1997) 364.

[8] Dixon *Textbook on International Law* 5th edn (2005) 105.

decision of the competent organ. *That decision has dispositive effect and is binding upon every member of the organization, regardless of how it voted or even whether it was a member of the organization at the time.*[9]

Admission confirms that the statehood of the admitted entity is opposable against all other members. This is not to say that UN admission establishes such opposability in the first place, or even that it is the only mechanism that might confirm it. A State is a State for reasons other than its admission to the UN, and, even as they have no duty formally to recognize it as such or to enter into any particular relations with it, other States are not free to act as if a given State does not exist.[10] UN admission, entailing the participation of all members in a multilateral treaty, may be described as putting a formal frame around the opposability of statehood toward all other UN members.

It would serve no purpose to revisit the extensive literature devoted to the question of the legal consequences of the recognition of States, a question evoking the more opaque aspects of a theological dispute.[11] As for the relation between recognition and admission to the United Nations, attempts have been made to establish that the latter entails the former. Manley Hudson in discussions on the Draft Declaration on the Rights and Duties of States proposed that admission to the UN be taken to constitute recognition 'by all the Members.'[12] Obstacles however exist to fully realizing an equation between admission and recognition. One obstacle is institutional: the UN is not clearly equipped to serve as a collective mechanism for recognition.[13] Another obstacle is political: the discretionary character of recognition has proved resilient.[14]

John Dugard in *Recognition and the United Nations* set out the main strands of thought concerning the relation between recognition and admission:

---

[9] Emphasis supplied. Rosenne *Treaties* 215.

[10] Compare Hans Blix's formulation:

> [B]y accepting treaties constituting international organizations, [the member States] must be deemed to have obliged themselves to accept the measure of relations which is necessary under these constitutions – but not more – with authorities which fulfill the international law criteria of governments of States members, although, in pursuit of a policy of non-recognition, they may refuse relations outside the framework of such organizations.

'Contemporary Aspects of Recognition' (1970 – II) 130 *Hag Rec* 589, 693.

[11] The legal 'nature' of recognition is considered *in extenso* in Grant *The Recognition of States: Law and Practice in Debate and Evolution* (1999) 1–82.

[12] ILC 1st sess 11th mtg, 27 Apr 1949 (Draft Declaration on the Rights and Duties of States) ¶ 21: ILC Ybk 1949 p. 85.

[13] For references to writers taking this view see Dugard 43–4.

[14] The *locus classicus* of the assertion of sovereignty in the matter of recognizing States is the statement in 1948 by former U.S. Permanent Representative Warren Austin: see citations Grant 'Hallstein Revisited: Unilateral Enforcement of Regimes of Nonrecognition since the Two Germanies' (2000) 36 *Stan JIL* 221, 248 n. 142.

The main objection to collective recognition by the United Nations is of a... formal nature. Many writers simply assert, with little examination of United Nations practice beyond the non-recognition of Israel by Arab States, that the recognition of States cannot be implied from admission to the United Nations. Support for this view is claimed from the fact that an amendment proposed by the Norwegian Delegation at the San Francisco Conference in 1945, designed to give the United Nations the power of recommending the collective recognition of new States, was not adopted. From this it is inferred that it was the intention of the founding fathers of the United Nations not to interpret admission to membership as equivalent to collective recognition of States.

Many writers, who favour collective recognition, acknowledge that admission to the United Nations has had a major impact on the law of recognition, but stop short of accepting it as an act of recognition in itself. Thus we find admission to the United Nations described as "a kind of collective recognition," "a step forward towards the principle of collective recognition," the "nearest analogue" to collective recognition, "a system of certification which has in substance fulfilled the function of collective recognition," "*prima facie* evidence of statehood," "tantamount to recognition of the member admitted as a State," and as a substitute, "to a large extent, but not for all aspects," of traditional recognition. In more futuristic vein, Chen declares that "[w]hen the United Nations shall have attained complete universality, the notion of 'recognition' will wither away, and membership of the United Nations will be the sole standard of relations between States."[15]

That recognition indeed appears to have lessened in importance as part of international practice over roughly the same period that the United Nations has so nearly approximated universality tends to support Chen's declaration. Yet recognition remains part of State practice, and admission to the UN remains at most a 'near analogue' to collective recognition. That its political character remains pronounced and that recognition is an act still left largely to the discretion of individual States – notwithstanding occasional indications in practice to the contrary[16] – both further suggest the qualified role of the UN in this connection.

As Brownlie says, 'Recognition, *as a public act of state*, is an optional and political act and there is no legal duty in this regard. However, in a deeper sense, if an entity bears the marks of statehood, other states put themselves at risk legally, if they ignore the basic obligations of state relations.'[17] The principle runs the other way as well, it being doubtful whether recognition of an unlawful situation, especially where the rule breached is *jus cogens*, will 'offset the original illegality.'[18] The question well may be put, as it was under the Stimson Doctrine, whether

---

[15] Dugard 44–5, citing Chen *The International Law of Recognition, with special reference to practice in Great Britain and the United States* (1951) 222. Citations to other works omitted.

[16] Grant *Recognition* 149–211.

[17] Emphasis original. Brownlie *Principles* 6th edn 89–90.

[18] Brownlie *Principles* 5th edn 78.

recognition of an unlawful situation itself is an unlawful act.[19] It certainly may be an *unfriendly* act, as against the party which the underlying unlawfulness has injured.[20] Insofar as one may draw analogy between admission to the UN and recognition, the same considerations as apply to recognition would apply *mutatis mutandis.*[21]

7.1.2 *International Responsibility*

Where a State holds an international obligation and conduct attributable to the State constitutes a breach of the obligation, the State has committed an internationally wrongful act which, in turn, entails the international responsibility of the State.[22] Difficulties of attribution, and thus of responsibility, arise when a State acts under cover of an international organization. The problem is connected with membership, for it potentially arises whenever a State participates as a member of an organization. The membership that follows admission, then, has as one legal consequence the potential shielding of the member State from international responsibility for acts which the law otherwise might impute to it.

The ILC when working on the topic of responsibility of international organizations was cognizant that a member State might claim the organization as a shield against responsibility for its own misconduct. The draft articles reflect this in their extensive provision for attaching responsibility to the member State. Draft articles 25 through 30, which set out situations in which a member State might

---

[19] See Grant 'Doctrines, Stimson etc' in Wolfrum ed *Max Planck Encyclopedia of Public International Law* (forthcoming).

[20] See Art. 5(3), Definition of Aggression, GA res 3314 (XXIX), 14 Dec 1974 Annex: 'No territorial acquisition or special advantage resulting from aggression is or shall be recognized as lawful.' A similar statement is included under the first principle of the Friendly Relations Declaration: GA res 2625 (XXV), 24 Oct 1970 Annex.

[21] Draft art. 45(1) on responsibility of international organizations would provide as follows:
> No State or international organization shall recognize as lawful a situation created by a serious breach [by an international organization of an obligation arising under a peremptory norm of general international law], nor render aid or assistance in maintaining that situation.
ILC Rpt on the work of its 59th sess, 7 May–5 June and 9 July–10 Aug 2007, GAOR 62nd sess Supp No 10: A/62/10 ¶ 344 p. 218. Gaja Fifth Report, A/CN.4/583 p 19 ¶ 64 and Comment (7) to draft art. 45, A/62/10 ¶ 344 p. 220, mention the requirement of non-recognition of the unlawful annexation of Kuwait by Iraq in SC res 662, 9 Aug 1990 ¶ 2; and the statement that '[t]he Community and its member States will not recognize entities which are the result of aggression' contained in the Declaration by the European Community on Yugoslavia and on the Guidelines on the Recognition of New States, 16 Dec 1991, (1992) 31 ILM 1485, 1487. Admission of an entity to membership, where States and international organizations are under an obligation to refrain from acts tending to confirm or consolidate the status of the entity, is a breach of the obligation. This is the clear case of admission as wrongful act.

[22] ARSIWA Arts 1, 2.

be responsible, are by way of exception but significant nevertheless for their effect of mitigating what otherwise would be a major ellipsis in responsibility.[23]

The situation may differ between admission to the UN and admission to considerably smaller organizations. An international organization with only a handful of members may be open to greater scrutiny, if membership in the organization (or its very creation) is to give legal cover to its members for acts for which they otherwise would have to answer directly. Scrutiny does not necessarily result however in removal of the legal cover. The House of Lords took a hard look at the Sixth Tin Council and the member States remained insulated from responsibility.[24] It may not always be that way. In the *NATO* cases, the lack of jurisdiction meant that the ICJ did not need to reach the question of attribution. Germany, among other States, said that responsibility does not arise 'for reason of membership for measures taken by…NATO…'[25] Yet there were some indications that NATO would not have been a defense against responsibility. Yugoslavia, unsurprisingly, assumed that the member States were responsible.[26] Such a position taken by one State engaged in contentious proceedings is not necessarily persuasive on its own as evidence of a general position. The Court however admonished the Parties that a failure of jurisdiction does not absolve States of their obligation to abide by international law, including the rule that disputes are to be resolved by peaceful means. The Court's admonishment was in careful terms: 'whether or not States accept the jurisdiction of the Court, they remain in any event responsible for acts attributable to them that violate international law, including humanitarian law.'[27] This did not say whether acts done in the framework of NATO number among "acts attributable to them." If however acts done in the framework of NATO could be attributed to the member States of that organization under no circumstance whatever, then it would be

---

[23] See Crawford 'Holding International Organisations and Their Members to Account' Fifth Steinkraus-Cohen International Law Lecture, School of Oriental and African Studies, London 15 March 2007.

[24] *Maclaine Watson & Co Ltd v International Tin Council* [1990] 2 AC 418. A number of States constituted the Sixth International Tin Council. The price of tin collapsed. The Council became insolvent. The Council's creditors pursued the matter in English court and found that only the Council, not its constituent States, could be proceeded against. This was recourse to legal process but without result: the Council had no money.

[25] A/CN.4/556 p. 65.

[26] See e.g. excerpts from Yugoslavia's pleadings in *Legality of Use of Force (Yugoslavia v Canada)* ICJ Rep 1999 pp. 259, 268 ¶ 24.

[27] *Legality of Use of Force (Yugoslavia v United States of America)* Request for the Indication of Provisional Measures (Removal from the List) Order of 2 June 1999, ICJ Rep 1999 pp. 916, 925 ¶ 31; *Legality of Use of Force (Yugoslavia v Spain)* ibid., p. 773 ¶ 37.

hard to justify even the Court's glancing reference to continued responsibility. The Court while leaving the matter open saw fit to mention it.[28]

And to consider specialized organizations (metals leagues, military alliances and the like) is not to say that they are the only types of organization that member States might use to shield themselves from international responsibility. Member States well might use a universal organization for legal cover as well. The possibility exists that mandates of the Security Council will shield States from attribution, though, as seen in *Al-Jedda*, national courts (among others) are likely to push back against any tendency to relieve States of responsibility under such cover.[29]

7.1.3   *Access to the International Court of Justice*

Only States may be parties to cases before the International Court of Justice (ICJ Statute Article 34(1)). All member States of the UN are '*ipso facto* parties to the Statute' of the Court (Charter Article 93(1)). A further consequence of membership, then, is access to the ICJ.

It is not however necessary to be a member State of the UN in order to be a party to a case. Before admission to the UN, a State may become a party to the Statute of the ICJ, and in this way may be a party to a case in the ICJ: the Court 'shall be open to the States Parties to the...Statute' (ICJ Statute Article 35(1)).

Becoming a party to the Statute, for a non-member State, is by way of action taken under Charter Article 93(2):

> A State which is not a Member of the United Nations may become a party to the Statute of the International Court of Justice on conditions to be determined in each case by the General Assembly upon the recommendation of the Security Council.

Switzerland was the first to become a party to the Statute without first having been admitted as a member State to the UN. Swiss participation thus presents a curious pair of bookends to universality: Switzerland was the first State to take steps that helped achieve universal participation in the Court and among the last to join the UN. Acting under Article 93(2), the General Assembly determined

---

[28] For works addressing the relation between the member States and NATO in connection with the Kosovo operations, see citations in Gaja Second Report A/CN.4/541, 2 Apr 2004 p. 4 ¶ 7 n. 9.

[29] See e.g. Lord Bingham of Cornhill at ¶¶ 23–4 in *R (on the application of Al-Jedda) (FC) v Secretary of State for Defence (Justice and another intervening)* Judgment of 12 Dec. 2007, House of Lords Appellate Committee, [2007] UKHL 58, [2008] 2 W.L.R. 31 (on appeal from [2006] EWCA Civ 327).

Switzerland will become a party to the Statute of the Court on the date of the deposit with the Secretary-General of the United Nations of an instrument, signed on behalf of the Government of Switzerland and ratified as may be required by Swiss constitutional law, containing:

    (a) Acceptance of the provisions of the Statute of the International Court of Justice;

    (b) Acceptance of all the obligations of a Member of the United Nations under Article 94 of the Charter;

    (c) An undertaking to contribute to the expenses of the Court such equitable amount as the General Assembly shall assess from time to time after consultation with the Swiss Government.[30]

Japan, Liechtenstein, San Marino, and Nauru later became parties to the Statute in the same way. The conditions for each were the same as for Switzerland.[31] When conditions were set for Switzerland to become a party to the Statute, a Security Council Committee of Experts emphasized however that the conditions for one State under Article 93(2) are not necessarily the same as for another:

> The conditions on which a State which is not a member of the United Nations may become a party to the Statute are to be determined *in each case* by the General Assembly upon the recommendation of the Security Council. Accordingly, the conditions recommended above as appropriate to the case of Switzerland are not intended to constitute a precedent to be followed either by the Security Council or by the General Assembly in any future case under Article 93, paragraph 2, of the Charter.[32]

In practice, the 'conditions recommended' did not change, and one therefore might draw the conclusion after a half century that a precedent now has been established. The plain language of Charter Article 93, paragraph 2 nevertheless remains. The Charter basis thus remains for the conditions 'to be determined in each case by the General Assembly upon the recommendation of the Security Council.'

Writers have said that the universality of the United Nations removes the possibility of a non-member State seeking to become a party to the Statute, so Article 93(2) is unlikely again to be called into use. The situation of 'new States com[ing] into existence without applying for membership in the United Nations,' wrote Karin Oellers-Frahm in 2006, 'seems to be rather hypothetical.'[33] The declaration of independence of Kosovo in the face of objections of

---

[30] GA res 91(I), 11 Dec 1946.

[31] Oellers-Frahm 'Article 93 UN Charter' in *Statute Commentary* 153, 157 ¶ 6.

[32] Report and Recommendation of the Committee of Experts of the Security Council concerning the conditions on which Switzerland may become a Party to the Statute of the International Court of Justice ¶ 6: included as Annex to GA res 91(I), 11 Dec 1946.

[33] Oellers-Frahm 'Article 93 UN Charter' in *Statute Commentary* 153, 158 ¶ 11.

permanent members of the Security Council perhaps makes the situation rather less hypothetical.

It is also possible for a State neither a member State of the UN nor a party to the Statute of the ICJ to be party to a case. Article 35(2) of the Statute provides as follows:

> The conditions under which the Court shall be open to other States shall, subject to the special provisions contained in treaties in force, be laid down by the Security Council, but in no case shall such conditions place the parties in a position of inequality before the Court.

The clause 'the special provisions contained in treaties in force' has been limited, 'without any textual warrant,' to treaties in force in 1945, so its practical significance is small, if any remains.[34] Still operative is the phrase 'conditions under which the Court shall be open to other States...shall be laid down by the Security Council.' The Security Council adopted resolution 9 (1946) to lay down conditions pursuant to Article 35(2):

> The International Court of Justice shall be open to a State which is not a party to the Statute of the International Court of Justice, upon the following condition, namely, that such State shall previously have deposited with the Registrar of the Court a declaration by which it accepts the jurisdiction of the Court, in accordance with the Charter of the United Nations and with the terms and subject to the conditions of the Statute and Rules of the Court, and undertakes to comply in good faith with the decision or decisions of the Court and to accept all the obligations of a Member of the United Nations under Article 94 of the Charter.[35]

Resolution 9 is the instrument which operationalizes Article 35(2) of the Statute.[36]

For States not members of the UN, the conditions now laid down for gaining access to the Court are not as stringent as the criteria for being admitted to the UN. This is the effect of Charter Article 93(2), Statute Article 35(2), and associated practice. A State under Charter Article 93(2) or Security Council resolution 9 (1946) gains access to the Court by affirming its commitment to the Statute and to Article 94 of the Charter and by assuming certain financial obligations. The conditions are therefore the same specified for non-member States seeking to become parties to the Statute; and for non-Statute States seeking access to the Court. Setting a uniform condition apparently was intended. According to the Committee of Experts,

---

[34] Crawford & Grant 'International Court of Justice' in Weiss & Daws eds *Oxford Handbook* 193, 207 n. 10.

[35] SC res 9, 15 Oct 1946 ¶ 1.

[36] On the (perhaps problematic) relation between Art. 35(2) and Art. 36(2), see Zimmermann 'Article 35' *Statute Commentaries* 565, 585–6 ¶¶ 78–80.

> The [Committee's] intention in inserting the second suggested condition is the same as that which caused it to recommend the identical wording appearing in paragraph (1) of [SC res 9(I)] setting out the conditions under which the Court shall be open to States not parties to the Statute. The obligations imposed by Article 94 of the Charter upon a Member of the United Nations should, in the opinion of the Committee, apply equally to non-members of the United Nations which become parties to the Statute and to non-parties which are allowed access to the Court.[37]

Yet, as pointed out above, notwithstanding consistent practice, it was not the Charter that determined the conditions for Switzerland to become party to the Statute. The General Assembly determined the conditions acting on the recommendation of the Security Council under Charter Article 93(2). Different conditions could be set in a future case. The conditions set out in Security Council resolution 9 (1946) are expressly applicable to all States seeking access under Statute Article 35(2) – but only for so long as resolution 9 remains in effect. Those conditions, too, then, are not necessarily permanent. The Security Council in resolution 9

> reserve[d] the right to rescind or amend this resolution by a resolution which shall be communicated to the Court, and on receipt of such communication and to the extent determined by the new resolution, existing declarations shall cease to be effective except in regard to disputes which are already before the Court.[38]

The conditions which have applied to date, both for non-UN members to become party to the Statute and for non-Statute parties to gain access to the Court, in practice could be changed.

Indeed neither the Charter nor the Statute specifies what the scope of the conditions for becoming party or gaining access might be. As noted, the existing conditions for a non-UN member State to gain access to the ICJ are not as stringent as the criteria for being admitted to the UN. The non-UN member, whether seeking access by way of accession to the Statute or under Statute Article 35(2), does so by affirming its commitment to the Statute and to Article 94 of the Charter and by assuming certain financial obligations. The Article 94 commitment entails other, but not all other, Charter commitments. The Committee of Experts said,

> [T]he obligations of a Member of the United Nations under Article 94 include the complementary obligations arising under Articles 25 and 103 of the Charter insofar as the provisions of those Articles may relate to the provisions of Article 93, and non-members of the United Nations which become parties to the Statute (and non-parties which have access to the Court) become bound by these complementary

---

[37] GA res 91(I), 11 Dec 1946 Annex ¶ 4.
[38] SC res 9, 15 Oct 1946 ¶ 4.

obligations under Articles 25 and 103 in relation to the provisions of Article 94 (but not otherwise), when they accept "all the obligations of a Member of the United Nations under Article 94."[39]

This is still only part of the total obligations that the UN Charter entails for member States. The requirement of Charter Article 4(1) that a State, to be admitted, 'accept the obligations contained in the present Charter' means that the State accept *all* the obligations. The non-member State seeking access to the ICJ plainly does not need to do as much – at least under the current (and now half-century long) disposition. The commitment to Article 94, etc. for purposes of gaining access to the ICJ thus can be thought of as an abridged version of the full commitment required under Article 4(1) of the Charter for purposes of admission to the UN. The less stringent requirements for ICJ participation reflect the relative urgency of the goal of achieving universal subscription to the principle that international disputes are to be resolved by pacific means.

It is not immediately clear whether any constitutional provision would prevent the General Assembly under Charter Article 93(2) or the Security Council under Statute Article 35(2) from requiring the non-member State to satisfy more stringent conditions. A situation might be hypothesized in which the General Assembly and the Security Council are divided as to the role to give a State in UN processes, the Security Council veto preventing admission to the UN, but a General Assembly majority favouring the State. This was the division of opinion before the package deal. The definition of Security Council 'recommendation' under Charter Article 4(2), as affirmed in the *Competence* Advisory Opinion, would apply again if dispute arose as to the meaning of the same term under Charter Article 93(2). A conceivable – though, again, hypothetical – bargain would be that the Security Council require as a condition for access to the Court even more stringent conditions than those set down in Article 4(1) for admission to membership.[40] The State would be free to reject such terms and seek adjudication elsewhere. In any case, such conditions could not 'place the parties in a position of inequality before the Court.'

The provisions of the UN Charter, ICJ Statute, and Security Council resolution 9 (1946) under which States are given standing before the Court would appear straightforward. It might have been said at one time, and to an extent might still be maintained, that the main preliminary question likely to arise in an ICJ proceeding is the question of the consent of a State to jurisdiction –

---

[39] GA res 91(I), 11 Dec 1946 Annex ¶ 4.

[40] That the conditions for access to the Court by non-member States may be varied upon decision of the competent UN organs suggests a comparison to the accession provisions of the European Union under Title VII, Art O (Final Provisions) of the Treaty on European Union, signed 7 Feb 1992, entered into force 1 Nov 1993: 1757 UNTS 4, 156. The EU accession provisions, too, may be varied from one applicant to another; but unlike the conditions for access to the Court, they actually have been varied (and considerably) in practice.

e.g., a question as to the effectiveness or scope of a compromissory clause for purposes of Article 36(1) of the Statute.[41] But difficult questions of standing, too, will arise, where the relationship is unclear between the UN and the State seeking access to the Court. The disintegration of Yugoslavia gave rise to a situation in which the relationship between the UN and a certain State was indeed in doubt, and the State was engaged, both as respondent and applicant, in multiple cases in the Court. The ambiguity as to the relationship between the United Nations and Yugoslavia (later titled Serbia and Montenegro) has been discussed already (see Chapter 6 above). A comparatively clean solution was available where jurisdiction was lacking.[42] A far less satisfactory approach took shape where the problem of UN membership was not as easy to avoid (or where the Court failed to avoid it). One still may ask (and writers have)[43] whether the Court in 2004 in truth needed to take as categorical position as it did on the membership question.

7.1.4   *Participation in Other UN Processes*

As seen immediately above, UN membership automatically entails access to the International Court of Justice; but the Court is open on other terms to non-member States as well. The situation with respect to participation in other UN processes is somewhat different: membership does not necessarily assure that a State will belong to any given functional organ of the UN. The Human Rights Council, to give one example, does not include all States of the UN.[44] However, as with the ICJ, a non-member State on terms fashioned to particular circumstances may participate in certain UN processes that, presumptively, are open only to member States. An example may be drawn from UN processes concerning administration of territory.

The UN in recent years has become engaged in the administration of territory to an extent once thought unlikely to be matched again after the winding down

---

[41] For the cases and discussion, see Tomuschat 'Article 36' in Zimmermann, Tomuschat & Oellers-Frahm *The Statute of the International Court of Justice. A Commentary* (2006) 588, 612–26.

[42] For example, in the *NATO cases*, the U.S. had not consented to jurisdiction under Art. 38(5) of the Rules of Court, *Legality of Use of Force (Yugoslavia v USA)* Request for Indication of Provision Measures (Removal from the List) Order of 2 June 1999, ICJ Rep 1999 pp. 916, 925 ¶ 28; and Spain was not subject to compulsory jurisdiction because it had made a valid reservation as to reciprocity under Art. 36(2) of the Statute: ibid., *(Yugoslavia v Spain)* ICJ Rep 1999 pp. 761, 770–1 ¶ 25.

[43] See e.g. Dimitrijevic & Milanovic 'The strange story of the Bosnian Genocide Case' (2008) 21 *Leiden JIL* 65, 81–2. cf. Blum 'Was Yugoslavia a Member of the United Nations in the Years 1992–2000?' (2007) 101 *AJ* 800, 818. Blum says that the problem mainly arose from the failure of the General Assembly and Security Council to adopt a definitive position.

[44] GA res 60/251, 15 Mar 2006.

of the trusteeship system. The main contemporary instances – Kosovo and East Timor – have gone considerably further than extending a mandate to a single State to administer territory; they have involved the UN in discharging the whole array of administrative functions associated with territorial responsibility.[45] All of the Contact Group States involved in Kosovo have been UN members. An historic example, however, demonstrates that a non-member State also might participate in such an administrative process.

Italy, upon being designated administering State for the Trust Territory of Somaliland in 1950,[46] was not a UN member. This was an anomalous situation. Politically, it was referable to the necessity of regularizing the Italian administration in the Horn of Africa. Legally, it was not clearly consistent with the Charter. Article 86 of the Charter makes provision for membership in the Trusteeship Council only of member States of the UN, and among the members of the Council are to be 'those Members [of the United Nations] administering trust territories.' In light of the purpose of the Trusteeship Council to place the entirety of the system of administration of Trust Territories under UN supervision, this latter provision well may be interpreted as meaning that *all* States administering trust territories are to be members of the Council. If this interpretation is accepted (and practice supports it), then a question arises as to what the legal basis was for Italy's designation as a State responsible for a Trust Territory and for Italy's participation in the Trusteeship Council. By Trusteeship Council resolution 310 (VIII),[47] the Trusteeship Council requested that the General Assembly include the matter of Italy's participation in the agenda. That the Trusteeship Council chose to ask reflects the member States' sense that Italy's non-membership was problematic. France proposed a draft General Assembly resolution which would refer to Trusteeship Council resolution 310 (VIII) and to Italy's 'exercising its responsibilities towards the United Nations as an Administering Authority' under Chapters XII and XIII. The French draft '[c]onsider[ed] that Italy should be enabled to exercise those responsibilities with complete effectiveness.'[48] This is the language which the General Assembly adopted shortly afterward.[49] The General Assembly also called on the Security

---

[45] The main recent works are Kiderlen *Von Triest nach Osttimor. Der völkerrechtliche Rahmen für die Verwaltung von Krisengebieten durch die Vereinten Nationen* (2008); Knoll *The Legal Status of Territories Subject to Administration by International Organisations* (2008); Stahn *The Law and Practice of International Territorial Administration. Versailles to Iraq and Beyond* (2008); Wilde *International Territorial Administration: How Trusteeship and the Civilizing Mission Never Went Away* (2008).

[46] By GA res 442 (V), 2 Dec 1950, which approved the Trusteeship Agreement.

[47] 23 Feb 1951: 9–1:2, USSR against, New Zealand and United Kingdom abstaining.

[48] A/C.4/L.142, 26 Nov 1951.

[49] GA res 550 (VI) ('Question of the full participation of Italy in work of the Trusteeship Council'), 7 Dec 1951.

Council to address the application of Italy for admission to membership in the UN – which further suggested that full participation in the Trusteeship Council under Charter Article 86 indeed was only for States members of the UN. Italy nevertheless remained a non-member State.

The solution for the Trusteeship Council was to adopt Supplementary Rules granting Italy the right to participate without vote on proceedings relative to the Somaliland Trust Territory and general questions of the International Trusteeship System.[50] The Committee had been set up expressly to deal with the question of Italian participation. This improvised solution may be taken as illustrating the proposition that it is necessary for the efficient functioning of an organization – or for the efficient functioning of a body within an organization – for it to include the States involved in the tasks it exists to fulfill.

Thus, while the Charter expressly provides for extending participation in the ICJ to non-member States, ad hoc approaches can be developed to extend participation in other UN processes. On the one hand, this tends to qualify the significance of membership: States and non-States alike may participate. On the other hand, the need for special decisions, whether under provisions of the Charter such as Article 93(2) or wholly improvised, tends to show that membership has specific consequences relative to the rights of a State within the UN system: where membership is lacking, such decisions are required; where membership obtains, they are not. As will be suggested in the second part of this Chapter, membership retains considerable importance for States in other respects as well.

7.1.5   *The Presumption of Continuity of Membership*

The continuity of statehood in international law is an entrenched presumption, as noted in Chapter 4 above. As noted already in this Chapter, a degree of relation exists between statehood and UN membership. The two however are not synonymous, and so it does not necessarily follow that a presumption exists that, once a member, a State remains a member. Yet since 1945 no State has been expelled from the UN under Charter Article 6; nor has any State been suspended from the exercise of its rights and privileges under Article 5. Membership in the UN, once attained, is not readily lost – if it now can be lost at all. Writers have examined expulsion and suspension *in extenso*.[51] We may consider

---

[50] T/847 adopted 20, 21 & 23 Feb 1951 as drafted by a Trusteeship Council special committee, the Committee on Rules of Procedure (Argentina, Australia, Belgium, Iraq, Thailand, US).

[51] The fullest treatment of expulsion and suspension is that by Magliveras *Exclusion from Participation in International Organizations: The Law and Practice behind Member States' Expulsion and Suspension of Membership* (1999). See also Sohn 'Expulsion or Forced Withdrawal from an

the practice here briefly, with a view to its tendency to reinforce the universality of membership in the United Nations.

Looking at the history, one sees that expulsion from a general international organization is not entirely out of the question. An attempt was made under the League of Nations to expel a member – Liberia – and another member in fact was expelled – Russia. In the Liberian case, the problem was forced labour imposed on the Kru tribes. Louis Sohn doubted whether there was legal basis for expulsion of Liberia in 1934[52] and did not think that expulsion would be an effective mechanism for disciplining a member in any event.[53] Doubt as to the practical utility of expulsion as a sanction has been expressed by Schermers as well.[54] As action in the end was not taken, the Liberian precedent is essentially negative.

The USSR, after invading Finland, was expelled from the League. The League Council resolution of 14 December 1939 effectuating expulsion is noteworthy as the single example of its type (i.e., the single example of either the League or the UN expelling a member State):

The Council,

Having taken cognisance of the resolution adopted by the Assembly on December 14th, 1939, regarding the appeal of the Finnish Government;

1. Associates itself with the condemnation by the Assembly of the action of the Union of Soviet Socialist Republics against the Finnish State; and
2. For the reasons set forth in the resolution of the Assembly, in virtue of Article 16, paragraph 4, of the Covenant, finds that, by its act, the Union of Soviet Socialist Republics has placed itself outside the League of Nations. It follows that the Union of Soviet Socialist Republics is no longer a Member of the League.[55]

The League Assembly had determined that Russia was in breach of Article 12 of the Covenant; and also of specific political agreements with Finland; that Russia had denounced a non-aggression pact with Finland without justification; and had refused to appear before the Council and the Assembly for purposes of presenting its dispute with Finland for examination. The Assembly and Council both described the USSR as having 'placed itself outside the League [or Covenant],' a form of words tending to take the onus off the organization and to underscore the discretion of the member State. If accepted on these terms, the

---

International Organization' (1964) 77 *Harv LR* 1381; Bowett *Law of international institutions* 4th edn 392–4; Jenks 'Expulsion From the League of Nations' (1935) 16 *BY* 155.
[52] Sohn (1964) 77 *Harv LR* 1381, 1385–97.
[53] Ibid., 1382. See also Magliveras, 19–21.
[54] *International Institutional Law* § 110 pp. 73–4.
[55] *LONSOJ* p. 506 (Council resolution); p. 540 (Assembly resolution).

resolution simply ratified a decision taken already by Russia and expressed by way of aggression against a State. Indeed, it has been asked whether the USSR, as a formal matter, was really expelled from the League.[56] It seems somewhat formalistic to argue whether this was an expulsion or a withdrawal. Whether or not one takes a position, the functional purpose of the relevant League transactions was clear enough: Russia was no longer to be treated as a member State of the organization, and the League adopted this new position in authoritative statements. In any event, general European war already had erupted, and international conditions quickly deteriorated to such a degree that, politically, Russia's expulsion was beside the point. The disappearance of the League after World War II cut short any constitutional development to which the incident might otherwise have led.

Article 6 of the UN Charter provides that '[a] member of the United Nations which has persistently violated the Principles contained in the present Charter may be expelled from the Organization by the General Assembly upon the recommendation of the Security Council.' Under Article 5, a State against which preventive or enforcement action has been taken by the Security Council may be formally 'suspended from the exercise of the rights and privileges of membership.' The same constitutional process obtains – decision of the Assembly upon recommendation of the Council.

Individual member States from time to time called for Article 5 or Article 6 measures against Israel.[57] It was clear that Israel was to remain a member in good standing; the question of suspending or expelling Israel was the preoccupation of a small minority of member States (though support among the Non-Alligned bloc was sufficient for a General Assembly resolution stating that Israel was not a peace-loving State – a resolution that says more about the General Assembly than about Israel).[58] Opposition to South Africa during the *Apartheid* regime, however, was much more widespread and led to a search in earnest for means to curtail South Africa's participation in the Organization. This led member States eventually to turn to the credentials procedures, by which a delegation is accepted (or not) for participation in the General Assembly. The transactions

---

[56] Gross 'Was the Soviet Union Expelled from the League of Nations?' (1945) 39 *AJ* 35. Gross's doubt sprang from procedural irregularities. He also noted objections by States at the time to phrasing ('placed itself') in the two League resolutions: ibid., at 43.

[57] E.g., Kuwait, GAOR 40th sess 37th plen mtg, 16 Oct 1985; Libya, Letter dated 18 June 1981 from the Chargé d'affaires ad interim of the Libyan Arab Jamahiriya addressed to the President of the Security Council, S/14559, SCOR 36th yr Supp for April-June 1981 (following Israeli operations against Iraqi nuclear facilities); Syria, SCOR 27th yr 1651st mtg ¶ 195. See generally Halberstam 'Excluding Israel from the General Assembly by a Rejection of its Credentials' (1984) 78 *AJ* 179.

[58] GA res ES-9/1, 5 Feb 1982.

leading to South Africa's temporary cessation of participation in the General Assembly are the main example of an attempt to expel a member State from the UN.

It was widely agreed by the 1970s that the UN should take steps against South Africa in response to its institutionalized system of racial control and separation. Member States were not however in agreement as to the precise steps to be taken. Expulsion was considered from time to time. Kenya, Mauritania, Cameroon, and Iraq in 1974, for example, put forward a draft resolution in the Security Council which, with reference to Article 6, would have recommended expulsion of South Africa.[59] The resolution was rejected.[60] A different approach was needed, if measures were to be taken with regard to South Africa's participation in the UN.

The approach that in the end bore some, if limited, fruit was to turn to the credentialing process. In the mid-1960s, challenges were made in the Credentials Committee against the presence of South African representatives in the General Assembly. The Commonwealth already had compelled South Africa to withdraw from that organization (in 1961).[61] Opinion had not yet shifted among States within the UN Credentials Committee however to the extent that a definitive vote against South Africa could be obtained.[62]

The twenty-fifth General Assembly session (1970) was a turning point within the Assembly as a whole. As was the practice, the General Assembly at the start of its session adopted a resolution accepting the decision of the Credentials Committee that the credentials of the delegations of the member States had been received and found valid. However, resolution 2636 A (XXV) of 13 November 1970 added by way of amendment the words 'except with regard to the credentials of the representative of the Government of South Africa.'[63] The resolution was adopted 71 votes to 2 with 45 abstentions.

The General Assembly President quickly moved to qualify the exception clause. According to the President, the clause 'would not seem ... to mean that the South African delegation is unseated or cannot continue to sit in this Assembly; ... it will not affect the rights and privileges of membership of South Africa.'[64] This apparently was based on the advice of the UN legal counsel, who said that a member State could be denied representation only by action taken under

---

[59] S/11543: Four-Power Draft Resolution, SCOR 29th yr 1802nd mtg, 25 Oct 1974.

[60] SCOR 29th year 1808th mtg, 30 Oct 1974 (10:3–2).

[61] Dugard (1998) 92 *AJ* 187, 202 n. 123.

[62] See e.g., GAOR 21st sess, Annexes, a.i. 3, A/6620, ¶¶ 14, 15, 18; GAOR 23rd sess, Annexes, a.i. 3, A/7228, ¶¶ 13, 20 (rejecting proposal to declare South African representatives' credentials invalid (5–3:1)).

[63] *Rep UN* (1970–78) p. 98 ¶ 44.

[64] GAOR 25th sess 1901st plen mtg ¶ 286.

Article 5.[65] Thus what might have seemed a reasonably clear statement by the General Assembly that the credentials of South Africa had not been accepted was denied that effect. The General Assembly incorporated the same 'except...South Africa' limitation into its credentials resolutions at the start of the 26th and 27th sessions (1971 and 1972).[66] So too in those sessions did the President qualify the 'except...South Africa' clause by placing such an interpretative gloss on it as to assure continued representation of South Africa in the Assembly.[67] Sensing a deadlock, the opponents of South Africa sought in 1973 to reject South Africa's credentials directly. This meant taking the matter back to the Credentials Committee itself. The Committee rejected a proposal to reject South Africa's credentials, but, this time, by a margin of only 5 to 4.[68]

In 1974, the General Assembly determined that South Africa was in 'flagrant violation of the principles of the Charter of the United Nations and the Universal Declaration of Human Rights.' The Assembly called upon the Security Council 'to review the relationship between the United Nations and South Africa in the light of the constant violation by South Africa.'[69] At this stage, a member State requested the (new) General Assembly President to guide the member States as to the proper interpretation of the 'except...South Africa' clause and to define a further course of General Assembly action respecting South Africa's participation. The President set out guidance in the following terms:

> It would...be a betrayal of the clearly and repeatedly expressed will of the General Assembly to understand this to mean that it was merely a procedural method of expressing its rejection of the policy of *apartheid*. On the basis of the consistency with which the General Assembly has regularly refused to accept the credentials of the delegation of South Africa, one may legitimately infer that the General Assembly would in the same way reject the credentials of any other delegation authorized by the Government of the Republic of South Africa to represent it, which is tantamount to saying in explicit terms that the General Assembly refuses to allow the delegation of South Africa to participate in its work.
>
> Thus it is, as President of the twenty-ninth session of the General Assembly, that I interpret the decision of the General Assembly, leaving open the question of the status of the Republic of South Africa as a Member of the United Nations, which as we all know, is a matter requiring a recommendation from the Security Council. My interpretation refers exclusively to the position of the delegation of South Africa within the strict framework of the rules of procedure of the General Assembly.[70]

---

[65] *UN Jurid Ybk* 1970 pp. 169–71.

[66] GA res 2862 (XXVI), 20 Dec 1971 (103–1:16); GA res 2948 (XXVII), 8 Dec 1972 (103–1:16).

[67] E.g., on 30 Sept 1974: *Rep UN* (1970–78) p. 99 ¶ 57.

[68] Tanzania was sponsor of the proposal: GAOR 28th sess Annexes, a.i. 3, A/9179, First Report of the Credentials Committee 4 Oct 1973 ¶¶ 7, 12.

[69] GA res 3207 (XXIX) ('Relationship between the United Nations and South Africa') 30 Sept 1974 (125–1:9).

[70] GAOR 29th sess 2281st plen mtg, 12 Nov 1974.

In one respect, the President's guidance was cautious: it recognized the authority of the Security Council over Article 6 matters. To have done otherwise would have been to trigger a full-blown constitutional crisis. As it stood, this nevertheless was a *volte-face* from the previous President's position. Member States challenged the new interpretation, and it drew rebuke subsequently from writers.[71] The General Assembly nevertheless upheld it.[72] The representatives of South Africa thus were barred from participating in the work of the Assembly from September 1974 through the end of *Apartheid*.[73] A 'back door to the suspension of membership rights' had been discovered in credentials procedure.[74]

But even given that aperture, carrying through specific measures required a certain amount of legal convolution. The question arises, if action under Article 6 or Article 5 was impossible even with respect to the perpetrator of *Apartheid*, the Bantustans, and unlawful occupation of Namibia, under what circumstances might those Charter provisions actually operate. The statement of the General Assembly on 5 February 1982 that Israel, by its occupation of Arab territories, was not a peace-loving State and in breach of obligations under the Charter,[75] in the eyes of its sponsors perhaps looked like the predicate to Article 6 action, but no such action was taken. The truly clear case was Security Council reaction to the Iraqi invasion of Kuwait in 1990. In that case, there was no question of self-defense, and no question but that the aggressor was acting with intent to disrupt the territorial integrity of a State. Invasion followed by formal pronouncements that the State territory in its entirety was henceforward to be a province of the invading State left little room for interpretation. Yet Iraq remained a member State throughout the period of unlawful annexation and the period of armed enforcement action, sanctions, and international diplomatic isolation that followed. The practice suggests that once a member State, always a member State.

---

[71] E.g., Gross 'Editorial Comment: On the Degradation of the Constitutional Environment of the United Nations' (1983) 77 *AJ* 569; Bowett *Law of International Institutions* 4th edn 395–7.

[72] GAOR 29th sess 2281st plen mtg (91–22:19), 12 Nov 1974. The basis for the Presidents' interpretations of the 'except…South Africa' clause was contested. It could be that the interpretations were equally valid, the several years of General Assembly practice intervening between the former (Hambro) and latter (Bouteflika) having generated by accretion a shift in law. For the division of support in the General Assembly for the competing positions over time, see Amerasinghe 128–9.

[73] GA res 48/258 A, 23 June 1994 ¶ 7.

[74] Fleischhauer 'Panel Remarks: Compliance and Enforcement in the United Nations System' (1991) 85 *ASIL Proc* 428, 421. Not all attacks on participation by way of credentialing will succeed. Consider Yugoslavia's failed attack on Bosnia. Yugoslavia argued, *inter alia*, that the Bosnian government was not competent to represent Bosnia: 'at the time of the filing of the Application, Mr. Izetbegovic was recognized, in particular by the United Nations, as the Head of State of Bosnia and Herzegovina,' ICJ Rep 1996 at 621–2 ¶ 44.

[75] GA res ES-9/1, 5 Feb 1982.

A member State, to be sure, may voluntarily decline to participate in the General Assembly or other UN proceedings, though there is no express provision in the Charter for a member State to withdraw from the UN. The case that comes closest to withdrawal suggests that the tendency is to preserve membership at some level, even as against the expressed position of the member State to terminate its membership. The case that might have been treated as withdrawal was that of Indonesia. By letter of its Foreign Minister dated 20 January 1965 to the Secretary-General, Indonesia announced its withdrawal from the United Nations: the seating of Malaysia in the Security Council, according to the letter, left Indonesia 'no alternative... but withdrawal from the United Nations.' Therefore, 'Indonesia has decided at this stage and under the present circumstances to withdraw from the United Nations.'[76] The position may appear to have been unequivocal, but Indonesia resumed participation in September 1966. The earlier measure apparently had not been a 'withdrawal' in a sense such that it would have terminated membership. It had been, instead, a 'cessation of co-operation.' By telegram dated 19 September 1966, Indonesia told the Secretary-General that it 'has decided to resume full co-operation with the United Nations and to resume participation in its activities.'[77] The statement to the Secretary-General was short, almost perfunctory. It notably referred only to Indonesia 'decid[ing],' which suggested that the contemplated measure was one involving only a unilateral operation by the (member?) State. As far as the UN was concerned, this was correct: resumption of 'co-operation' and 'participation' did not require (re)admission.[78]

Cuba, subjected to membership sanction by the OAS, continued, of course, as a fully participating member of the UN.[79]

---

[76] SCOR 20th yr Supp for Jan–March S/6157.

[77] A/6419, S/7498.

[78] Statement of President of the General Assembly upon seating of the delegation of Indonesia: GAOR 21st sess 1420th plen mtg ¶¶ 7–9, 28 Sept 1966. See Amerasinghe 120. For citation to writers on the problems associated with absence of a withdrawal provision in the Charter, see Schwelb 'Withdrawal from the United Nations: The Indonesian Intermezzo' (1967) 61 *AJ* 661, 661 n. 2.

[79] The OAS suspended Cuba's participation in the organization from 1962: American Union, Eighth Meeting of Consultation, Background Memorandum on the Convocation of the Meeting 1 (OEA/Ser.F/II.8, Doc. 2) (1962) cited by Sohn (1964) 77 *Harv LR* 1381, 1417 n. 185. This was on the ground that the government of Cuba had voluntarily separated itself from OAS principles – a somewhat constructed position but one which nevertheless allows the organization to say that Cuba's membership as such has not been terminated. The OAS Charter does not provide a clear mechanism for termination of the membership of a State. Cuba sought ICJ review of the decision, and its lawfulness was contested in the UN Security Council and OAS Council: Sohn 1418–20. The ambiguity as to the position of Cuba as a State within

The durability of membership is consistent with the general presumption favouring continuity of the rights of statehood in international law. It also has been said to be consistent with considerations of comity and the objective of maintaining international peace and security. Argentina, in its submissions in the *Competence* advisory proceedings, characterized suspension and expulsion as 'extreme and punitive measures which, as countries are involved, are not easy to adopt because of the reactions they may provoke and because they jeopardize peaceful international existence and co-operation.'[80] Israel has indicated that curtailment of rights of participation would be inconsistent with the 'principle of universality.'[81] Schermers doubts whether expulsion is consistent with universality.[82] If the UN is to be universal, it must not only admit all States; it must retain all States as well.

In light of the preponderance of support that would be needed in the Assembly and Council to effectuate either an Article 5 or Article 6 measure against a State, the suspension or expulsion of a State would be unlikely to cause a general breakdown of 'peaceful international existence' as Argentina feared it might. Consensus would be a prerequisite to suspension or expulsion. The point on co-operation however seems right; and exclusion of a State, even in the presence of consensus that it should be excluded, would not seem to advance co-operation. The involvement of multiple States, most seeking in most situations to avoid or mitigate friction with other States, is the political factor making implementation of measures under Articles 5 and 6 difficult in practice. It could be that the entrenched presumption of universality is a legal consideration also militating against removal of a member State on whatever terms. The measures against *apartheid* South Africa can be reconciled with this, by observing that the UN did not reject the continued membership of the State of South Africa but instead shifted the challenge to a distinct question: namely, whether a particular set of political organs in truth constituted the government entitled to represent that State at international level.

The effectiveness of Charter Article 5 and Article 6 must be questioned, as against the *de minimus* operation of those provisions in practice since 1945. States commencing membership in the Organization do not have the option of adopting reservations to their membership,[83] a constraint on States that would seem symmetrical with a rule (if unwritten) that the Organization does not have

---

(or without) the OAS in the 1970s presented a jurisdictional question to the Inter-American Commission on Human Rights: see remarks by Farer (2002) 96 *ASIL Proc* 95, 106.

[80] ICJ Pldgs 1950 p. 134.

[81] Letter dated 27 October 1986 from the Permanent Representative of Israel to the United Nations addressed to the Secretary-General, A/41/766.

[82] *International Institutional Law*, §§ 30, 108–22.

[83] Bowett *Law of International Institutions* 4th edn 384–5.

the option of rescinding or diminishing the rights of States once admitted. Each State, in short, takes the UN as a package deal; and the UN takes each State as such as well.

7.2   *Universality and the Future of International Organization*

Admission works its effects both in legal and sociological spheres. We have just considered the legal effects above. Also, admission has both specific and general effects. That is to say, admission has effects relative to each admitted State; and admission – especially the aggregate of all admissions under a presumption of universality – has effects relative to the international system and to the UN as a component of that system. We now may turn to consider the extra-legal effects of admission, both on the individual State admitted and generally.

7.2.1   *Minimum Access to Processes of International Relations*

Admission to the United Nations guarantees the admitted State at least minimum access to processes of international relations. As noted, one rationale to seeking UN membership is that membership permits the admitted State to consolidate its diplomatic operations, establishing links to many other States through the single institutional apparatus of the Organization. This may be a compelling rationale in some instances, especially for the very small or very poor States for which the maintenance of international ties to many States otherwise might be impracticable in view of competing demands on the public purse. The effect of UN membership in this dimension is heightened by the aggregate of admissions to membership: that the UN now is a near-universal organization means that membership entails contact between each member State and virtually all other States.

Universal admission and the minimum access to processes of international relations that membership guarantees may have certain corollary effects. Considering the character of membership as a guarantee of minimum access, universal admission has removed an impediment in the way of a community seeking to establish its independence as a new State. One therefore may hypothesize that a corollary effect is to encourage the creation of new States. UN membership, by the logic of the Charter, is conclusive as to the statehood of the entity admitted – a point which the International Court was clear about in the *Bosnian Genocide* case.[84]

---

[84] See discussion earlier this Chapter.

Membership brings security;[85] it brings access to multilateral diplomacy;[86] it brings introductions to the network of global aid and credit institutions.[87] Membership is the starting point for inclusion in the international trade regime and for protection of intellectual property rights.[88] The significant involvement of the UN in maintenance of the international security architecture, including even administration of territory, is a project in which a State may participate more readily after admission.[89] So too are member States better positioned than non-members to participate in the law-drafting projects of the UN, e.g., in the framework of the ILC[90] – and the admitted State has an absolute advantage over the non-member as a participant in the formation of law through the practice of the principal and other organs.

UN membership in this light is a valuable public good. It is not however one the supply of which is restricted with respect to the entities eligible to acquire it. The result of the march to universality since the mid-1950s is that all (or nearly all) States are UN members, and it is barely conceivable that the UN, under the current constitutional disposition, would turn down any large number of applications. It once was the case that a community emerging as a State was not guaranteed that it would be automatically admitted to the Organization; under

---

[85] Consider the response to the invasion of Kuwait: SC resns 660, 2 Aug 1990; 661, 6 Aug 1990; 662, 9 Aug 1990; 678, 29 Nov 1990. To be sure, it is hard to conceive any other response to the unlawful invasion and forcible annexation of a State – which suggests that the security of Kuwait in 1990–1 may be referred to its statehood. This still, if slightly less directly, refers security to UN admission, for, as already noted, admission is conclusive as to that status.

[86] A point Dugard makes in noting the function of the UN as a centre of multilateral diplomacy: Dugard *Recognition* 77–8.

[87] On the position of the IMF and World Bank within the UN system generally, see Woods 'Bretton Woods Institutions' in Weiss & Daws eds *Oxford Handbook* 233–53. See also Brown 'IMF governance, the Asian financial crisis, and the new financial architecture' in Yee & Tieya eds *International Law in the Post-Cold War World: Essays in memory of Li Haopei* (2001) 131. The question of State access to finance is not limited to international public institutions. Private institutions, too, are unlikely to enter into credit relations with entities – or with private parties within the territory of entities – whose international legal status is insecure. This has been a consideration in seeking a resolution of the status of Kosovo.

[88] Zamora 'Economic Relations and Development' in Joyner ed *The United Nations and International Law* (1997) 232, 239–58, 280–85.

[89] Recall the special measures that the Trusteeship Council had to adopt to engage Italy in its work.

[90] This proposition holds, even as the constituents of the ILC are not representatives of the States of their nationality, but rather 'persons of recognized competence in international law.' The ILC members are chosen from a list nominated by the member States: ILC Statute Art. 3 (GA res 174 (II) 21 Nov 1947 as amended); and the drafting process involves questionnaires and other forms of consultation with the governments of the member States: ILC Statute Art. 16.

a different course of constitutional development admission might have continued to be a less certain result. Doubt as to whether the State would become a
member State could have certain effects. In particular, as hypothesized, it could
have effects on the decision-making process that leads a community to elect to
establish itself as an independent State.

The emergence of a community as an independent State requires deliberate
steps, involving severance of existing legal and political ties and the articulation of a claim to constitute itself as juridically separate from all other States.
Whether and when to take the steps to statehood will be decided in view of
multiple considerations. A number of considerations militate against statehood.
Persistent claim by an existing State (such as by China with respect to Taiwan)
is one consideration. Another is the consideration that independence entails
loosing the benefits of participation in a larger national community that well
may have provided protection against economic and other risks. A community
may further consider that, as an independent State, it could become isolated
from the international community; the State of which it was formerly part held
an established position in international relations and, through that State, the
community had itself enjoyed a degree of international access. To be sure, one
ground for the community to pursue independence may be that the existing
State denies it such access; but the case where the incumbent State has completely suppressed the rights of some part of its polity only arises sometimes,
the more common case being that in which access will have existed at least to
a degree. A prospect of isolation from the international community could deter
a community from becoming an independent State.

Admission to the UN, however, as said, assures at least minimum access to
the processes of international relations. Universal admission means that no State
need consider that it might have less than such minimum access. The universal admission of States to the UN thus makes it unnecessary to consider that
independence might impose a more or less thorough international isolation on
the independent community. Universality removes what would otherwise count
among the potential risks of independence.[91]

Given the multiple dimensions of UN membership as an international public good, if no substantive limit is placed on admission, then the incentive for
independence is increased. Among the significant number of new independent
States in the 20th century, some have not succeeded in providing basic public
order at municipal level. The problem of such deficits in government has been
pervasive enough that writers, States, and international organizations have treated

---

[91] Some of the general problems for a putative State of being excluded from the UN were pointed
out by Van Dr Vyver: 'Self-Determination of the Peoples of Quebec under International Law'
(2000) 10 *J Trans L & Pol'y* 1, 35–6.

it as a distinct sociological (if not legal) phenomenon. The problem of 'failed States' – perhaps better termed a problem of failed governments[92] – has not generally been treated as a problem of the admission practice of the UN; but perhaps it should. If the first States to emerge out of decolonization had not been admitted rapidly to the UN and thereby integrated into international relations, then, perhaps, other communities would not have followed so rapidly on the course to independence. This is not to ignore that to have continued colonial administration would have presented enormous problems. The conundrum of colonialism indeed was that to continue it indefinitely was unacceptable; but nobody knew how (or was willing) to engineer its ending so as to protect the interests of the inhabitants of the newly independent States.

7.2.2 Consolidation of the International Community as a Whole

Writers refer to the 'international community,'[93] and the expression turns up in international practice as well.[94] The identity and capacities of that community however remain unclear. The United Nations, at least in the rhetoric surrounding the 'international community,' occupies a central place. Judge Bustamante y Rivero referred to its predecessor, the League, as 'the first organized expression of the international community.'[95] The modern Organization is said to bear a number of relations to the community, such as being its chief institution,[96] acting

---

[92] The terminology of 'failed States' and 'State failure' is widely used. See, e.g., Sir Robert Jennings, 'Sovereignty and International Law' in Kreijan ed *State, Sovereignty, and International Governance* (2002) 27, 30; Kreijen *State failure, sovereignty and effectiveness: legal lessons from the decolonization of Sub-Saharan Africa* (2004) *passim*. The terminology is problematic however, not least of all for implying that it is the inhabitants of the States concerned who are principally to blame: Crawford *Creation* 2nd edn 718–23. The expression in Presidential Decision Directive 25 of May 1994 ('The Clinton Administration's Policy on Reforming Multilateral Peace Operations'), though less memorable, is more accurate: 'the collapse of governmental authority in some states.' cf reference to the 'failed state' as a case of 'degradation of internal sovereignty': Charpentier 'Le Phénomène Étatique à Travers les Grandes Mutations Politiques Contemporaines' in Société Française pour le Droit International *L'état souverain à l'aube du XXIe siècle* Colloque de Nancy (1994) 25–7.

[93] E.g. Kritsiotis 'Imagining the international community' (2002) 13 *EJIL* 961 and works cited ibid., 962 n. 16.

[94] E.g. GA res 60/1, 16 Sept 2005 (2005 World Summit Outcome) including in connection with the responsibility to protect: ibid., ¶ 139.

[95] *South West Africa Cases (Ethiopia v South Africa; Liberia v South Africa)* (Preliminary Objections) Judgment of 21 Dec 1962, Sep Op Bustamante, ICJ Rep 1962 p. 319, 351.

[96] Gattini 'A return ticket to "Communitarisme," please' (2002) 13 *EJIL* 1181, 1182, referring to the UN as 'a "material organ" of the international community as a whole'; De Wet 'The international constitutional order' (2006) 55 *ICLQ* 51, 54: 'The most important institution within the international community remains the UN.'

as agent for it,[97] etc.[98] The UN as a universal organization certainly encompasses a considerable portion of the actors which comprise it.

Putting a precise definition to the 'international community as a whole,' including its legal incidents, is difficult at a time when the development of that concept remains incomplete.[99] At least one fairly definite relation suggests itself: that between the international community and assertions of universal jurisdiction. To say that a particular right belongs to the 'international community as a whole' has been a shorthand for saying that universal jurisdiction exists for purposes of acting on the right. Judges Higgins, Kooijmans, and Buergenthal said in the *Arrest Warrant Case* that '[T]hose States and academic writers who claim the right to act unilaterally to assert a universal criminal jurisdiction...invoke the concept of acting as "agents for the international community." '[100] Belgium was an example of a State claiming the right in these terms: the normal requirements of territorial presence, Belgium said, were waived when an offence 'violated the fundamental interest of the international community.'[101] France saw the matter in a similar light.[102]

The assertion that the 'international community' is a formation having any legal relevance is contested on much the same grounds that it is promoted: universal jurisdiction exercised in the name of the community potentially extends the reach of every State into the affairs of any State – and, it is said, this presents a serious pitfall. Jurists have doubted the utility and even desirability of the expression 'international community' for the reason that its very imprecision could lead to unlimited assertions of jurisdiction in specific cases. Gilbert Guillaume, as President of the International Court, said as follows:

> The adoption of the United Nations Charter proclaiming the sovereign equality of States and the appearance on the international scene of new States, born of decolonization, have strengthened the territorial principle. International criminal law has itself undergone considerable development and constitutes today an impressive legal corpus. It recognizes in many situations the possibility, or indeed the obligation, for a State other than that on whose territory the offence was committed to confer

---

[97] Comment (2) to draft art. 19 ('Crimes against United Nations and associated personnel') ILC 48th sess ¶ 50: *ILC Ybk* 1996 Vol. II Pt. 2 p. 51.

[98] Such as giving the community a purported constitution: Dupuy 'The Constitutional Dimension of the Charter of the United Nations Revisited' (1997) 1 *Max Planck Ybk UN Law 1*, 19–33.

[99] Cf. Kritsiotis 13 *EJIL* at 964.

[100] *Case Concerning the Arrest Warrant of 11 April 2000 (Democratic Republic of the Congo v Belgium)* Joint Sep Op Higgins, Kooijmans, and Buergenthal, ICJ Rep 2002 pp. 3, 78 ¶ 51.

[101] ICJ Rep 2002 pp. 3, 65 ¶ 8, citing Belgian Counter-Memorial, ¶¶ 3.3.44 to 3.3.52.

[102] *Case Concerning Certain Criminal Proceedings in France (Republic of the Congo v France)* Request for the Indication of a Provisional Measures, Order of 17 June 2003, ICJ Rep 2003 pp. 102, 105 ¶ 11.

jurisdiction on its courts to prosecute the authors of certain crimes where they are present on its territory. International criminal courts have been created. But at no time has it been envisaged that jurisdiction should be conferred upon the courts of every State in the world to prosecute such crimes, wherever their authors and victims and irrespective of the place where the offender is to be found. To do this would, moreover, risk creating total judicial chaos. It would also be to encourage the arbitrary for the benefit of the powerful, purposefully acting as agent for an ill-defined "international community." Contrary to what is advocated by certain publicists, such a development would represent not an advance in the law but a step backward.[103]

The stated predicate to President Guillaume's criticism of the 'international community' is that territorial power in the hands of States is now complete. (It is at least very nearly so).[104] This is consistent with James Crawford's observation that the juridical template of statehood has become more uniform in modern international law.[105] New States have multiplied, and, though decolonization brought into being States of diverse political characteristics, they all are of familiar legal form. And, as James Crawford further observed, entities of unusual legal form, like Danzig of the interwar era, are now scarcely to be found. Little if any territory is left in the early 21st century except that under the jurisdiction of a State. The 'strengthened territorial principle' to which Guillaume refers follows as a direct consequence of the ascendance of statehood as the organizational principle in public order. In a world where the State remains so central – indeed, has become more central in the sense described (even as non-State forces grow in political strength) – it is all the more important that each State act within the limits of its own sovereignty. The concept of 'international community,' in President Guillaume's view, invites exercises in judicial overreach that would result in the limits being ignored. 'Judicial chaos,' he might have said, is only one of the potential difficulties: exorbitant claims of jurisdiction may provoke reaction among States, leading them to ignore international law, and thereby erode what gains law has made as against unregulated discretion in international relations.

Yet writers, States and jurists indeed continue to refer to the 'international community.' Their persistence in doing so suggests that practice has begun, if only fitfully, to vest in the community some element of a distinct legal personality. Judge Bustamante referred to 'a body designed to give organic structure and a

---

[103] Sep Op President Guillaume, ICJ Rep 2002 pp. 3, 43, ¶ 15.

[104] The resurgence of international administration of territory since the early 1990s perhaps qualifies the exclusivity of the State as actor responsible for territory. On the as-yet-underspecified responsibility of international organizations for their conduct as administrators of territory, see Kiderlen *Verwaltung von Krisengebieten*, 387–96; Stahn *International Territorial Administration* 579–644; Wilde *International Territorial Administration* 426–8.

[105] Crawford *Creation* 2nd edn 254.

general legal framework to the nations of the world as a whole.'[106] Though some
writers do, it certainly is too early to talk about the international community
engaging in particular acts – for example, adopting treaties – as if it already
had a coherent and fully defined corporate form.[107] If it is a 'legal framework,'
it is a very 'general' one; if it has 'organic structure,' it has it only skeletally.
Nevertheless, even if the development of the international community as a legal
formation has yet to proceed very far, the international community is assuming
a more definite existence as a political formation. It may be submitted that the
evolution of the United Nations into a universal representative body has fostered
the consolidation of this concept in international relations.

The main references to the 'international community' are in connection with
possible obligations owed to it by States or other actors. Comment (3) to draft
article 8 of the draft articles on responsibility of international organizations
lists as an entity to which an international obligation may be owed (and thus
against which a breach committed) 'the international community as a whole.'[108]
The proposition is by now well-established that *erga omnes* obligations exist in
international law – that is to say, obligations owed not to any one party but to
the entire community subject to the legal system. Though the idea is older,[109]
its modern appearance is associated with the following statement of the ICJ in
Barcelona Traction:

> 33. When a State admits into its territory foreign investments or foreign nationals,
> whether natural or juristic persons, it is bound to extend to them the protection
> of the law and assumes obligations concerning the treatment to be afforded them.
> These obligations, however, are neither absolute nor unqualified. In particular, an
> essential distinction should be drawn between the obligations of a State towards the
> international community as a whole, and those arising vis-a-vis another State in the
> field of diplomatic protection. By their very nature the former are the concern of

---

[106] *South West Africa Cases*, Sep Op Bustamante, ICJ Rep 1962 at 351.

[107] See e.g. Parent & Mayer-Robitaille 'Agriculture et Culture: Le défi de l'OMC de Prendre en
Compte les Considération Non Commerciales' (2007) 52 *McGill LJ* 415. See also Minnerop
(2003) 7 *Max Planck Ybk UN Law* 79, 89–96 on the international community as a 'legal
community.'

[108] ILC 57th sess: A/CN.4/L.666/Rev.1, 1 June 2005 p. 2.

[109] For example, the Concert of Europe acted as if it held certain rights and obligations concerning
general public order. The Concert was not an international organization (though it may have
been a progenitor of international organizations: see Amerasinghe *Institutional Law* 1–2). Its
legal interest in adopting a settlement in 1815 (and in maintaining the settlement adopted)
probably did not include an articulated interest in collective security, but that interest may
otherwise be likened to the interest which gives 'the international community as a whole' rights
and obligations with respect to certain aspects of public order today. On the Concert, especially
later but also at its point of origin, see Verosta *Kollektivaktion der Mächte des Europäischen
Konzerts (1886–1914)* (1988).

all States. In view of the importance of the rights involved, all States can be held to have a legal interest in their protection; they are obligations erga omnes.

34. Such obligations derive, for example, in contemporary international law, from the outlawing of acts of aggression, and of genocide, as also from the principles and rules concerning the basic rights of the human person, including protection from slavery and racial discrimination. Some of the corresponding rights of protection have entered into the body of general international law (*Reservations to the Convention on the Prevention and Punishment of the Crime of Genocide*, Advisory Opinion, ICJ Reports 1951, p. 23); others are conferred by international instruments of a universal or quasi-universal character.[110]

Barcelona Traction concerned investment protection and so the Court's disquisition on obligations 'towards the international community as a whole' was by way of contrast, if not *obiter*.[111] It is nevertheless a significant statement about the characteristics of legal rights in the international system.

States, in establishing institutions at international level since World War II, have tended to express their purposes in terms of the community, and various international authorities affirm the trend. The International Court of Justice, for example, it has been suggested, has a specific connection to the 'international community as a whole.' According to Judge Lachs, '[T]he Court is the guardian of legality for the international community as a whole, both within and without the United Nations.'[112] The ICJ is not the only judicial institution with a link to the international community. The International Criminal Court is connected to the international community by the express terms of its Statute. The Criminal Court is an institution to establish the criminal responsibility of perpetrators of crimes against 'the international community as a whole.' Like the ICJ the Criminal Court exists 'in relationship with the United Nations system' (Rome Statute preambular paragraph 9).[113] The jurisdictional provision to be adopted in accordance with Articles 121 and 123 of the Statute 'shall be consistent with the relevant provisions of the Charter of the United Nations' (Rome Statute Article 5(2)).[114] Claus Kress suggests that vesting the prosecutorial function in such 'a genuine community organ' is the way to avoid the problem, which President Guillaume noted, of a State abusing the notion of universal

---

[110] ICJ Rep 1970 pp. 3, 32 ¶¶ 33–4.

[111] E.g. Bassiouni 'International Recognition of Victims' Rights' (2006) 6 *HR L Rev* 203, 239; Shelton 'Normative Hierarchy in International Law' (2006) 100 *AJ* 291, 318 refers to it as *dicta*.

[112] *Questions of Interpretation and Application of the 1971 Montreal Convention arising from the Aerial Incident at Lockerbie (Libyan Arab Jamahiriya v United Kingdom)* Request for the Indication of Provisional Measures, Order of 14 Apr 1992, Sep Op Lachs, ICJ Rep 1992 pp. 3, 26.

[113] 37 ILM at 1002.

[114] Ibid., 1004.

jurisdiction.[115] In any event, the logic is plain that one would turn to the United Nations when addressing a matter of 'concern to the international community as a whole.' The Statute of the International Criminal Court is an example of the logic implemented in practice. It is a further example of the 'international community as a whole' undergoing a degree of institutionalization within the UN framework.

A relation between the UN and the international community as a whole has been inherent from the start. Charter Article 1 says that the Organization's work is to be directed to general purposes, in particular preservation of peace and security. Such purposes are not the concern of individual States alone. They are general concerns. The relevance of international organization to community interests is inscribed in other instruments as well. Draft article 22, paragraph 1(a) on responsibility of international organizations acknowledges that the UN's work (or for that matter the work of any international organization) may be directed to community interests. Article 22 excludes necessity as a ground for precluding wrongfulness. However, it sets out as an exception that an otherwise wrongful act '[i]s the only means for the organization to safeguard against a grave and imminent peril an essential interest of the international community as a whole when the organization has, in accordance with international law, the function to protect that interest.'[116] To set out an exception in terms of the organization having the function to protect 'an essential interest of the international community as a whole' can only have meaning if an organization indeed can have that function. And it makes sense to assign such a function to an international organization only if the 'international community as a whole' has some existence at least at political level, even if not as a legal person.

The notion of the UN acting to protect the interests of the international community, or of the international community acting through the UN to promote its shared policies, or of the UN giving rise to new institutions having as their purpose to promote those policies, implies a distinction between the UN and the community. The UN indeed is not the same thing as the international community. The march toward universal membership has led to a situation in which the relation between the two is closer than ever. The early advocates of the liberal approach to admission of States to the UN, as we saw in Chapter 4 above, said that the result was required under the Charter from the start that all States be UN member States; it was just a matter of practical implementation of the (purportedly) mandated result. Whatever the legal basis for universality, even if the UN were to achieve and maintain complete participation by all States,

---

[115] Kress 'Universal jurisdiction over international crimes and the Institut de Droit International' (2006) 4 *J Int'l Crim Justice* 561, 572.

[116] Emphasis added. A/61/10 ¶ 91 p. 272. See also Comment (4) to draft art. 22 ibid., p. 274.

the international community as a whole however is conceptually separate from the UN. The main distinctions may be instanced.

For one, the international community is prior to the UN. Though all States and other international actors were not necessarily thought of as constituting a 'community' before the latter half of the 20th century,[117] the UN did not make its appearance against a backdrop of complete normative chaos. The international system may have been significantly underdeveloped, but it was not non-existent. Related to this is a further distinction, and that is that the international community, even as it has become more developed over recent decades, still lacks a definite institutional form. The UN by contrast is an institution. No single institution comes closer to including all States at governmental level, a situation giving credence to the notion that the UN has unique characteristics as a representative body. In the Draft Code of Crimes against the Peace and Security of Mankind (1996), the ILC said that attacks against UN personnel 'constitute violent crimes of exceptionally serious gravity which have serious consequences not only for the victims, but also for the international community.'[118] The UN was not equated with the international community; but UN personnel are 'persons who *represent* the international community.'[119]

The composition of the UN suggests a third distinction between the Organization and the community it represents. The UN is an organization of States. It has come to be an organization of very nearly all States – but not necessarily all. According to the International Court in the *Namibia* Advisory Opinion,

> As to non-member States, although not bound by Articles 24 and 25 of the Charter, they have been called upon … to give assistance in the action which has been taken by the United Nations with regard to Namibia. In the view of the Court, the termination of the Mandate and the declaration of the illegality of South Africa's presence in Namibia are opposable to all States in the sense of barring erga omnes the legality of a situation which is maintained in violation of international law.[120]

Erga omnes rules are opposable to all States, and this means non-member States and member States alike. The UN and the community of States, though overlapping considerably, are not necessarily coterminous.

---

[117] The 19th century tendency was to describe a society of European States, existing under certain rules *inter se* but in distinction against other States and polities: Keene *Beyond the Anarchical Society: Grotius, Colonialism, and Order in World Politics* (2002) 114.

[118] Comment (2) to draft art. 19 ('Crimes against United Nations and associated personnel') ILC 48th sess ¶ 50: *ILC Ybk* 1996 Vol. II Pt. 2 p. 51.

[119] Emphasis added. Ibid.

[120] *Legal Consequences for States of the Continued Presence of South Africa in Namibia (South West Africa) notwithstanding Security Council Resolution 276 (1970)* Advisory Opinion of 21 June 1971, ICJ Rep 1971 pp. 16, 56 ¶ 126.

And even if the UN comprised all States and continued to do so by way of some form of constitutional guarantee, the UN still would not be the same as the international community as a whole, for the community encompasses considerably more than States. Individuals insofar as they possess aspects of international legal personality are part of the community.[121] International organizations, though many of them are involved directly or indirectly in the UN system,[122] are not all part of that system – but they certainly are part of the international community. Entities proximate to States and the various non-State corporate formations, such as religions, transnational interest groups, non-governmental organizations, and the like, too, at least for certain purposes are constituents of the international community. The extensive involvement of non-governmental organizations in drafting recent multilateral conventions illustrates their relevance as community members.[123] Judge Lachs thus could properly speak of the international community existing 'both within and without the United Nations.'[124]

The UN, even as the universal organization of States, is not the same as the international community. The UN, as guarantor of general community interests, however, has given rise to various measures, including the establishment of permanent institutions like the Criminal Court, tending to consolidate the concept of the community. The concept, to the extent it has been consolidated, remains chiefly political. Universal membership, by making the UN an institution more nearly corresponding to the community, has contributed to the consolidation.

7.2.3   *Universal Vocation versus Sectoral Tasks*

An international organization exists to perform particular tasks. As we considered at the beginning of Chapter 1, the constitutive instrument of the organization often contains provisions specifying the tasks; those provisions and the provisions concerning admission of member States may be correlated with one another, for the States admitted to the organization in part will determine the political limits of what the organization can do.

Abdullah El-Erian as Special Rapporteur for Relations between States and inter-Governmental Organizations alluded to the connection between membership and functional capability. In his First Report on the topic, El-Erian set out

---

[121] See e.g. *LaGrand Case (Germany v United States of America)* ICJ Rep 2001 pp. 466, 494 ¶ 77.

[122] And some simultaneously are part of the UN system and another regional system – e.g., the Pan American Health Organization (PAHO): comments of the WHO, A/CN.4/545 pp. 27–8.

[123] NGO participation was extensive in the negotiations leading to adoption of the Convention on the Rights of Persons with Disabilities (CRPD): adopted 13 Dec 2006; entered into force 3 May 2008.

[124] See citation above. Writers have noted too that the community overlaps with, but is not coterminous with, the UN: Kritsiotis 13 *EJIL* at 972–4; De Wet 55 *ICLQ* at 54.

a classification of international organizations. This included several criteria for classification. One was 'classification... according to membership'[125] and another was 'classification... according to function.'[126] The proximate placement of these two classification criteria might suggest their mutual relevance. Moreover, the Special Rapporteur recognized that certain tasks require an organization to have a certain constituency. 'A regional organization can be general,' El-Erian reported, 'if its scope of activities is global within its region. But it is true that the universality of membership is important to enable the organization to fulfil the comprehensive tasks described...'[127] An organization created to perform 'comprehensive tasks' in El-Erian's view may require 'universality of membership.' INTERPOL, the coordinating body for international police activities, in comments made in connection with the draft articles on responsibility of international organizations, said that the tasks of certain organizations are such as to require even more than universal membership of States; non-State entities, e.g. 'non-independent territories,' participate in INTERPOL to equip it to discharge its global function.[128] This is to state the link between admission and task in fairly direct terms. El-Erian's concern was with organizations created to perform functions at the broadest level – he might have referred to 'universal purposes' or 'universal tasks.'

El-Erian in his First Report did not refer to tasks of narrower scope or purpose. Nor did he refer to restricted membership. Yet to say that 'comprehensive tasks' may require 'universality of membership' suggests its inverse: specialized tasks may require restricted membership. If the formulation is taken at a level of generality, it well could mean that the link between admission and task itself is comprehensive: for any level of generality or specificity of functions, the organization's membership should be correspondingly general or specific. El-Erian and the ILC later stepped back from stating this,[129] but the logic of the connection remains.

---

[125] El-Erian First Report 11 June 1963 ¶¶ 64–7 *ILC Ybk* 1963 Vol. II pp. 167–8.

[126] Ibid., ¶¶ 71–81 *ILC Ybk* 1963 Vol. II pp. 168–9.

[127] Ibid., ¶ 72 *ILC Ybk* 1963 Vol II. p. 168.

[128] Comments and observations received from Governments and international organizations, 12 May 2005, ILC 57th sess: A/CN.4/556 p. 11. Cf. Brownlie's statement, quoted ibid, that 'organizations are normally composed of States [but] a number of organizations have operated in effect a functional concept of membership compatible with their special purposes': *Principles* 6th edn (2003) 660.

[129] The drafting of Art. 1(1) of the Vienna Convention on the Representation of States in Their Relations with International Organizations of a Universal Character, adopted 14 Mar 1975, A/CONF.67/16; not yet entered into force (discussed in Chapter 4 above), was subject to discussion in the ILC. Some States proposed that the definition of 'international organization of a universal character' refer to 'object and purpose' of an organization. Instead, Art. 1(1) as adopted refers to 'responsibilities' of an organization. El-Erian said in 1971 that he 'doubts the

A consequence of universal membership is that the UN is suited to universal tasks. The UN therefore is ideally suited to certain tasks set out in the Charter.

One task that would be difficult to discharge if the Organization lacked universal membership is that of maintaining comity among States. The drafters of the Charter intended the UN to serve as a forum in which tensions arising from divergent interests might be relieved through diplomacy organized around the principle that all members are equal sovereigns. The role of the United Nations system in conciliating differences amongst regional subsystems of international law, for example through the activities of the International Law Commission and International Court of Justice, is also important.[130] The considerable differences of social and legal system among States, and their considerable differences of material interest, are perhaps the main justification for a forum of universal membership. It is a cliché to say that if the UN did not exist it would have to be invented, but the statement rings true. The heterogeneity of States is a heterogeneity of effective power – which is to say, States differ (and widely) in their ability to project power and even in their ability to communicate with other States. For a system comprised of diverse State constituents, it is submitted that it is necessary to have a forum of universal membership – and, moreover, for many, if not all, purposes within that organization, to generalize the rights of States to participate in its functions. Judge Palmieri was right when writing that the UN 'provide[s] a forum where peaceful discussions may displace violence as a means of resolving disputed issues.'[131] It exaggerates the potential of the Organization to turn such a characterization into a predication that the UN will turn any given sword into a ploughshare. The point instead is that a global forum is needed in which 'peaceful discussions *may* displace violence' – a forum in which at least the possibility for pacific resolution is presented. The UN, in its diplomatic vocation, then, is an enterprise of modest steps and, possibly, the occasional averted disaster; it is certainly not a panacea. But the enterprise even

---

need for changing the drafting of [the] sub-paragraph...to make it indicate clearly that the universal character of an international organization should derive from its object and purpose': El-Erian Sixth Report 2 & 29 Mar, 5, 9 & 26 Apr, 12 & 14 May 1971 ¶ 52 *ILC Ybk* 1971 vol. 2 Pt One p. 18.

[130] See Crawford & Grant 'The International Court of Justice' in Daws and Weiss eds *Oxford Handbook* 193–213. The role of the General Assembly in this regard is expressed in Article 13 of the Charter. See also the Foreword to *Reports of International Arbitral Awards* vol. I (1948) p. 4.

[131] *United States of America* v *Palestine Liberation Organization*, 695 F.Supp. 1456, 1459 (S.D.N.Y., 1988, Palmieri, D.J.). In seeking to widen participation in those 'peaceful discussions,' Judge Palmieri, in Rosalyn Higgins' words, 'was to proffer a judgment that matched for sheer pragmatism anything we have seen in the United Kingdom, Australia or Canada': 'The Concept of "The State": Variable Geometry and Dualist Perceptions' in Boisson de Chazournes & Gowlland-Debbas eds *The international legal system in quest of equality and universality: liber amicorum Georges Abi-Saab* (2001) 547, 552–4.

on these terms would be impossible, or much further from realization, if there existed no forum of universal participation. The Organization would be incapable of working in its appointed direction, if it did not include all potential (State) disputants. It certainly reflects the prejudices of certain blocks of States, and it all too frequently confuses process with result, but the General Assembly of the United Nations executes an indispensable function: it is a 'common clearing house,'[132] a *forum communis humanus* without which the jungle-like aspect of inter-State relations would likely increase. Universal admission was necessary for the General Assembly to realize this aspect of its vocation.

A further area of UN activity that universal membership has fostered is law-making. This already has been mentioned above in connection with comity. The UN provides a framework for formal processes of law-making, such as treaty-drafting and the adoption of resolutions, some of which may have binding effect and others of which, perhaps, may contribute to the consolidation of emergent rules. There are also the statements of governments through their representatives in the principal and other organs which may constitute evidence of the positions taken by States on particular legal questions.

Treaty-making, whether carried out within a UN framework or without, is the central modality of law-making at the international level. Treaties, like international organizations, may involve many States, or a very few States. Shabtai Rosenne considers the universal treaty in light of the distinction between contractual treaties and law-making treaties, a classic distinction and one noted in Chapter 1 above. Rosenne suggests that an association exists between contractual treaties and closed treaties – i.e., treaties which are either bilateral or to which only designated States may be party; and that an association also exists between law-making treaties and open treaties – i.e., treaties to which many or all States may be invited to be party. 'Closed' and 'open,' it should be said, here are relative terms. The problem which the ILC faced of whether to include an intermediate category of 'plurilateral' treaties, between 'bilateral' and 'multilateral,' hints at the problem of characterization and the range of variations that must be considered. 'Closed' and 'open' nevertheless usefully describe distinctions observable in treaty practice.

Rosenne says the following:

> [O]bservation has shown that to some extent the closed or open character of a treaty stands in some relationship to its presumed or postulated contractual or normative quality, to its being a *traité-contrat* or a *traité-loi*. This, in turn, has led

---

[132] As the League of Nations had been described: Graham *The League of Nations and the Recognition of States* (1933) 40–1. And the expression 'talk shop' has been applied to the General Assembly of the UN, as it had been to the League assembly, but the pejorative connotation arguably misses the point: Luck 'Prospects for Reform: Principal Organs' in Weiss & Daws eds *Oxford Handbook* 653, 659.

to the appearance of a theory of the universality of the law-making treaty regulating matters of universal concern, with its corollary that every State has a right, if it so desires, to become a party to such a universal treaty. In the United Nations and its related organisms, until 1974, for political reasons the participation clauses of this kind of treaty were usually drawn in exclusionary language… The resolution of the political issue which found expression in that policy has led to the introduction of a provision embodying the 'all States' formula for participation in this kind of treaty, but usage itself makes it doubtful if there has been any change in the fundamental rule that no State has a right under customary international law to become a party to any treaty it likes, not even one intended to be universal in time and space, and that the matter is always initially in the hands of the negotiating States.[133]

Rosenne here describes the development of international law toward relative openness of certain adopted instruments. The development gives rise to a number of considerations. First, 'universality' in this connection may mean at least two distinct things. A treaty may be 'universal' in that all States, or something close to all States, are actually parties to it. Universality, in this sense, is an accomplished fact. A treaty also however may be 'universal' in that it is maximally open – i.e., any State may accede to it. A treaty displaying openness in the sense described is not necessarily a treaty to which all States actually are parties at a given time. The 'universal' treaty is not necessarily universal in the accomplished sense of having universal participation. The term thus has a connotation of potentiality which, though pointing to the attainment of all-State scope, at the same time is a reminder of an aspiration in international law yet to be widely achieved.[134]

A second consideration is that the term 'universal' in the latter sense – the sense of a potential (and thus future) inclusion of all States – so far, too, in most, if not all, instruments that might merit being called 'universal' has remained relative. Rosenne, it is submitted, is right to say that, notwithstanding developments toward greater openness, a position is yet to be established in customary international law that a State possesses a right 'to become a party to any treaty it likes.' Customary international law by no means prevents the States which originally adopted a treaty from retaining a degree of mastery over future participation. The same goes for participation in international organizations as in treaties. The point was alluded to when the International Court in the *Case Concerning the Aerial Incident of July 27th, 1955* referred to Bulgaria being admitted to the United Nations not merely by a unilateral declaration on its own part – as would suffice for accession to certain 'open' treaties – but by

---

[133] Rosenne *Developments in the Law of Treaties 1945–1986* (1989) 185–6.

[134] The best candidates for 'universal' treaty in the fuller sense described are the Geneva Conventions of 1949, to which all States are party, as are entities such as Niue and the Cook Islands which, for purposes here relevant are assimilable into the category of 'States.' Respecting the two associated States in the Pacific, see Geneva Conventions Act 1958 (NZ), §§ 10(1), 10(3)(a), and 10(3)(b), referring to application of the Conventions to Niue and the Cook Islands.

two steps: application by the State and approval by the United Nations under Article 4.[135]

Rosenne in 1965 thought that 'participation in multilateral treaties of whatever kind had nothing whatever to do with the entirely different process of admission to international organizations, whether small or large, regional or universal.'[136] It is certainly right that the 'process of admission' to an international organization is not the same thing as the process of accession to a treaty. Yet it goes too far to say that the establishment of a universal organization has no relation 'whatever' to the adoption of various treaties intended to include all States as parties.

The developments in the admission practice of the United Nations which have been canvassed in this and the preceding Chapters, it is submitted, have mirrored the transition to a system of open treaties. Whatever its constitutional aspects, the UN Charter is also a treaty, so it must be doubted whether the concepts of universal organization and universal treaty may be totally separated. Moreover, the manner in which certain treaties have been drafted so as to facilitate universal participation is similar to that in which the UN Charter has been interpreted (or amended) to facilitate universal membership. The logic of the law-making treaty points toward maximum scope of participation. Certain substantive provisions in the drafts of such treaties have sometimes been moderated, even removed, in order to secure wider participation. The price of wider participation is measured in reduction (or at least modification) of the final substantive content of the treaty. The Statute of the International Criminal Court[137] is a famous example. Analogously, it may be that an international organization – itself the creation of a law-making treaty – later makes compromises to widen its membership, these including the liberalization, or even excision by amendment, of the substantive criteria for admission. A price of wider membership may be that the organization looses efficacy at carrying out narrower, sectoral tasks which require the more focused effort of States acting in recognition of shared interest. Widened participation, sometimes at the cost of efficacy in certain dimensions, has been seen both in multilateral treaties and in international organizations. If, as submitted, the admission provisions have disappeared in practice, then even the process of admission begins to look considerably more like the process of accession: the State seeking membership simply expresses its acceptance of the constitutive instrument, there being little possibility that procedural or substantive objections would prevent admission being granted, even though (unlike with other treaties) mechanisms still operate that could be used to block a given State.

The law-making character of multilateral treaties and the UN Charter is perhaps their most significant similarity. The UN Charter is a treaty with

---

[135] *Case Concerning the Aerial Incident of July 27th, 1955 (Israel v Bulgaria)* ICJ Rep 1959 pp. 127, 145.
[136] ILC 17th sess 793rd mtg, 1 June 1965 (Law of Treaties) ¶ 81: ILC Ybk 1965 Vol. I p. 129.
[137] Scheffer 'The United States and the International Criminal Court' (1999) 93 *AJ* 12.

law-making aspects in a double sense. The Charter establishes a constitutional system intended to be relevant to all States and governing an entity which possesses international legal personality. By creating the UN, the Charter creates law. The Charter also establishes institutions which themselves have the purpose of making new law and codifying existing law on the basis of participation by many States.[138] The UN is not unique among international organizations by virtue merely of the fact that it makes new law. The International Civil Aviation Organization, to give one example, makes law as well.[139] The UN Charter as a 'law making' instrument is distinctive because of the scope of membership and scope of activities of the Organization it creates: the UN is not restricted to one region or a narrow subject area; it thus undertakes law-making across a field which no other single organization encompasses. Practically every State is affected by law-making activities of such scope. This is significant, because, at least on democratic principles, it means that no State should be excluded from the UN law-making process. There exists a body of law, not strictly speaking the constitutional law of the United Nations, which was constituted, and continues to be constituted, in more or less formal processes, participation in which, though perhaps not necessarily limited to UN member States, is so closely connected to the Organization that a State not a member well may find itself excluded. Higgins referred to the UN as the 'focal point for State practice.'[140] The debates of the General Assembly and Security Council indeed are part of the law-making function of the UN, if in a less formal sense than are the activities of the ILC and the principal organs when they adopt instruments in pursuit of codification or progressive development. If any function of the United Nations supports the conclusion that universal membership – in the sense of actual, present participation by all States – is a constitutional necessity, then it is this law-making function.

Universality, one thus concludes, equips the Organization uniquely to function as a centre of law codification and progressive development, a workshop with a rich record in the pursuit of the vocation identified in Article 13(1)(a) of the Charter. The significance of the UN in that function is only heightened, if, as Rosenne suggests, in addition to making treaties, the UN can provide distinct rules for the interpretation of the treaties it makes.[141]

A paradox is presented however, for, 'even as [universality] is the source of its international authority,'[142] deficits in effective capacity result from universal

---

[138] On the UN as a mechanism for treaty-making, see Alvarez *International Organizations as Law-makers* (2005) 273–337; Rosenne *Treaties* 364–98; Higgins *Development*.

[139] Buergenthal *Law-Making in the International Civil Aviation Organization* (1969).

[140] Higgins *Development* 2.

[141] Rosenne *Treaties* 203–4.

[142] Letter Dated 20 April 1966 from the Acting Permanent Representative of the USSR Addressed to the President of the Security Council, S/7259 p. 2.

membership and these reduce the UN's authority. In a world of heterogeneous States, an organization of universal membership will be less efficient than more narrowly constituted organizations in the performance of certain tasks. As Henry Schermers says, 'Universal organizations are formed by governments with different political outlooks, varied cultures, and at different stages of development. This limits the confidence of the Members and their willingness to attribute any power to the organization.'[143] In certain fields, the universal organization well may be perceived as generating less legitimate decisions than organizations possessed of a stricter constitutional purpose and comprised of a narrower membership. The Human Rights Commission was the prime example of a UN body in which confidence was lost as a result of the inclusion of members not committed to its mission.[144] A challenge for international organization generally will be to balance the need for the UN as a body with universal membership with the need for regional and specialized organizations designed to carry out other tasks.[145]

---

[143] Schermers *International Institutional Law* (1980) § 31 pp. 22–3.

[144] For criticism by a national study group, see e.g. Task Force on the United Nations *The Imperative for Action, An Update of the Report of the Task Force on American Interests and UN Reform* Gingrich & Mitchell, chairmen (2005) 7. For internal UN criticism, see *In larger freedom: towards development, security and human rights for all* 21 Mar 2005, A/59/2005; and Addendum to the Report, Human Rights Council: Explanatory note by the Secretary-General, 23 May 2005, A/59/2005/Add.1 (cited by Scannella & Splinter 7 *Hum Rts LR* at 42 n. 4).

[145] The fragmentation of international law is among the difficulties that resort to regional organizations presents. For citations to literature on fragmentation, see 'Fragmentation of International Law: Difficulties Arising from the Diversification and Expansion of International Law,' Report of the ILC, 58th sess (2006), A/61/10, Ch. XII, ¶ 244, p. 402 n. 1011 (to appear in *ILC Ybk* 2006 vol. II pt. two). The ILC Study Group on the topic of fragmentation, Koskenniemi, Chairman, considered in particular the problem of regionalism producing conflicts with general international law: Report of the Study Group, 13 Apr 2006, A/CN.4/L.682, pp. 108–12 ¶¶ 211–217. See also Coicaud *Beyond the National Interest: The Future of UN Peacekeeping and Multilateralism in an Era of U.S. Primacy* (2007) 198, 210 (adverting to the 'battle between particularist and universalist conceptions of ethics'); Asmal 'International Law and Practice: Dealing with the Past in the South African Experience' (Second Annual Grotius Lecture) (2000) 94 *ASIL Proc* 1, 4. One answer to concerns about fragmentation is that, in any event, Article 103 of the Charter provides that Charter obligations prevail. See the ILC's Conclusions on fragmentation (Conclusions (35) and (41)): ibid., ¶ 251. It also may be said that a high degree of diversity in legal relations always has existed among States, each free to accept conventional obligations within the limits of *jus cogens*, and each in practice having such distinctive conventional obligations as to call into question notions of a monolithic international law. This is what got in the way of attempts to write a uniform international code of investor protection: see Crawford & Grant 'Responsibility of States for Injuries to Foreigners' in Barker & Grant eds *Harvard Research in International Law: Contemporary Analysis and Appraisal* (2007) 77, 124–6. There nevertheless remains a need for some core of universally accepted rules and principles, if one is to speak of an international legal system. The search is on-going: Orrego Vicuña *International dispute settlement* 6–7.

Conclusion

The United Nations exists in a world of heterogeneous States. Territorial extent, natural resources, population, wealth, military power, cultural potency – the incidents of what Keohane and Nye taxonomize under the related headings 'soft' and 'hard' power[1] – vary tremendously from State to State. So too vary the forms and practices of governments and the extent to which governments respect the human rights of the citizens and fulfil the international obligations of the States they represent. It is in this sense that States, even under the principle of sovereign (legal) equality, are heterogeneous. The present era is characterized by this high diversity among States. It also is characterized by a high degree of contact among States and among nationals of States. Since the 19th century, States have used intergovernmental institutions to regulate interstate contact, as well as to address problems not subject wholly to the jurisdiction of any one State. The number of such institutions has increased greatly since the mid-20th century. In a world of heterogeneous States and of many international organizations, the United Nations occupies a special place in at least one respect: it is the international organization that most nearly has attained universality of membership.

Yet achieving a universal membership roll is not necessarily the same as achieving the main goals of the founders of the UN. Indeed, it is common ground today that the United Nations has not carried out certain tasks fulfilment of which, it had been hoped, would lead to a stable and just world order. Among the failings commonly identified in the Organization are corruption and inefficiency in its peacekeeping missions; a top heavy secretariat; and disuse, if not breakdown, of the Chapter VII security apparatus. States and writers have identified the deficit of legitimacy that results when serial violators of human rights hold membership in its human rights organs as perhaps the most acute problem of a UN in crisis. This last failing relates most directly to membership. It suggests that universal membership, with respect to certain goals of the UN, impedes rather than fosters performance.

---

[1] Keohane & Nye *Power and Interdependence* 3rd edn (2001) 220.

Amerasinghe, in *Principles of the institutional law of international organizations*, said that '[c]onstitutions of international organizations, being organic instruments, may require change both in the light of experience in the organizations as well as in order to keep pace with developments in international society.'[2] Changes made to 'keep pace' with certain developments, however, though they may help achieve certain goals, may hinder the organization in the pursuit of other goals. It is not always the case in systems, legal or of whatever type, that modifying one part of the system in the pursuit of a particular objective will be a neutral act, with respect to all other objectives of the system. Improving efficacy in one part may decrease efficacy in another. The United Nations was established to perform certain functions at global level, and the Charter gives it authority and certain mechanisms to do so. In addition to the authority expressly conferred by the Charter, the UN has acquired further authority, by virtue of its achievement of near-universal membership of States. This achievement however has a cost: all-State participation hinders the Organization in the performance of other functions.

There may be no single solution to every problem facing the UN. Refining the institutional apparatus and reformulating particular UN mandates perhaps would solve, or at least ameliorate, some of the problems. The general, even constitutional, problem however remains. The UN is the universal representative body of States in a world of heterogeneous States. From rich, democratic States with governments effective in maintaining rule of law; to poor, authoritarian States; to States with few or no functioning public institutions, the spectrum is vast. Including all States in a single political organization was seen early in the UN era as beneficial to world public order. The existence of a general forum of States is still accepted as necessary to the system of international relations. Since the UN has become an organization in which membership of States is nearly universal, however, the tensions and conflicts inherent in a world of heterogeneous sovereigns leave their mark on the UN. This at times has meant paralysis within the Organization. And herein lies a paradox, for universality both gives the UN authority and, by way of the limits it places on effectiveness, takes authority away.

Understanding admission criteria is central to understanding how the UN came to be as it is today. States are not born members of the UN; they are admitted under decisions taken by existing members. Universal admission might be described as the result of application of a self-evident Charter principle. The better view is that it resulted from choices of the member States when implementing the admission criteria of the Charter.

---

[2] Amerasinghe 2nd rev edn (2005) 447.

The UN Charter, in Article 4, paragraph 1, sets out criteria for membership in the UN. As we have seen, the criteria are that an applicant for admission be a State; peace-loving; committed to the purposes and principles of the Charter; and willing and able to fulfil its commitment to the purposes and principles of the Charter. The International Court of Justice in 1948 was clear, in its Advisory Opinion on *Conditions of Admission of a State for Membership in the United Nations*, that the member States of the UN must apply these criteria when they vote whether to admit a new member. The Court also said that it is up to member States to scrutinize the merits of each application for admission. In practice, however, the criteria of Article 4(1) scarcely have been applied at all.

It would serve no purpose to talk about expelling member States in good standing. Nor can one readily conceive a legal doctrine of involuntary 'de-recognition' without overturning much of modern international law. Striking States from the rolls would not necessarily make sense as policy either. However, in view of the character and severity of the crisis in international organization, the time perhaps has come to apply admission criteria more rigorously than heretofore has been the practice. This would have at least two dimensions.

First, a stricter approach might be taken toward future applications for UN membership. We tend to think of the current number of States – 194 in total, 192 members of the UN – as a 'settled' or 'right' number; but, over time, the number has fluctuated, and widely. In CE 1618, there were around 3000 States; by 1914, scarcely over 60. Since then, the number of States has more than trebled. Managing change in the number of States – and, it is submitted, their identity and character – is a role that we well may need an organization in the future to fill – and the UN, if used properly, could fill it. The prevailing, permissive approach to UN admission has done nothing to discourage the creation of States; it perhaps even has been an incentive. A stricter approach to UN admission could place a deterrent in the way of precipitous independence. This in turn would have a stabilizing effect in international relations.

Second, the selective principle behind Article 4(1) could be revived also to regulate which States participate in the key functional organs of the UN. A vetting process based on the criteria could, for example, keep human rights violators out of the bodies responsible for monitoring human rights. The importance of this particular objective was recognized by the Gingrich-Mitchell Task Force.[3] The United States indeed made a proposal (among others) that the new Human Rights Council be closed to States against which Security Council sanctions are in force.[4] While Article 4(1) addresses the prior question of which States to admit

---

[3] Gingrich & Mitchell Report (2005) 6.
[4] Bolton *Surrender is not an Option: Defending America at the United Nations and Abroad* (2007) 234–8.

to membership in the UN as a whole, the criteria it embodies could be applied for internal purposes as well. Substantive criteria for participation by member States of an organization in the organization's subsidiary, functional organs are supported specifically in the jurisprudence of the International Court;[5] and they make sense as part of the logic of international organization generally.

Managing the process by which certain applicants become UN member States and regulating which UN member States perform specific tasks within the Organization have the potential to play a significant role. This could extend beyond the UN, for one could adopt a selective approach to membership in other organizations – including organizations yet to be established. It is submitted that the efficacy of new international organizations, whether a League of Democracies or other body, will depend in large part on how the authors of their constitutive instruments define the criteria for admission – and how the original member States in practice apply them.

The United Nations is the way it is, because its membership criteria have been applied permissively rather than restrictively. The result is universal membership, and universal membership determines what the UN can and cannot do. The UN has proved effective in doing those things that require the participation of all States. In particular, universality has benefitted the Organization with respect to its role in providing a universal diplomatic forum and a framework for codification and progressive development of international law. The Charter however envisaged the UN performing more than these roles, as important in themselves as they are. The broad sense of 'purposes and principles' of the UN Charter entails active involvement in matters of general human dignity – especially in formulating, monitoring, and enforcing rules and standards of human rights. If the UN is to act more effectively with respect to human rights, it needs better to control which States participate in the mechanisms having tasks in that field.

The Permanent Representative of Costa Rica, the Reverend Benjamín Núñez Vargas, in 1955 offered a justification for opening the United Nations to all States. The setting was the General Assembly, immediately after sixteen new member States had been accepted for admission. It was the day the ten-year logjam, viewed by many member States as intolerable, finally had been broken. Father Núñez said that one group of States among those admitted that day possessed 'political and social systems deserv[ing] our full sympathy and approval because they are in keeping with that respect for human dignity and freedom which is the essence of...democracy.' A second group were ruled under 'totalitarian doctrines which violate the dignity of the peoples concerned, as well as

---

[5] *Constitution of the Maritime Safety Committee of the Inter-Governmental Maritime Consultative Organization*, Advisory Opinion of 8 June 1960, ICJ Rep 1960 p. 150.

their right to self-determination.' The Costa Rican Permanent Representative said the following about the two groups:

> We welcome the first group of countries in the certainty that they will strengthen the eagerness of the United Nations to affirm human freedom, to promote social welfare and to maintain international peace. We welcome the second group in the confidence that proximity to so many peace-loving nations will show them the road to complete freedom along which their people yearn to travel, and that their contact with us will make it easier for them to fulfil the intention and the promise which they make on being admitted to this body, namely, that they will henceforth conduct themselves in accordance with the principles of the United Nations Charter, and especially with the requirements of Article 4.[6]

Article 4, as seen in the Chapters above, indeed entailed certain requirements. The greater significance of those requirements, however, would have been in their rigorous application as a control on admission, not as a basis for asserting obligations on member States, over whom the Organization, *ex post* admission, would hold considerably less leverage.

It is difficult today to see, in light of its historic purpose and evolution, how the UN could be anything other than the 'parliament of man'[7] into which it evolved over the first decades of its existence. Nor would it be desirable to qualify this universality. Its value is well-recognized. As the representative of Italy said in 1975 during discussions on admission of Viet Nam,

> [O]ur aim should be to make the United Nations a genuine world forum where the views of all countries can be heard whether they be large or small, rich or poor, or whatever their political system may be. Our goal, at any rate, is a world organization that genuinely represents the people of this world.[8]

The role of the UN as a 'genuine world forum' is now a central aspect of the Organization. The problem with lapse of the admission criteria of Article 4(1), which Chapter 4 above examined, is that tasks exist that an organization of universal membership in a world of heterogeneous States is ill-suited to perform.

The wider point – one that might be taken as an axiom of international organization – is that what States are let in determine what the organization can do; membership criteria – in constitutive instruments and in practice – control what States are let in; membership criteria therefore determine what the organization

---

[6] Mr Núñez (Costa Rica) GAOR 555th mtg 14 Dec 1955 ¶ 88. Núñez had been actively engaged in Costa Rican politics at the time of the 1948 civil war – and the permanent demilitarization of the country that followed.

[7] Paul Kennedy's preferred title; Alfred, Lord Tennyson's expression originally: Kennedy *The parliament of man: the past, present, and future of the United Nations* (2006) xi, quoting Tennyson 'Locksley Hall' (1837).

[8] Mr Cavaglieri (for Italy): SCOR 1834th mtg 6 Aug 1975 p. 9 ¶ 97.

can do. This is obvious at a certain level. It is however all too readily ignored when considering how international organizations actually work. International organizations are not politically organic entities. To be sure, like States, they are international legal persons. As international legal persons, international organizations are separate from the member States which comprise them. The separate legal personality of international organizations has major consequences, not least of all in the field of international responsibility. As a matter of the operations and decisions of an international organization, however, the goals and interests of individual member States remain extremely significant. The functional realities of an international organization therefore must be distinguished from its legal form: Judge Dillard was not wrong to say that the members of an international organization 'are linked together by the constitution, and their relationships are governed by the constitution.'⁹ But Philippe Sands, equally, is right to say that we are in 'a world of desegregated international institutions which are nothing more than the sum of their parts, namely, their membership.'¹⁰ The latter observation even may have implications for the legal personality of the international organization, which Alain Pellet, among others, has cautioned (one may imagine *pace* Judge Dillard) not to over-generalize.¹¹ The European Union

---

⁹ *Appeal Relating to the Jurisdiction of the ICAO Council (India v Pakistan)*, Separate Opinion of Judge Dillard, ICJ Rep 1972 pp. 46, 30 ¶ 3. The relevant passage is as follows:

> Whatever the nature of its legal personality may be, each organization has a constitution which provides it with a general rule to which all its members are subject. Their rights and obligations towards each other flow from this constitution. It is the fact that the organization is a legal person which prevents the legal relationships between its members being considered as governed by a series of independent bilateral treaties. The life of the organization is not governed disjunctively by an accumulation of bilateral treaties. Members of the organization are linked together by the constitution, and their relationships are governed by the constitution. Such relationships are those resulting from the status of member of the organization, and not the status of a party to bilateral treaties. This is of the very essence of organizations; it is required by the common interest, and is a necessity for their functioning and effectiveness.

¹⁰ Sands, comment on symposium panel: 'World Trade and the Environment' (1999) 19 *New York Law School Journal of International & Comparative Law* 163, 183–4. Kelsen saw international organizations in a similar light: *Principles of International Law* (New York: Rinehart, 1952) 172.

¹¹ Pellet, rejecting the Special Rapporteur's view that international organizations possess 'sovereignty,' said that '... international organizations [are] no more than instruments at the service of their member States and of the aims jointly pursued by those States': Discussions in connection with the Fourth Report on Relations between States and international organizations, ILC 42nd sess 2178th mtg 21 June 1990 ¶ 18, *ILC Ybk* 1990 Vol. I p. 215. Pellet expressed concern to avoid an over-generalization from the legal personality of international organizations which 'themselves were prone to seek considerable extensions of their privileges and immunities' – concern justified where there as yet exist few mechanisms for adjudication against them; ibid., ¶ 20 p. 216. Cf. Francis Mahon Hayes, saying that the rights and duties of the international organization derive from the purposes and functions defined in its constituent instrument, not from 'the

may be an exception – the one international organization to have turned into a more highly integrated entity and thus to contain internal processes which are autonomous to a meaningful degree from the member States.[12] If the EU is an exception, then it belongs to its own category. What an international organization can do – what it is capable of doing – depends on the States constituting it. The control mechanism placed on admission of States therefore shapes the international organization in a fundamental way.

The United Nations as a universal organization is indispensable in a fractious world. It is clear however that its capacities are not without limit. Among the things the UN cannot do are tasks that equally cannot be performed by a single State. Between the national and the universal there thus exists a void. To the extent that other specialized or regional organizations have stepped in to fill the void, this has been made possible by application of their own, more restrictive admission criteria. If an international organization is to further all the purposes which the Costa Rican permanent representative attributed to that 'first group' of States – 'to affirm human freedom, to promote social welfare and to maintain international peace' – then those are the purposes that must be considered, when deciding whether to admit a candidate to membership.

---

fact of international personality': ILC 42nd sess 2176th mtg 19 June 1990 ¶ 6, *ILC Ybk* 1990 vol. I p. 201.

[12] Consider Schermers' distinction between 'supranational' and 'intergovernmental' organizations: *International Institutional Law* (1980) §§ 40–47 pp. 27–31. See also Morand 'La Souveraineté, Un Concept Dépassé à l'heure de la Mondialisation?' in Boisson de Chazournes & Gowlland-Debbas eds (2001) 153, 162–5. For the Czech view as to what type of organization the UN is, see ICJ Pldgs 1948 p. 117 ('*leur* pouvoir discrétionnaire').

Bibliography

Acevska, Ljubica, 'The Republic of Macedonia: An Atypical Balkan Country' (1997) 20 *Ford ILJ* 1521

Ackermann, Alice, *Making Peace Prevail – Preventing Violent Conflict in Macedonia* (Syracuse: Syracuse University Press, 2000)

Akande, Dapo, 'The Jurisdiction of the International Criminal Courts over Nationals of Non-Parties: Legal Basis and Limits' (2003) 1 *J Int'l Crim Justice* 618

Alger, Chadwick F., 'Widening Participation' in Weiss, Thomas George and Daws, Sam eds, *The Oxford Handbook on the United Nations* (Oxford: Oxford University Press, 2007)

Alvarez, José E., *International Organizations as Law-makers* (Oxford: Oxford University Press, 2005)

Amerasinghe, C.F., *Principles of the institutional law of international organisations* 2nd rev edn (Cambridge: Cambridge University Press, 2005)

Anand, Ram Prakash, 'Sovereign Equality of States in International Law' (1986) 197 *Hag Rec* 9

Ando, Nisuke, *Surrender, Occupation, and Private Property in International Law: An Evaluation of U.S. Practice in Japan* (Oxford: Oxford University Press, 1991)

Anzilotti, Dionisio, *Cours de Droit International* 3rd edn, trans to French from Italian by Gilbert Gidel (Paris: Receuil Sirey, 1929)

Araujo, Robert John, 'Objective Meaning of Constituent Instruments and Responsibility of International Organizations' in Ragazzi, Maurizio ed, *International Responsibility Today. Essays in Memory of Oscar Schachter* (Leiden: Martinus Nijhoff, 2005)

Asmal, Kader, 'International Law and Practice: Dealing with the Past in the South African Experience' (Second Annual Grotius Lecture) (2000) 94 *ASIL Proc* 1

Audeoud, Olivier, 'Les Collectivités Intra-Étatiques dans la Vie Internationale' in Société française pour le droit international *Colloque de Nancy: L'Etat souverain à l'aube du XXIᵉ siècle* (Paris: Pedone, 1994)

Bailey, Sydney D. & Daws, Sam, *The Procedure of the UN Security Council* 2nd edn (Oxford: Oxford University Press, 1998)

—— *The Procedure of the UN Security Council* 3rd edn (Oxford: Clarendon Press, 1998)

Bailey, Thomas A., *Diplomatic History of the American People* 10th edn (Englewood Cliffs: New Jersey: Prentice-Hall, 1980)

Bashkurti, Lisen, 'Political Dynamics Within the Balkans: The Cases of Bosnia & Herzegovina, Macedonia, Bulgaria, Serbia, and Montenegro' (2005) 80 *Chicago-Kent L Rev* 49

Bassiouni, M. Cherif, 'International Recognition of Victims' Rights' (2006) 6 *HR L Rev* 203

Bastid, Suzanne, *Droit des Gens: Principes généreux* (Paris: Institut d'Etudes politiques, Les Cours de Droit, 1960) (collected lectures)

Beaulac, William L., *Franco: Silent Ally in World War II* (Carbondale: Southern Illinois University Press, 1986)

Ben Achour, Yadh, 'État, Cultures, et Mondialisation' in Boisson de Chazournes, Laurence & Gowlland-Debbas, Vera eds, *The international legal system in quest of equality and universality: liber amicorum Georges Abi-Saab* (The Hague: Martinus Nijhoff, 2001)

Blix, Hans, 'Contemporary Aspects of Recognition' (1970 – II) 130 *Hag Rec* 589

Blokker 'Beyond "Dili": On the Powers and Practice of International Organization' in Kreijen, Gerard ed, *State, Sovereignty, and International Governance* (Oxford: Oxford University Press, 2002)

Bluemel, Erik B., 'Unraveling the Global Warming Regime Complex: Competitive Entropy in the Regulation of the Global Public Good' (2007) 155 *U Penn L Rev* 1981

Blum, Yehuda Z., 'The Soviet Union's Seat at the United Nations' (1992) 3 *EJIL* 354

—— 'UN Membership of the "New" Yugoslavia: Continuity or Break?' (1992) 86 *AJ* 830

—— 'Was Yugoslavia a Member of the United Nations in the Years 1992–2000?' (2007) 101 *AJ* 800

Bokor-Szegő, Hanna, 'Questions of State Identity and State Succession in Eastern and Central Europe' in Mrak, Mojmir ed, *Succession of States* (Leiden: Martinus Nijhoff, 1999)

Bolton, John, *Surrender is not an Option: Defending America at the United Nations and Abroad* (New York: Threshold Editions, 2007)

Bowett, Derek W., *The Law of International Institutions* 4th edn (London: Stevens & Sons, 1982)

Breau, Susan C., 'The constitutionalisation of the international legal order' (2008) 21 *Leiden JIL* 545

Brown, Bartram S., 'IMF governance, the Asian financial crisis, and the new financial architecture' in Yee, Sienho & Tieya, Wang eds, *International Law in the Post-Cold War World: Essays in memory of Li Haopei* (London: Routledge, 2001)

Brownlie, Ian, *Principles of Public International Law* 5th edn (Oxford: Oxford University Press 1998)

—— *Principles of Public International Law* 6th edn (Oxford: Oxford University Press, 2003)

Brunnbauer, Ulf, 'The Implementation of the Ohrid Agreement: Ethnic Macedonian Resentments' 1/2002 *J on Ethnopolitics and Minority Issues in Europe*

Buckley, Roger, *Occupation diplomacy: Britain, the United States, and Japan, 1945–1952* (Cambridge: Cambridge University Press, 1982)

Buergenthal, Thomas, *Law-Making in the International Civil Aviation Organization* (Syracuse: Syracuse University Press, 1969)

Bühler, Konrad K., *State Succession and Membership in International Organizations* (The Hague: Kluwer Law International, 2001)

Burke, Edmund, *Reflections on the revolution in France, and on the proceedings in certain societies in London relative to that event. In a letter intended to have been sent to a gentleman in Paris* (Dublin, 1790)

Byers, Michael, *Custom, Power and the Power of Rules: International relations and customary international law* (Cambridge: Cambridge University Press, 1999)

Caty, Gilbert, *Le Statut Juridique des États Divisés* (Paris: Éditions A. Pedone, 1969)

Cazala, Julien, 'L'Accession du Monténégro à l'Indépendance' (2006) 52 *AFDI* 160

Charney, Jonathan I. & Prescott, J.R.V., 'Resolving Cross-Strait Relations between China and Taiwan' (2000) 94 *AJ* 453

Charpentier, Jean, 'Le Phénomène Étatique à Travers les Grandes Mutations Politiques Contemporaines' in Société Française pour le Droit International *L'état souverain à l'aube du XXIᵉ siècle* Colloque de Nancy (Paris: Pedone, 1994)

Chen, Frederick Tse-Shyang, 'The Meaning of 'States' in the Membership Provisions of the United Nations Charter' (2001) 12 *Ind Int'l & Comp LR* 25

Chen, Ti-Chiang, *The International Law of Recognition, with special reference to practice in Great Britain and the United States* (London: Stevens & Sons, 1951)

Cheng, Bin, *Studies in International Space Law* (Oxford: Clarendon Press, 1997)

Church, Clive H., *The Politics and Government of Switzerland* (New York: Palgrave Macmillan, 2004)

Ciobanu, Dan, 'Credentials of Delegations and Representation of Member States at the United Nations' (1976) 25 *ICLQ* 351

Claude, Inis L., *Swords into Plowshares* 4th edn (New York: Random House, 1984)

Cohen (later Higgins), Rosalyn, 'The Concept of Statehood in United Nations Practice' (1961) 109 *U Pa LR* 1127

Coicaud, Jean-Marc, *Beyond the National Interest: The Future of UN Peacekeeping and Multilateralism in an Era of U.S. Primacy* (Washington, DC: United States Institute of Peace Press, 2007)

Cotran, Eugene, 'Some Legal Aspects of the Formation of the United Arab Republic and the United Arab States' (1959) 8 *ICLQ* 346

Craven, Matthew C.R., 'What's in a Name? The Former Yugoslav Republic of Macedonia and Issues of Statehood' (1995) 16 *Australian YBIL* 199

—— 'The *Genocide* Case, the Law of Treaties and State Succession' (1997) 68 *BY* 127

—— 'The Problem of State Succession and Identity Under International Law' (1998) 9 *EJIL* 142

Crawford, James & Grant, Thomas D., 'International Court of Justice' in Weiss, Thomas George and Daws, Sam eds, *The Oxford Handbook on the United Nations* (Oxford: Oxford University Press, 2007)

—— 'Responsibility of States for Injuries to Foreigners' in Barker, Craig J. & Grant, John P. eds, *Harvard Research in International Law: Contemporary Analysis and Appraisal* (Buffalo: W.S. Hein, 2007)

Crawford, James, 'Democracy and the body of international law' in Fox, Gregory H., & Roth, Brad R. eds, *Democratic Governance and International Law* (Cambridge: Cambridge University Press, 2000)

—— ed., *The International Law Commission's Articles on State Responsibility: Introduction, Text and Commentaries* (Cambridge: Cambridge University Press, 2002)

—— *Creation of States in International Law* 2nd edn (Oxford: Oxford University Press 2006)

—— 'Holding International Organisations and Their Members to Account' Fifth Steinkraus-Cohen International Law Lecture, School of Oriental and African Studies, London 15 March 2007

Crook, John ed, 'Diplomatic and Consular Relations: U.S. Relations with Republic of Macedonia' (2005) 99 *AJ* 254

David, Eric, 'La Responsabilité des États Fédéraux dans les Relations Internationales' in Institut de Sociologie *Les États fédéraux dans les relations internationales: actes du colloque de Bruxelles* (Brussels: Bruylant, 1984)

de Marco, Guido & Bartolo, Michael, *A Second Generation United Nations for Peace and Freedom in the 21st Century* new edn (London: Kegan Paul, 2002)

de Visscher, *Problèmes d'interprétation judiciaire en droit international public* 140 (1969)

De Wet, Erika, 'The international constitutional order' (2006) 55 *ICLQ* 51

Delbrück, Jost, 'Book Review and Notes' (1990) 84 *AJ* 817

Detwiler, Donald S., 'Spain and the Axis During World War II' (1971) 33(1) *Review of Politics* 36

Dickinson, Edwin, *Equality of States in International Law* (Cambridge: Harvard University Press, 1920)

Diez, Emanuel, 'UNO-Beitritt und Neutralitäts-erklärung' in Dutoit, Bernard & Grisel, Etienne eds, *Recueil de Travaux Offerts à M Georges Perrin* (Lausanne: Diffusion Payot, 1984)

Dimitrijevic, Vojin & Milanovic, Marko, 'The strange story of the Bosnian Genocide Case' (2008) 21 *Leiden JIL* 65

Dixon, Martin, *Textbook on International Law* 3rd edn (London: Blackstone, 1996)

—— *Textbook on International Law* 5th edn (Oxford: Oxford University Press, 2005)

Dolan, Edward, 'The Member-Republics of the USSR as Subjects of the Law of Nations' (1955) 4 *ICLQ* 629

Dronova, Natalia V., 'The Division of State Property in the Case of State Succession in the Former Soviet Union' in Eiseman, Pierre Michel & Koskenniemi, Martti eds, *State Succession: Codification Tested Against the Facts* (Hague Academy, 2000)

Dugard, John and Van den Wyngaert, Christine, 'Reconciling Extradition with Human Rights' (1998) 92 *AJ* 187

Dugard, John, *Recognition and the United Nations* (Cambridge: Grotius Publications, 1987)

Dupuy, Pierre-Marie, 'The Constitutional Dimension of the Charter of the United Nations Revisited' (1997) 1 *Max Planck Ybk UN Law 1*

Duursma, Jorri C., *Fragmentation and the International Relations of Micro-States. Self-determination and Statehood* (Cambridge, Cambridge University Press, 1996)

Eitel, Tono, 'The UN Security Council and its Future Contribution in the Field of International Law. What may we expect?' (2000) 4 *Max Planck Ybk UN Law* 53

Elleman, Bruce A., 'Secret Sino-Soviet Negotiations on Outer Mongolia, 1918–1925' (1993–4) 66 *Pacific Affairs* 539

Epstein, Julius J., Epstein, Philip G. & Koch, Howard, *Casablanca* (Warner Bros, 1942)

Farer, Tom, 'Bombing for Peace: Collateral Damage and Human Rights' (2002) 96 *ASIL Proc* 95

Fawcett, JES, *The British Commonwealth in International Law* (London: Stevens & Sons, 1963)

Feinberg, Nathan, 'L'admission de nouveaux membres à l'Organisation des Nations Unies' (1952) LXXX *Hag Rec* 299

Fidler, David P., 'A Kinder, Gentler System of Capitulations? International Law, Structural Adjustment Policies, and the Standard of Liberal, Globalized Civilization' (2000) 35 *Tex ILJ* 387

Finkelstein, Lawrence S., 'International Cooperation in a Changing World: A Challenge to United States Foreign Policy' (1969) 23(3) *Int'l Org* 559

Fischer-Lescano, Andreas, 'Die Emergenz der Globalverfassung' (2003) 63 *ZaöVR* 715

Fitzmaurice, Sir Gerald, 'The Law and procedure of the International Court of Justice: Treaty Interpretation and Certain Other Treaty Points' (1951) 28 *BY* 8

—— *The Law and Procedure of the International Court of Justice* (Cambridge: Grotius 1986)

Fleischhauer, Carl-August, 'Panel Remarks: Compliance and Enforcement in the United Nations System' (1991) 85 *ASIL Proc* 428

Franck, Thomas M., 'Legitimacy and the democratic entitlement' in Fox, Gregory H., & Roth, Brad R. eds, *Democratic Governance and International Law* (Cambridge: Cambridge University Press, 2000)

Freudenschuß, Helmut, 'Collective Security' in Cede, Franz & Sucharipa-Behrmann, Lilly eds, *The United Nations Law and Practice* (Leiden: Martinus Nijhoff, 2001)

Frowein, Jochen Abr., 'The Reunification of Germany' (1992) 86 *AJ* 152

Fuller, C. Dale, 'Soviet Policy in the United Nations' (1949) 263 *Annals of the Am Acad of Pol & Soc'l Science* 141

Gattini, Andrea, 'A return ticket to "Communitarisme," please' (2002) 13 *EJIL* 1181

Gelberg, Ludwik, 'The Warsaw Treaty of 1970 and the Western Boundary of Poland' (1982) 76 *AJ* 119

Gillespie, Alexander & Burns, William C.G. eds, *Climate Change in the South Pacific: Impacts and Responses in Australia, New Zealand and Small Island States* (Dordrecht: Kluwer, 1999)

Gillespie, Alexander, 'Small Island States in the Face of Climatic Change' (2004) 22 *UCLA J Env L & Pol'y* 107

Ginsburgs, George, 'The Soviet Union, the Neutrals and International Law in World War II' (1962) 11 *ICLQ* 171

Ginther, Konrad, 'Article 4' in Simma, Bruno ed, *Charter of the United Nations: A Commentary* 2nd edn (Oxford: Oxford University Press, 2002)

Graham, Malbone W., *The League of Nations and the Recognition of States* (Berkeley: University of California Press, 1933)

Grant, Thomas D., 'Internationally Guaranteed Constitutive Order: Cyprus and Bosnia as Predicates for a New Nontraditional Actor' (1998) 8 *J Trans L & Pol'y* 1

—— *The Recognition of States: Law and Practice in Debate and Evolution* (Westport: Praeger, 1999)

—— 'Defining Statehood: The Montevideo Convention and its Discontents' (1999) 37 *Colum J Trans'l L* 403

—— 'Hallstein Revisted: Unilateral Enforcement of Regimes of Nonrecognition since the Two Germanies' (2000) 36 *Stan JIL* 221

—— 'States Newly Admitted to the United Nations: Some Implications' (2000) 39 *Colum J Trans'l L* 177

—— 'United States Practice Relating to the Baltic States, 1940–2000' (2001) 1 *Baltic YBIL* 23

—— 'Doctrines, Stimson etc' in Wolfrum, Rudiger ed, *Max Planck Encyclopedia of Public International Law* (Oxford: Oxford University Press) (forthcoming)

—— 'Micro-States' in Wolfrum, Rudiger ed, *Max Planck Encyclopedia of Public International Law* (Oxford: Oxford University Press) (forthcoming)

Green, Elizabeth E., 'China and Mongolia: Recurring Trends and Prospects for Change' (1986) 26 *Asian Survey* 1337

Grieg, D.W., 'The Advisory Jurisdiction of the International Court and the Settlement of Disputes between States' (1966) 15 *ICLQ* 325

Gross, Leo, 'Was the Soviet Union Expelled from the League of Nations?' (1945) 39 *AJ* 35

—— 'Progress Towards Universality of Membership in the United Nations' (1956) 50 *AJ* 781

—— 'Editorial Comment: On the Degradation of the Constitutional Environment of the United Nations' (1983) 77 *AJ* 569

Gunter, Michael M., 'Switzerland and the United Nations' (1976) 30 *Int'l Org* 129

Halberstam, Malvina, 'Excluding Israel from the General Assembly by a Rejection of its Credentials' (1984) 78 *AJ* 179

Hall, William E., *A Treatise on International Law* 8th edn (Oxford: Clarendon Press, 1924)

Hannum, Hurst, *Sovereignty and Self-Determination: The Accommodation of Conflicting Rights* (Philadelphia: University of Pennsylvania Press, 1990)

Haug, Hans, 'Die allfällige Mitgliedschaft der Schweiz in den Vereinten Nationen und das Internationale Komitee Roten Kreuzes' in Diez, Emanuel, Monnier, Jean, Müller, Jörg Paul, Reimann, Heinrich & Wildhaber, Luzius eds, *Festschrift für Rudolf Bindschedler zum 65. Geburtstag* (Bern: Verlag Stampfli & Cie, 1980)

Hebrew University of Jerusalem Study Group, *Israel and the United Nations* (New York: Manhattan Publishing Group for the Carnegie Endowment for International Peace, 1956)

Higgins, Rosalyn, 'The Concept of "The State": Variable Geometry and Dualist Perceptions' in Boisson de Chazournes, Laurence & Gowlland-Debbas, Vera eds, *The international legal system in quest of equality and universality: liber amicorum Georges Abi-Saab* (Leiden: Martinus Nijhoff, 2001)

Hoffmeister, Frank, 'Changing requirements for membership' in Ott, Andrea & Inglis, Kirstyn eds *Handbook on European Enlargement: A Commentary on the Enlargement Process* (The Hague: TMC Asser Press, 2002)

Honig, Frederick, 'The International Court of Justice 1947–1950' (1951/52) 14 *ZaöRV* 497

Hotz, Alfred J., 'The United Nations Since 1945: An Appraisal' (1961) *Annals of the American Academy of Political & Social Science* 127

Huang, Eric Ting-Lun, 'Taiwan's Status in a Changing World: United Nations Representation and Membership for Taiwan' (2003) 9 *Ann Surv Int'l & Comp L* 55

Hudson, Manley O., 'The Twenty-Ninth Year of the World Court' (1951) 45 *AJ* 1

Jaenicke, Günther, 'Die Aufnahme neuer Mitglieder in die Organisation der Vereinten Nationen' (1950/51) 13 *ZaöRV* 291

Jākobsone, Ieva, 'Latvia: The Claim for Independence' (2001) 1 *Baltic YBIL* 233

Jakštonytė, Sigutė & Cvelich, Michail, 'Constitutional and International Documents Concerning the International Legal Status of Lithuania' (2001) 1 *Baltic YBIL* 301

Janev, Igor, 'Legal Aspects of the Use of a Provisional Name for Macedonia in the United Nations System' (1999) 93 *AJ* 155

Japanese Association of International Law Study Group, *Japan and the United Nations* (New York: Manhattan Publishing Co, 1958)

Jay, Russell A., *United Nations Observer Status: An Accumulation of Contemporary Documents* (Washington: World Association of Lawyers, 1976)

Jenks, Clarence Wilfred, 'Expulsion From the League of Nations' (1935) 16 *BY* 155

Jennings, Sir Robert, 'Sovereignty and International Law' in Kreijan, Gerard ed, *State, Sovereignty, and International Governance* (Oxford: Oxford University Press, 2002)

Joseph, Sarah, Schultz, Jenny & Castan, Melissa, *The International Covenant on Civil and Political Rights: Cases, Materials and Commentary* 2nd edn (Oxford: Oxford University Press, 2004)

Juillard, Patrick, 'The External Debt of the Former Soviet Union: Succession or Continuation?' in Burdeau, Geneviève & Stern, Brigitte eds, *Dissolution, Continuation et Succession en Europe de l'Est: succession d'états et relations économiques internationales* (Paris: Montchrestien, 1994)

Ǩalimas, Dainius, 'Legal Issues on the Continuity of the Republic of Lithuania' (2001) 1 *Baltic YBIL* 1

Kearney, Michael G., *The Prohibition of Propaganda for War in International Law* (Oxford: Oxford University Press, 2007)

Keene, Edward, *Beyond the Anarchical Society: Grotius, Colonialism, and Order in World Politics* (Cambridge: Cambridge University Press, 2002)

Kelsen, Hans, 'The Principle of Sovereign Equality of States as a Basis for International Organization' (1944) 53 *Yale LJ* 207

—— *Principles of International Law* (New York: Rinehart, 1952)

Kennedy, Paul, *The parliament of man: the past, present, and future of the United Nations* (New York: Random House, 2006)

Keohane, Robert O. & Nye, Joseph S., *Power and Interdependence* 3rd edn (New York: Longman, 2001)

Kerr, Rachel, *The International Criminal Tribunal for the Former Yugoslavia. An exercise in law, politics, and diplomacy* (Oxford: Oxford University Press, 2004)

Kewenig, Wilhelm, 'Sonderprobleme einer Deutschen Mitgliedschaft in den Vereinten Nationen' in Scheuner, Ulrich & Lindemann, Beate eds, *Die Vereinten Nationen und die Mitarbeit der Bundesrepublik Deutschland* (Munich: R. Oldenbourg Verlag, 1973)

Khabarov, Sergei, 'Introductory Note' (1995) 34 ILM 1298

Kharad, R., 'La reconnaissance internationale des États baltes' (1992) 96 *RGDIP* 843

Kiderlen, Hans Fabian, *Von Triest nach Osttimor. Der völkerrechtliche Rahmen für die Verwaltung von Krisengebieten durch die Vereinten Nationen* (Heidelberg: Springer Verlag, 2008)

Klein, R.A., *Sovereign Equality Among States: The History of an Idea* (Toronto: University of Toronto Press, 1974)

Koskenniemi, Martti & Lehto, Marja, 'La succession d'Etats dans l'ex URSS, en ce qui concerne particulièrement les relations avec la Finlande' (1992) 38 *AFDI* 905

Koskenniemi, Martti, 'The Present State of Research Carried Out by the English-Speaking Section of the Centre for Studies and Research' in Eiseman, Pierre Michel & Koskenniemi, Martti eds, *State Succession: Codification Tested Against the Facts* (Hague Academy, 1996)

—— *From Apology to Utopia. The Structure of International Legal Argument* (Cambridge: Cambridge University Press, 2005)

Kreijen, Gerard, *State failure, sovereignty and effectiveness: legal lessons from the decolonization of Sub-Saharan Africa* (Leiden: Martinus Nijhoff, 2004)

Kress, Claus, 'Universal jurisdiction over international crimes and the Institut de Droit International' (2006) 4 *J Int'l Crim Justice* 561

Kritsiotis, Dino, 'Imagining the international community' (2002) 13 *EJIL* 961

Kunz, Josef L., 'Austria's Permanent Neutrality' (1956) 50 *AJ* 418

Langer, William L. and Gleason, S. Everett, *The Undeclared War, 1940–41* 1st edn (New York: Council on Foreign Relations, 1953)

Lauterpacht, Hersch, *The Development of International Law by the International Court* (London: Stevens & Son Ltd, 1958)

Lee, Thomas H., 'International Law, International Relations Theory, and Preemptive War: The Vitality of Sovereign Equality Today' (2004) 67 *Law & Contemporary Problems* 147

Lejeune, Yves, 'Les Competences des Communautés et des Regions Belges en Matière Internationale' in Institut de Sociologie *Les États fédéraux dans les relations internationales: actes du colloque de Bruxelles* (Brussels: Bruylant, 1984)

Liang, Yuen-Li, 'Admission of Indian States to the United Nations' (1949) 43 *AJ* 144

—— 'Conditions of Admission of a State to Membership in the United Nations' (1949) 43 *AJ* 288

Lloyd, David O., 'Succession, Secession, and State Membership in the United Nations' (1994) 26 *NYU J Int'l L & Pol* 761

Luck, Edward C., 'Prospects for Reform: Principal Organs' in Weiss, Thomas George and Daws, Sam eds, *The Oxford Handbook on the United Nations* (Oxford: Oxford University Press, 2007)

Ludlow, David J., 'Preventive Peacekeeping in Macedonia: An Assessment of UN Good Offices Diplomacy' 2003 *Brigham Young L Rev* 761

Lukashuk, Igor I., 'Special Capitol Hill Session: State Succession and Relations with Federal States: Discussion' (1992) *86 ASIL Proc* 23

Lupu, Yonatan, 'Rules, Gaps and Power: Assessing Reform of the U.N. Charter' 24 *Berkeley JIL* 881 (2006)

MacDonald, Ronald St John & Johnston, Douglas M. eds, *Towards World Constitutionalism, Issues in the Legal Ordering of the World Community* (Leiden: Martinus Nijhoff, 2005)

Magiera, Siegfried, 'Article 9' in Simma, Bruno ed, *Charter of the United Nations: A Commentary* 2nd edn (Oxford: Oxford University Press, 2002)

Magliveras, Konstantinos D., *Exclusion from Participation in International Organizations: The Law and Practice behind Member States' Expulsion and Suspension of Membership* (The Hague: Kluwer Law International, 1999)

Mälksoo, Lauri, *Illegal Annexation and State Continuity: the Case of the Incorporation of the Baltic States by the USSR* (Leiden: Martinus Nijhoff, 2003)

McDougal, Myres S., Lasswell, Harold D. & Miller, James C., *The Interpretation of International Agreements and World Public Order: Principles of Content and Procedure* (Dordrecht: Martinus Nijhoff, 1994)

McNair, Arnold D., *Law of Treaties: British Practice and Opinions* (Oxford: Clarendon Press, 1938)

McWhinney, Edward, 'The International Court of Justice and International Law-Making: The Judicial Activism/Self-Restraint Antinomy' (2006) 5 *Chinese JIL* 3

Mettraux, Guénaël, *International Crimes and the* Ad Hoc *Tribunals* (Oxford: Oxford University Press, 2005)

Mills, William B. & Hancock, Katherine, *Small Island States in Indian and Atlantic Oceans: Vulnerability to Climate Change and Strategies for Adaptation* (Reston, Virginia: American Society of Civil Engineers, 2005)

Minnerop, Petra, 'The Classification of States and the Creation of Status within the International Community' (2003) 7 *Max Planck Ybk UN Law* 79

Mockli, Deniel, 'The Long Road to Membership: Switzerland and the United Nations' in Gabriel, Jürg Martin & Fischer, Thomas eds, *Swiss Foreign Policy, 1945–2002* (New York: Palgrave Macmillan, 2003)

Moinuddin, Hasan, *The Charter of the Islamic Conference and Legal Framework of Economic Cooperation among its Member States* (Oxford: Clarendon Press, 1987)

Morand, Charles-Albert, 'La Souveraineté, Un Concept Dépassé à l'heure de la Mondialisation?' in Boisson de Chazournes, Laurence & Gowlland-Debbas, Vera eds, *L'Ordre Juridique International. Un Système en Quête d'Équité et d'Universalité. Liber Amicorum Georges Abi-Saab* (The Hague: Martinus Nijhoff, 2001)

Mosely, Philip E., 'Soviet Policy in the United Nations' (1947) 22 *Procs of the Academy of Pol'l Science* 28

Movsesian, Mark L., 'The Persistent Nation State and the Foreign Sovereign Immunities Act' 18 *Cardozo L Rev* 1083 (1996)

Mower, Alfred Glenn, 'Observer Countries: Quasi Members of the United Nations' (1966) 20 *Int'l Org* 266

Müller, Joachim ed, *Reforming the United Nations: the struggle for legitimacy and effectiveness* (Leiden: Martinus Nijhoff, 2006)

Müllerson, Rein, 'The Continuity and Succession of States, by Reference to the Former USSR and Yugoslavia' (1993) 42 *ICLQ* 473

Murphy, Sean D., 'Democratic legitimacy and the recognition of States and governments' in Fox, Gregory H. & Roth, Brad R. eds, *Democratic Governance and International Law* (Cambridge: Cambridge University Press, 2000)

—— 'Assessing the Legality of Invading Iraq' (2004) 92 *Georgetown LJ* 173

Neroni Slade, Tuiloma, 'The Making of International Law: The Role of Small Island States' (2003) 17 *Temple Int'l & Comp LJ* 531

Noortmann, Math, *Enforcing International Law: From Self-help to Self-contained Regimes* (Burlington, VT: Ashgate, 2005)

O'Keefe, Roger, 'The Admission to the United Nations of the Ex-Soviet and Ex-Yugoslav States' (2001) 1 *Baltic Yearbook of International Law* 167

Oellers-Frahm, Karin, 'Article 93 UN Charter' in Zimmermann, Andreas, Tomuschat Christian & Oellers-Frahm, Karin eds, *The Statute of the International Court of Justice. A Commentary* (Oxford: Oxford University Press, 2006)

Oppenheim, Lassa, *International Law: A Treatise* 1st edn (London: Longmans, Green & Co, 1905)

—— *International Law: a treatise* 5th edn (Sir Hersch Lauterpacht ed) (London: Longman, 1935 and 1937)

—— *International Law: a treatise* 8th edn (Sir Hersch Lauterpacht ed) (London: Longman, 1955)

Orakhelashvili, Alexander, 'Statehood, Recognition and the United Nations System: A Unilateral Declaration of Independence in Kosovo' (2008) 12 *Max Planck Ybk UN Law* 1

Orrego Vicuña, Francisco, *International dispute settlement in an evolving global society: constitutionalization, accessibility, privatization* (Cambridge: Cambridge University Press, 2004)

Ostrowski, Stephen T., 'Preventive Deployment of Troops as Preventive Measures: Macedonia and Beyond' (1998) 30 *NYU J Int'l L & Pol* 793

Parent, Geneviève & Mayer-Robitaille, Laurence, 'Agriculture et Culture: Le défi de l'OMC de Prendre en Compte les Considération Non Commerciales' (2007) 52 *McGill LJ* 415

Pazartzis, Photini, 'La reconnaissance d' "une ex-République Yougoslave": La question de l'ancienne République Yougoslave de Macédoine (ARYM)' (1995) 41 *AFDI* 281

Pellet, Alain, 'The Opinions of the Badinter Arbitration Committee: A Second Breath for the Self-determination of Peoples' (1992) 3 *EJIL* 178

Pomerance, Michla, 'Seeking Judicial Legitimation in the Cold War: U.S. Foreign Policy and the World Court, 1948–1962' (1995) 5 *Ind Int'l & Comp LR* 303

Ponsonby, Baron Arthur, *Democracy and Diplomacy: A Plea for Popular Control of Foreign Policy* (London: Meuthen & Co Ltd, 1915)

Popetrevski, Vasko & Latifi, Veton, 'The Ohrid Framework Agreement Negotiations,' June

2004, occasional paper on theme *The 2001 Conflict in FYROM – Reflections*, Conflict Studies Research Centre (available at www.defac.ac.uk/colleges/csrc/document-listings/balkan/csrc_mpf-2004–07–22/04(15)-Chap3–JP.pdf/)

Poulakidas, Dean M., 'Macedonia: Far More than a Name to Greece' (1995) 18 *Hastings Int'l & Comp L Rev* 397

Probst, Raymond R., *'Good Offices' in the Light of Swiss International Practice and Experience* (Dordrecht: Martinus Nijhoff, 1989)

Rabkin, Jeremy A., *The Case for Sovereignty: Why the World Should Welcome American Independence* (Washington, DC: The AEI Press, 2004)

Radan, Peter, 'Post-Secession International Borders: A Critical Analysis of the Opinions of the Badinter Arbitration Commission' (2000) 24 *Melbourne Univ LR* 50

Ramet, Sabrina P., 'Views From Inside: Memoirs concerning the Yugoslav Breakup and War' (2002) 61 *Slavic Review* 558

Reisman, W. Michael, Arsanjani, Mahnoush H., Wiessner, Siegfried & Westerman, Gayl S., *International Law in Contemporary Perspective* (New York: Foundation Press, 2004)

Reuter, Paul, *Institutions internationales* 3rd edn (Paris: Presses Universitaires de France, 1962)

Rich, Roland, 'Recognition of States: The Collapse of Yugoslavia and the Soviet Union' (1993) 4 *EJIL* 36

Roberts, Adam & Kingsbury, Benedict, 'Introduction: The UN's Roles in International Society since 1945' in Roberts, Adam & Kingsbury, Benedict eds, *United Nations, Divided World: The UN's Roles in International Relations* 2nd edn (Oxford: Clarendon Press, 1993)

Robinson, Jacob, 'Metamorphosis of the United Nations' (1958) 94 *Hag Rec* 497

Rolland, Sonia E., 'Developing Country Coalitions at the WTO: In Search of Legal Support' (2007) 48 *Harv ILJ* 483

Rosenne, Shabtai, (with assistance of Yaël Ronen) *The law and practice of the International Court, 1920–2005* 4th ed (Leiden: Martinus Nijhoff, 2006)

Rosenne, Shabtai, *Developments in the Law of Treaties 1945–1986* (Cambridge: Cambridge University Press, 1989)

Rosenstock, Robert, 'The Declaration of Principles of International Law Concerning Friendly Relations: A Survey' (1971) 65 *AJ* 713

Rousseau, Charles E., *Droit International Public* (Paris: Recueil Sirey, 1953)

Russell, Ruth B. (with assistance of Jeannette E. Muther), *A History of the United Nations Charter* (Washington, DC: Brookings Institution, 1958)

Saideman, Lewis, 'Do Palestinian Refugees Have a Right of Return to Israel?' (2004) 44 *Virg JIL* 829

Salmon, Jean, 'Internal Aspects of the Right to Self-Determination: Towards a Democratic Legitimacy Principle?' in Tomuschat, Christian ed, *Modern Law of Self-Determination* (Dordrecht: Martinus Nijhoff, 1993)

Salulaid, Jaan, 'Restoration of the Effect of Estonian International Treaties' (2001) 1 *Baltic YBIL* 225

Sands, Philippe, 'World Trade and the Environment' (1999) 19 *New York Law School Journal of International & Comparative Law* 163

Scannella & Splinter 7 *Hum Rts LR* at 42 n. 4.

Schabas, William A., *The UN International Criminal Tribunals: The Former Yugoslavia, Rwanda and Sierra Leone* (Cambridge: Cambridge University Press, 2006)

Schachter, Oscar, 'State Succession: The Once and Future Law' (1993) 33 *Virg JIL* 253

Schaller, Christian, 'Die Sezession des Kosovo und der völkerrechtliche Status der internationalen Präsenz (2008) 46 *AdV* 131

Schaller, Michael, *The American occupation of Japan: the origins of the Cold War in Asia* (New York: Oxford University Press, 1985)

Scharf, Michael P., 'Musical Chairs: The Dissolution of States and Membership in the United Nations' (1995) 28 *Cornell ILJ* 29

Scheffer, David J., 'The United States and the International Criminal Court' (1999) 93 *AJ* 12

Schermers, Henry G., *International Institutional Law* (Alphen aan den Rijn: Sijthoff & Noordhoff, 1980)

Schermers, Henry G. & Blokker, Niels M., *International Institutional Law: unity within diversity* 3rd rev edn (Leiden: Martinus Nijhoff, 1995)

—— *International Institutional Law: unity within diversity* 4th rev edn (Leiden: Martinus Nijhoff, 2003)

Schermers, Henry, 'Different Aspects of Sovereignty' in Kreijen, Gerard ed, *State, Sovereignty, and International Governance* (Oxford: Oxford University Press, 2002)

Schindler, Dietrich, 'Die Lehre von den Vorwirkungen der Neutralität' in Diez, Emanuel, Monnier, Jean, Müller, Jörg Paul, Reimann, Heinrich & Wildhaber, Luzius eds, *Festschrift für Rudolf Bindschedler zum 65.Geburtstag* (Bern: Verlag Stampfli & Cie, 1980) 563

Schwarzenberger, Georg, *A Manual of International Law* vol. I 4th edn (London: Stevens & Sons, 1960)

Schwelb, Egon, 'Withdrawal from the United Nations: The Indonesian Intermezzo' (1967) 61 *AJ* 661

Serdy, Andrew, 'Bringing Taiwan into the International Fisheries Fold: the legal personality of a fishing entity' (2004) 75 *BY* 183

Shaw, Malcolm N., 'State Succession Revisited' (1994) 34 *Finn YBIL* 5

—— *International Law* 5th edn (Cambridge: Cambridge University Press, 2003)

Shelton, Dinah, 'Normative Hierarchy in International Law' (2006) 100 *AJ* 291

Silber, Laura & Little, Allan, *Yugoslavia: Death of a Nation* rev ed (New York: Penguin, 1997)

Simms, Brendan, *Unfinest Hour: Britain and the Destruction of Bosnia* (London: Allen Lane, 2001)

Slaughter, Anne-Marie, *A New World Order* (Princeton: Princeton University Press, 2004)

Sloane, Blaine, 'The United Nations as a Constitution' (1989) 1 *Pace YBIL* 61

Soder, Josef, *Die Idee der Völkergemeinschaft: Francisco de Vitoria und die philosophischen Grundlagen des Völkerrecht* (Frankfurt/Main: Alfred Metzner Verlag, 1955)

—— *Die Vereinten Nationen und die Nichtmitglieder: Zum Problem der Weltstaatenorganisation* (Bonn: Ludwig Röhrscheid Verlag, 1956)

Sohn, Louis, *Cases and Materials on United Nations Law* (London: Stevens & Sons, 1956)

—— 'Expulsion or Forced Withdrawal from an International Organization' (1964) 77 *Harv LR* 1381

Stahn, Carsten, 'The Agreement on Succession Issues of the Former Socialist Federal Republic of Yugoslavia' (2002) 96 *AJ* 379

—— *The Law and Practice of International Territorial Administration. Versailles to Iraq and Beyond* (Cambridge: Cambridge University Press, 2008)

Stürchler, Nikolas, *The Threat of Force in International Law* (Cambridge: Cambridge University Press, 2007)

Suny, Ronald Grigor, *The Making of the Georgian Nation* 2nd edn (Bloomington: Indiana University Press, 1994)

Talmon, Stefan, *Recognition of Governments in International Law: With Particular Reference to Governments in Exile* (Oxford: Clarendon Press, 1998)

Task Force on the United Nations, *The Imperative for Action, An Update of the Report of the Task Force on American Interests and UN Reform*, Newt Gingrich & George Mitchell, chairmen (Washington, DC: United States Institute of Peace, 2005)

Thirlway, Hugh W.A., *Non-Appearance before the International Court of Justice* (Cambridge: Cambridge University Press, 1985)

Thomas, M.A., 'When the Guests Move In: Permanent Observers to the United Nations Gain the Right to Establish Permanent Missions in the United States' 78 *Ca L Rev* 197 (1990)

Thornberry, Patrick, 'The Democratic or Internal Aspect of Self-Determination with Some Remarks on Federalism' in Tomuschat, Christian ed, *Modern Law of Self-Determination* (Dordrecht: Martinus Nijhoff, 1993) 101

Tomuschat, Christian & Thouvenin, Jean-Marc eds, *The Fundamental Rules of the International Legal Order: Jus Cogens and Obligations Erga Omnes* (Leiden: Martinus Nijhoff, 2006)

Tomuschat, Christian, 'Article 36' in Zimmermann, Andreas, Tomuschat, Christian & Oellers-Frahm, Karin eds, *The Statute of the International Court of Justice. A Commentary* (Oxford: Oxford University Press, 2006) 588

Trask, Roger R., 'Spruille Braden versus George Messersmith: World War II, The Cold War, and Argentine Policy, 1945–1947' (1984) 26(1) *Journal of Interamerican Studies & World Affairs* 69

Türk, Danilo, 'Recognition of States: A Comment' (1993) 4 *EJIL* 66

Vagts, Detlev F., 'Switzerland, International Law and World War II' (1997) 91 *AJ* 466

Van Der Vyver, Jonathan D., 'Self-Determination of the Peoples of Quebec under International Law' (2000) 10 *J Trans L & Pol'y* 1

Van Staden, Alfred & Vollaard, Hans, 'The Erosion of State Sovereignty: Towards a Post-territorial World?' in Kreijen, Gerard ed, *State, Sovereignty, and International Governance* (Oxford: Oxford University Press, 2002)

Verdross, Alfred, 'Austria's Permanent Neutrality and the United Nations Organization' (1956) 50 *AJ* 61

Verosta, Stephan, *Kollektivaktion der Mächte des Europäischen Konzerts (1886–1914)* (Vienna: Verlag der Österreichischen Akademie der Wissenschaften, 1988)

Waldock, Humphrey, *General Course on Public International Law*, (1962) 106(II) *Hag Rec* 20

Warbrick, Colin & Tierney, Stephen eds, *Towards an International Legal Community? The Sovereignty of States and the Sovereignty of International Law* (London: British Institute of International and Comparative Law, 2006)

Warbrick, Colin, 'The principle of sovereign equality' in Lowe, Vaughan & Warbrick, Colin eds, *The United Nations and the Principles of International Law: Essays in memory of Michael Akehurst* (London, Routledge, 1994)

—— 'Recognition of States: Recent European Practice' in Evans, Malcolm D. ed., *Aspects of Statehood and Institutionalism in Contemporary Europe* (Aldershot: Dartmouth Publishing, 1996)

Wedgwood, Ruth, 'The ICJ Advisory Opinion on the Israeli Security Fence and the Limits of Self-Defense' (2005) 99 *AJ* 52

Weil, Prosper, 'Le droit international en quête de son identité' (1992) 237 *Hag Rec* (VI) 13

Weiss, Thomas G., Forsythe, David P., Coate, Roger A. & Pease, Kelly-Kate, *The United Nations and Changing World Politics* 5th edn (Boulder, Colorado: Westview Press, 2007)

Weller, Marc, 'The International Response to the Dissolution of the Socialist Federal Republic of Yugoslavia' (1992) 86 *AJ* 569

Weston, Burns H., Falk, Richard A. & Charlesworth, Hilary, *International Law and World Order: A Problem-Oriented Coursebook* 3rd edn (St. Paul: West Group, 1997)

Wheaton, Henry, *Elements of International Law* 8th edn (Boston: Little, Brown, and Company, 1866)

Wilde, Ralph, *International Territorial Administration: How Trusteeship and the Civilizing Mission Never Went Away* (Oxford: Oxford University Press, 2008)

Williams, Paul R., 'The Treaty Obligations of the Successor States of the Former Soviet Union, Yugoslavia, and Czechoslovakia: Do They Continue in Force?' (1994) 23 *Denver JIL & Pol'y* 1

Wilson, Carolyn L., 'Changing the Charter: The United Nations Prepares for the Twenty-first Century' (1996) 90 *AJ* 115

Wolfrum, Rüdiger, *Die Internationalisierung Staatsfreier Räumer: die Entwicklung einer internationalen Verwaltung für Antarktis, Weltraum, hohe See und Meeresboden* (Berlin: Springer-Verlag, 1984)

Wood, Michael C., 'Participation of Former Yugoslav States in the United Nations and in Multilateral Treaties' (1997) 1 *Max Planck Ybk UN Law* 231

Woods, Ngaire, 'Bretton Woods Institutions' in Weiss, Thomas George and Daws, Sam eds, *The Oxford Handbook on the United Nations* (Oxford: Oxford University Press, 2007)

Woods, Randall B., 'Conflict or Community? The United States and Argentina's Admission to the United Nations' (1977) 46(3) *Pacific Historical Review* 363

Woodward, Susan L., *Balkan Tragedy: Chaos and Dissolution After the Cold War* (Washington, DC: Brookings Institution, 1995)

Yakemtchouk, Romain, 'La Communauté des États Indépendants CEI' (1995) 41 *AFDI* 245

Ydit, Méir, *Internationalised Territories: From the 'Free City of Cracow' to the 'Free City of Berlin'* (Leyden: A.W. Sythoff, 1961)

Young, Richard, 'The State of Syria: New or Old?' (1962) 56 *AJ* 484

Zacklin, Ralph, *The Amendment of the Constitutive Instruments of the United Nations and Specialized Agencies* (Leiden: Martinus Nijhoff, 1968, reissued with forward by Henry G Schermers, 2005)

Zamora, Stephen, 'Economic Relations and Development' in Joyner, Christopher C. ed, *The United Nations and International Law* (Cambridge: Cambridge University Press and American Society of International Law, 1997)

Zegveld, Liesbeth, *Accountability of Armed Opposition Groups in International Law* (Cambridge: Cambridge University Press, 2002)

Zieger, Gottfried, 'Deutsche Einheit und Europäische Integration' in Zieger, Gottfried, Meissner, Boris & Blumenwitz, Dieter eds, *Deutschland als Ganzes: Rechtliche und Historische Überlegungen: anlasslich des 70. Geburtstages von Herbert Czaja* (Cologne: Verlag Wissenschaft und Politik Berend von Nottbeck, 1985)

Ziemele, Ineta, *State Continuity and Nationality: Baltic States and Russia: Past, Present and Future as Defined by International Law* (Leiden: Martinus Nijhoff, 2005)

Zimmermann, Andreas, 'Article 35' in Zimmermann, Andreas, Tomuschat, Christian & Oellers-Frahm, Karin eds, *The Statute of the International Court of Justice. A Commentary* (Oxford: Oxford University Press, 2006)

Index